Full Moon
O Sagashite

2

Story & Art by Arina Tanemura

Table of Contents

♥Full Moon o Sagashite

Please stop me from crying,
help me win this fight.

Whisper to the wind, the water,
the cherry blossoms of the night...

Help my smile awake
with a joy unsurpassed,

Even if such gentle things
were never meant to last.

I remember all the feelings
you gave me,

And when I think of you,
my soul flies free.

Even while my heart
aches deeply,

Memories of you let me
treat others sweetly.

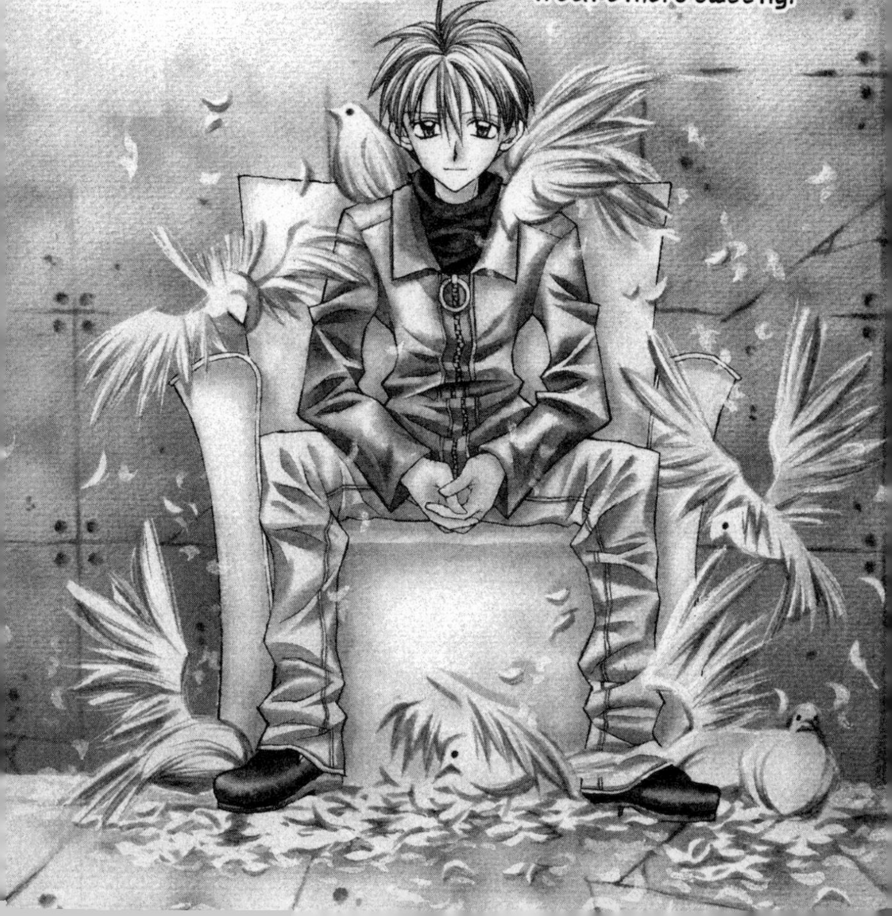

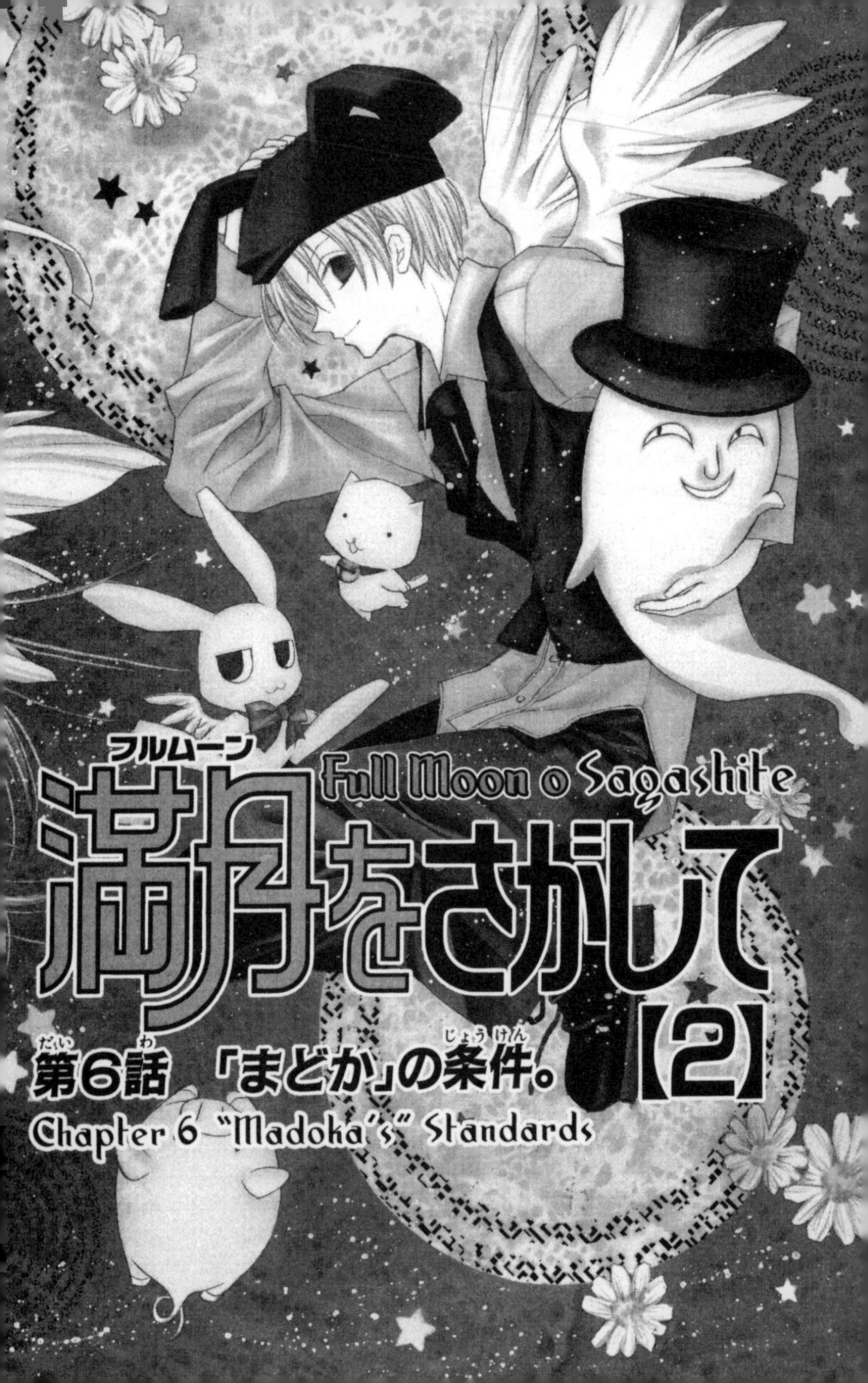

フルムーン
Full Moon o Sagashite
満月をさがして
【2】
第6話　「まどか」の条件。
Chapter 6 "Madoka's" Standards

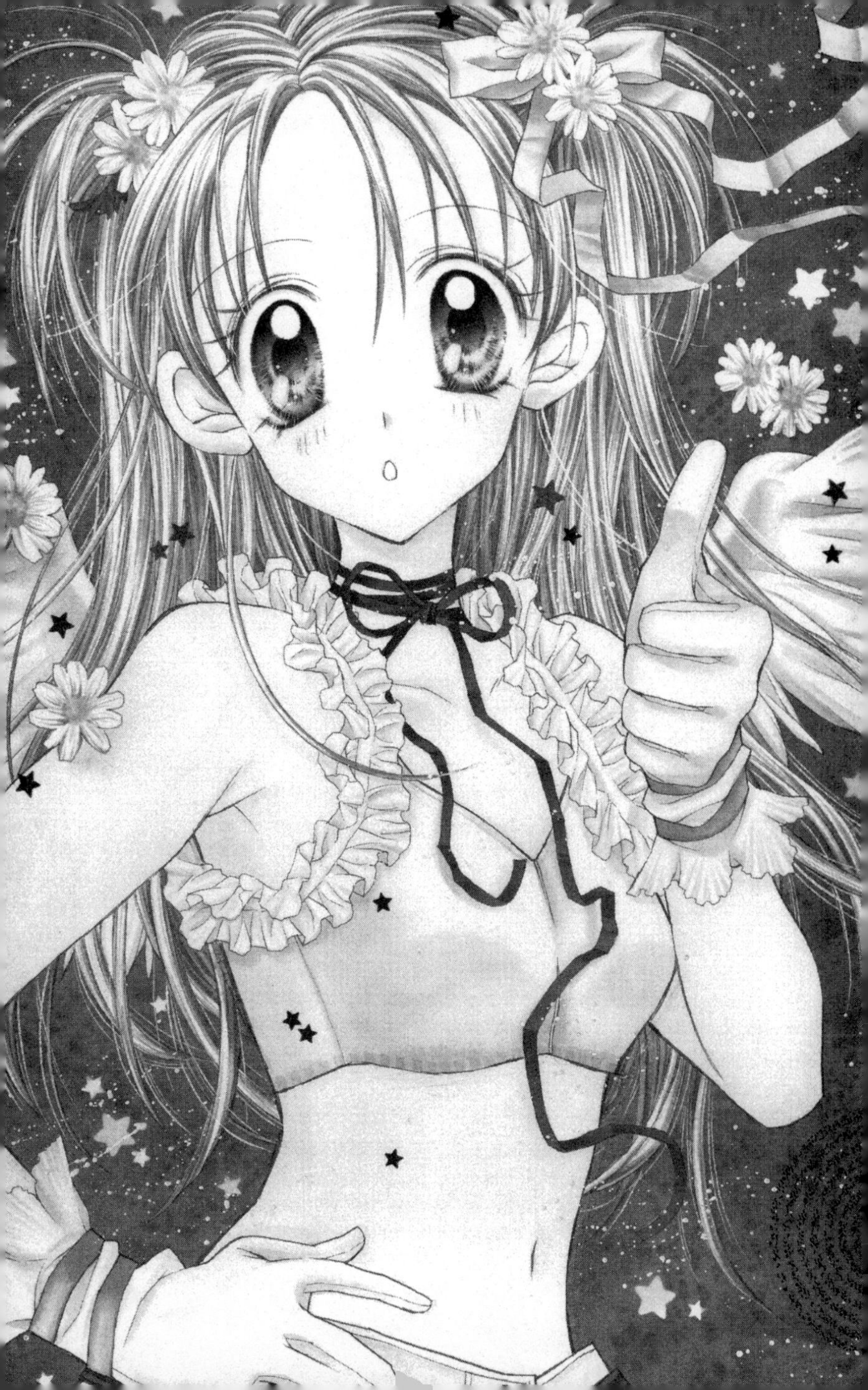

CHARACTER INTRODUCTIONS

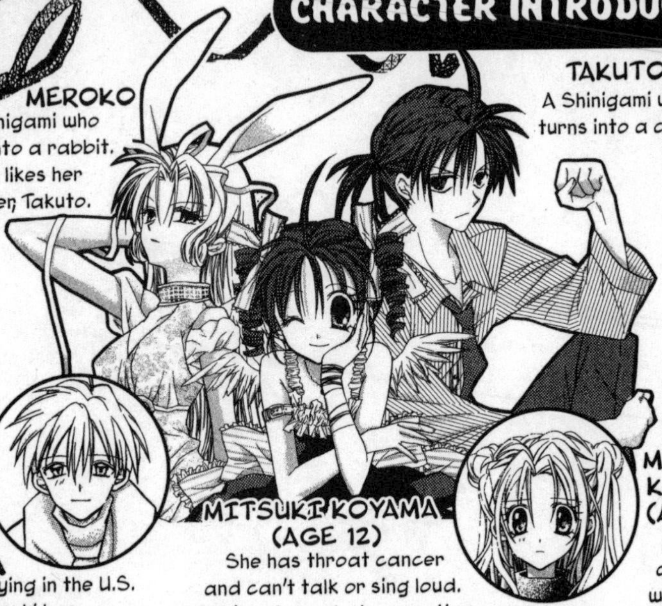

MEROKO
A Shinigami who turns into a rabbit. She likes her partner, Takuto.

TAKUTO
A Shinigami who turns into a cat.

EICHI
He's studying in the U.S. Mitsuki has loved him since she was little.

MITSUKI KOYAMA (AGE 12)
She has throat cancer and can't talk or sing loud. She's not good at competing or quarreling.

MITSUKI KOYAMA (AGE 16)
Mitsuki's alter ego, who debuts as the singer "Fullmoon."

Full Moon o Sagashite

Mitsuki is 12. She loves Eichi, who's studying in the U.S., and she dreams of fulfilling her promise to him by becoming a singer. Mitsuki has a form of cancer in her throat called sarcoma, and her doctor has recommended that she have an operation. But she refuses to go through with it, since the operation would destroy her singing voice. One day, a pair of Shinigami named Takuto and Meroko appear, and tries to stop Mitsuki from going to an audition. However, Takuto is moved by Mitsuki's ardent wish to become a singer and helps her audition by transforming her into a healthy 16-year-old. Mitsuki is able to sing in her new body and wins the competition. She makes her musical debut as "Fullmoon." Mitsuki's first CD is doing well, and she gets an offer do a shampoo commercial. The job offer is a competition between Mitsuki and a girl named Madoka Wakamatsu. Both of them will write lyrics for the same melody and perform their version. Mitsuki manages to write the lyrics with Takuto and Meroko's help, but on the day of the competition, the song Madoka starts to sing is the same as Mitsuki's...

THE STORY THUS FAR

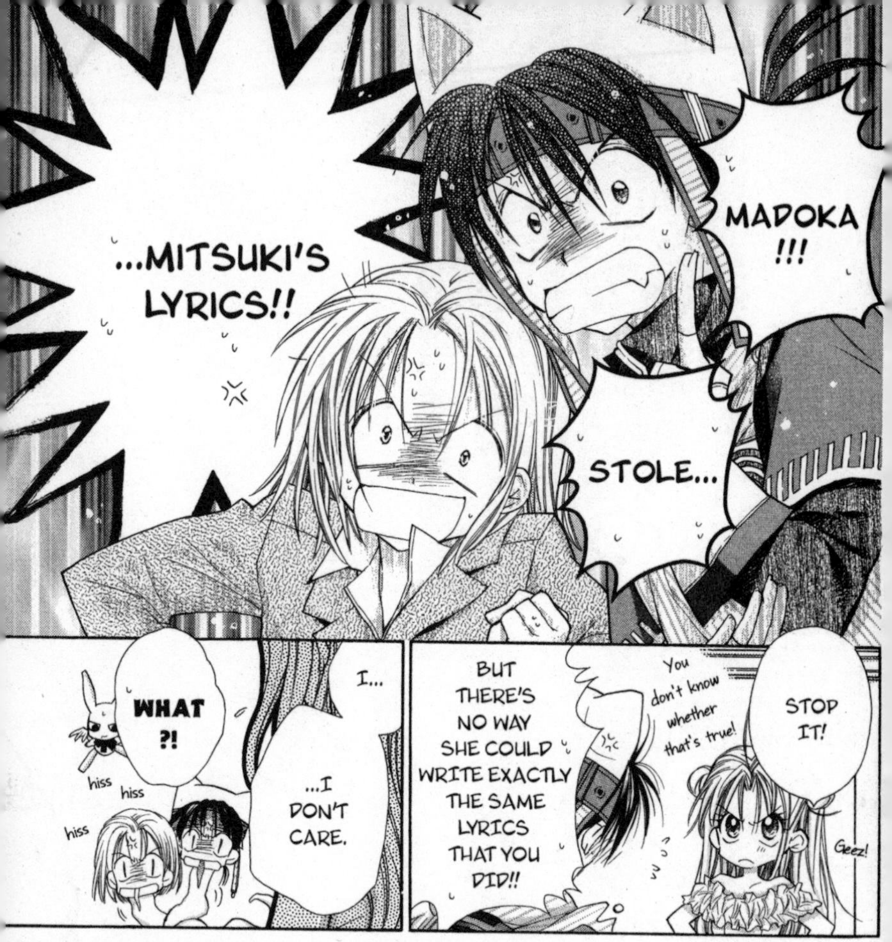
MADOKA !!!
STOLE...
...MITSUKI'S LYRICS!!
STOP IT!
You don't know whether that's true!
Geez!
BUT THERE'S NO WAY SHE COULD WRITE EXACTLY THE SAME LYRICS THAT YOU DID!!
I...
...I DON'T CARE.
WHAT ?!
hiss
hiss
hiss

Chapter 6 "Madoka's" Standards (Spoilers follow) **Cover Copy** **I will keep on singing. Until my voice reaches you...**

The cover illustrations is, "Mitsuki-chan and Shinigamiiz" as the theme. Plus Gut-chan

You'll understand why Izumi is not in animal form if you read Chapter Nine. (☺) Mitsuki-chan grew wings with the idea of being the fifth Shinigami. Mitsuki-chan's posing seems a bit stiff. Big illustrations are hard to draw. Sheesh...

About the story...it was fun drawing the staff members...I'd like to draw them again. Also, Takuto feeling rivalry towards Eichi is cute. So cute!

Lonely, unrequited love really suits Takuto (I shouldn't be saying that).

By the way, Meroko in the last two pages of this chapter was really popular. Uhohoooo ♪ Are you Arale-chan from Dr. Slump, or what?

In this chapter, I changed my ink from Kaimei Drawing Sol K to Kaimei Sumi Ink. I used Kaimei Sumi Ink for my debut and up to my fourth work, so I'm back to it now, and I think my decision is correct. The previous ink was hard (the particles seemed rough), so now my inking takes less time.

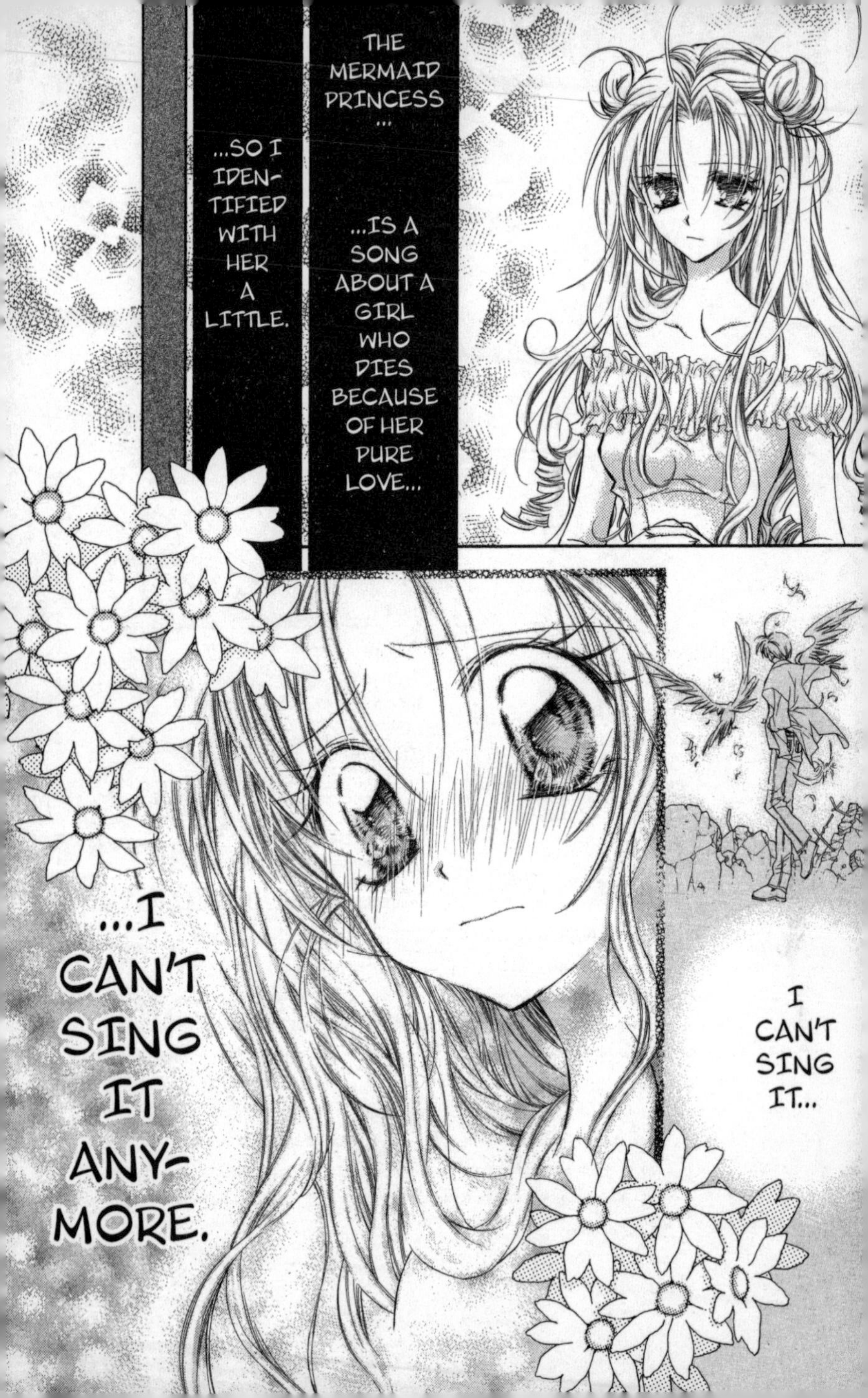
THE MERMAID PRINCESS ...
...IS A SONG ABOUT A GIRL WHO DIES BECAUSE OF HER PURE LOVE...
...SO I IDEN-TIFIED WITH HER A LITTLE.
I CAN'T SING IT...
...I CAN'T SING IT ANY-MORE.

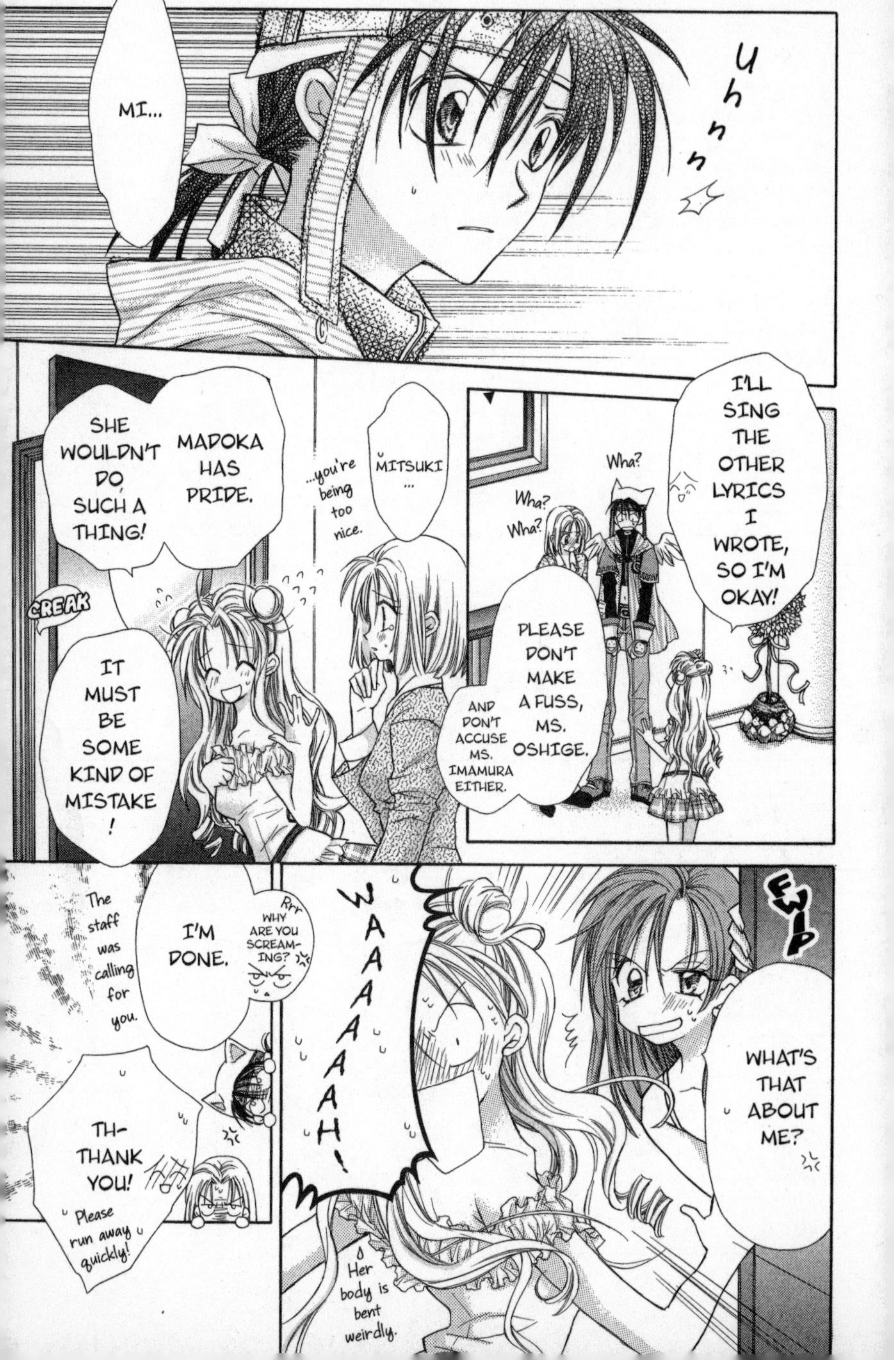
Uhnnn
MI...
I'LL SING THE OTHER LYRICS I WROTE, SO I'M OKAY!
Wha?
Wha? Wha?
PLEASE DON'T MAKE A FUSS, MS. OSHIGE.
AND DON'T ACCUSE MS. IMAMURA EITHER.
MITSUKI...
...you're being too nice.
MADOKA HAS PRIDE.
SHE WOULDN'T DO SUCH A THING!
CREAK
IT MUST BE SOME KIND OF MISTAKE!
FWIP
WHAT'S THAT ABOUT ME?
WAAAAAAAH!
Her body is bent weirdly.
I'M DONE.
The staff was calling for you.
Rrr
WHY ARE YOU SCREAMING?
TH-THANK YOU!
Please run away quickly!

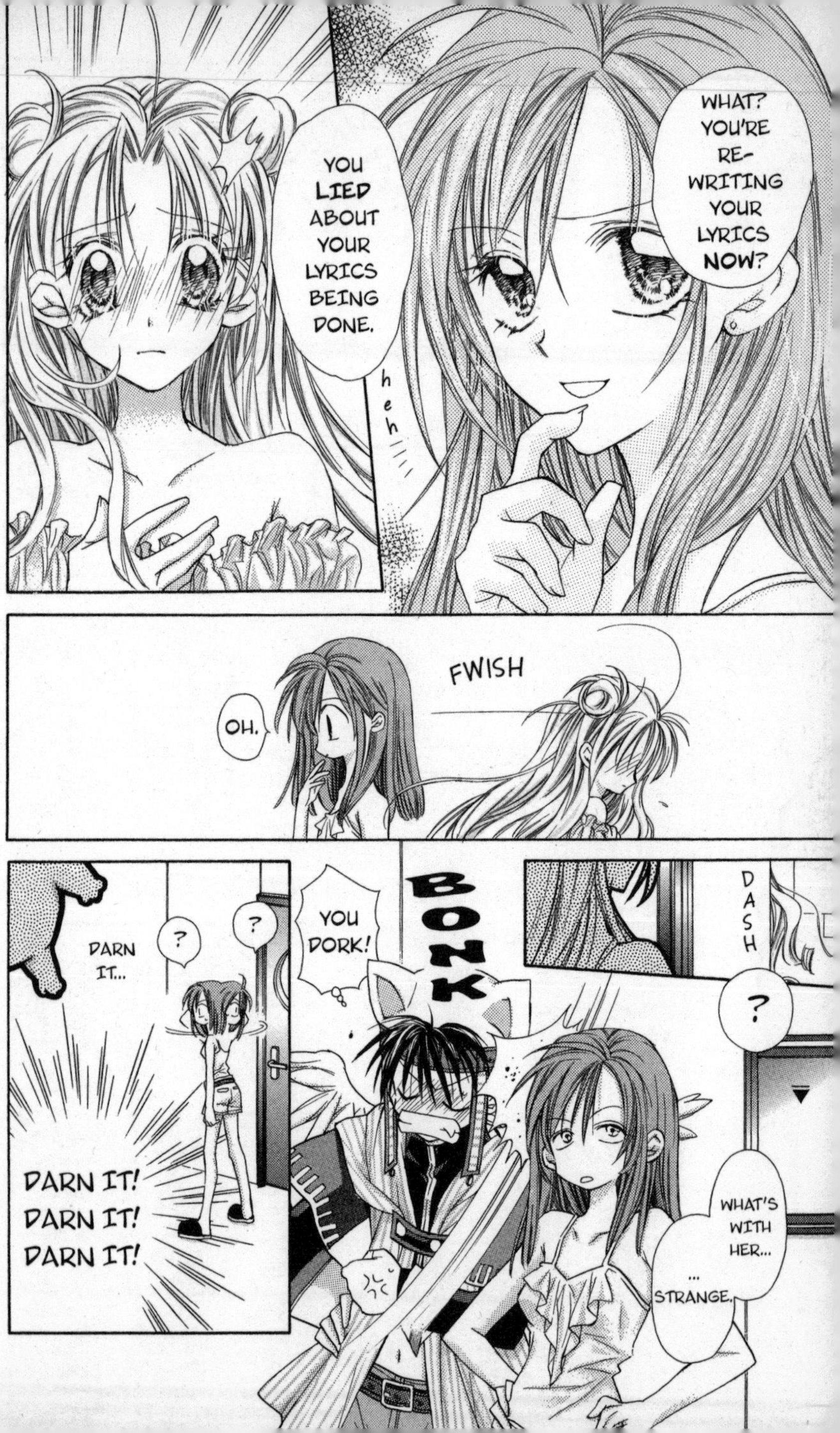
WHAT? YOU'RE RE-WRITING YOUR LYRICS NOW?
heh
YOU LIED ABOUT YOUR LYRICS BEING DONE.
FWISH
OH.
DASH
?
BONK
YOU DORK!
WHAT'S WITH HER...
...STRANGE.
?
?
DARN IT...
DARN IT! DARN IT! DARN IT!

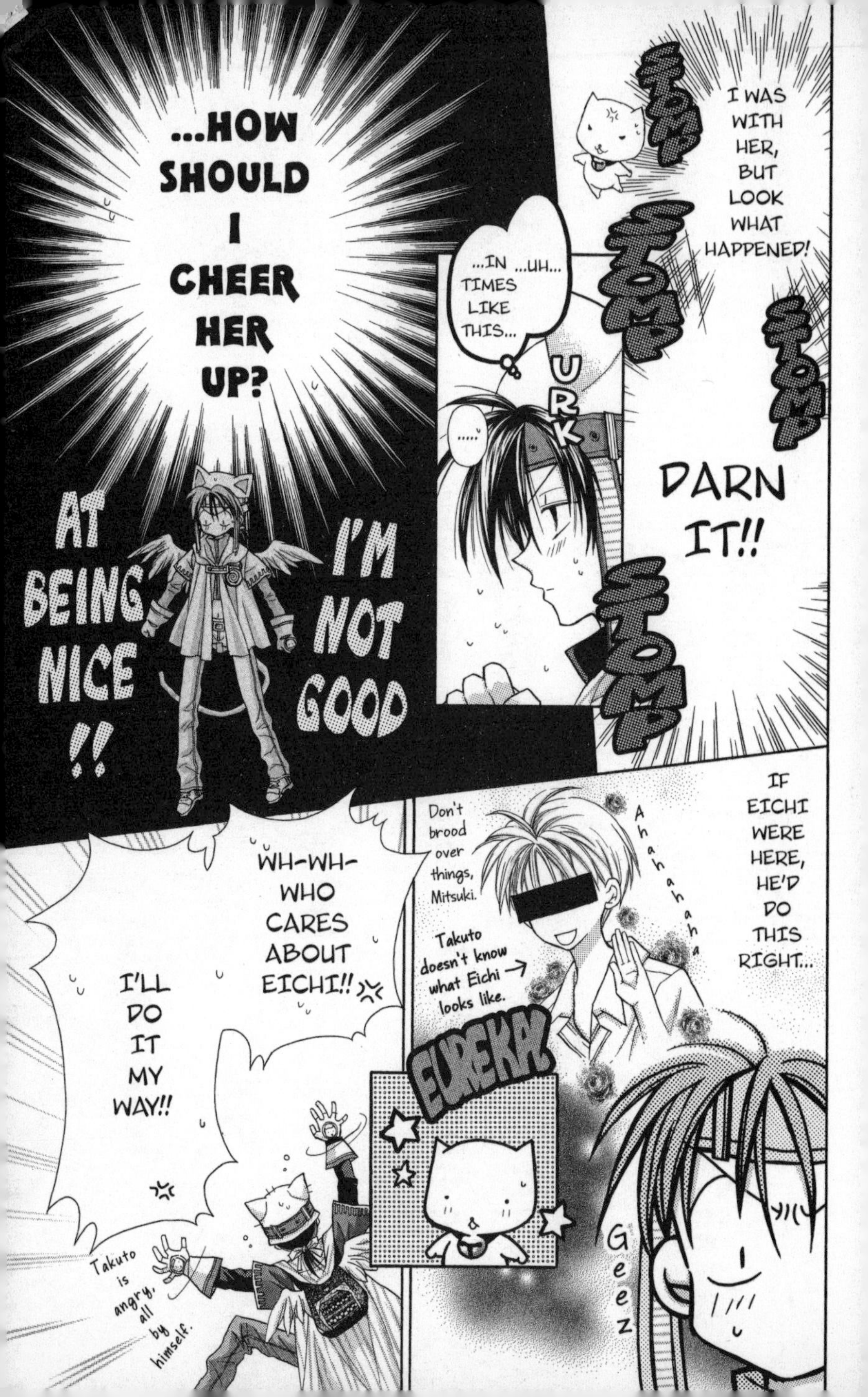
STOMP
I WAS WITH HER, BUT LOOK WHAT HAPPENED!
STOMP
STOMP
DARN IT!!
STOMP
...IN ...UH... TIMES LIKE THIS...
URK
.....
...HOW SHOULD I CHEER HER UP?
I'M NOT GOOD AT BEING NICE!!
IF EICHI WERE HERE, HE'D DO THIS RIGHT...
Don't brood over things, Mitsuki.
Ahahahaha
Takuto doesn't know what Eichi looks like.
EUREKA!
Geez
WH-WH-WHO CARES ABOUT EICHI!!
I'LL DO IT MY WAY!!
Takuto is angry, all by himself.

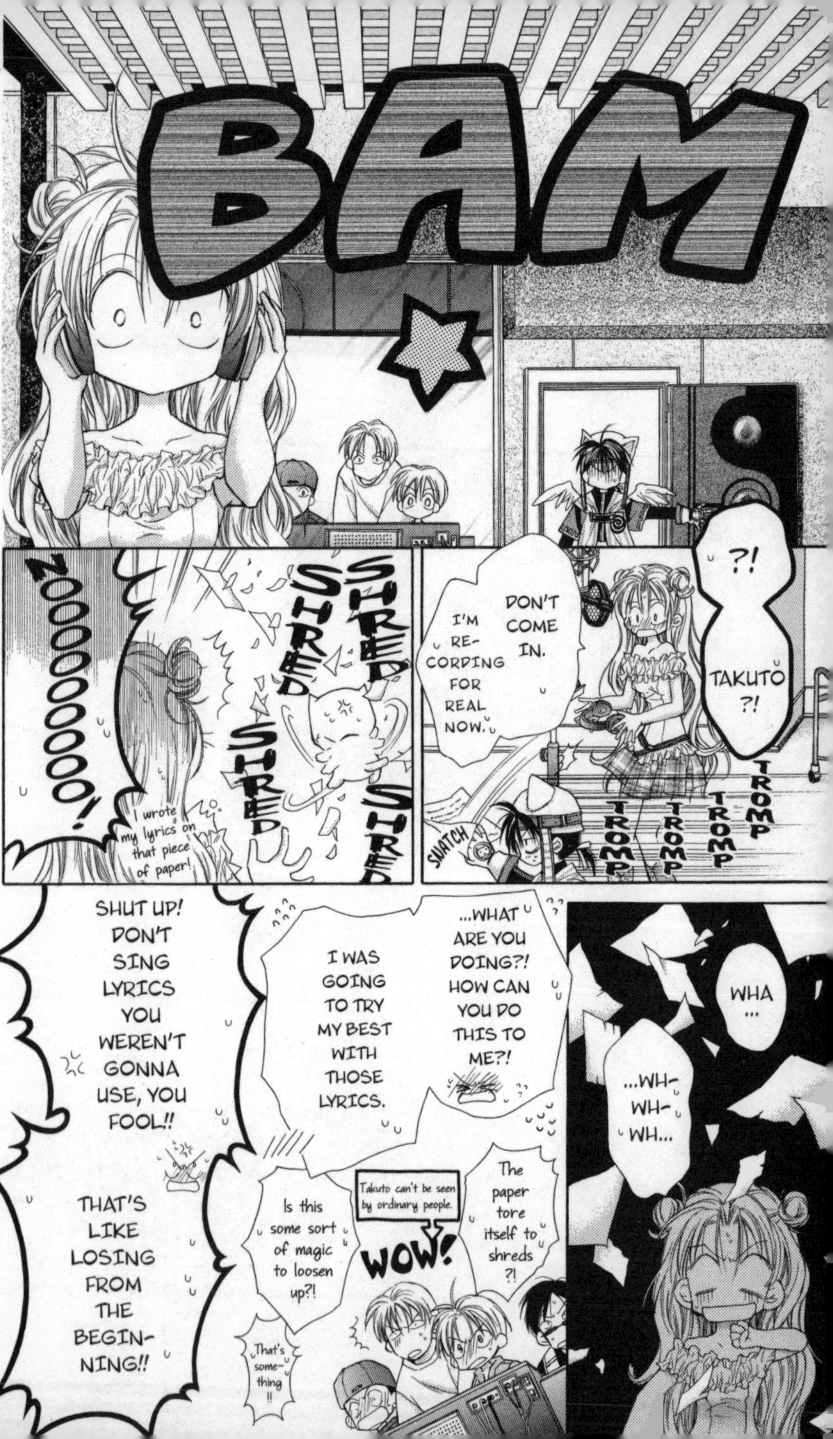
BAM
?!
TAKUTO ?!
DON'T COME IN.
I'M RE-CORDING FOR REAL NOW.
TROMP TROMP TROMP TROMP
SNATCH
SHRED SHRED SHRED SHRED
NOOOOOOOO!
I wrote my lyrics on that piece of paper!
WHA...
...WH-WH-WH...
...WHAT ARE YOU DOING?! HOW CAN YOU DO THIS TO ME?!
I WAS GOING TO TRY MY BEST WITH THOSE LYRICS.
The paper tore itself to shreds?!
Takuto can't be seen by ordinary people.
WOW!
Is this some sort of magic to loosen up?!
That's some-thing!!
SHUT UP! DON'T SING LYRICS YOU WEREN'T GONNA USE, YOU FOOL!!
THAT'S LIKE LOSING FROM THE BEGIN-NING!!

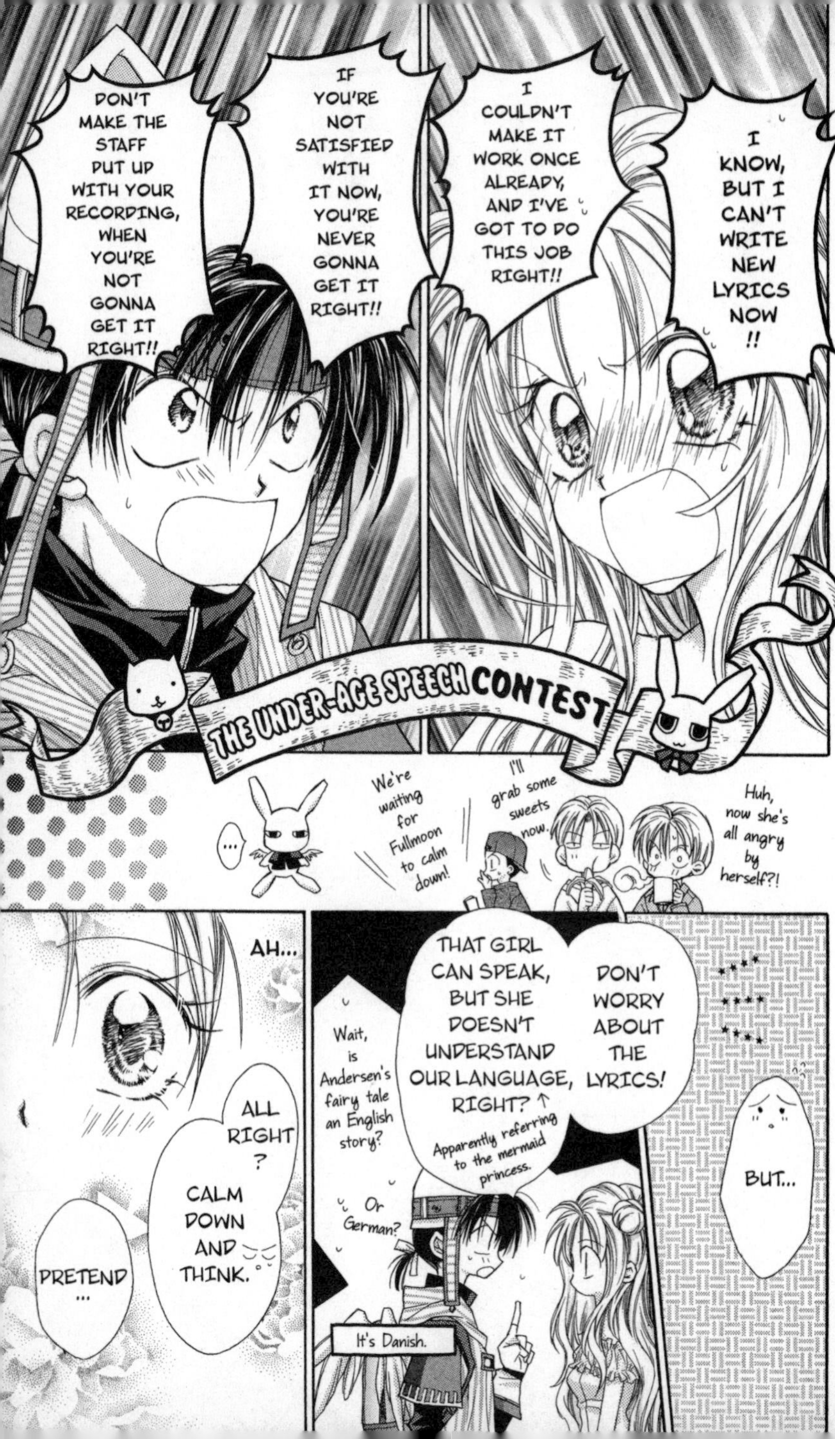
I KNOW, BUT I CAN'T WRITE NEW LYRICS NOW!!
I COULDN'T MAKE IT WORK ONCE ALREADY, AND I'VE GOT TO DO THIS JOB RIGHT!!
IF YOU'RE NOT SATISFIED WITH IT NOW, YOU'RE NEVER GONNA GET IT RIGHT!!
DON'T MAKE THE STAFF PUT UP WITH YOUR RECORDING, WHEN YOU'RE NOT GONNA GET IT RIGHT!!
THE UNDER-AGE SPEECH CONTEST
Huh, now she's all angry by herself?!
I'll grab some sweets now.
We're waiting for Fullmoon to calm down!
...
BUT...
DON'T WORRY ABOUT THE LYRICS!
THAT GIRL CAN SPEAK, BUT SHE DOESN'T UNDERSTAND OUR LANGUAGE, RIGHT? ↑
Apparently referring to the mermaid princess.
Wait, is Andersen's fairy tale an English story?
Or German?
It's Danish.
AH...
ALL RIGHT?
CALM DOWN AND THINK.
PRETEND...

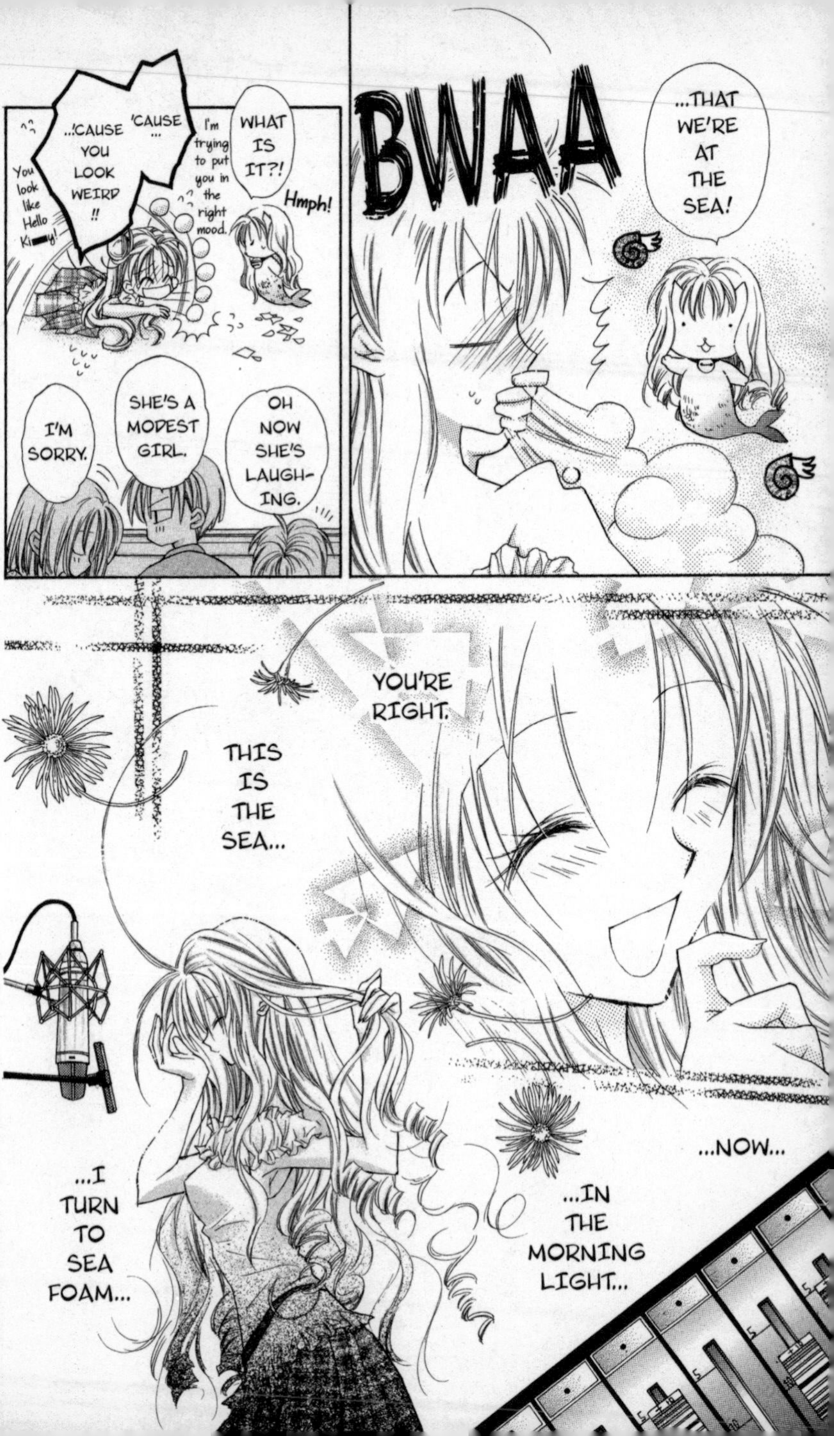
BWAA
...THAT WE'RE AT THE SEA!
WHAT IS IT?!
I'm trying to put you in the right mood.
Hmph!
'CAUSE ...
...'CAUSE YOU LOOK WEIRD !!
You look like Hello Ki[redacted]y!
OH NOW SHE'S LAUGHING.
SHE'S A MODEST GIRL.
I'M SORRY.
YOU'RE RIGHT.
THIS IS THE SEA...
...NOW...
...IN THE MORNING LIGHT...
...I TURN TO SEA FOAM...

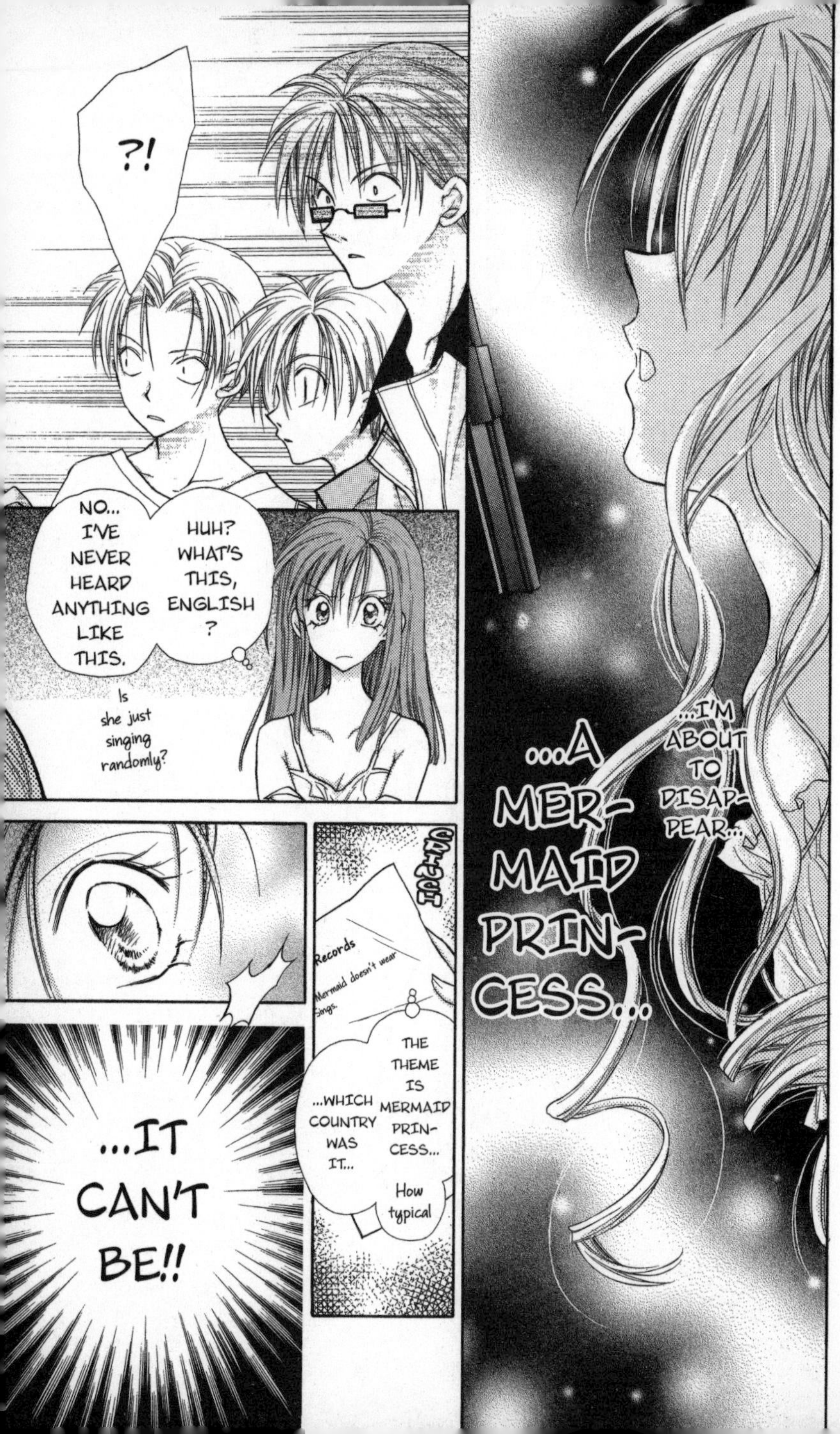
...I'M ABOUT TO DISAPPEAR...
...A MERMAID PRINCESS...
?!
HUH? WHAT'S THIS, ENGLISH?
NO... I'VE NEVER HEARD ANYTHING LIKE THIS.
Is she just singing randomly?
Records
Mermaid doesn't wear
Sings.
THE THEME IS MERMAID PRINCESS...
How typical
...WHICH COUNTRY WAS IT...
...IT CAN'T BE!!

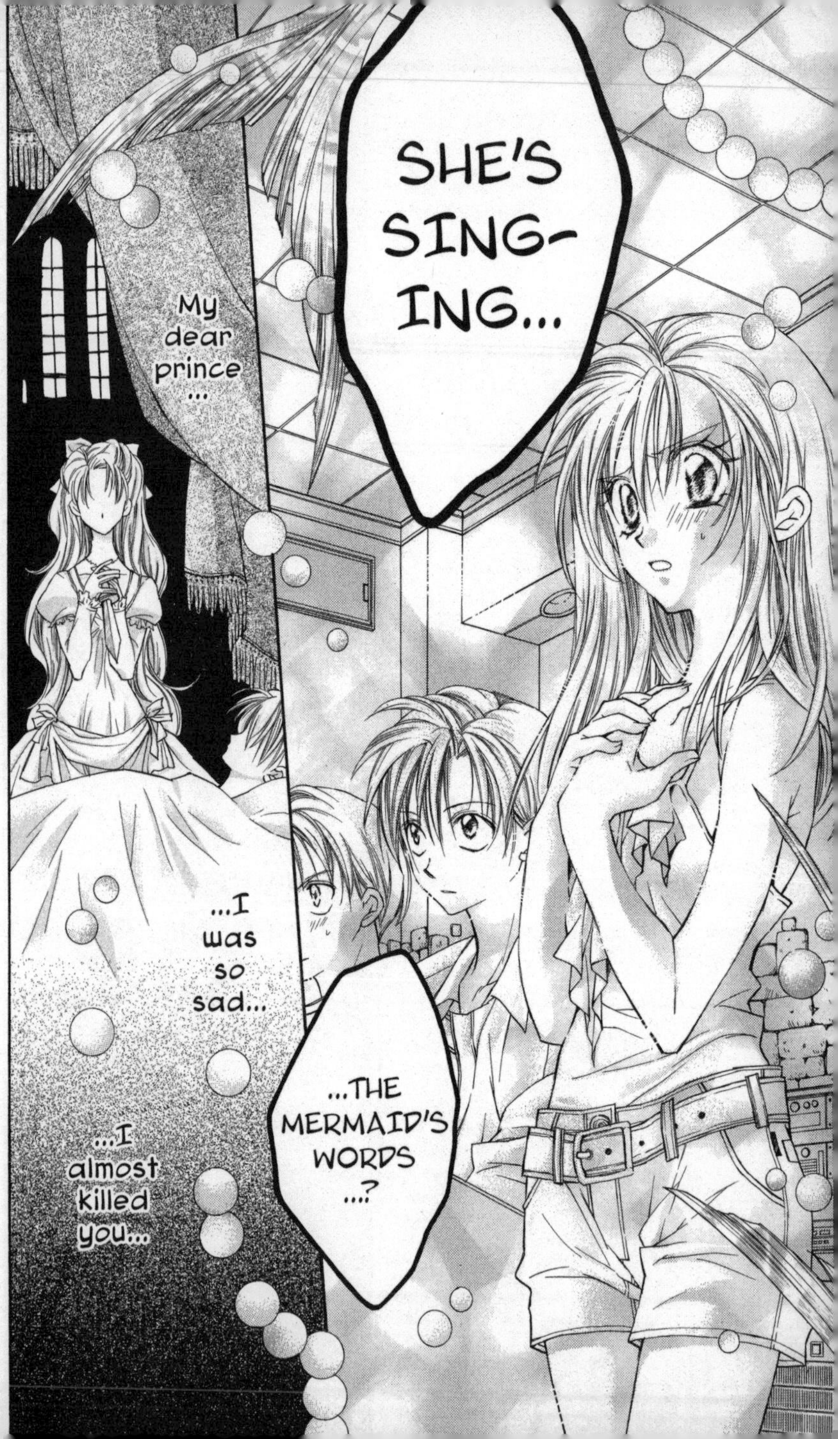
SHE'S SING-ING...
...THE MERMAID'S WORDS ...?
My dear prince ...
...I was so sad...
...I almost killed you...

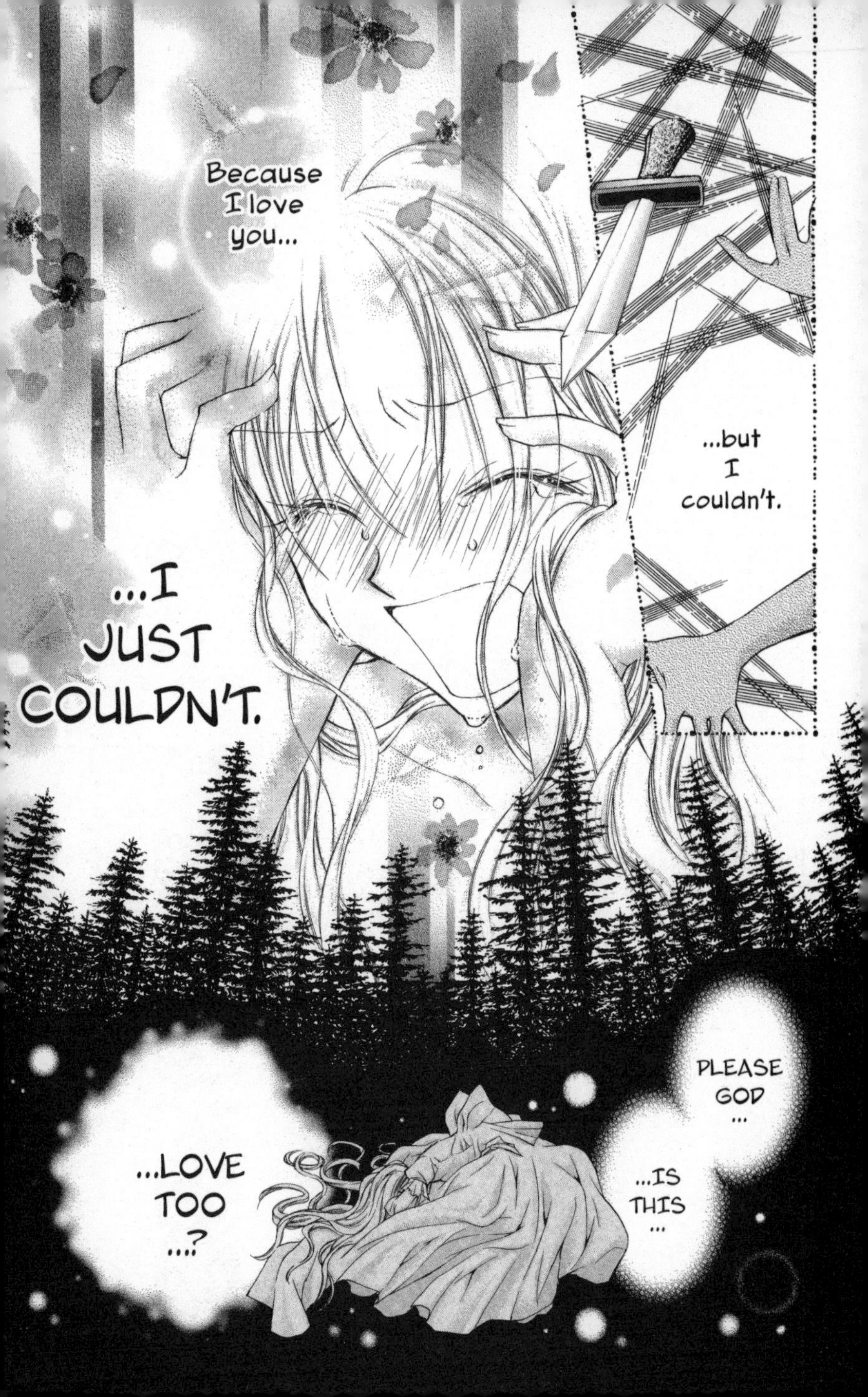
...but I couldn't.
Because I love you...
...I JUST COULDN'T.
PLEASE GOD ...
...IS THIS ...
...LOVE TOO ...?

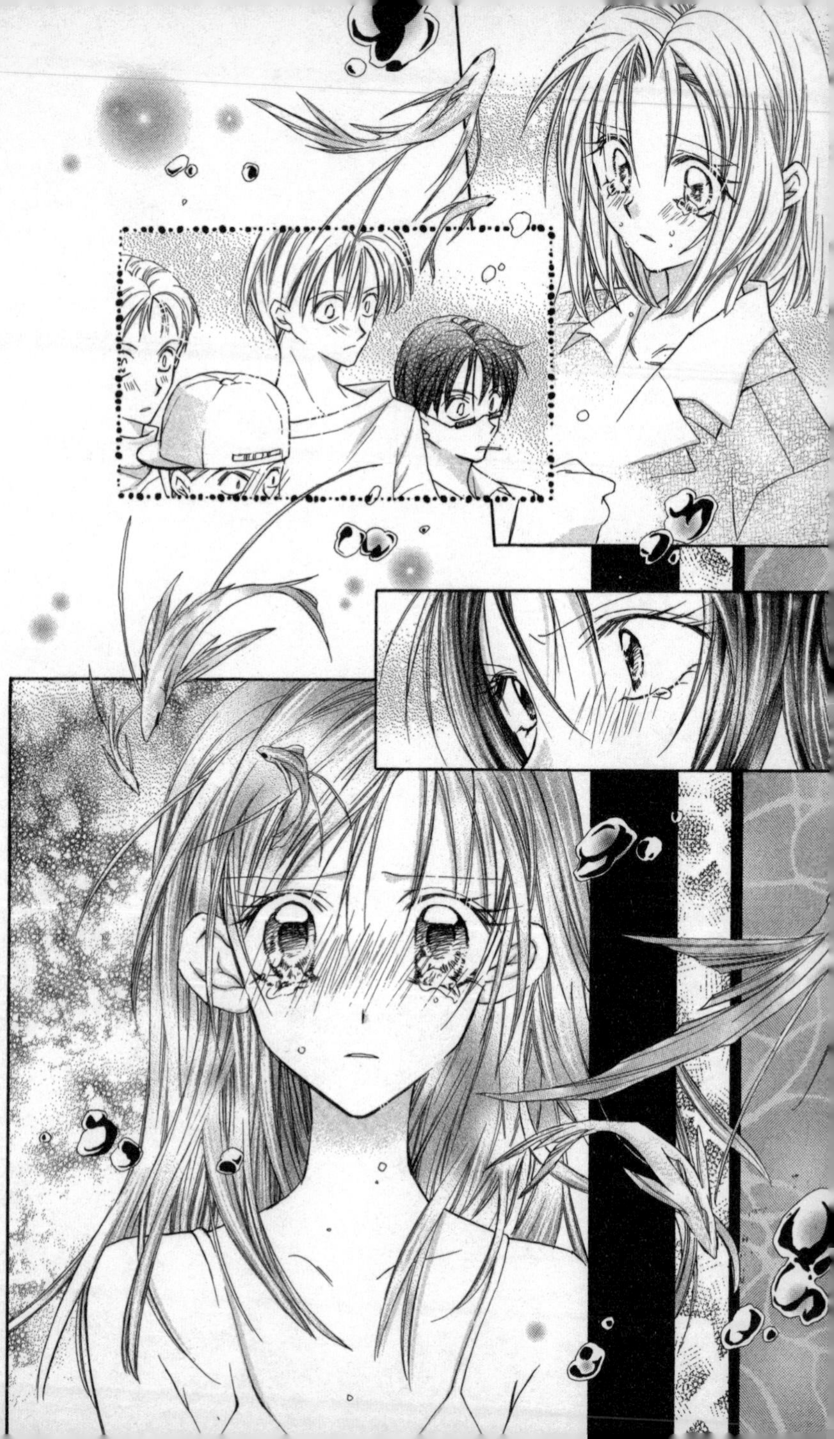

HOWDY

Hello! I'm Arina Tanemura.
I came to deliver you "Fullmoon o Sagashite" Vol.②. I'd like talk about things a bit here.

First, for character introductions (continued from Vol. ①)

Masami Oshige (age 28)

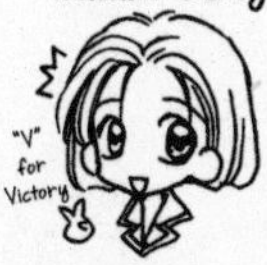
"V" for Victory

She used to be an idol named Yuina Hanakazari. Oshige-san's name was taken from editors' names, mixed up. And because all of them (there were three) liked drinking, Oshige-san became a drinker too. Thank you... She's um... I like her. (Evil grin)

Izumi Lio

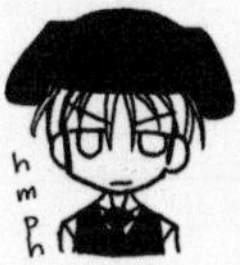
hmph

I thought people wouldn't like him, but it hasn't been that way. I like him. It's easy to draw him (you like him because of that?). After he appeared, the story (the characters?) really started moving, so I'm thankful to him.

Jonathan

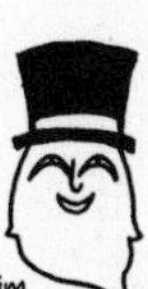

The mysterious ghost (?). He is a Shinigami, too. I think the good part about him is that it's not clear whether he likes Izumi, or whether he's making fun of him.

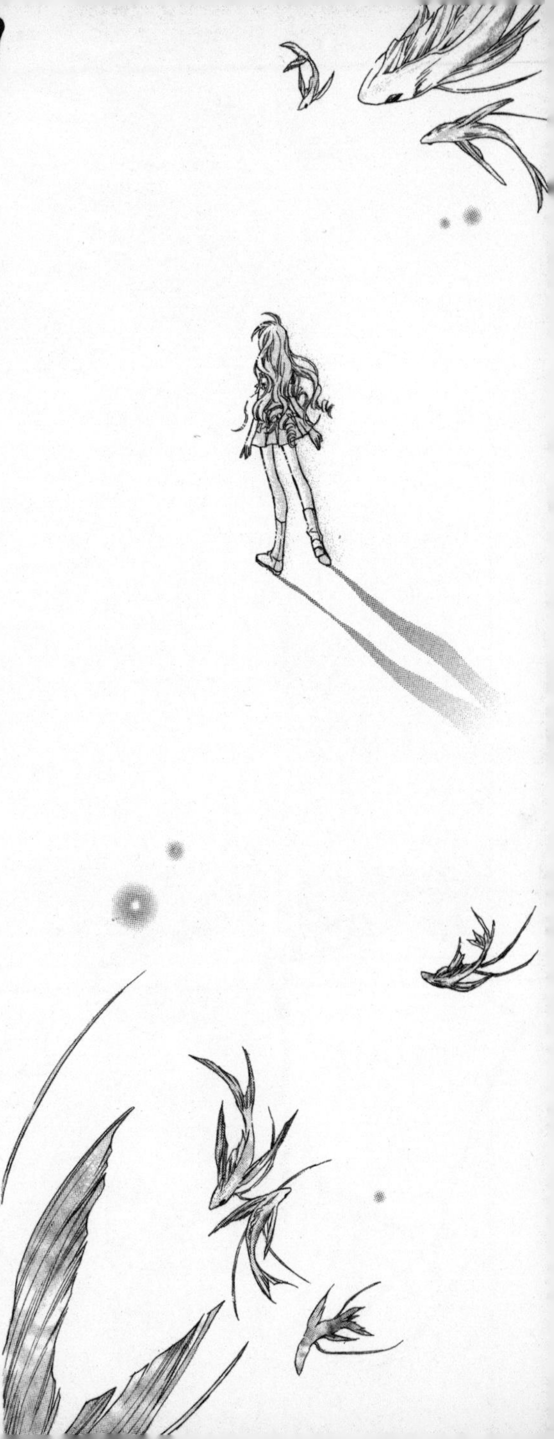

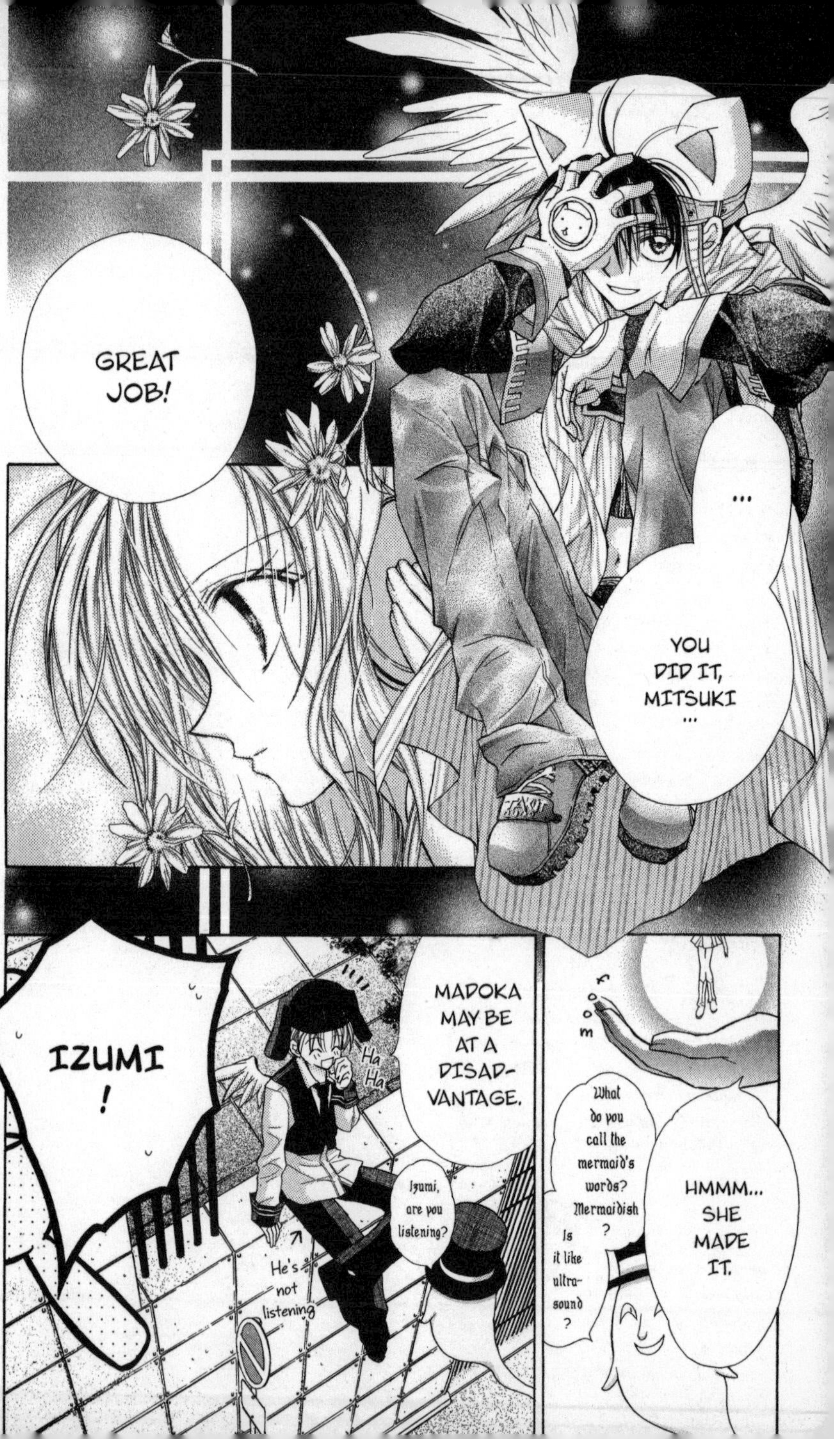
GREAT JOB!
...
YOU DID IT, MITSUKI ...
foom
HMMM... SHE MADE IT.
What do you call the mermaid's words? Mermaidish?
Is it like ultra-sound?
MADOKA MAY BE AT A DISAD-VANTAGE.
Ha Ha
Izumi, are you listening?
He's not listening
IZUMI!

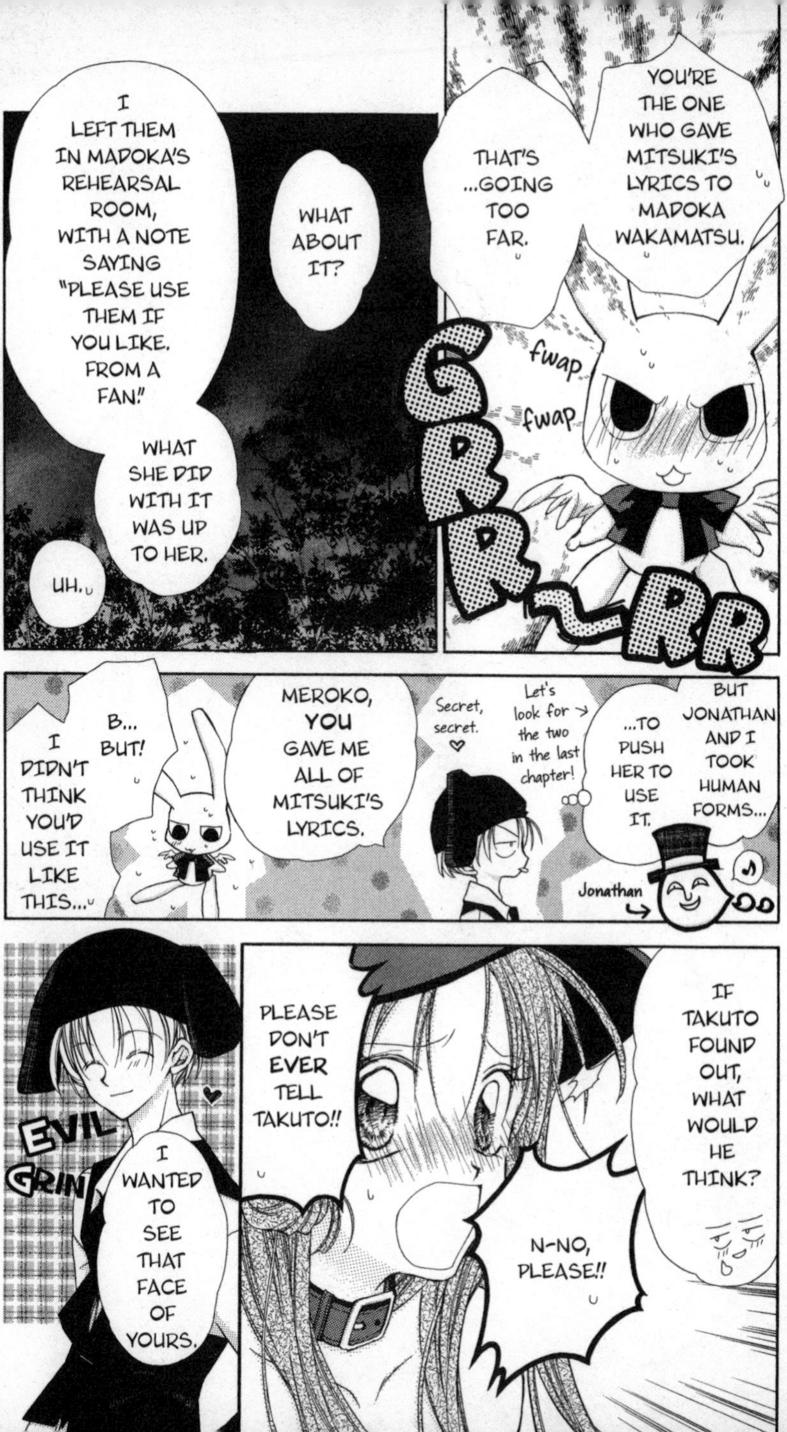
YOU'RE THE ONE WHO GAVE MITSUKI'S LYRICS TO MADOKA WAKAMATSU.
THAT'S ...GOING TOO FAR.
fwap
fwap
GRR~RR
WHAT ABOUT IT?
I LEFT THEM IN MADOKA'S REHEARSAL ROOM, WITH A NOTE SAYING "PLEASE USE THEM IF YOU LIKE. FROM A FAN."
WHAT SHE DID WITH IT WAS UP TO HER.
UH.
BUT JONATHAN AND I TOOK HUMAN FORMS...
...TO PUSH HER TO USE IT.
Let's look for the two in the last chapter!
Jonathan
Secret, secret. ♥
MEROKO, YOU GAVE ME ALL OF MITSUKI'S LYRICS.
B... BUT!
I DIDN'T THINK YOU'D USE IT LIKE THIS...
IF TAKUTO FOUND OUT, WHAT WOULD HE THINK?
PLEASE DON'T EVER TELL TAKUTO!!
N-NO, PLEASE!!
I WANTED TO SEE THAT FACE OF YOURS.
EVIL GRIN

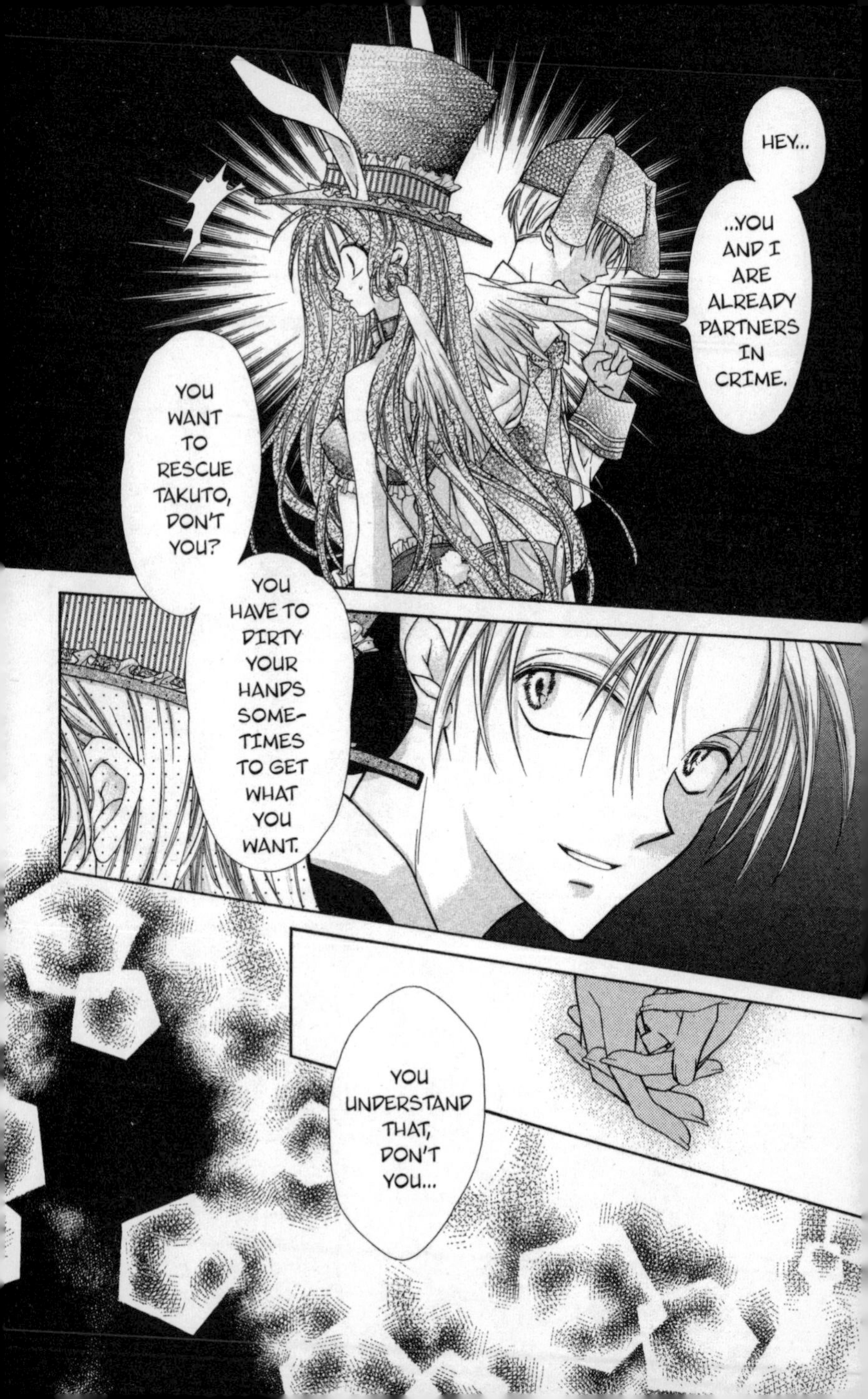
HEY...
...YOU AND I ARE ALREADY PARTNERS IN CRIME.
YOU WANT TO RESCUE TAKUTO, DON'T YOU?
YOU HAVE TO DIRTY YOUR HANDS SOME-TIMES TO GET WHAT YOU WANT.
YOU UNDERSTAND THAT, DON'T YOU...

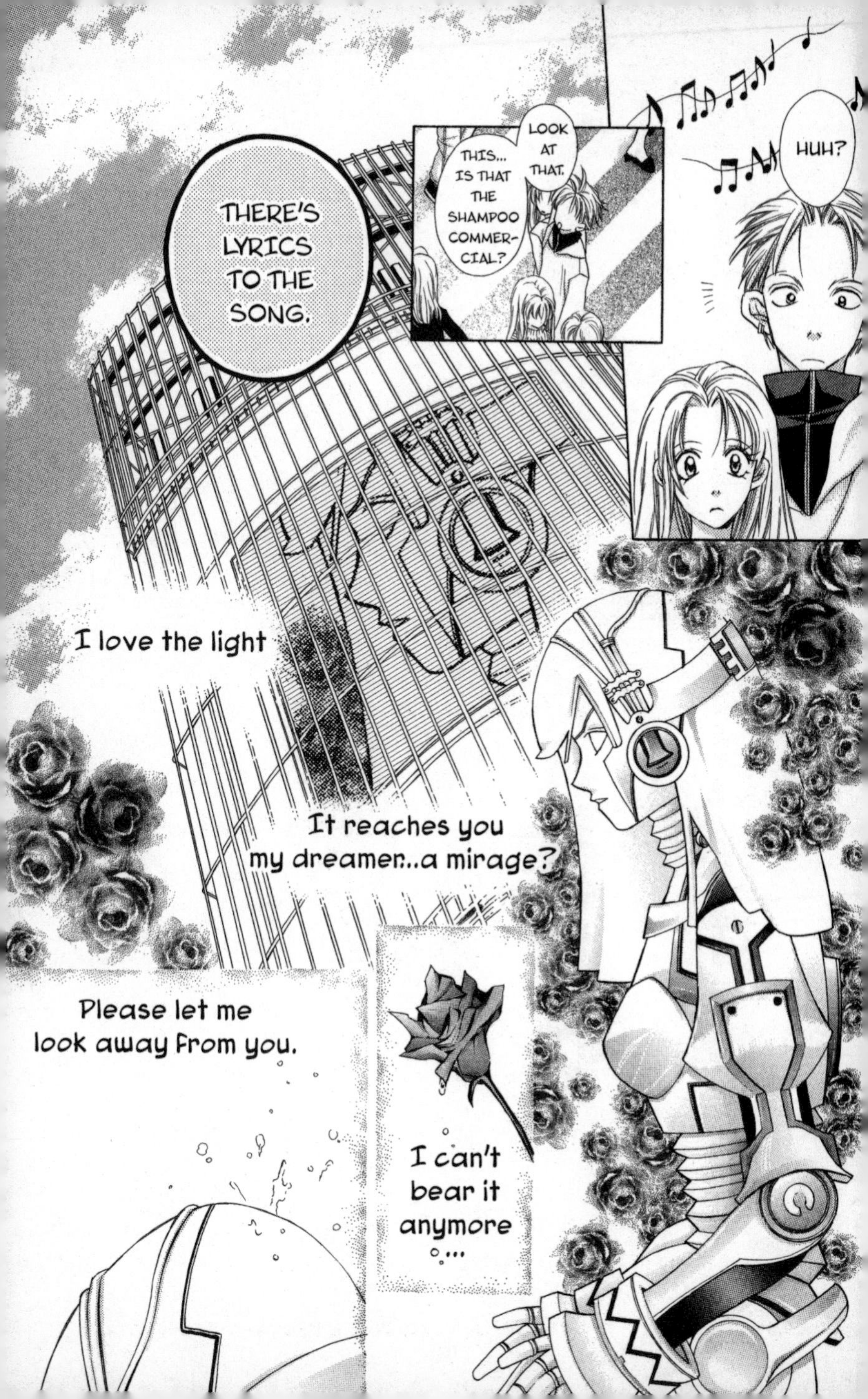
HUH?
LOOK AT THAT.
THIS... IS THAT THE SHAMPOO COMMERCIAL?
THERE'S LYRICS TO THE SONG.
I love the light
It reaches you my dreamer...a mirage?
I can't bear it anymore...
Please let me look away from you.

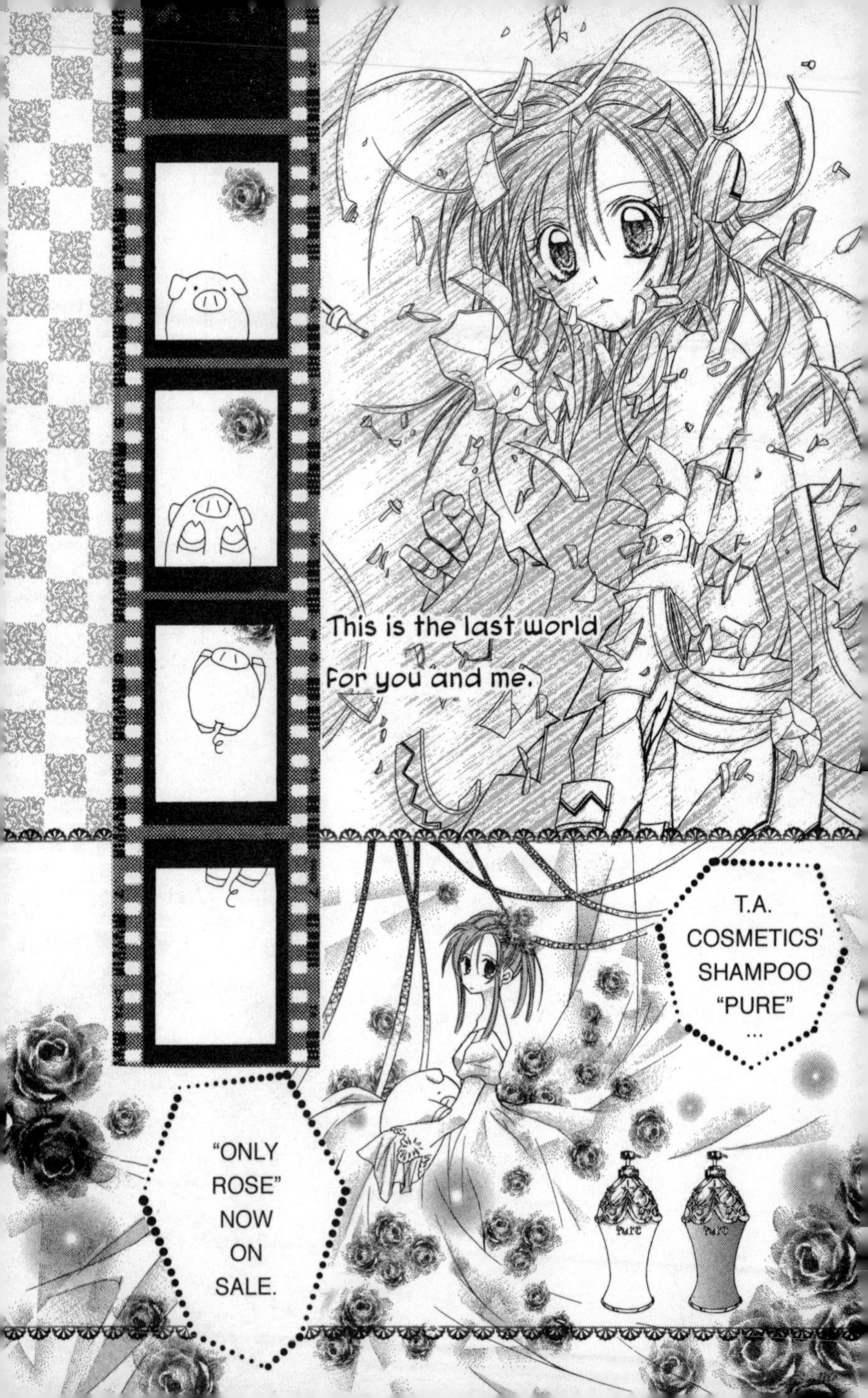
This is the last world
for you and me.
T.A. COSMETICS' SHAMPOO "PURE" ...
"ONLY ROSE" NOW ON SALE.

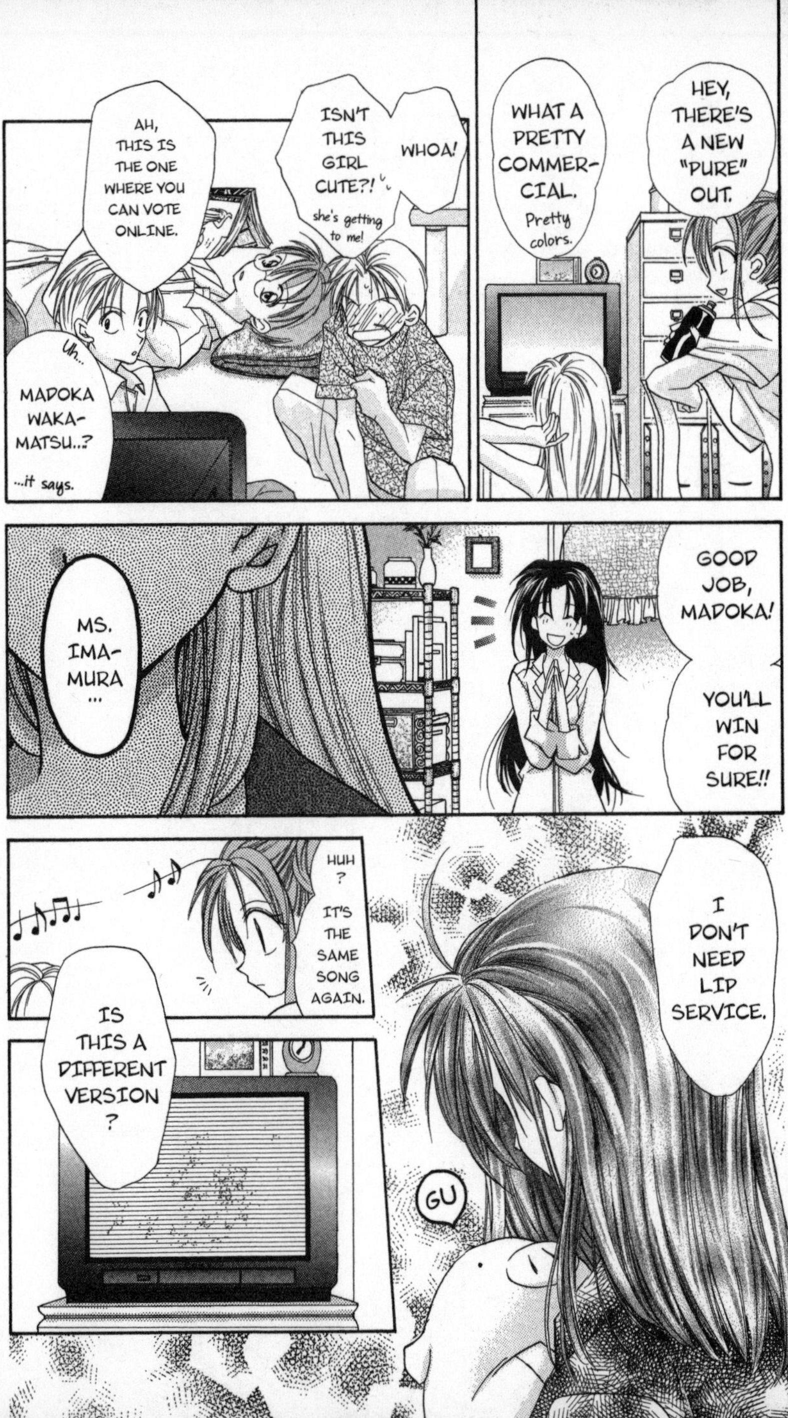
HEY, THERE'S A NEW "PURE" OUT.
WHAT A PRETTY COMMERCIAL.
Pretty colors.
WHOA!
ISN'T THIS GIRL CUTE?!
she's getting to me!
AH, THIS IS THE ONE WHERE YOU CAN VOTE ONLINE.
Uh...
MADOKA WAKAMATSU...?
...it says.
GOOD JOB, MADOKA!
YOU'LL WIN FOR SURE!!
MS. IMAMURA...
I DON'T NEED LIP SERVICE.
GU
HUH? IT'S THE SAME SONG AGAIN.
IS THIS A DIFFERENT VERSION?

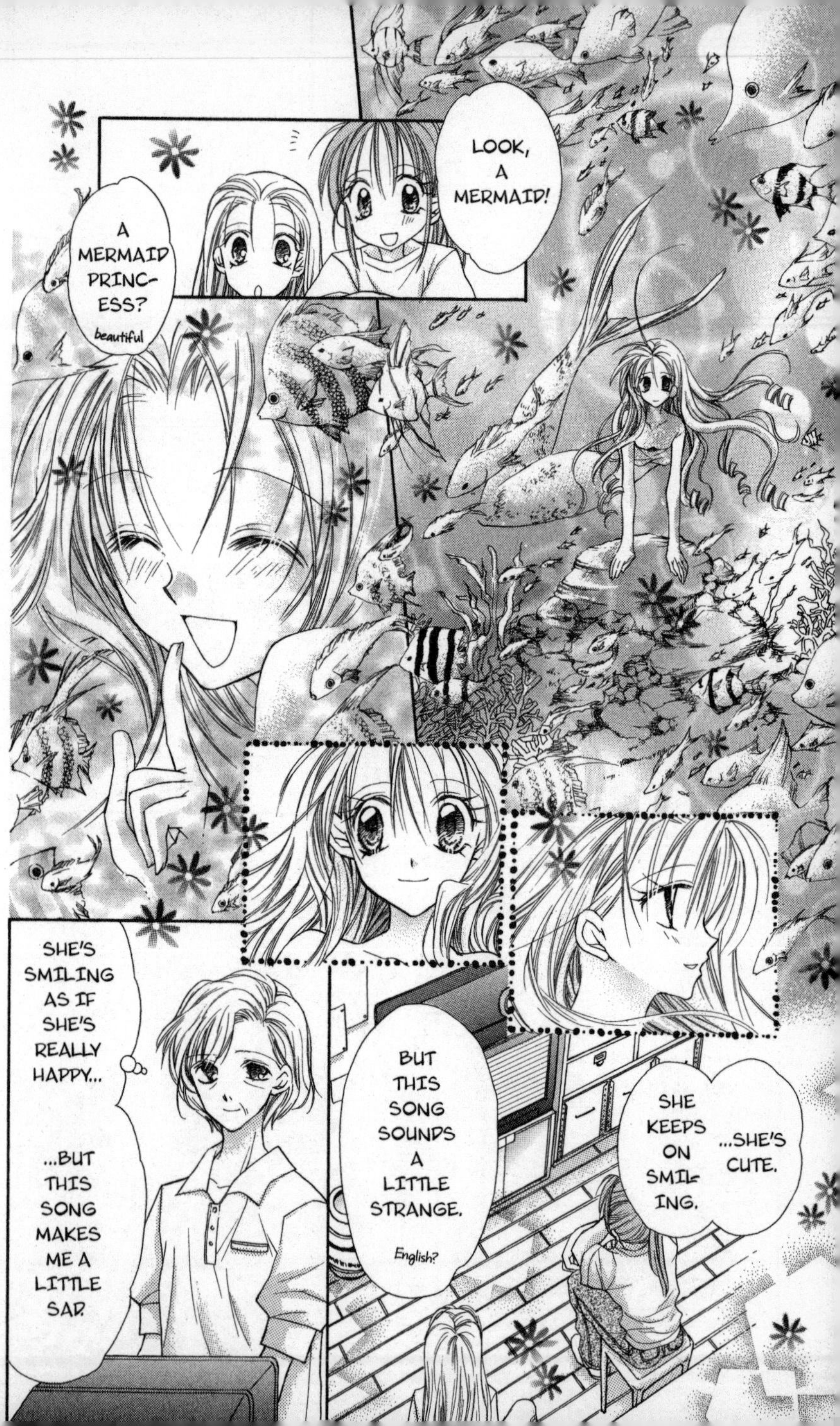
LOOK, A MERMAID!
A MERMAID PRINCESS?
beautiful
SHE KEEPS ON SMIL-ING.
...SHE'S CUTE.
BUT THIS SONG SOUNDS A LITTLE STRANGE.
English?
SHE'S SMILING AS IF SHE'S REALLY HAPPY...
...BUT THIS SONG MAKES ME A LITTLE SAD.

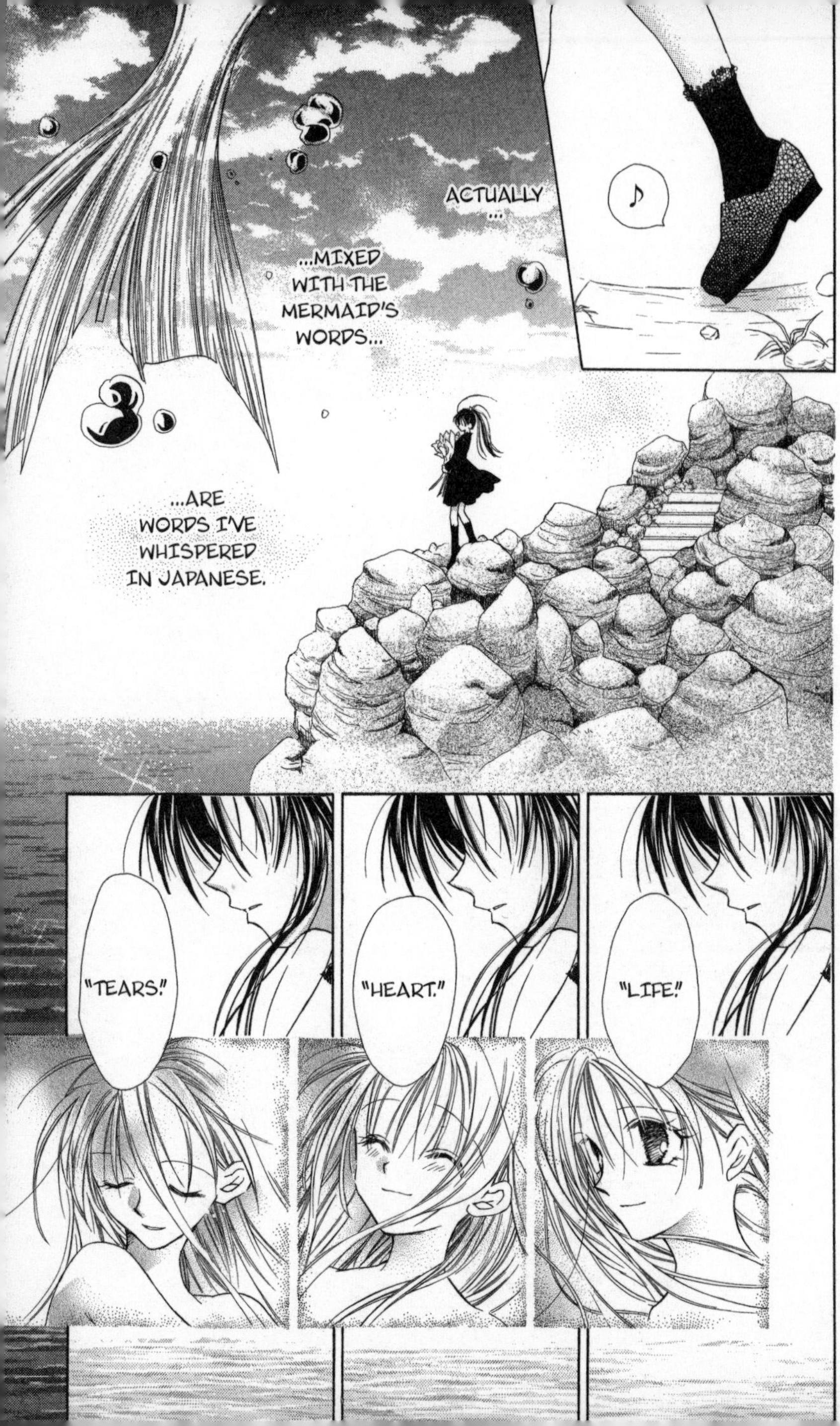
♪
ACTUALLY ...
...MIXED WITH THE MERMAID'S WORDS...
...ARE WORDS I'VE WHISPERED IN JAPANESE.
"LIFE."
"HEART."
"TEARS."

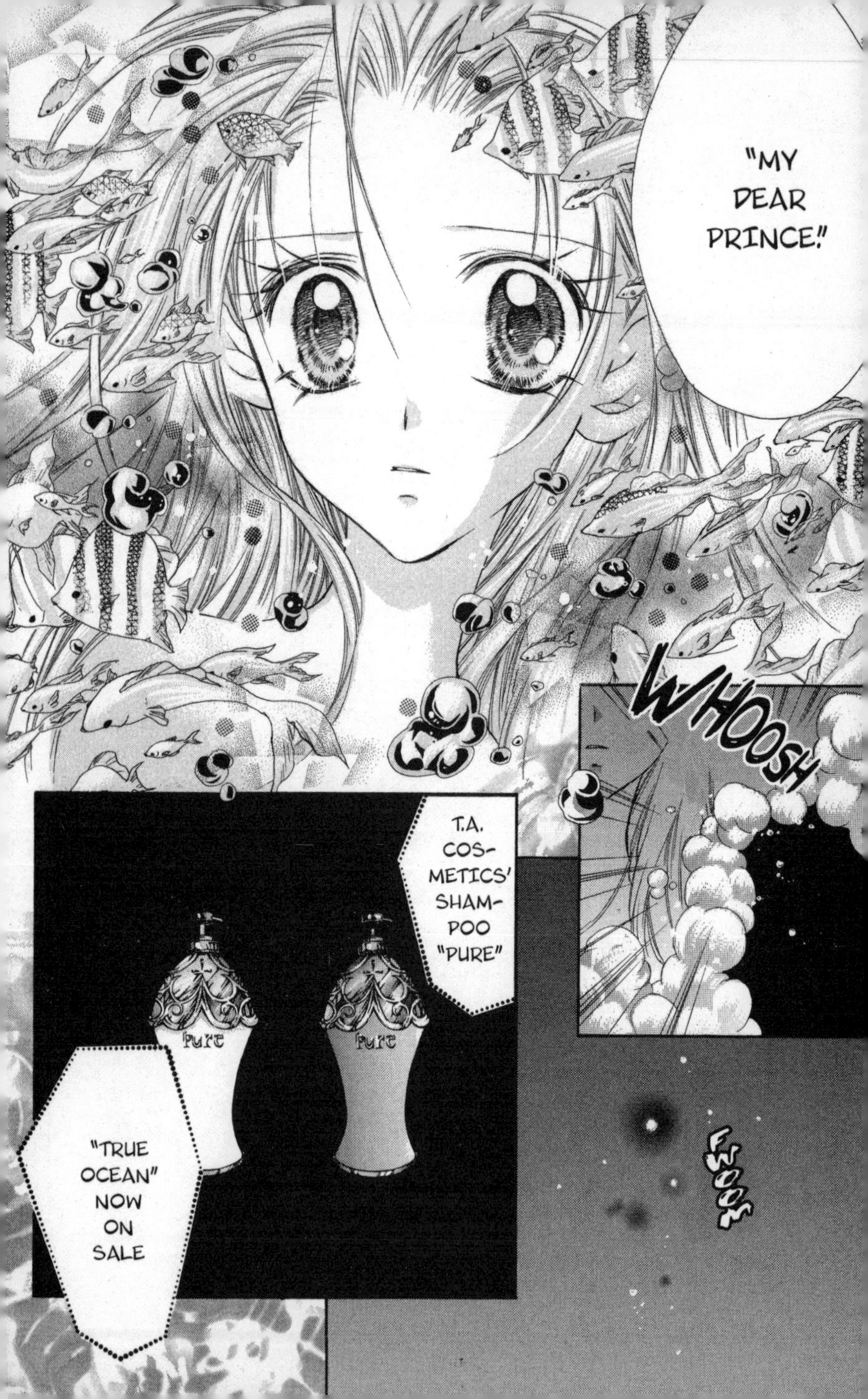
"MY DEAR PRINCE!"
WHOOSH
FWOOM
T.A. COS-METICS' SHAM-POO "PURE"
pure
pure
"TRUE OCEAN" NOW ON SALE

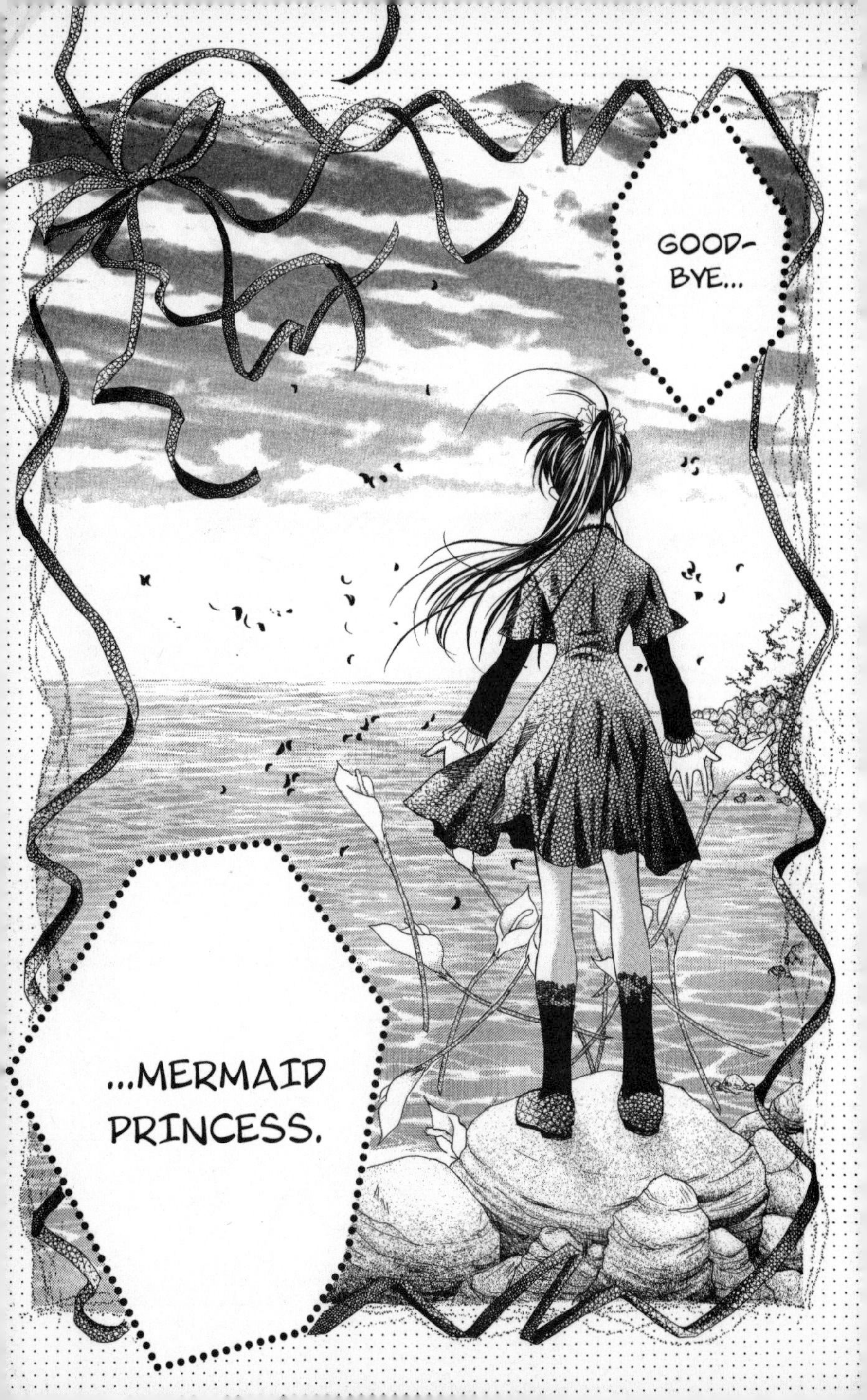
GOOD-BYE...
...MERMAID PRINCESS.

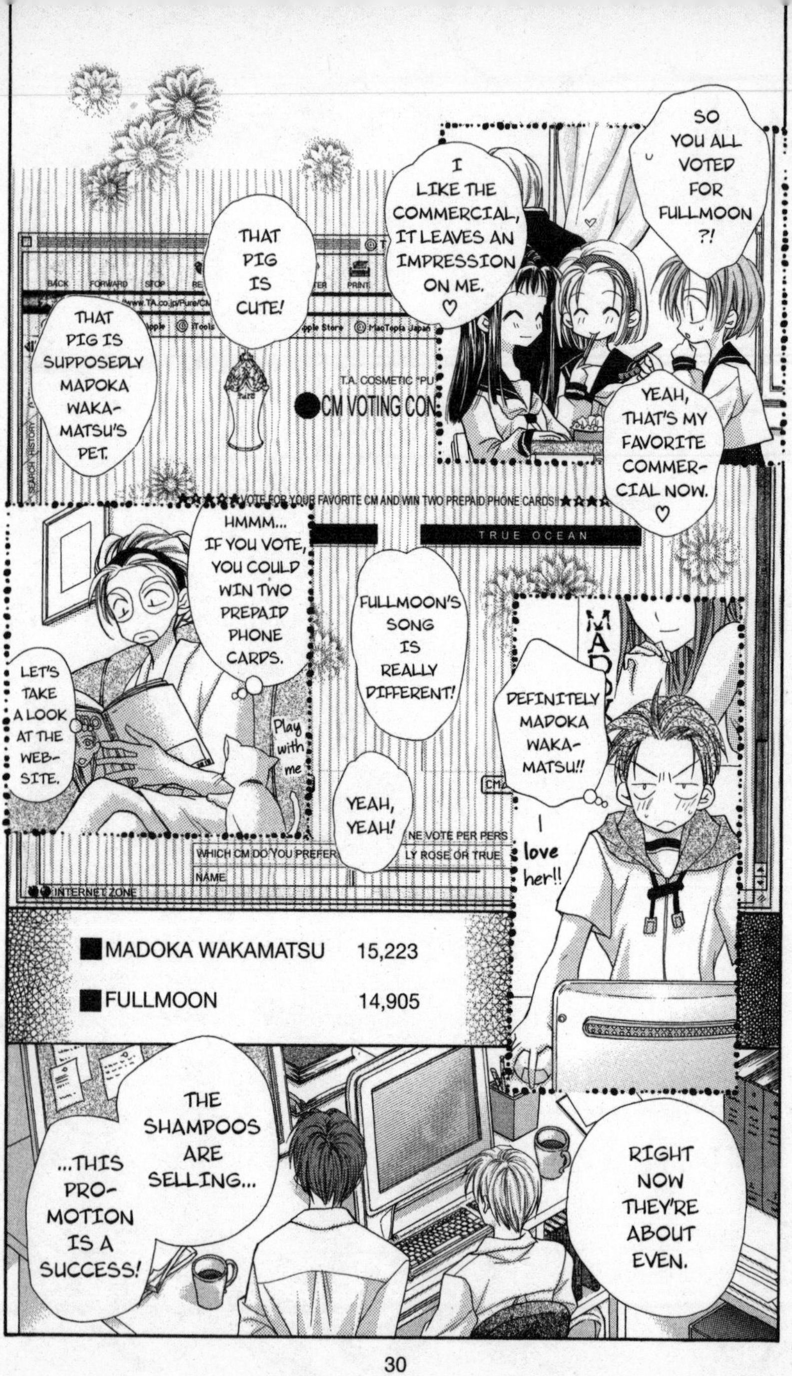
SO YOU ALL VOTED FOR FULLMOON?!
I LIKE THE COMMERCIAL, IT LEAVES AN IMPRESSION ON ME. ♡
YEAH, THAT'S MY FAVORITE COMMERCIAL NOW. ♡
THAT PIG IS CUTE!
THAT PIG IS SUPPOSEDLY MADOKA WAKAMATSU'S PET.
BACK FORWARD STOP PRINT
CM VOTING CON
VOTE FOR YOUR FAVORITE CM AND WIN TWO PREPAID PHONE CARDS!!
TRUE OCEAN
DEFINITELY MADOKA WAKAMATSU!!
I love her!!
FULLMOON'S SONG IS REALLY DIFFERENT!
YEAH, YEAH!
HMMM... IF YOU VOTE, YOU COULD WIN TWO PREPAID PHONE CARDS.
LET'S TAKE A LOOK AT THE WEB-SITE.
Play with me
WHICH CM DO YOU PREFER
NAME
INTERNET ZONE
MADOKA WAKAMATSU 15,223
FULLMOON 14,905
RIGHT NOW THEY'RE ABOUT EVEN.
THE SHAMPOOS ARE SELLING...
...THIS PROMOTION IS A SUCCESS!

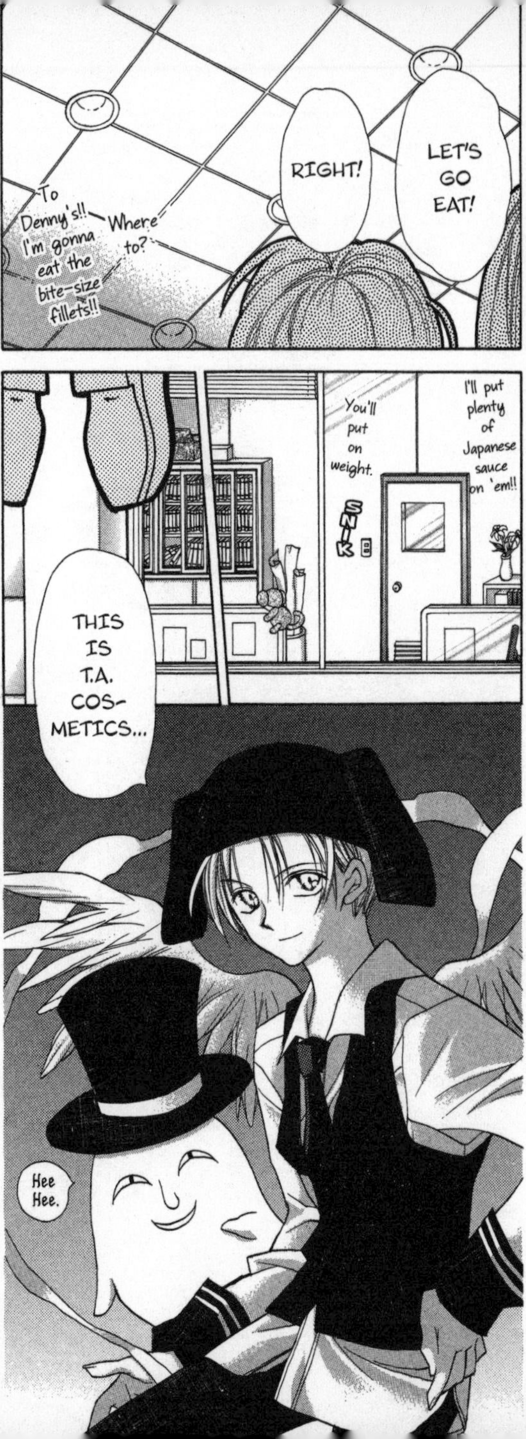
LET'S GO EAT!
RIGHT!
Where to?
To Denny's!! I'm gonna eat the bite-size fillets!!
I'll put plenty of Japanese sauce on 'em!!
You'll put on weight.
SNIK
THIS IS T.A. COSMETICS...
Hee Hee.

The agency president.

He is Imamura's older brother. Um... I wanted to draw an airhead. I want to make him even sillier. I'll say it myself, but he's like Noin, isn't he.

From "Kamikaze Kaito Jeanne"

the Aha guy

The boss.

He's Takuto and Meroko and Izumi and Jonathan's boss. He's the head of the pediatrics ward. The boss doesn't go retrieve souls himself anymore, unless it's absolutely necessary. Since there aren't any characters that look like Death, I made the boss look like it.

Shinigami costume

...there's space here, so please enjoy the dazzling world of neko-kun.

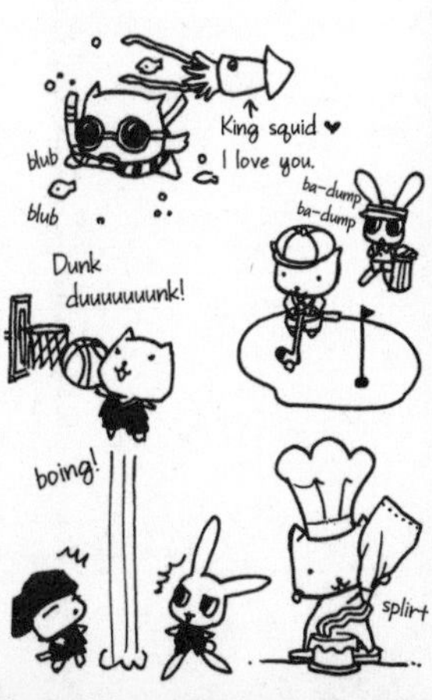
King squid ♥
I love you.
blub
blub
ba-dump
ba-dump
Dunk
duuuuuuunk!
boing!
splirt

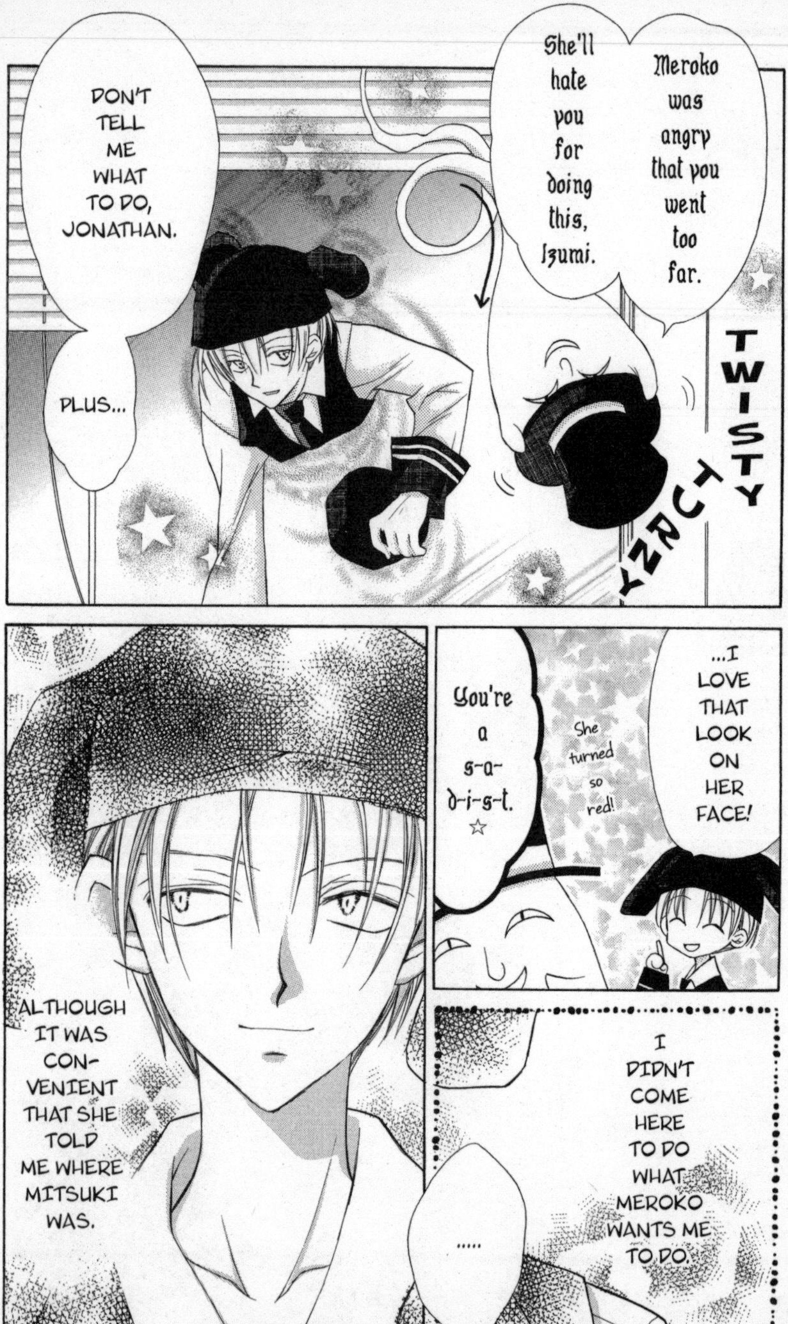

TWISTY
TURNY
Meroko was angry that you went too far.
She'll hate you for doing this, Izumi.
DON'T TELL ME WHAT TO DO, JONATHAN.
PLUS...
...I LOVE THAT LOOK ON HER FACE!
She turned so red!
You're a s-a-d-i-s-t. ☆
I DIDN'T COME HERE TO DO WHAT MEROKO WANTS ME TO DO.
.....
ALTHOUGH IT WAS CON-VENIENT THAT SHE TOLD ME WHERE MITSUKI WAS.

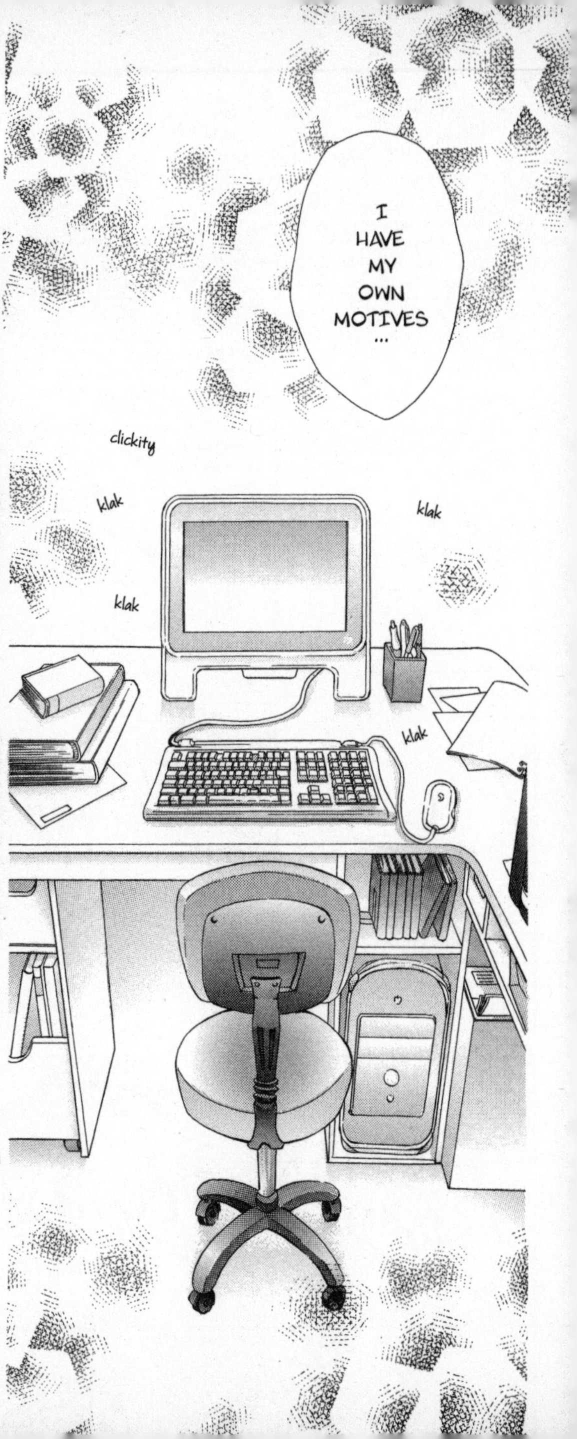
I HAVE MY OWN MOTIVES...
klak
clickity
klak
klak
klak

Arina Tanemura's "Penchi DE Shakin'"☆

Episode 50

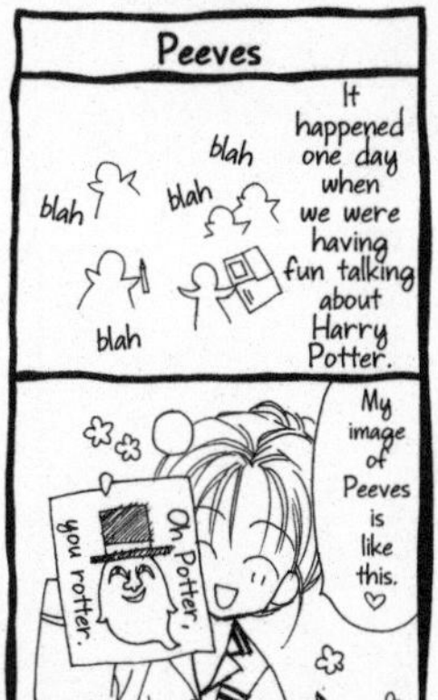
Peeves
It happened one day when we were having fun talking about Harry Potter.
blah
blah
blah
blah
My image of Peeves is like this.
Oh Potter, you rotter.
No way!
blah
There's no description like that!!
Peeves is supposed to look human!
blah
Oh...
...no way, huh...
I didn't want to waste it, so I used it for my new character.

I named it "Jonathan" without much thought... It's a common foreign name, but it has a jolly image for me...

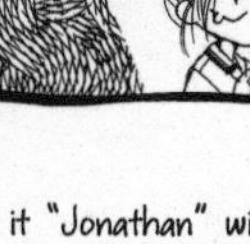
Oh really?

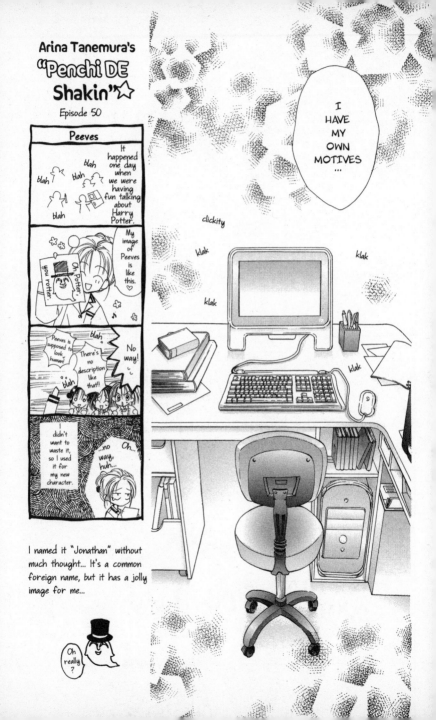

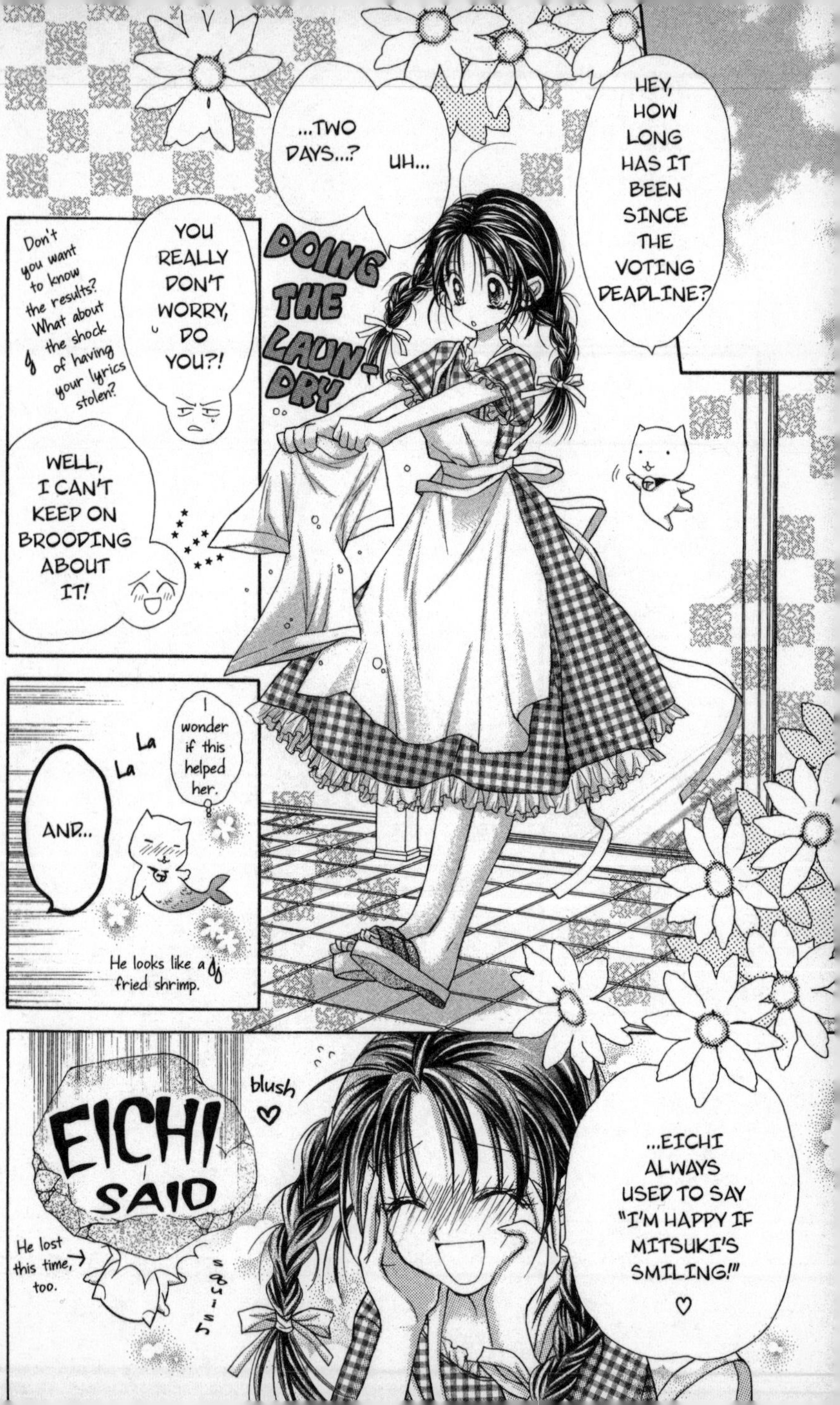
HEY, HOW LONG HAS IT BEEN SINCE THE VOTING DEADLINE?
UH...
...TWO DAYS...?
DOING THE LAUNDRY
YOU REALLY DON'T WORRY, DO YOU?!
Don't you want to know the results? What about the shock of having your lyrics stolen?
WELL, I CAN'T KEEP ON BROODING ABOUT IT!
I wonder if this helped her.
La
La
AND...
He looks like a fried shrimp.
...EICHI ALWAYS USED TO SAY "I'M HAPPY IF MITSUKI'S SMILING!" ♡
blush ♡
EICHI SAID
squish
He lost this time, too.

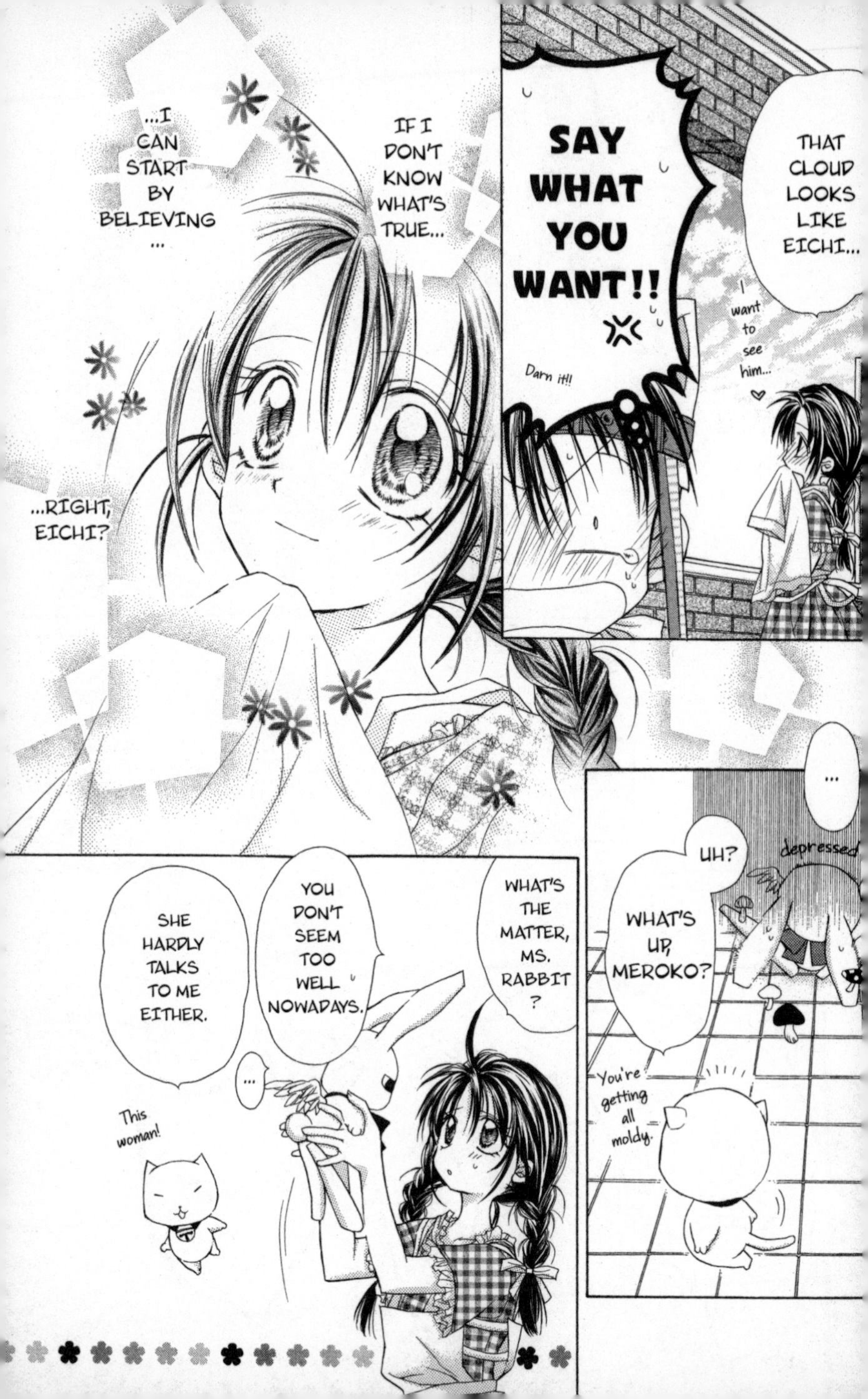

THAT CLOUD LOOKS LIKE EICHI...
I want to see him...
SAY WHAT YOU WANT!!
Darn it!!
IF I DON'T KNOW WHAT'S TRUE...
...I CAN START BY BELIEVING ...
...RIGHT, EICHI?
...
UH?
depressed
WHAT'S UP, MEROKO?
You're getting all moldy.
WHAT'S THE MATTER, MS. RABBIT?
YOU DON'T SEEM TOO WELL NOWADAYS.
...
SHE HARDLY TALKS TO ME EITHER.
This woman!

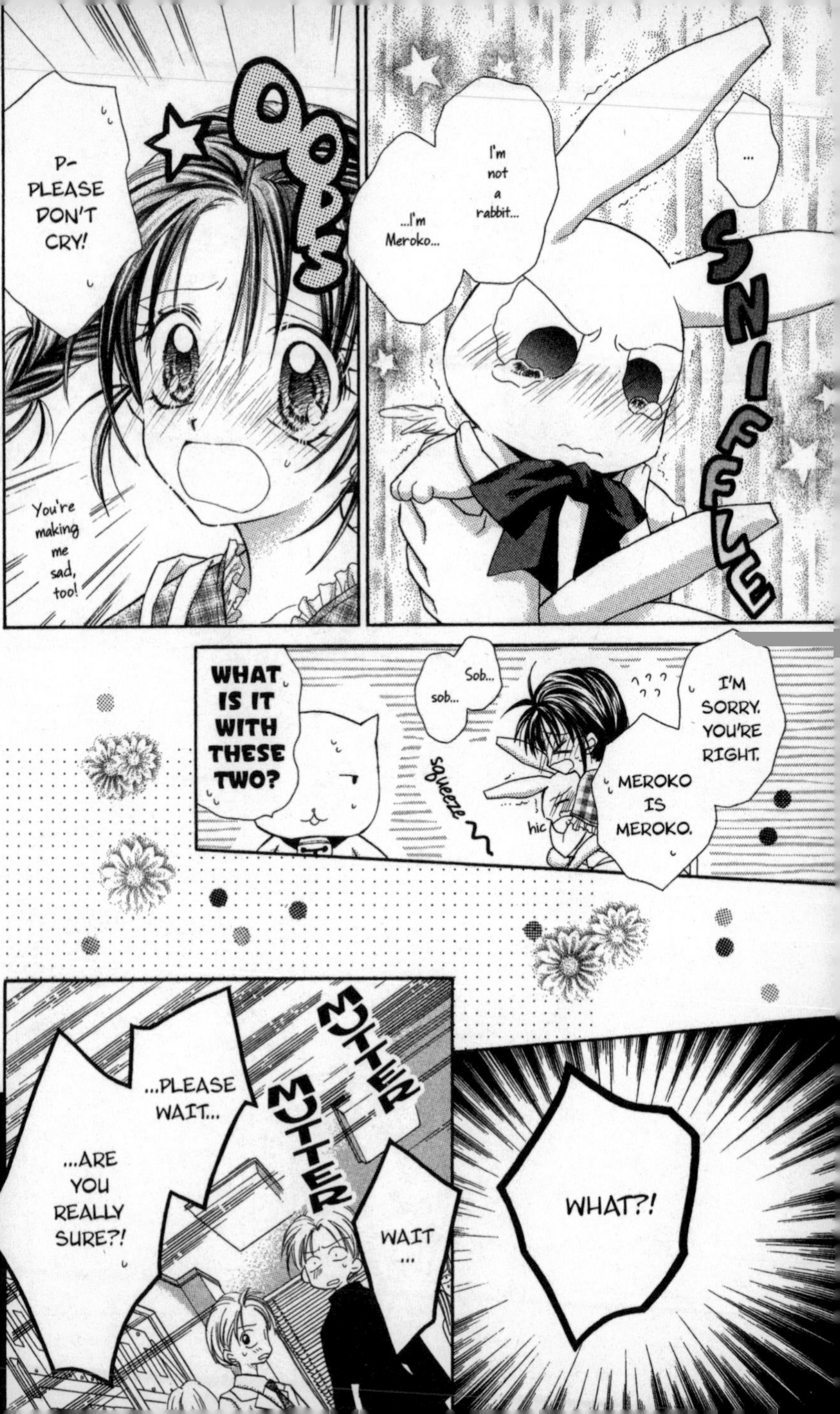
...
SNIFFLE
I'm not a rabbit...
...I'm Meroko...
OOPS
P-PLEASE DON'T CRY!
You're making me sad, too!
I'M SORRY. YOU'RE RIGHT.
MEROKO IS MEROKO.
hic
Sob... sob...
squeeze
WHAT IS IT WITH THESE TWO?
WHAT?!
WAIT ...
MUTTER MUTTER
...PLEASE WAIT...
...ARE YOU REALLY SURE?!

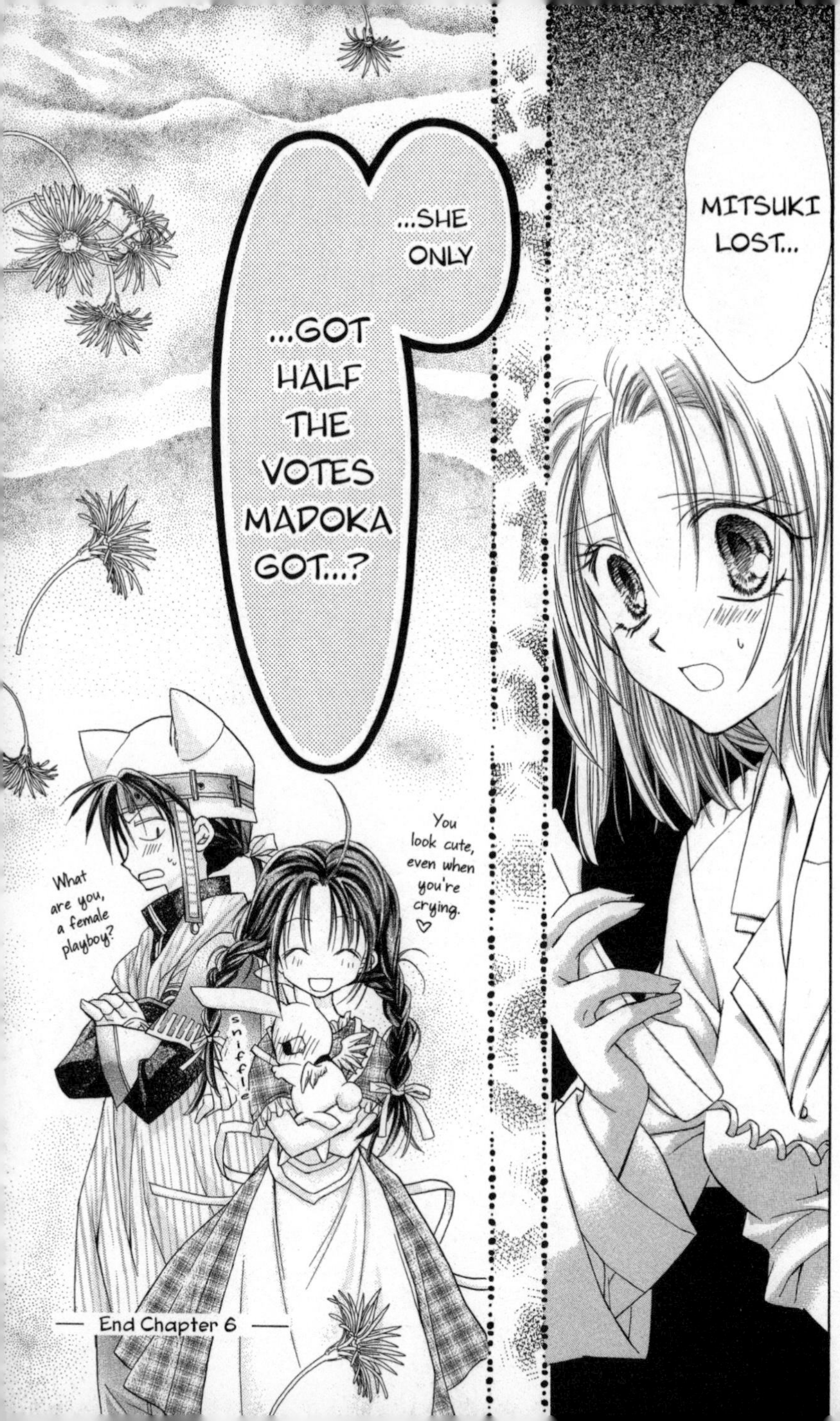
MITSUKI LOST...
...SHE ONLY
...GOT HALF THE VOTES MADOKA GOT...?
You look cute, even when you're crying. ♡
sniffle
What are you, a female playboy?
— End Chapter 6 —

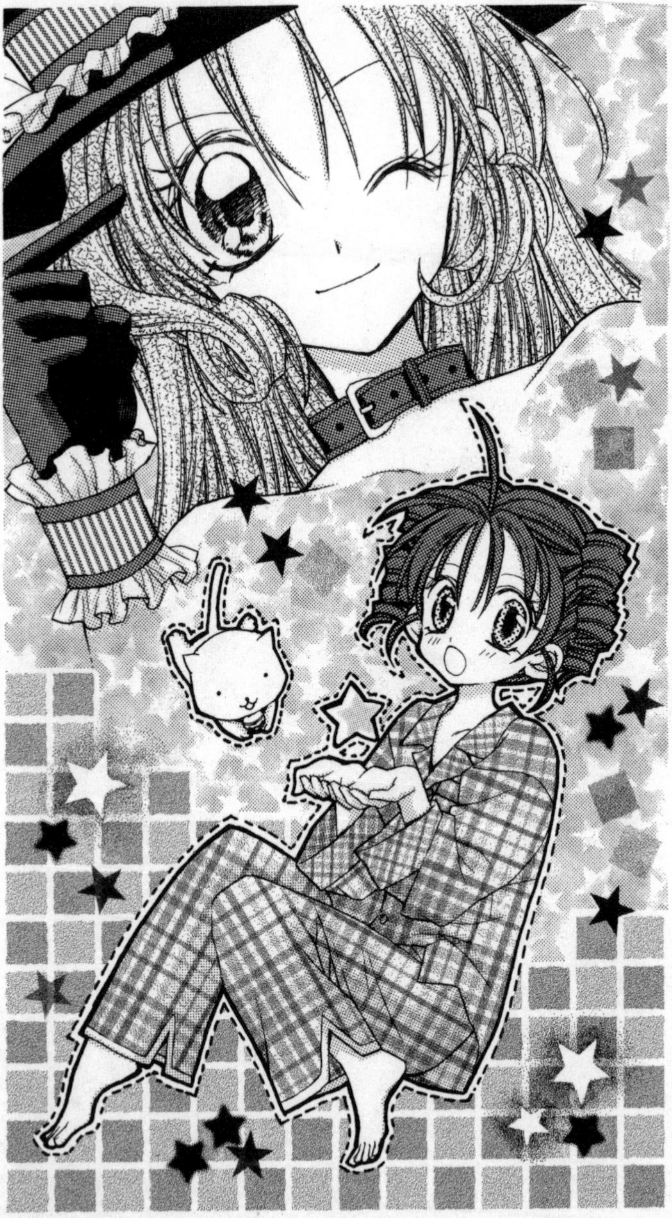

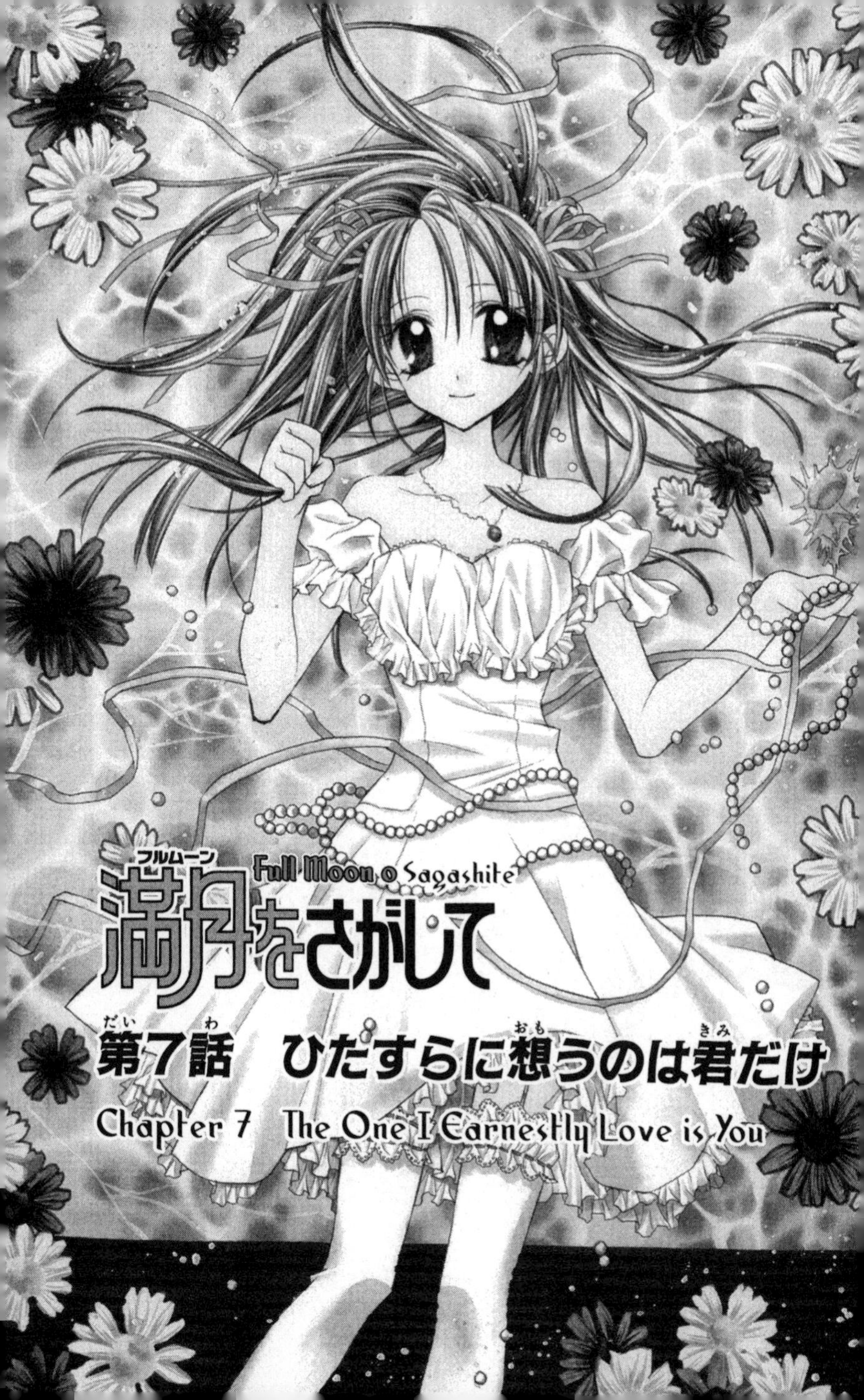
満月をさがして
Full Moon o Sagashite
第7話　ひたすらに想うのは君だけ
Chapter 7　The One I Earnestly Love is You

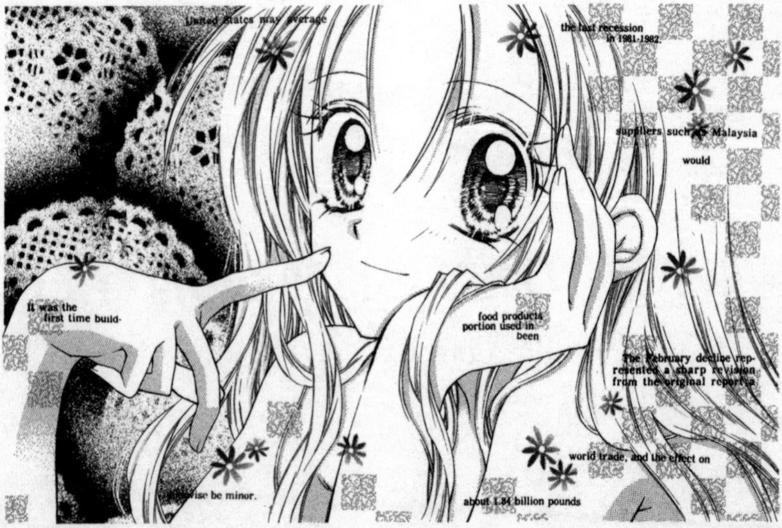
the last recession
in 1981-1982.
United States may average
suppliers such as Malaysia
would
food products
portion used in
been
It was the
first time build-
The February decline rep-
resented a sharp revision
from the original report
world trade, and the effect on
about 1.84 billion pounds
wise be minor.

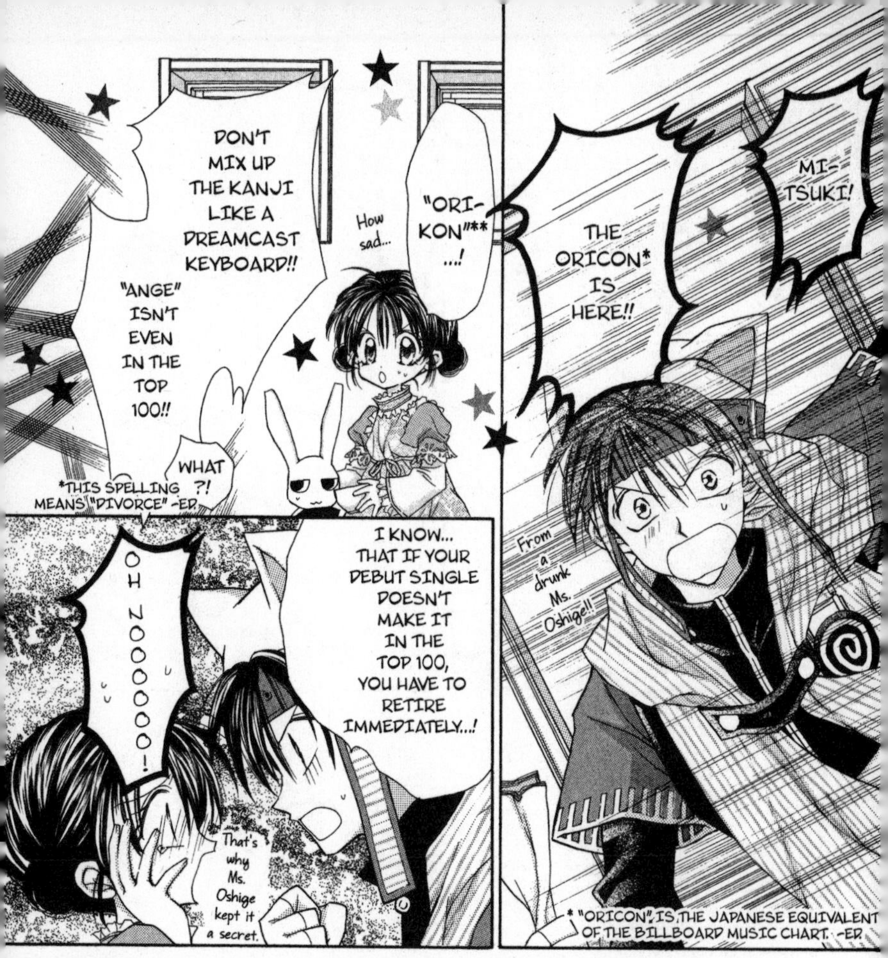
MI-TSUKI!
THE ORICON* IS HERE!!
From a drunk Ms. Oshige!!
* "ORICON" IS THE JAPANESE EQUIVALENT OF THE BILLBOARD MUSIC CHART. -ED.
"ORI-KON"** ...!
How sad...
DON'T MIX UP THE KANJI LIKE A DREAMCAST KEYBOARD!!
"ANGE" ISN'T EVEN IN THE TOP 100!!
WHAT ?!
*THIS SPELLING MEANS "DIVORCE" -ED.
I KNOW... THAT IF YOUR DEBUT SINGLE DOESN'T MAKE IT IN THE TOP 100, YOU HAVE TO RETIRE IMMEDIATELY...!
That's why Ms. Oshige kept it a secret.
OH NOOOOOOO!

Spoiler below!

Chapter 7 The One I Earnestly Love is You Cover Copy A pure voice. A pure feeling.

↑ I like this cover copy, Koike-san.

Since the story was about the mermaid princess, the cover illustration was drawn in that image. "I want a dress like this...but my upper arms aren't thin enough" was what I was thinking when I drew this, a sad memory. I gained weight again...I love rice!!! ♥ The theme of this story is that the Madoka episode is over for now, so before getting into the Izumi episode, I wanted to bring together the structure of all the unrequited loves. (I choose the title to reflect that too. The one I love is you alone—only that one person—and, you are the only one I love! are two versions with the same meaning.) ← Is my Japanese strange?

I love the Eichi♥Mitsuki coupling!! (Although I like the Takuto♥Mitsuki and the Izumi♥Meroko coupling too.) ← At work everyone has different opinions. Eichi♥Mitsuki banzai!! How happy ~!! By the way, panel 2 of this page appeared in a Dreamcast magazine. (Apparently a reader sent a letter to the section that reveals strange typos by the Dreamcast keyboard.) Thank you.

Note: When you type in Japanese, the characters automatically get converted to kana on-screen, and then you hit the space bar to transform the kana into kanji. If you don't get the kanji that you want, you keep hitting the space bar until the right one shows up. This can lead to weird typos. —Ed.

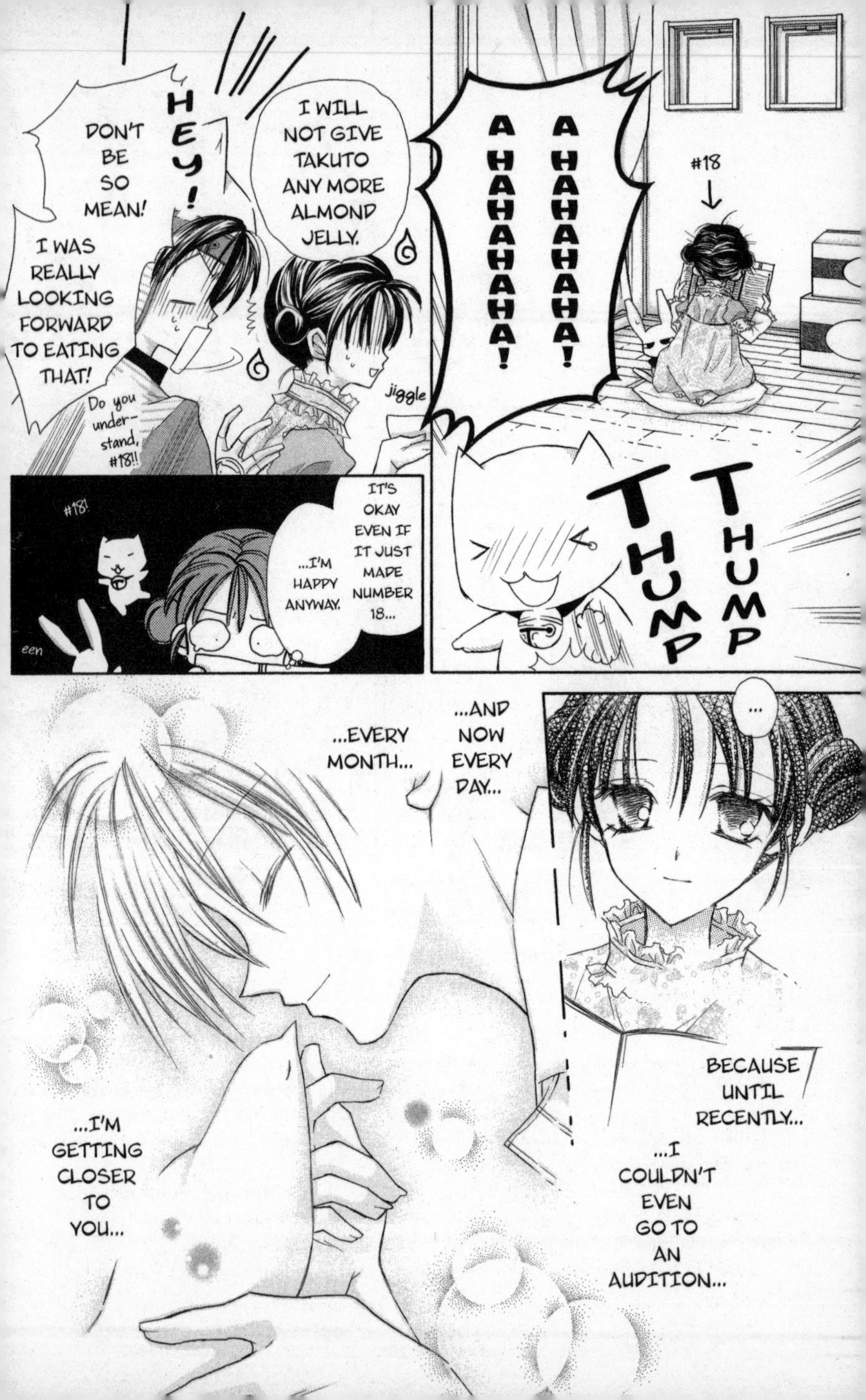
#18
AHAHAHAHA! AHAHAHAHA!
I WILL NOT GIVE TAKUTO ANY MORE ALMOND JELLY.
HEY!
DON'T BE SO MEAN!
I WAS REALLY LOOKING FORWARD TO EATING THAT!
jiggle
Do you under-stand, #18!!
THUMP THUMP
IT'S OKAY EVEN IF IT JUST MADE NUMBER 18...
...I'M HAPPY ANYWAY.
#18!
een
...
BECAUSE UNTIL RECENTLY...
...I COULDN'T EVEN GO TO AN AUDITION...
...AND NOW EVERY DAY...
...EVERY MONTH...
...I'M GETTING CLOSER TO YOU...

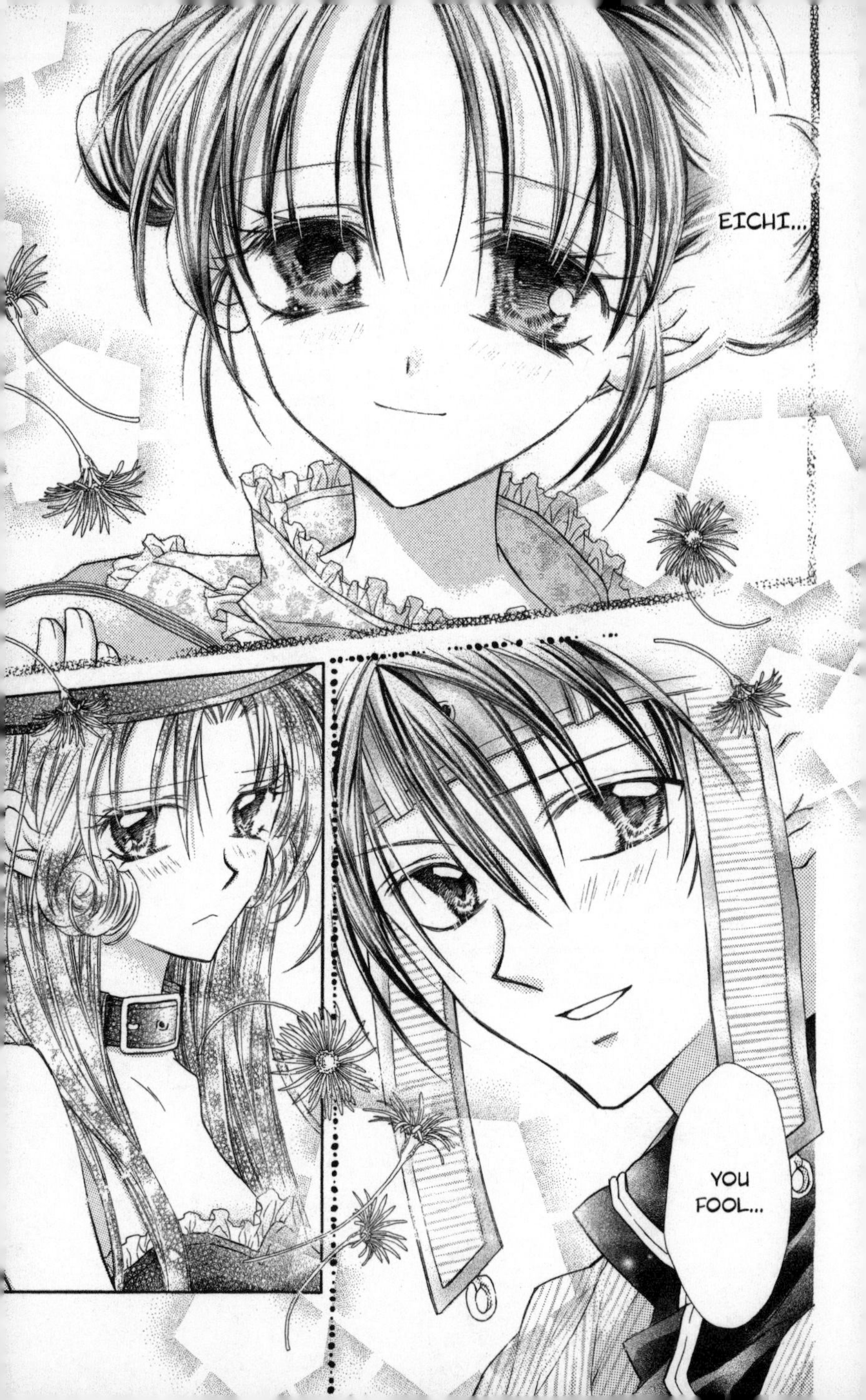
EICHI...
YOU FOOL...

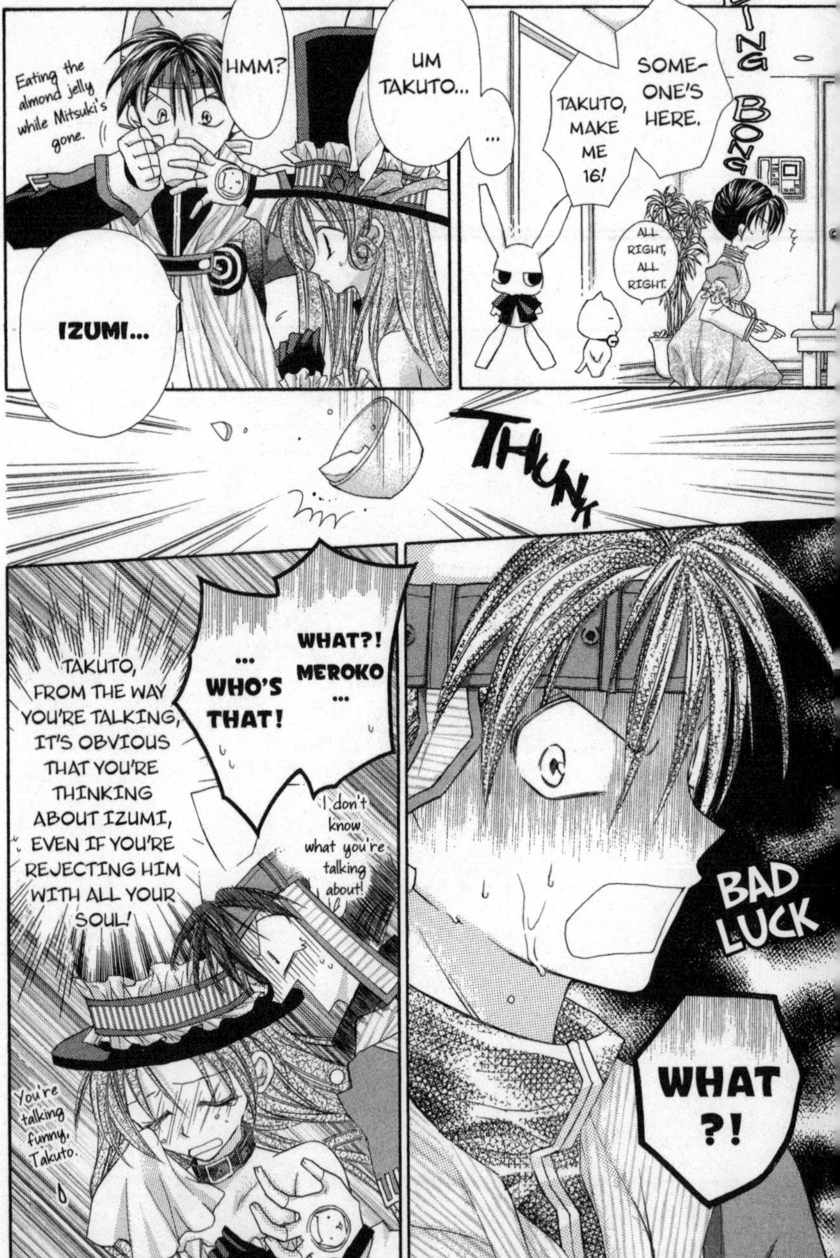
BING BONG
SOME-ONE'S HERE.
TAKUTO, MAKE ME 16!
ALL RIGHT, ALL RIGHT.
UM TAKUTO...
...
HMM?
Eating the almond jelly while Mitsuki's gone.
IZUMI...
THUNK
BAD LUCK
WHAT ?!
WHAT?! MEROKO ...
... WHO'S THAT!
TAKUTO, FROM THE WAY YOU'RE TALKING, IT'S OBVIOUS THAT YOU'RE THINKING ABOUT IZUMI, EVEN IF YOU'RE REJECTING HIM WITH ALL YOUR SOUL!
I don't know what you're talking about!
You're talking funny, Takuto.

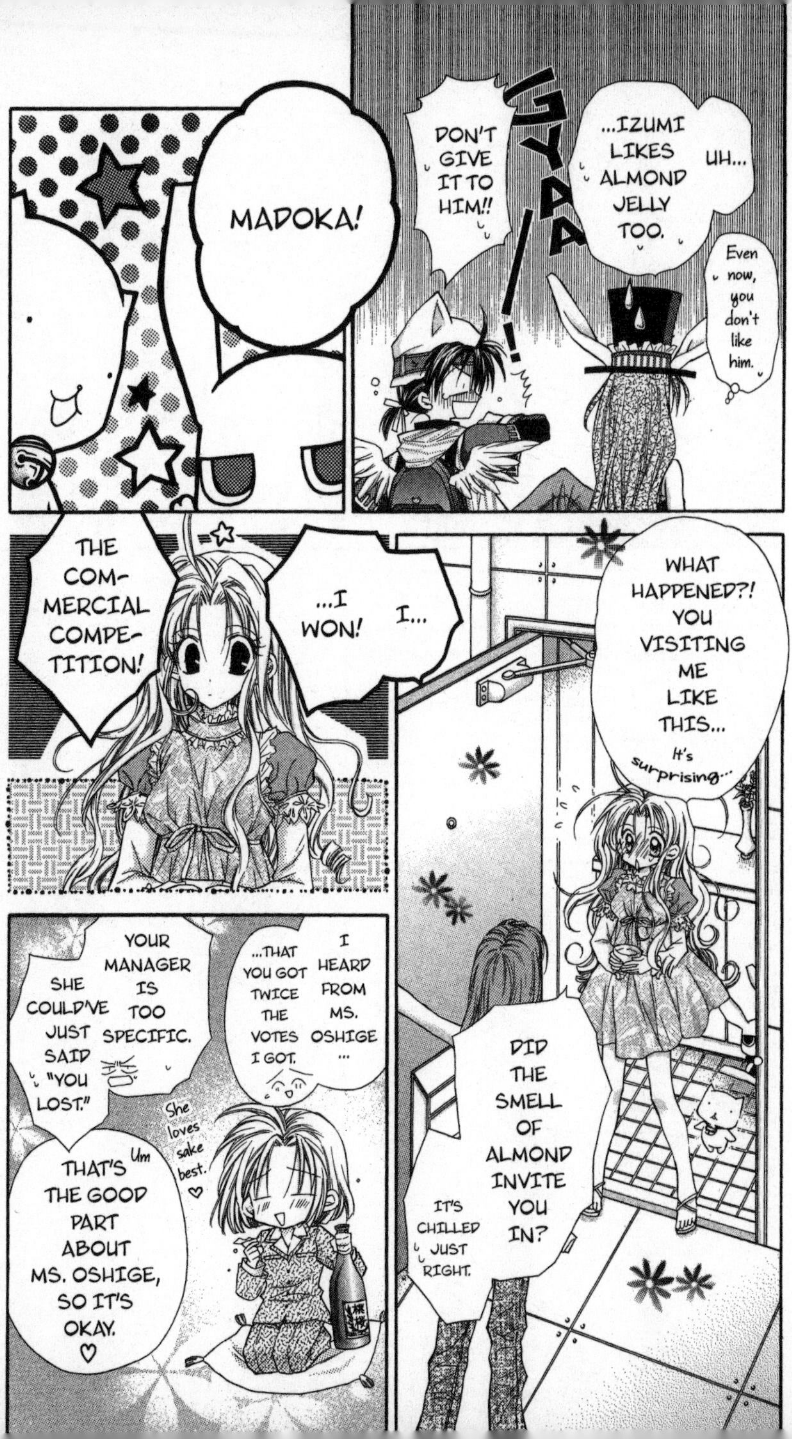
UH...
...IZUMI LIKES ALMOND JELLY TOO.
GYAA!!
DON'T GIVE IT TO HIM!!
Even now, you don't like him.
MADOKA!
WHAT HAPPENED?! YOU VISITING ME LIKE THIS...
It's surprising...
DID THE SMELL OF ALMOND INVITE YOU IN?
IT'S CHILLED JUST RIGHT.
I...
...I WON!
THE COMMERCIAL COMPETITION!
I HEARD FROM MS. OSHIGE...
...THAT YOU GOT TWICE THE VOTES I GOT.
YOUR MANAGER IS TOO SPECIFIC.
SHE COULD'VE JUST SAID "YOU LOST."
Um
She loves sake best.
THAT'S THE GOOD PART ABOUT MS. OSHIGE, SO IT'S OKAY. ♡

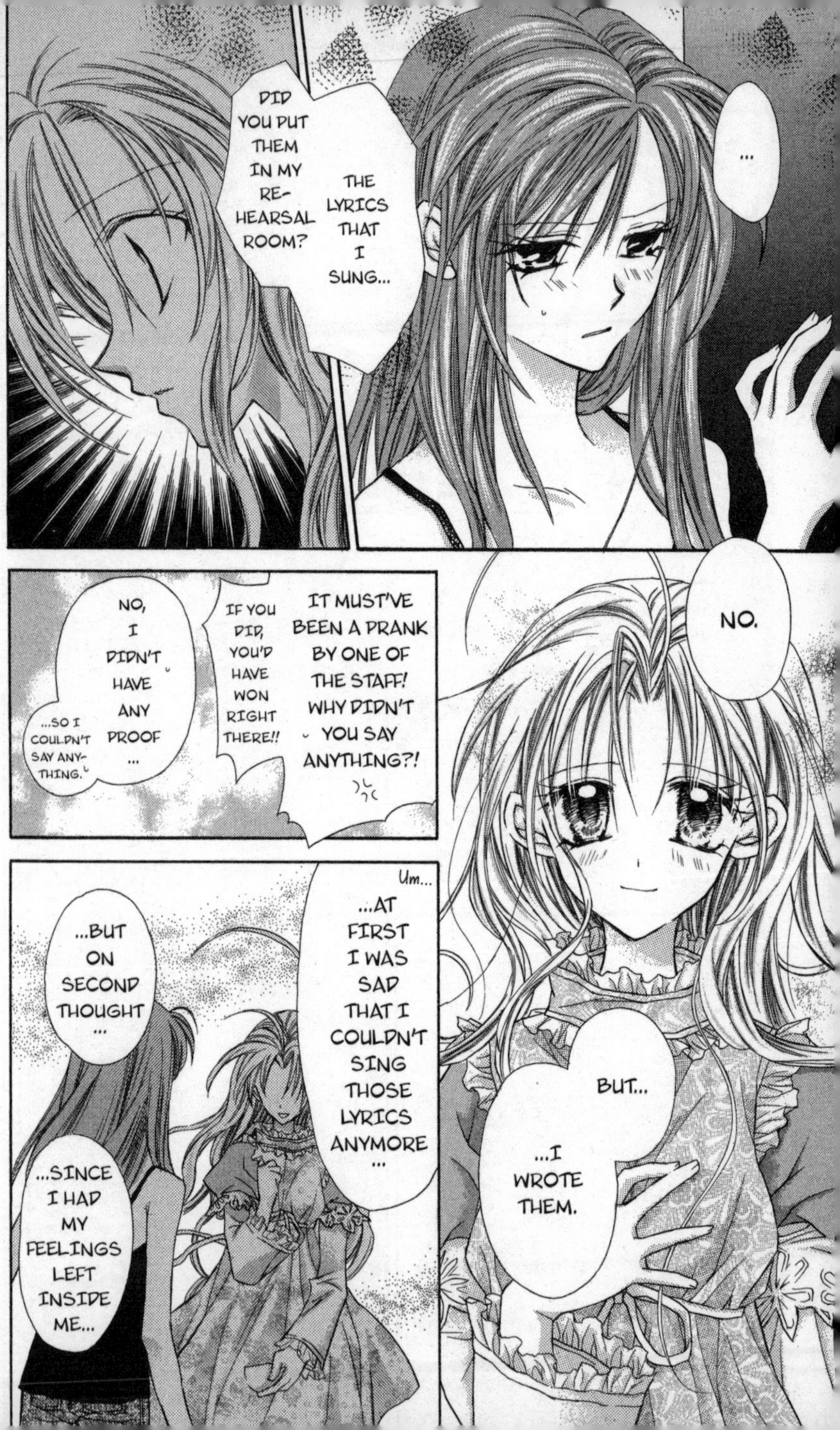
...
THE LYRICS THAT I SUNG...
DID YOU PUT THEM IN MY RE-HEARSAL ROOM?
NO.
BUT...
...I WROTE THEM.
IT MUST'VE BEEN A PRANK BY ONE OF THE STAFF! WHY DIDN'T YOU SAY ANYTHING?!
IF YOU DID, YOU'D HAVE WON RIGHT THERE!!
NO, I DIDN'T HAVE ANY PROOF...
...SO I COULDN'T SAY ANY-THING.
Um...
...AT FIRST I WAS SAD THAT I COULDN'T SING THOSE LYRICS ANYMORE...
...BUT ON SECOND THOUGHT...
...SINCE I HAD MY FEELINGS LEFT INSIDE ME...

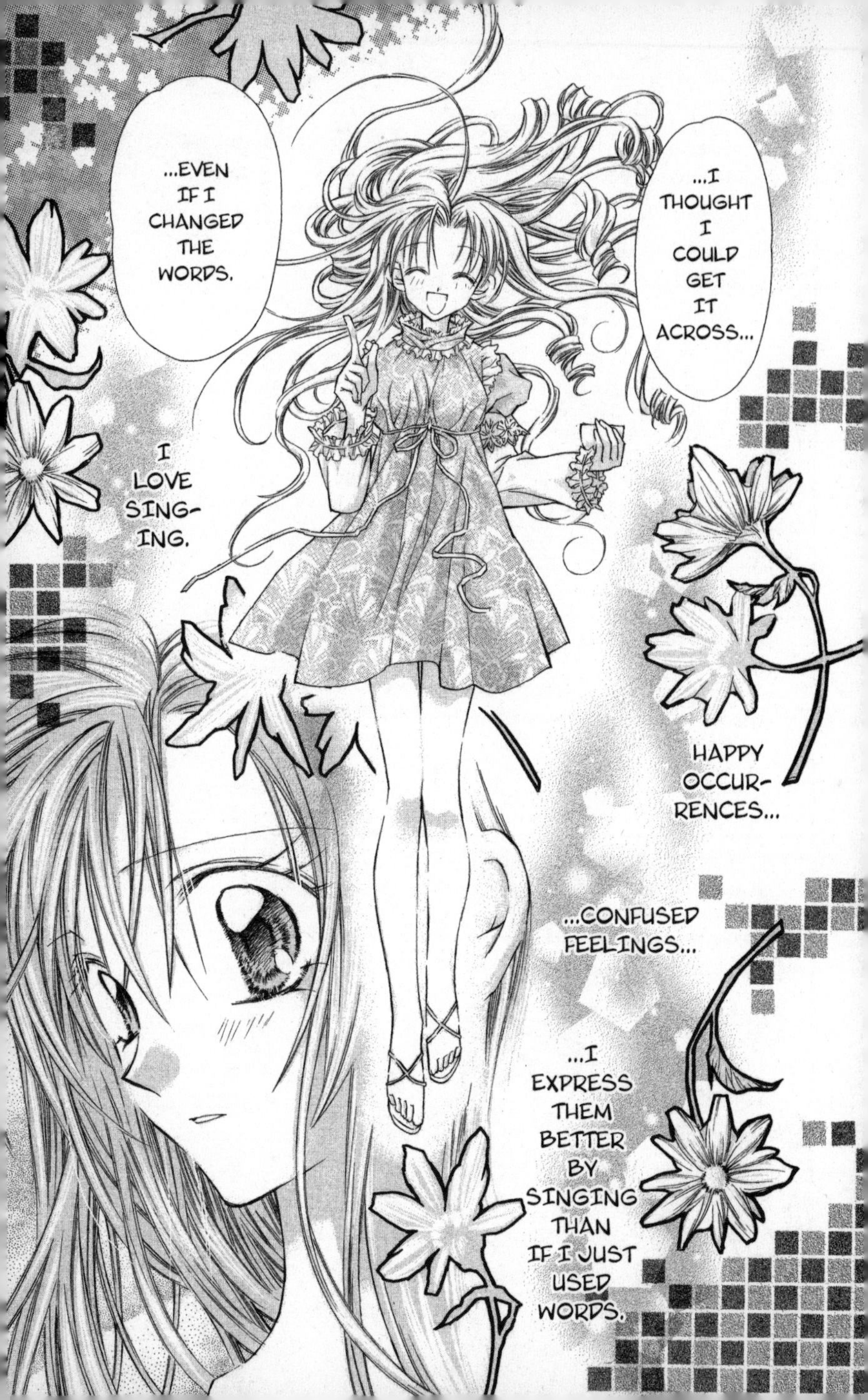
...I THOUGHT I COULD GET IT ACROSS...
...EVEN IF I CHANGED THE WORDS.
I LOVE SING-ING.
HAPPY OCCUR-RENCES...
...CONFUSED FEELINGS...
...I EXPRESS THEM BETTER BY SINGING THAN IF I JUST USED WORDS.

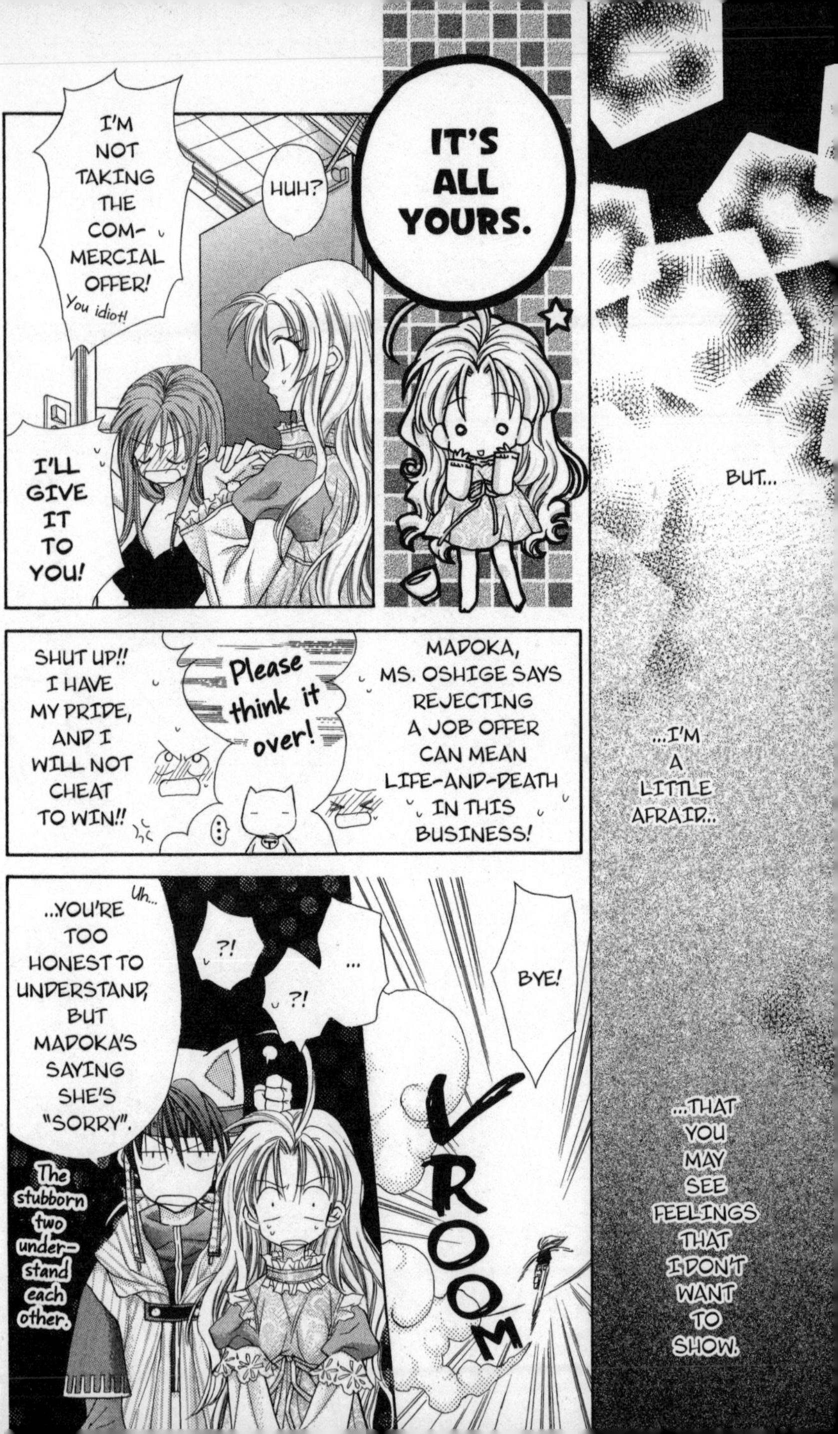
BUT...
...I'M A LITTLE AFRAID...
...THAT YOU MAY SEE FEELINGS THAT I DON'T WANT TO SHOW.
IT'S ALL YOURS.
HUH?
I'M NOT TAKING THE COM-MERCIAL OFFER!
You idiot!
I'LL GIVE IT TO YOU!
MADOKA, MS. OSHIGE SAYS REJECTING A JOB OFFER CAN MEAN LIFE-AND-DEATH IN THIS BUSINESS!
Please think it over!
...
SHUT UP!! I HAVE MY PRIDE, AND I WILL NOT CHEAT TO WIN!!
BYE!
VROOM
?!
...
?!
Uh...
...YOU'RE TOO HONEST TO UNDERSTAND, BUT MADOKA'S SAYING SHE'S "SORRY".
The stubborn two under-stand each other.

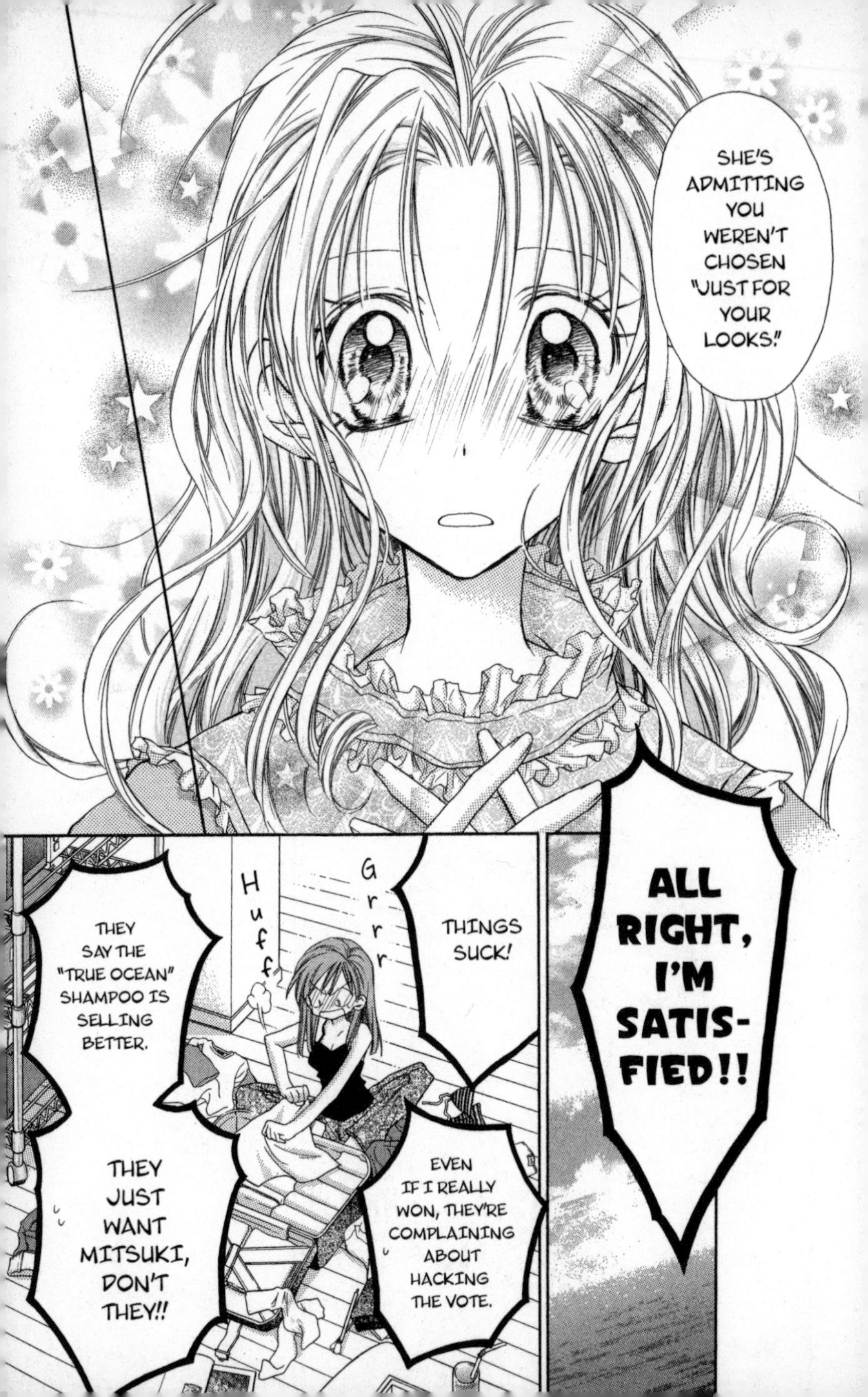
SHE'S ADMITTING YOU WEREN'T CHOSEN "JUST FOR YOUR LOOKS."
ALL RIGHT, I'M SATIS-FIED!!
THINGS SUCK!
Grrr
Huff
THEY SAY THE "TRUE OCEAN" SHAMPOO IS SELLING BETTER.
EVEN IF I REALLY WON, THEY'RE COMPLAINING ABOUT HACKING THE VOTE.
THEY JUST WANT MITSUKI, DON'T THEY!!

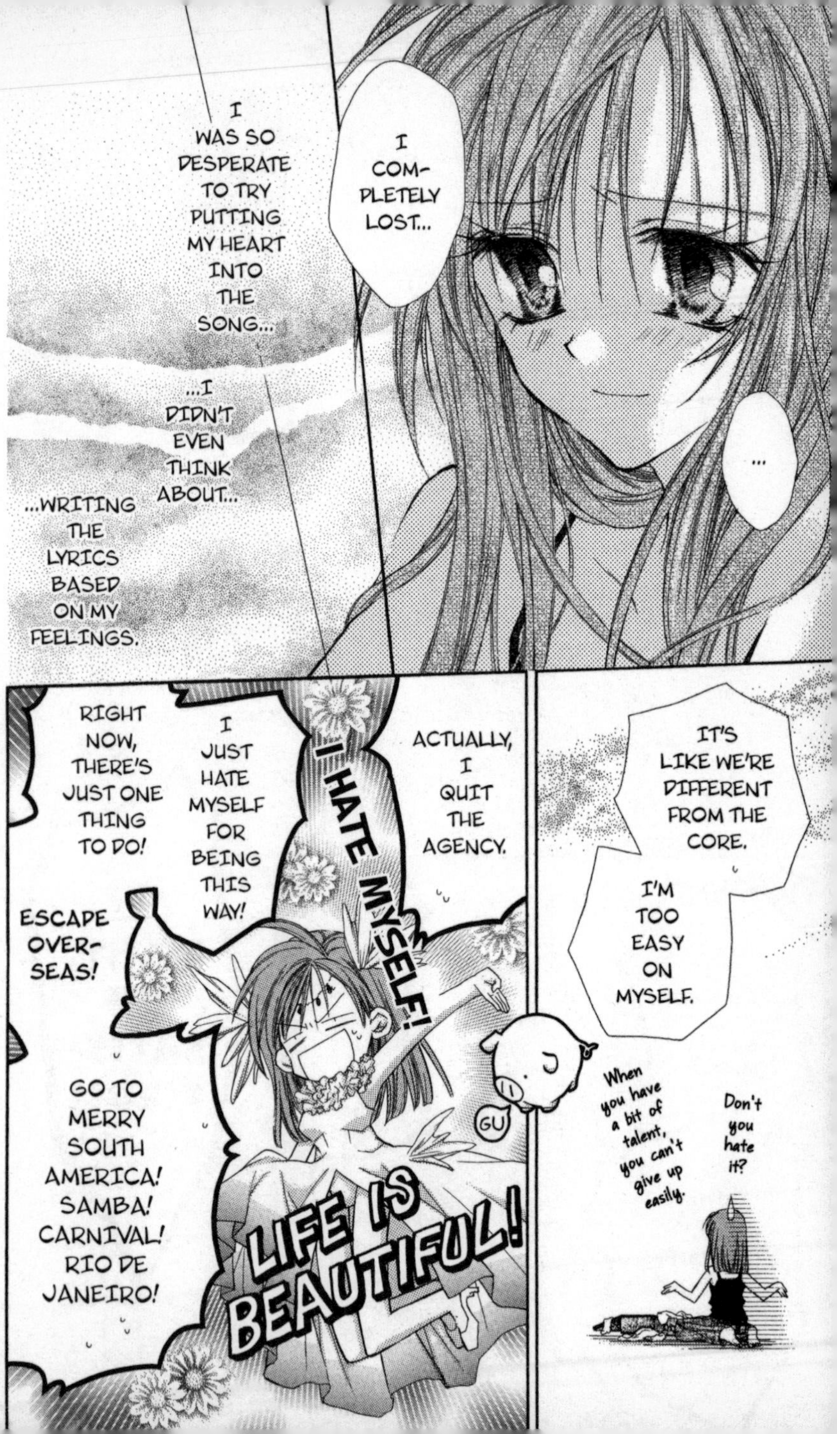
I COMPLETELY LOST...
I WAS SO DESPERATE TO TRY PUTTING MY HEART INTO THE SONG...
...I DIDN'T EVEN THINK ABOUT...
...
...WRITING THE LYRICS BASED ON MY FEELINGS.
IT'S LIKE WE'RE DIFFERENT FROM THE CORE.
I'M TOO EASY ON MYSELF.
Don't you hate it?
When you have a bit of talent, you can't give up easily.
ACTUALLY, I QUIT THE AGENCY.
I HATE MYSELF!
I JUST HATE MYSELF FOR BEING THIS WAY!
RIGHT NOW, THERE'S JUST ONE THING TO DO!
ESCAPE OVERSEAS!
GU
GO TO MERRY SOUTH AMERICA! SAMBA! CARNIVAL! RIO DE JANEIRO!
LIFE IS BEAUTIFUL!

● My Recent Favorites ●

POPEE the Performer

This is a computer animated cartoon being broadcast on Kids Station (it's been re-broadcast now). Cable TV.

The story is about Popee, a clown in a circus, performing his tricks (practicing?) with his assistant Kedamono. Eventually, Popee's father Papee joins, and there's a lot of dark(?) and violent (-__-) gags. (I'm sorry this explanation is hard to understand. ^-) I love all three of them.

The title song is very good, and there is a maxi single out, which I recommend. (The promo clip being broadcast on Kids Station is the best!) It's in the DVD too.

My favorite episodes are "SLEEP," "MIRROR," "OPENING," "LONELINESS," "FACE," "POISON," "DREAM," "KARATE SHOW," and "GUNMAN" (that's a lot).

● New: Storm of Love ●

The well-known(?!) drama on Fuji-TV (Afternoons 1:30-2:00). It may be over when this tankobon is out, but I love this. (One reason is that Takeshi is being played by G3) of Kamen Rider Agito.

When the master died, we were working on **Full Moon**, so me and assistant Airi were really sad. Airi loves the drama, too.

We love the drama so much that when Ishihara Yoshizumi-san appears on the 5-o'clock Super News weather, we get really angry at him. (I'm sorry Yoshizumi-san.)

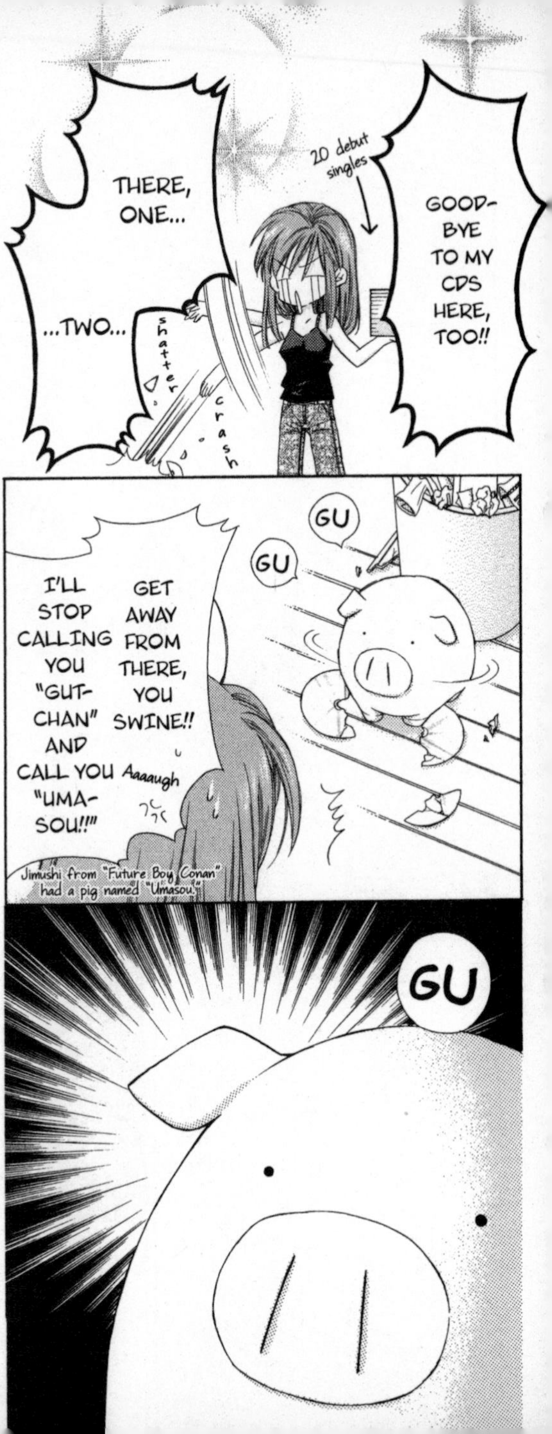
GOOD-BYE TO MY CDS HERE, TOO!!
20 debut singles
THERE, ONE...
...TWO...
shatter
crash
GU
GU
GET AWAY FROM THERE, YOU SWINE!!
I'LL STOP CALLING YOU "GUT-CHAN" AND CALL YOU "UMA-SOU!!"
Aaaaugh
Jimushi from "Future Boy Conan" had a pig named "Umasou."
GU

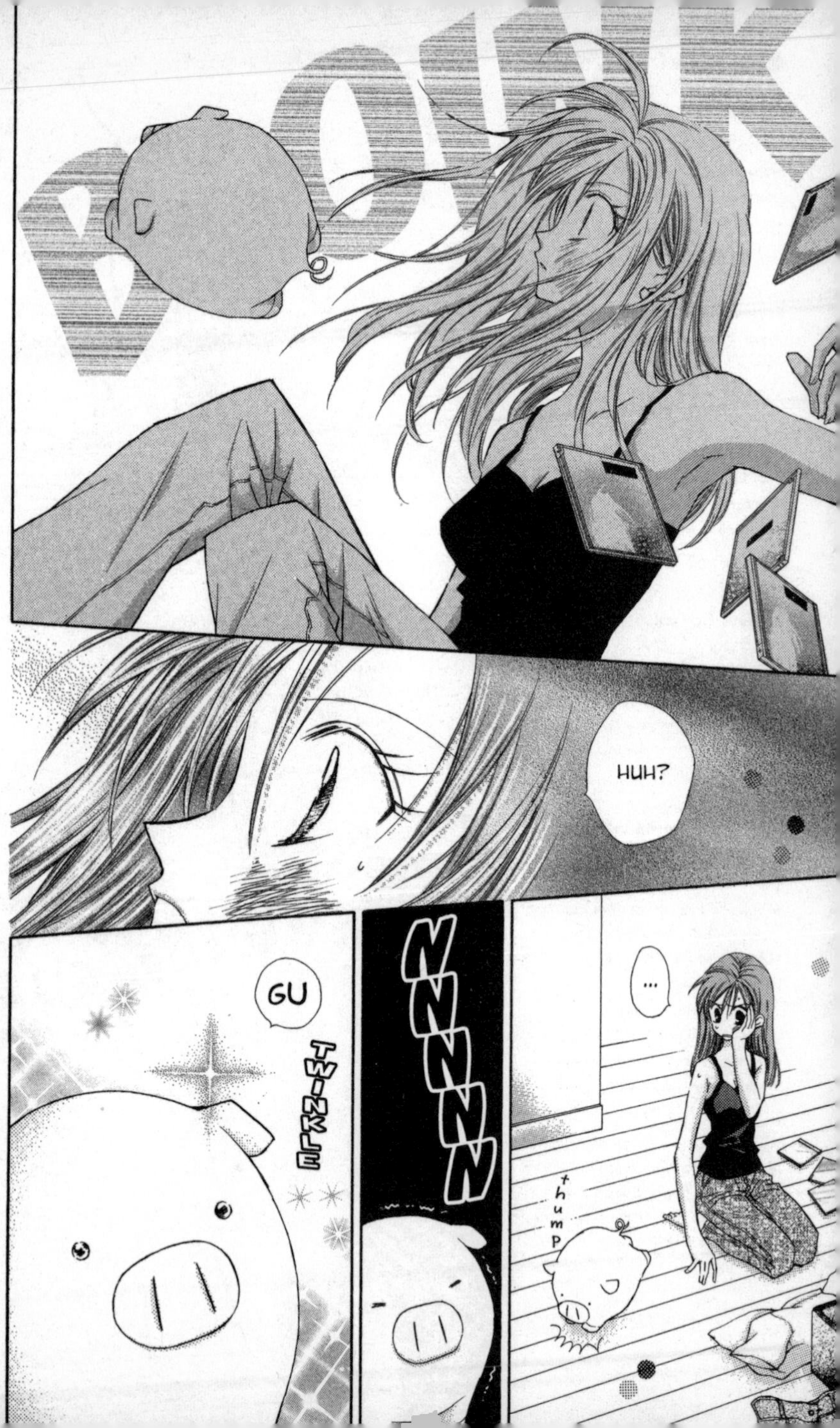
BOINK
HUH?
...
thump
NNNNNN
GU
TWINKLE

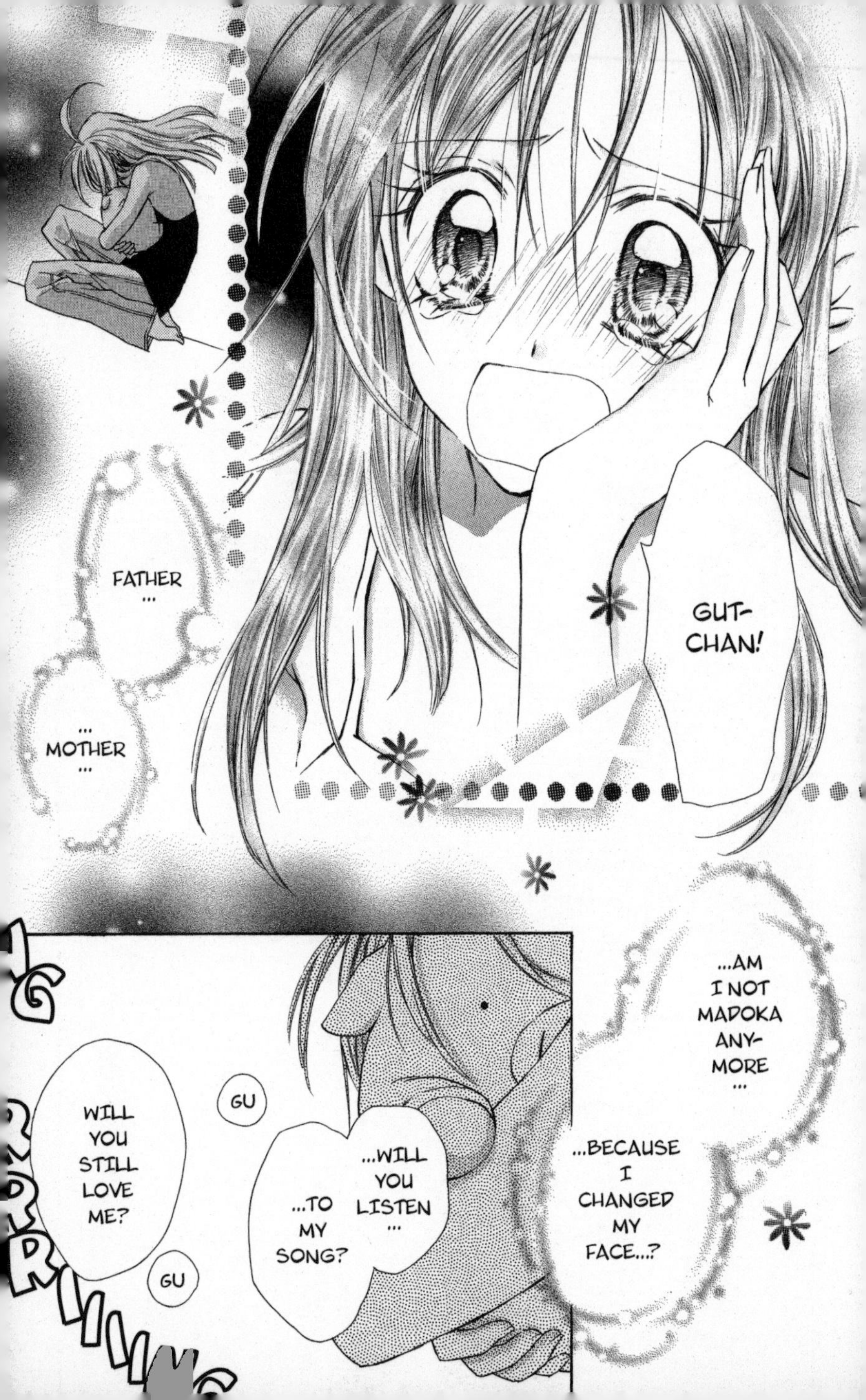
GUT-CHAN!
FATHER ...
... MOTHER ...
...AM I NOT MADOKA ANYMORE ...
...BECAUSE I CHANGED MY FACE...?
...WILL YOU LISTEN ...
...TO MY SONG?
GU
WILL YOU STILL LOVE ME?
GU

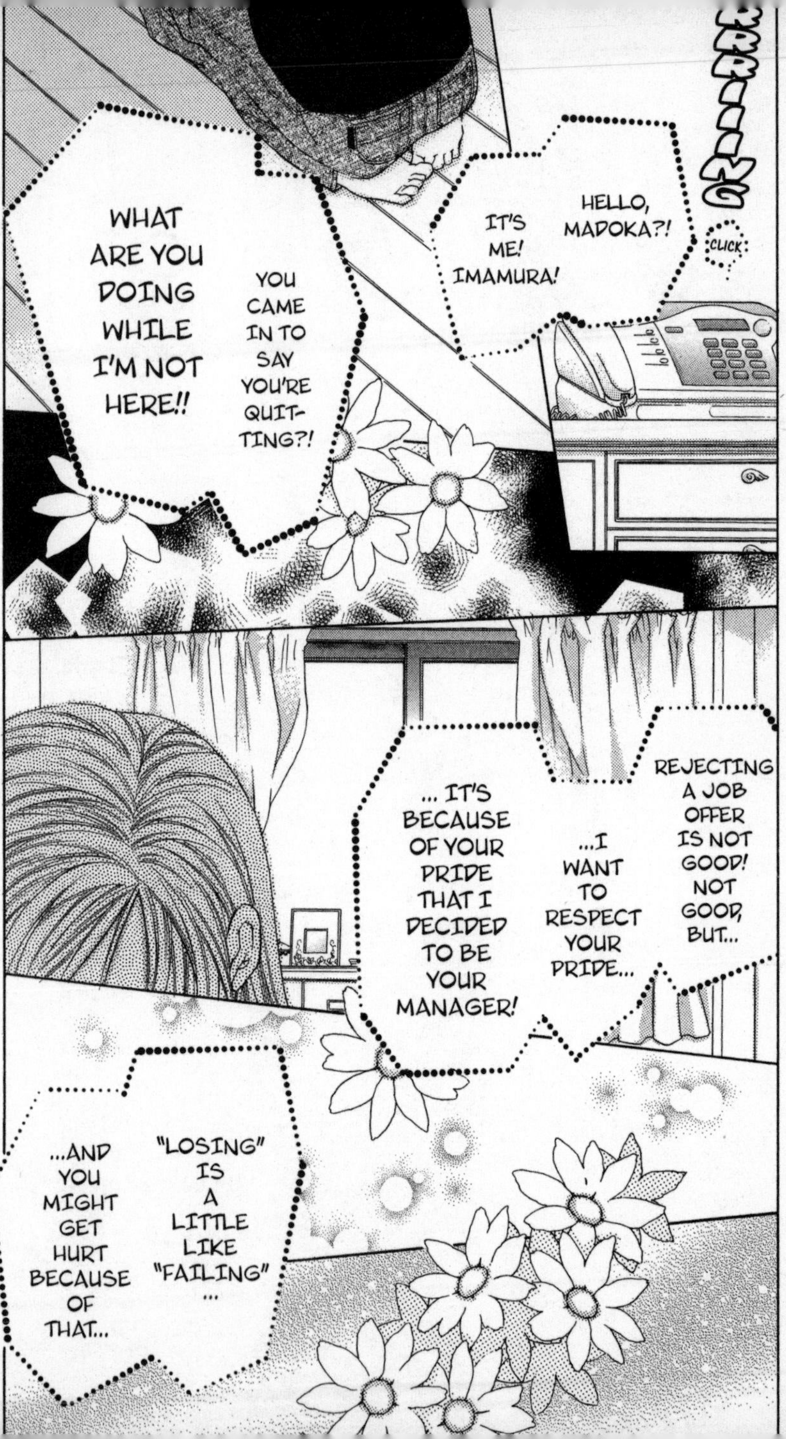
RRRIIING
CLICK
HELLO, MADOKA?!
IT'S ME! IMAMURA!
YOU CAME IN TO SAY YOU'RE QUIT-TING?!
WHAT ARE YOU DOING WHILE I'M NOT HERE!!
REJECTING A JOB OFFER IS NOT GOOD! NOT GOOD, BUT...
...I WANT TO RESPECT YOUR PRIDE...
... IT'S BECAUSE OF YOUR PRIDE THAT I DECIDED TO BE YOUR MANAGER!
"LOSING" IS A LITTLE LIKE "FAILING"...
...AND YOU MIGHT GET HURT BECAUSE OF THAT...

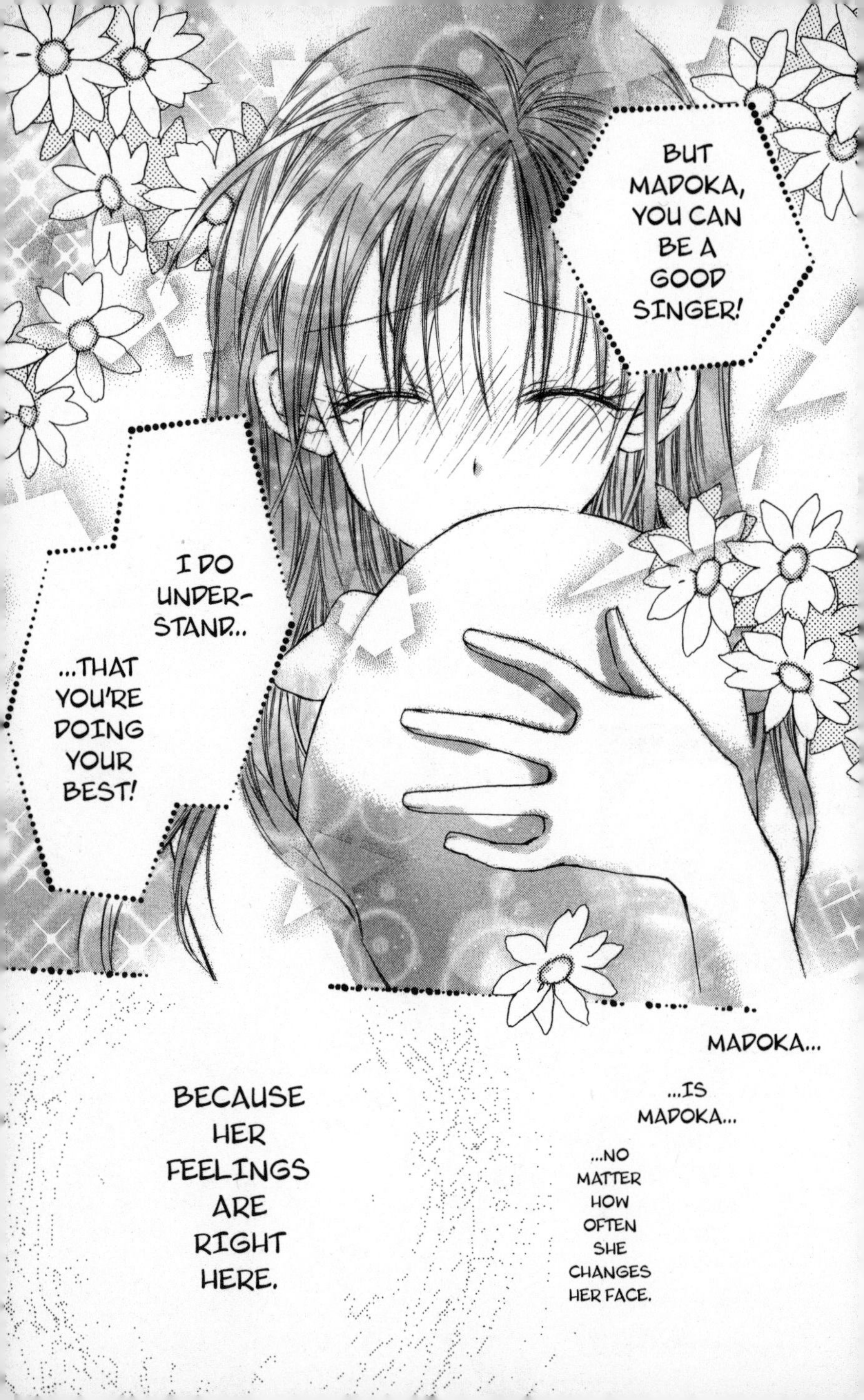
BUT MADOKA, YOU CAN BE A GOOD SINGER!
I DO UNDERSTAND...
...THAT YOU'RE DOING YOUR BEST!
MADOKA...
...IS MADOKA...
...NO MATTER HOW OFTEN SHE CHANGES HER FACE.
BECAUSE HER FEELINGS ARE RIGHT HERE.

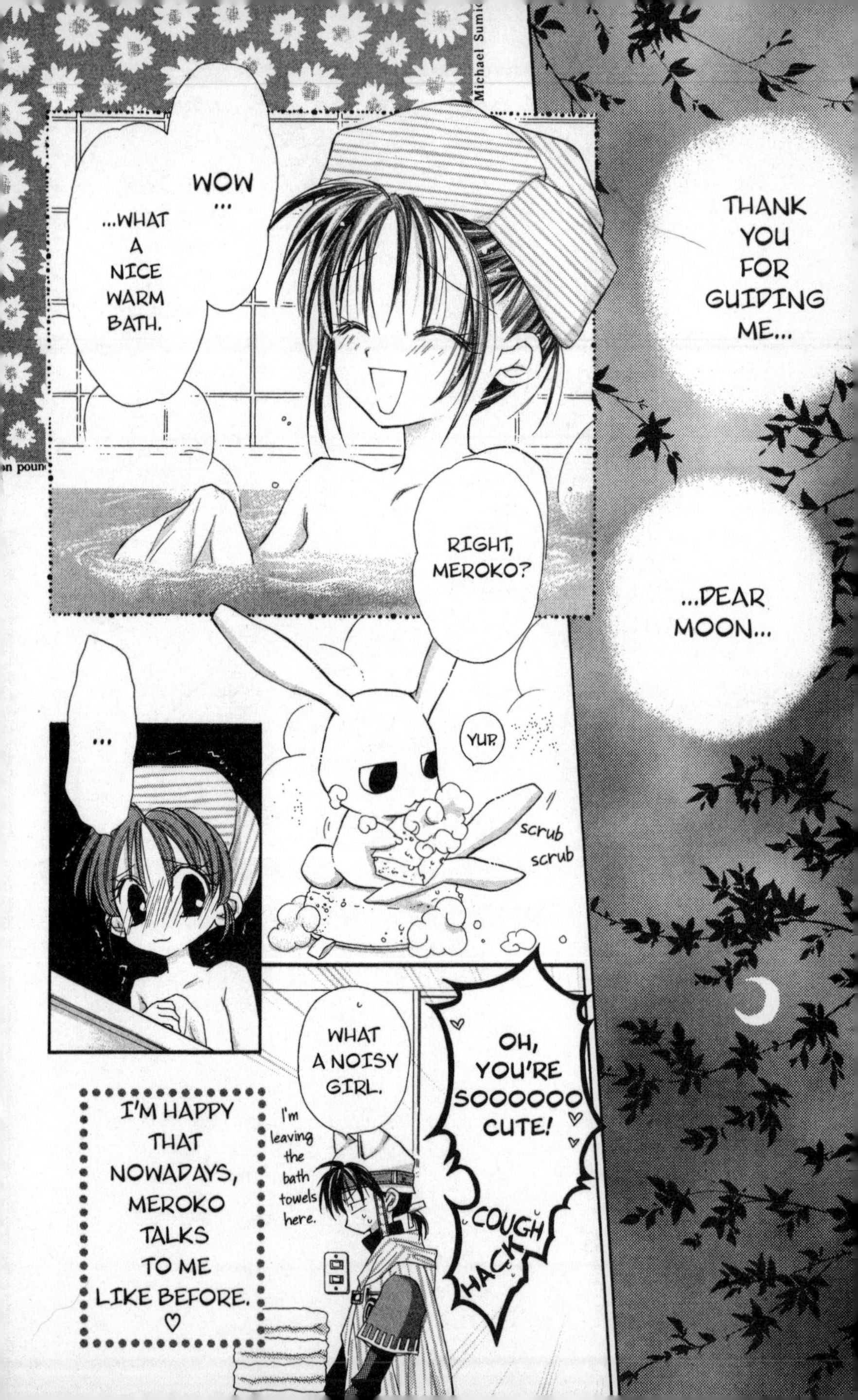
THANK YOU FOR GUIDING ME...
...DEAR MOON...
WOW...
...WHAT A NICE WARM BATH.
RIGHT, MEROKO?
YUP.
scrub scrub
...
OH, YOU'RE SOOOOOO CUTE!
COUGH HACK
WHAT A NOISY GIRL.
I'm leaving the bath towels here.
I'M HAPPY THAT NOWADAYS, MEROKO TALKS TO ME LIKE BEFORE. ♡

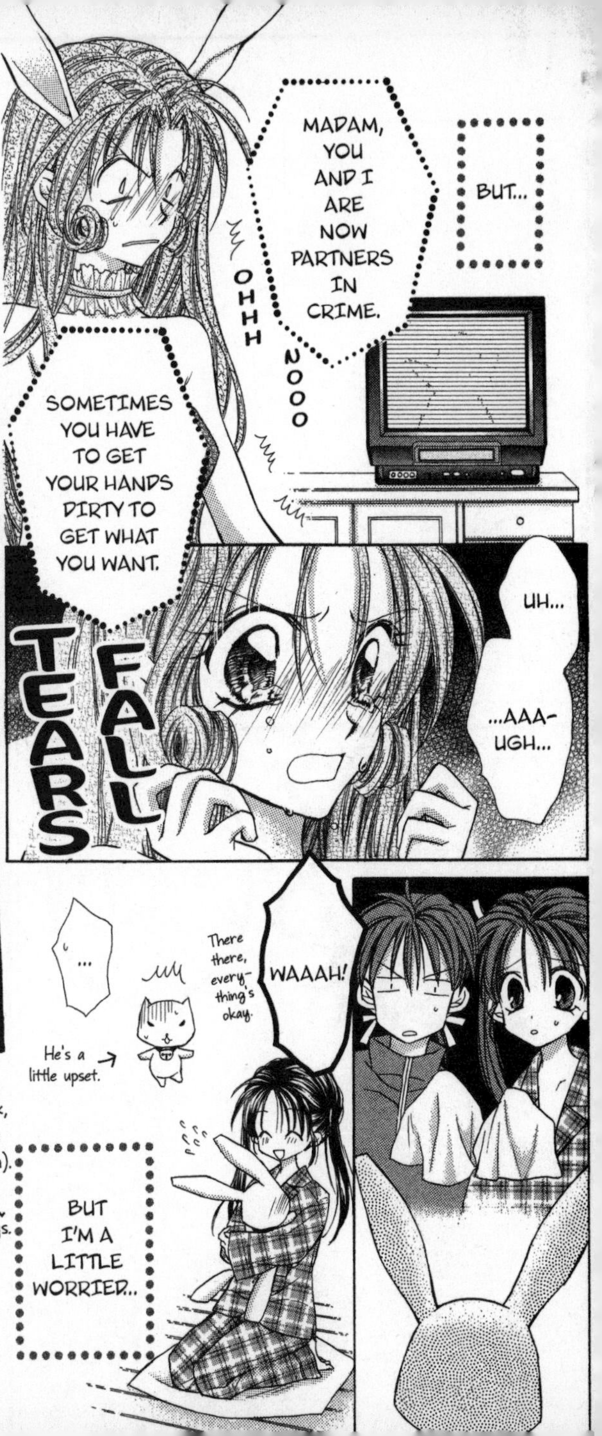
BUT...
MADAM, YOU AND I ARE NOW PARTNERS IN CRIME.
OHHH NOOO
SOMETIMES YOU HAVE TO GET YOUR HANDS DIRTY TO GET WHAT YOU WANT.
UH...
...AAA-UGH...
TEARS FALL
WAAAH!
There there, every-thing's okay.
...
He's a little upset.
BUT I'M A LITTLE WORRIED...

ARINA TANEMURA'S "PENCHI DE SHAKIN"

Episode 51

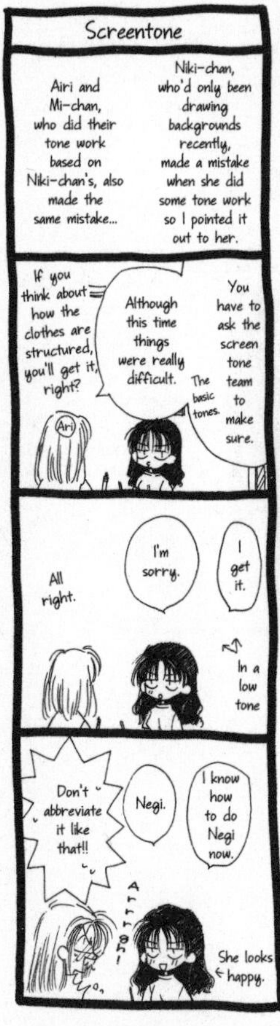
Screentone
Niki-chan, who'd only been drawing backgrounds recently, made a mistake when she did some tone work so I pointed it out to her.
Airi and Mi-chan, who did their tone work based on Niki-chan's, also made the same mistake...
You have to ask the screen tone team to make sure.
The basic tones.
Although this time things were really difficult.
If you think about how the clothes are structured, you'll get it, right?
Ari
I get it.
I'm sorry.
All right.
In a low tone
I know how to do Negi now.
Negi.
Don't abbreviate it like that!!
She looks happy.

Negi means "Negi-ramen." The mistake is not in this book, so you may not notice (We've corrected it for the tankobon).

Kanan-kotsu, Airi, Mi-chan, Akoko-tan, thank you always.

Thank you Niki-chan too.

I'm always asking you for help when deadlines are tight.

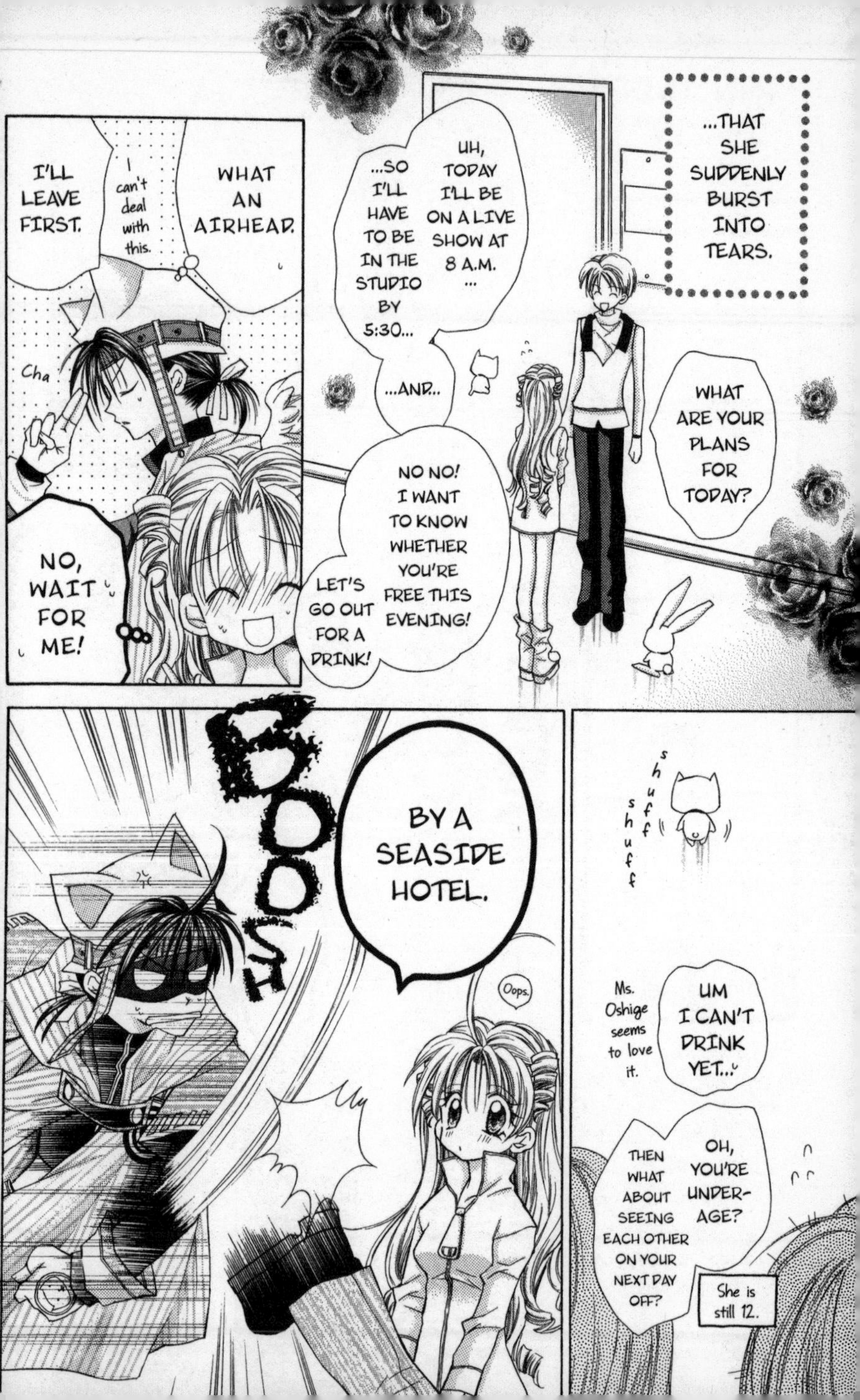
...THAT SHE SUDDENLY BURST INTO TEARS.
WHAT ARE YOUR PLANS FOR TODAY?
UH, TODAY I'LL BE ON A LIVE SHOW AT 8 A.M. ...
...SO I'LL HAVE TO BE IN THE STUDIO BY 5:30...
...AND...
NO NO! I WANT TO KNOW WHETHER YOU'RE FREE THIS EVENING!
LET'S GO OUT FOR A DRINK!
WHAT AN AIRHEAD.
I can't deal with this.
I'LL LEAVE FIRST.
Cha
NO, WAIT FOR ME!
shuff shuff
UM I CAN'T DRINK YET...
Ms. Oshige seems to love it.
OH, YOU'RE UNDER-AGE?
THEN WHAT ABOUT SEEING EACH OTHER ON YOUR NEXT DAY OFF?
She is still 12.
BY A SEASIDE HOTEL.
BOOSH
Oops.

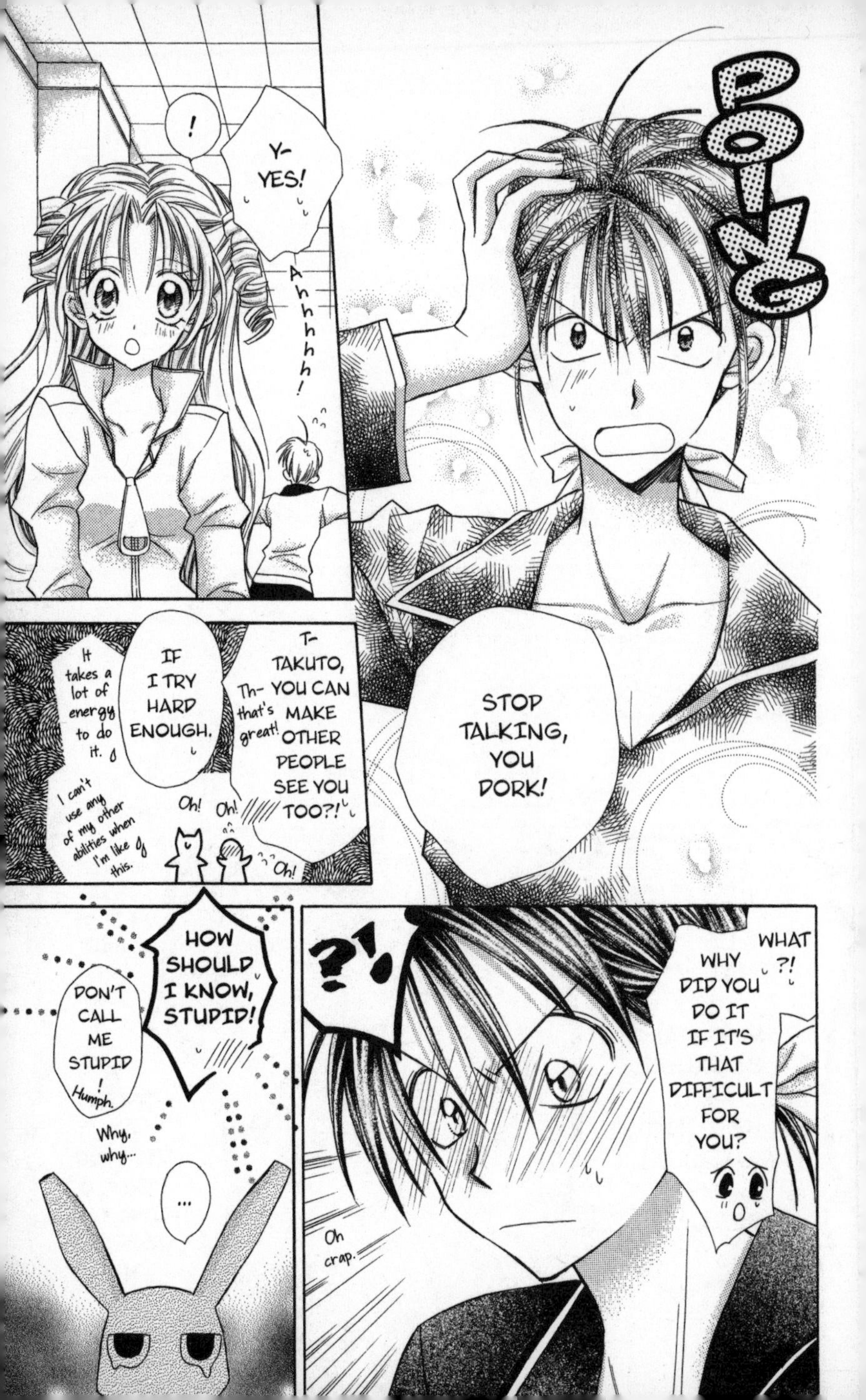
POING
STOP TALKING, YOU DORK!
Y- YES!
!
Ahhhhh!
T- TAKUTO, YOU CAN MAKE OTHER PEOPLE SEE YOU TOO?!
Th- that's great!
IF I TRY HARD ENOUGH.
It takes a lot of energy to do it.
Oh!
Oh!
Oh!
I can't use any of my other abilities when I'm like this.
?!
WHAT?!
WHY DID YOU DO IT IF IT'S THAT DIFFICULT FOR YOU?
Oh crap.
HOW SHOULD I KNOW, STUPID!
DON'T CALL ME STUPID!
Humph.
Why, why...
...

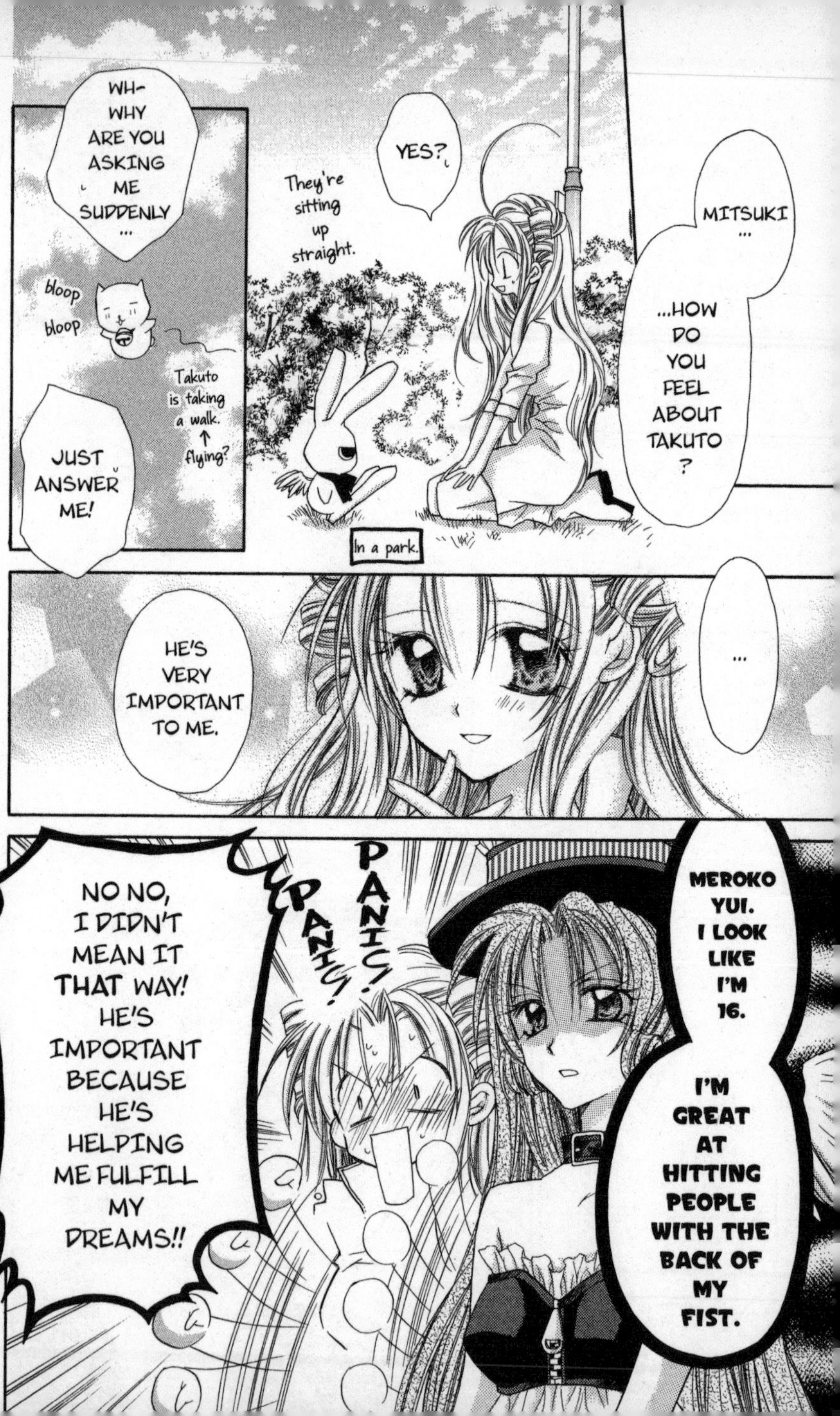
MITSUKI...
...HOW DO YOU FEEL ABOUT TAKUTO?
YES?
They're sitting up straight.
In a park.
WH-WHY ARE YOU ASKING ME SUDDENLY...
bloop bloop
Takuto is taking a walk. ↑ flying?
JUST ANSWER ME!
...
HE'S VERY IMPORTANT TO ME.
MEROKO YUI. I LOOK LIKE I'M 16.
I'M GREAT AT HITTING PEOPLE WITH THE BACK OF MY FIST.
PANIC! PANIC!
NO NO, I DIDN'T MEAN IT THAT WAY! HE'S IMPORTANT BECAUSE HE'S HELPING ME FULFILL MY DREAMS!!

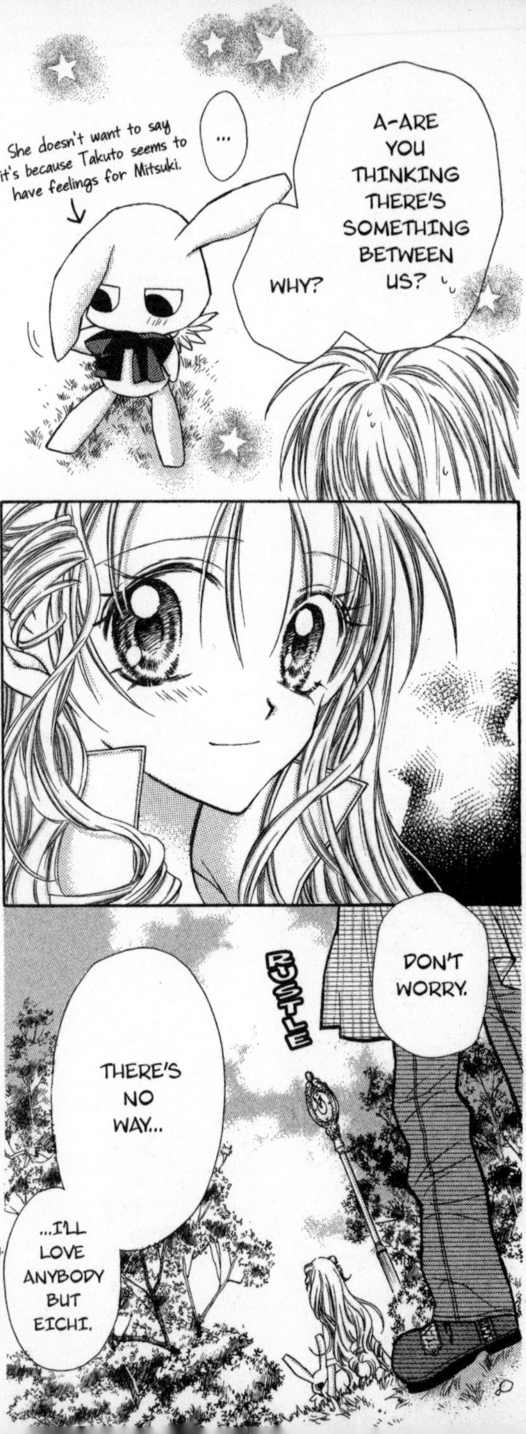
A-ARE YOU THINKING THERE'S SOMETHING BETWEEN US?
WHY?
...
She doesn't want to say it's because Takuto seems to have feelings for Mitsuki.
DON'T WORRY.
RUSTLE
THERE'S NO WAY...
...I'LL LOVE ANYBODY BUT EICHI.

●My Favorites, Part ②●

.hack//SIGN (a TV Tokyo anime)
I love this. I'm having great fun watching it. I love Subaru (The wings.)
(I love Sora and Kurimu and BT too) ← I love the other characters too but I especially love him...
I'm in the middle of getting all the DVDs. ♪ Love!

ICO (a Playstation2 game)
I was late starting this game, but I really got into it. (I wanted to play it for a long time, but I didn't have enough time to do it.)
But, um...I'm not very good at playing action games. I'm not too good with my hands, so I wasn't too good at it. I have no patience.

So I had Asano-san and Airi play it. But even then, it was difficult, so we bought the guidebook. ← I played the navigator, book in hand. (Hee.)
(Uh, I buy guidebooks for, say FF, after finishing the game once so I can play deeper (?))
I saw the second round.
(I got the hidden items too.)
It was good. I love Yolda (Ico too.)
(Asano-san keeps on saying Elda. I've told her many times, but she keeps on saying Elda. Please help me.)

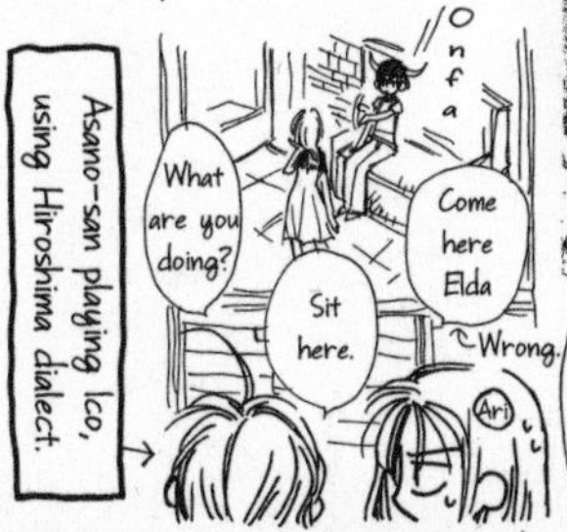
Asano-san playing Ico, using Hiroshima dialect.
Onfa
What are you doing?
Come here Elda
Sit here.
Wrong.
Airi

Ico pushing boxes...he's strong and I like that. ← when pulling he's even stronger...

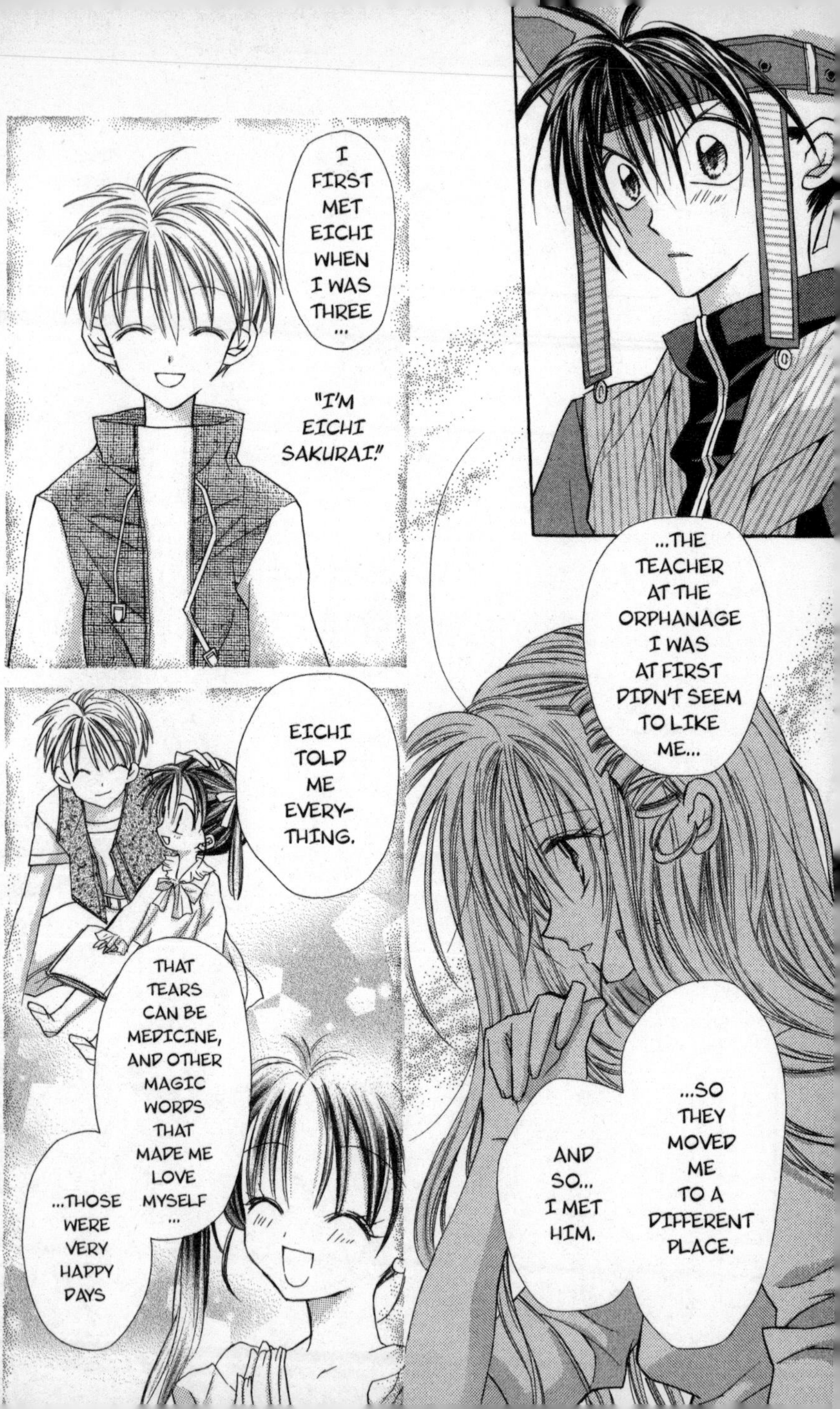
...THE TEACHER AT THE ORPHANAGE I WAS AT FIRST DIDN'T SEEM TO LIKE ME...
...SO THEY MOVED ME TO A DIFFERENT PLACE.
AND SO... I MET HIM.
I FIRST MET EICHI WHEN I WAS THREE ...
"I'M EICHI SAKURAI!"
EICHI TOLD ME EVERY-THING.
THAT TEARS CAN BE MEDICINE, AND OTHER MAGIC WORDS THAT MADE ME LOVE MYSELF ...
...THOSE WERE VERY HAPPY DAYS

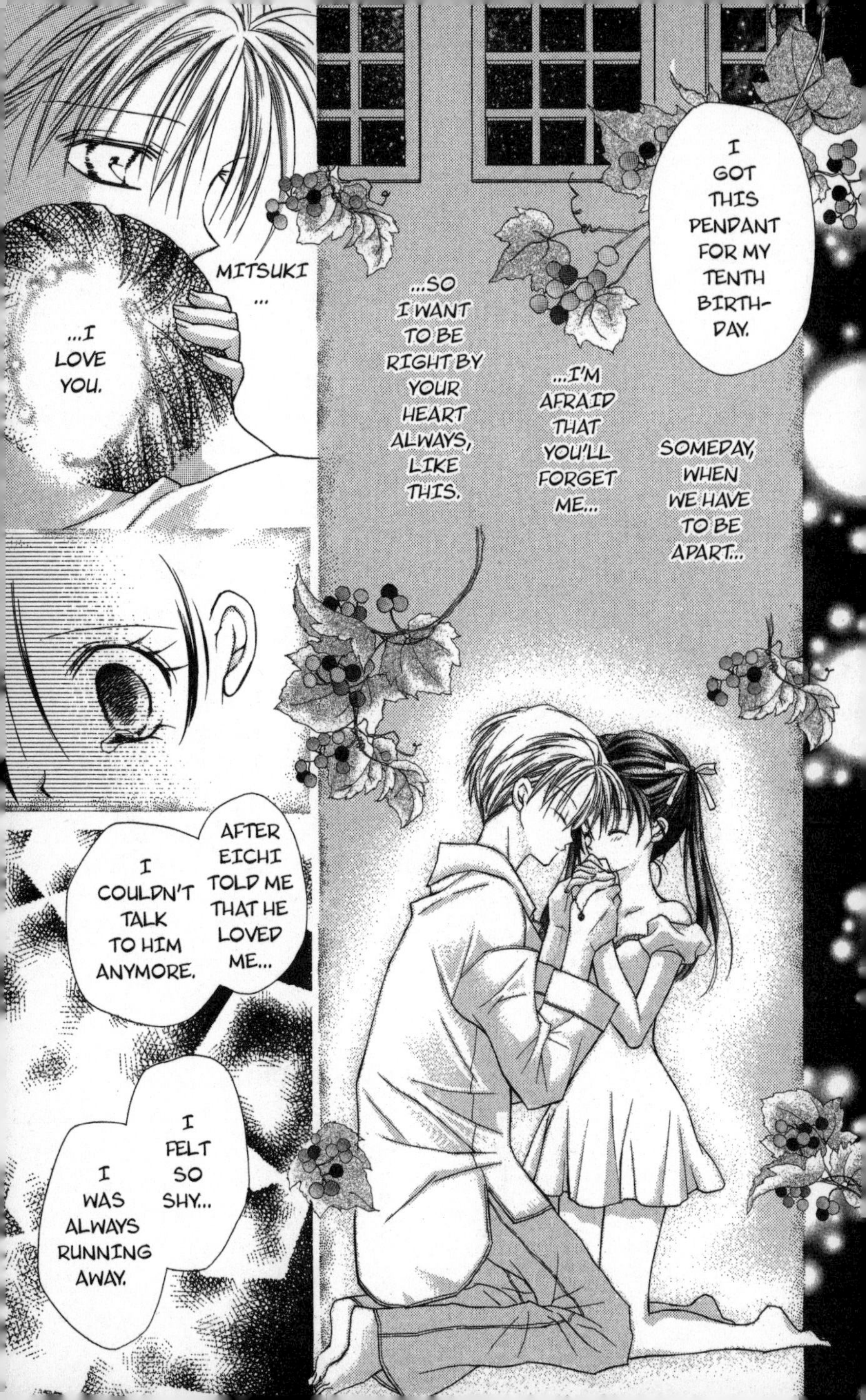
I GOT THIS PENDANT FOR MY TENTH BIRTHDAY.
SOMEDAY, WHEN WE HAVE TO BE APART...
...I'M AFRAID THAT YOU'LL FORGET ME...
...SO I WANT TO BE RIGHT BY YOUR HEART ALWAYS, LIKE THIS.
MITSUKI...
...I LOVE YOU.
AFTER EICHI TOLD ME THAT HE LOVED ME...
I COULDN'T TALK TO HIM ANYMORE.
I FELT SO SHY...
I WAS ALWAYS RUNNING AWAY.

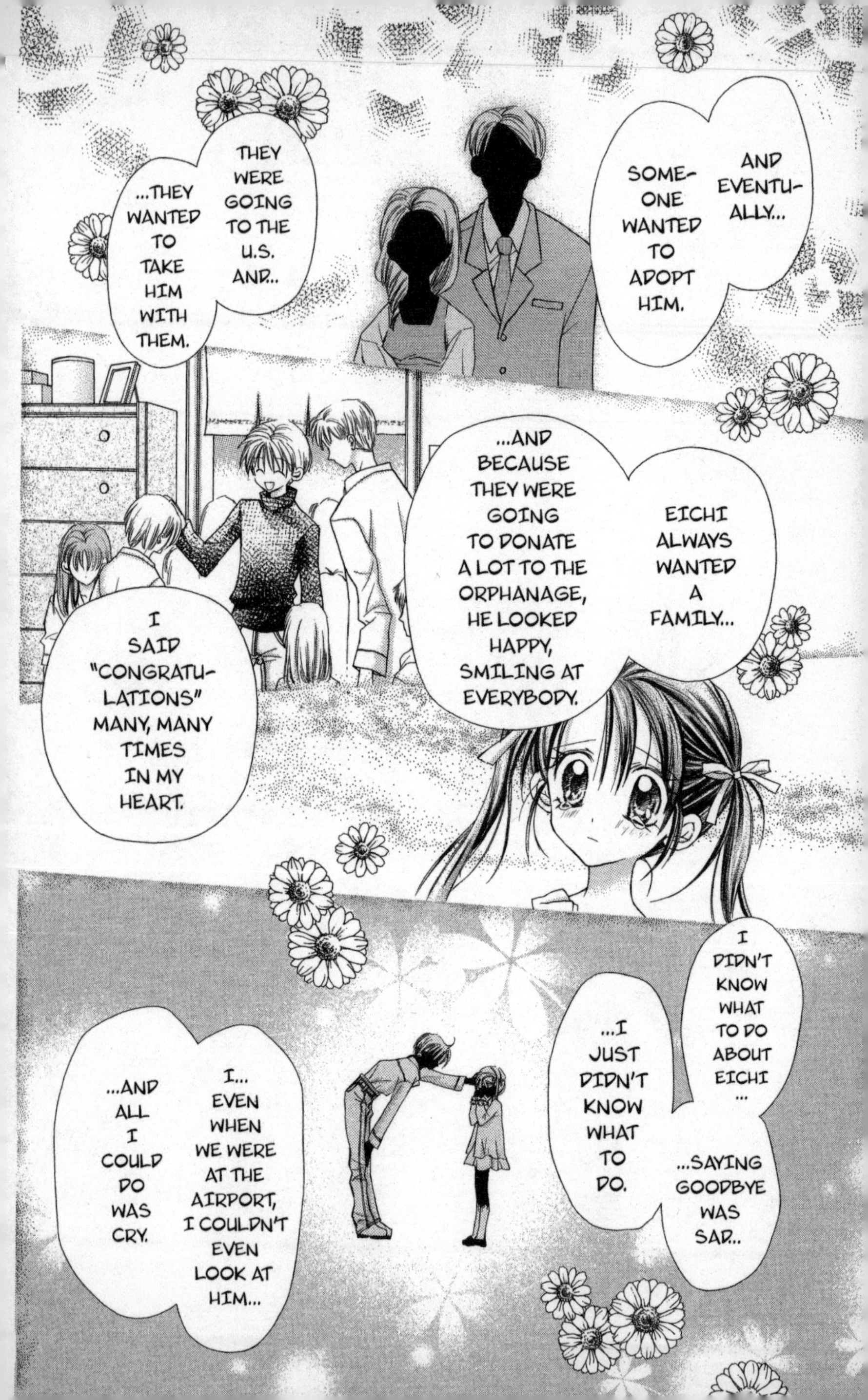
AND EVENTUALLY...
SOMEONE WANTED TO ADOPT HIM.
THEY WERE GOING TO THE U.S. AND..
...THEY WANTED TO TAKE HIM WITH THEM.
EICHI ALWAYS WANTED A FAMILY...
...AND BECAUSE THEY WERE GOING TO DONATE A LOT TO THE ORPHANAGE, HE LOOKED HAPPY, SMILING AT EVERYBODY.
I SAID "CONGRATULATIONS" MANY, MANY TIMES IN MY HEART.
I DIDN'T KNOW WHAT TO DO ABOUT EICHI...
...SAYING GOODBYE WAS SAD..
...I JUST DIDN'T KNOW WHAT TO DO.
I... EVEN WHEN WE WERE AT THE AIRPORT, I COULDN'T EVEN LOOK AT HIM...
...AND ALL I COULD DO WAS CRY.

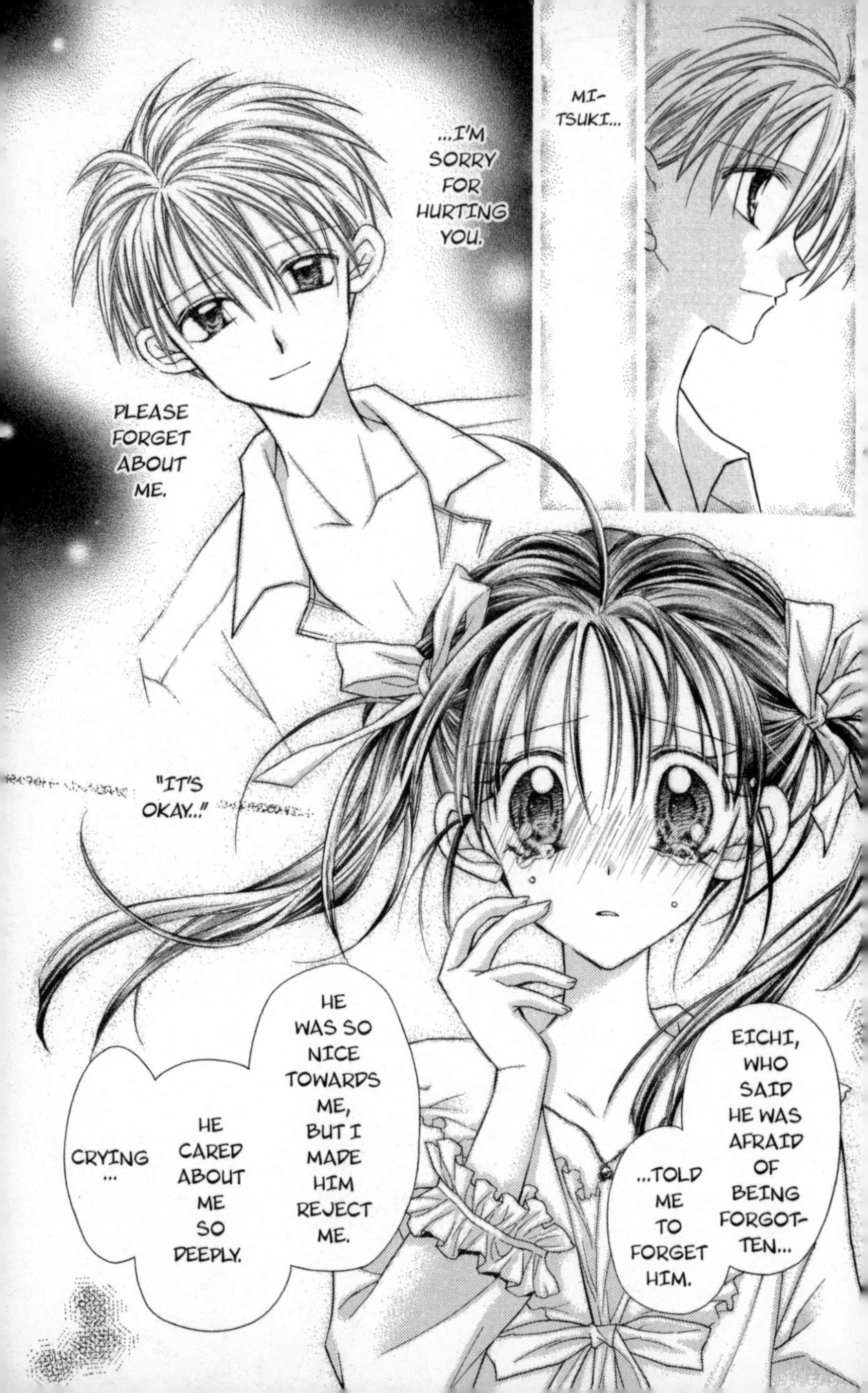
MI-TSUKI...
...I'M SORRY FOR HURTING YOU.
PLEASE FORGET ABOUT ME.
"IT'S OKAY.."
EICHI, WHO SAID HE WAS AFRAID OF BEING FORGOT-TEN...
...TOLD ME TO FORGET HIM.
HE WAS SO NICE TOWARDS ME, BUT I MADE HIM REJECT ME.
HE CARED ABOUT ME SO DEEPLY.
CRYING...

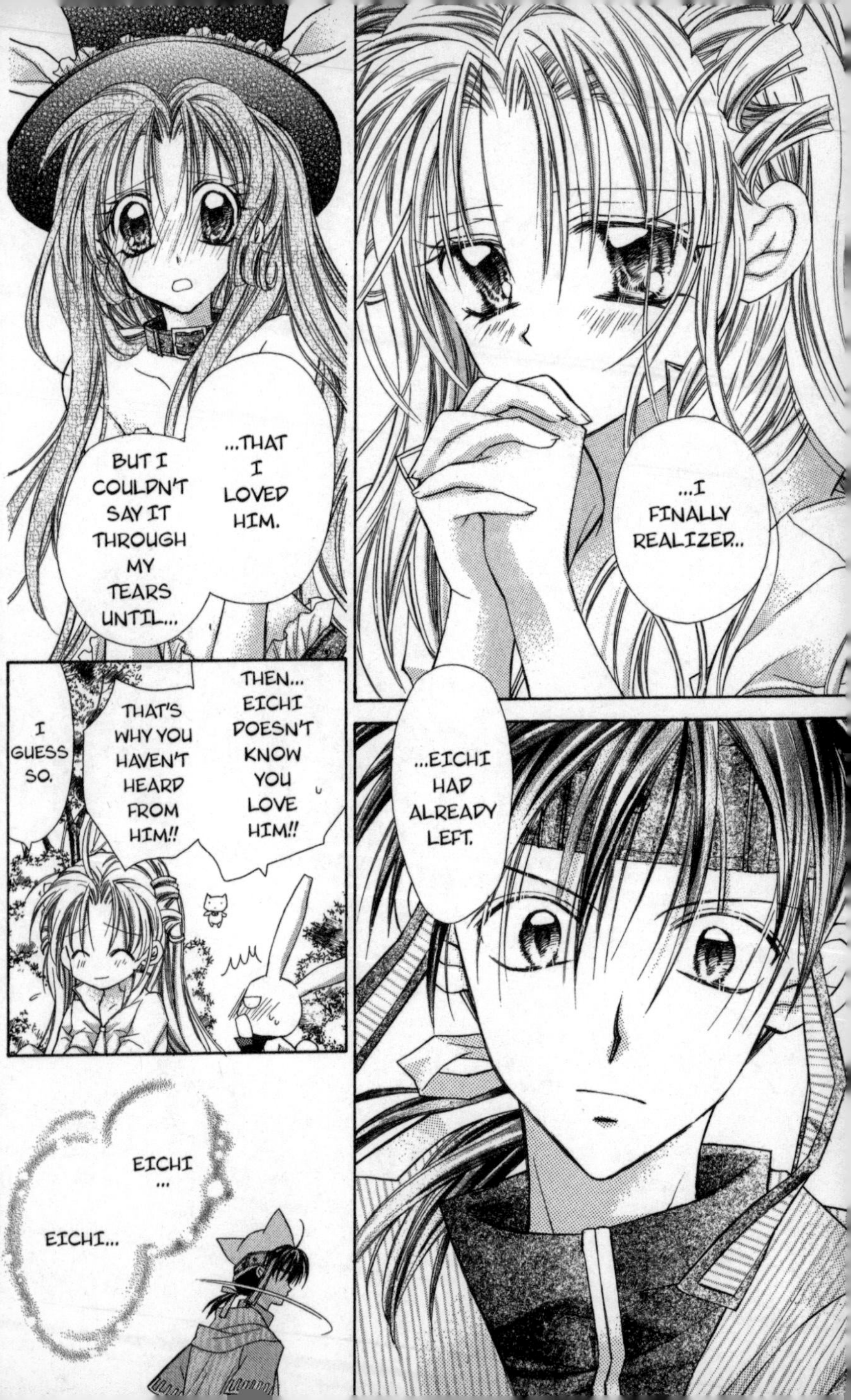
...I FINALLY REALIZED..
...THAT I LOVED HIM.
BUT I COULDN'T SAY IT THROUGH MY TEARS UNTIL...
...EICHI HAD ALREADY LEFT.
THEN... EICHI DOESN'T KNOW YOU LOVE HIM!!
THAT'S WHY YOU HAVEN'T HEARD FROM HIM!!
I GUESS SO.
EICHI ...
EICHI...

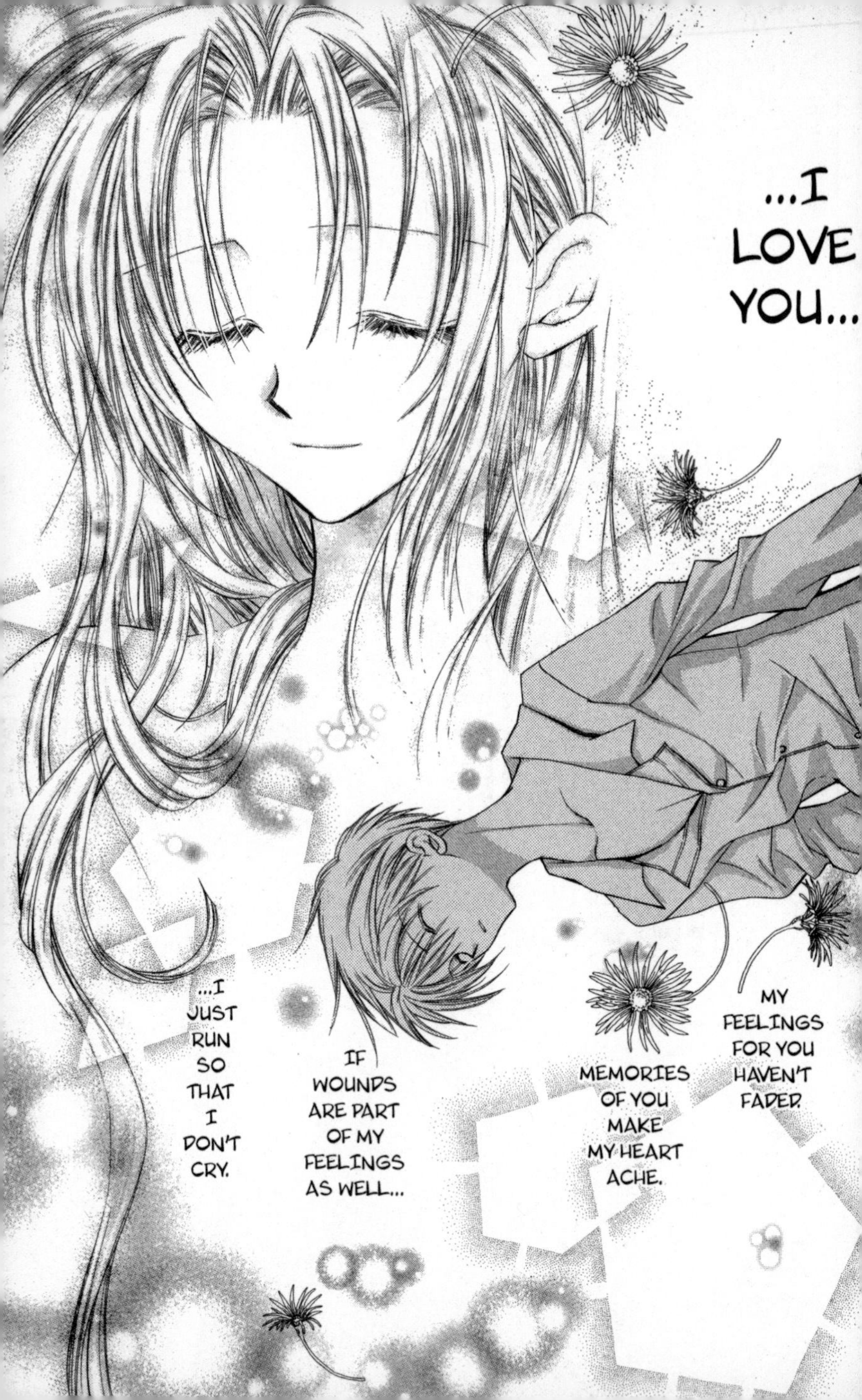
...I LOVE YOU...
MY FEELINGS FOR YOU HAVEN'T FADED.
MEMORIES OF YOU MAKE MY HEART ACHE.
IF WOUNDS ARE PART OF MY FEELINGS AS WELL...
...I JUST RUN SO THAT I DON'T CRY.

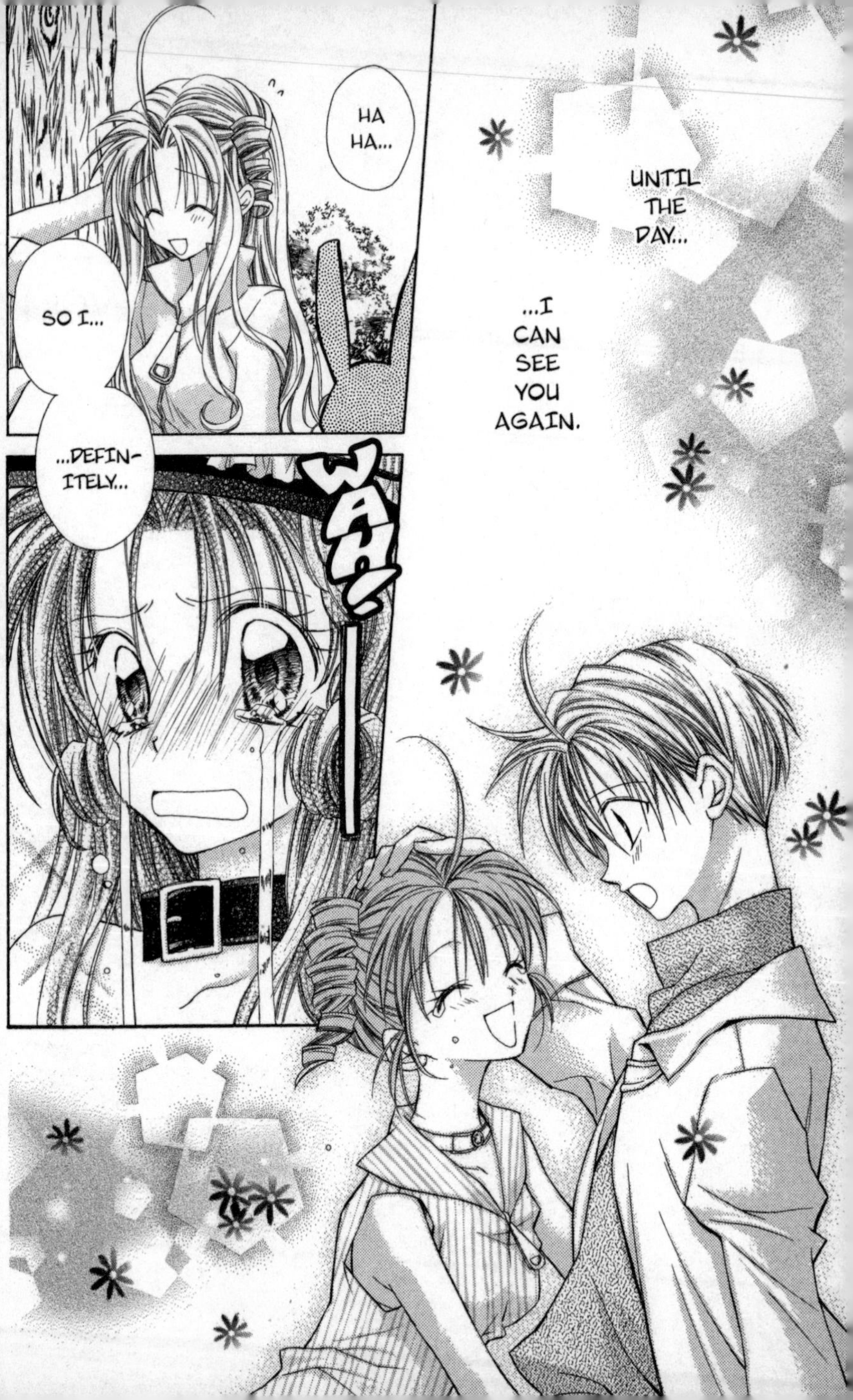
HA HA...
SO I...
...DEFIN-ITELY...
WAAH!
UNTIL THE DAY...
...I CAN SEE YOU AGAIN.

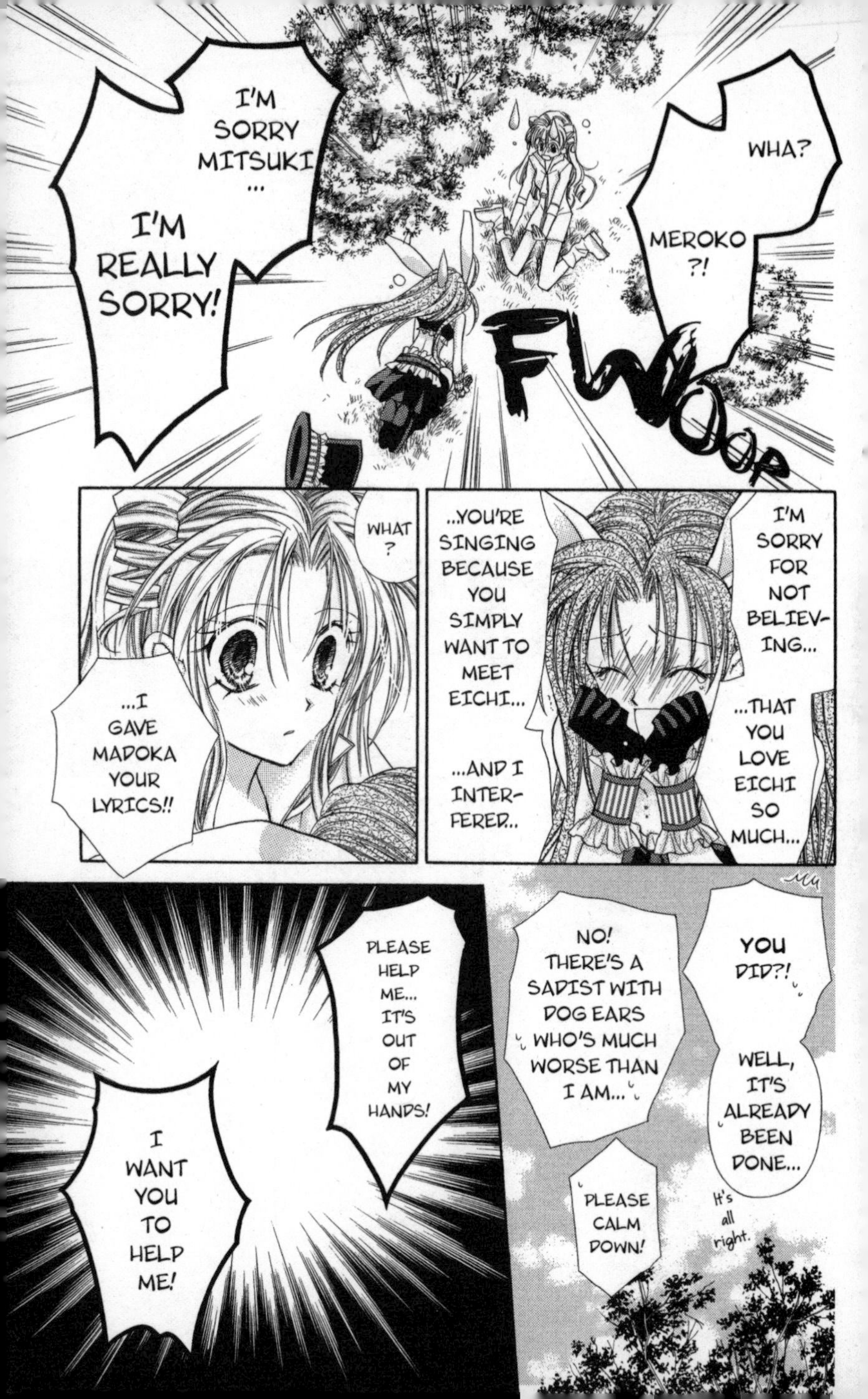

WHA? MEROKO?!
I'M SORRY MITSUKI... I'M REALLY SORRY!
FWOOP
I'M SORRY FOR NOT BELIEVING...
...THAT YOU LOVE EICHI SO MUCH...
...YOU'RE SINGING BECAUSE YOU SIMPLY WANT TO MEET EICHI...
...AND I INTERFERED...
WHAT?
...I GAVE MADOKA YOUR LYRICS!!
YOU DID?!
WELL, IT'S ALREADY BEEN DONE...
NO! THERE'S A SADIST WITH DOG EARS WHO'S MUCH WORSE THAN I AM...
PLEASE CALM DOWN!
It's all right.
PLEASE HELP ME... IT'S OUT OF MY HANDS!
I WANT YOU TO HELP ME!

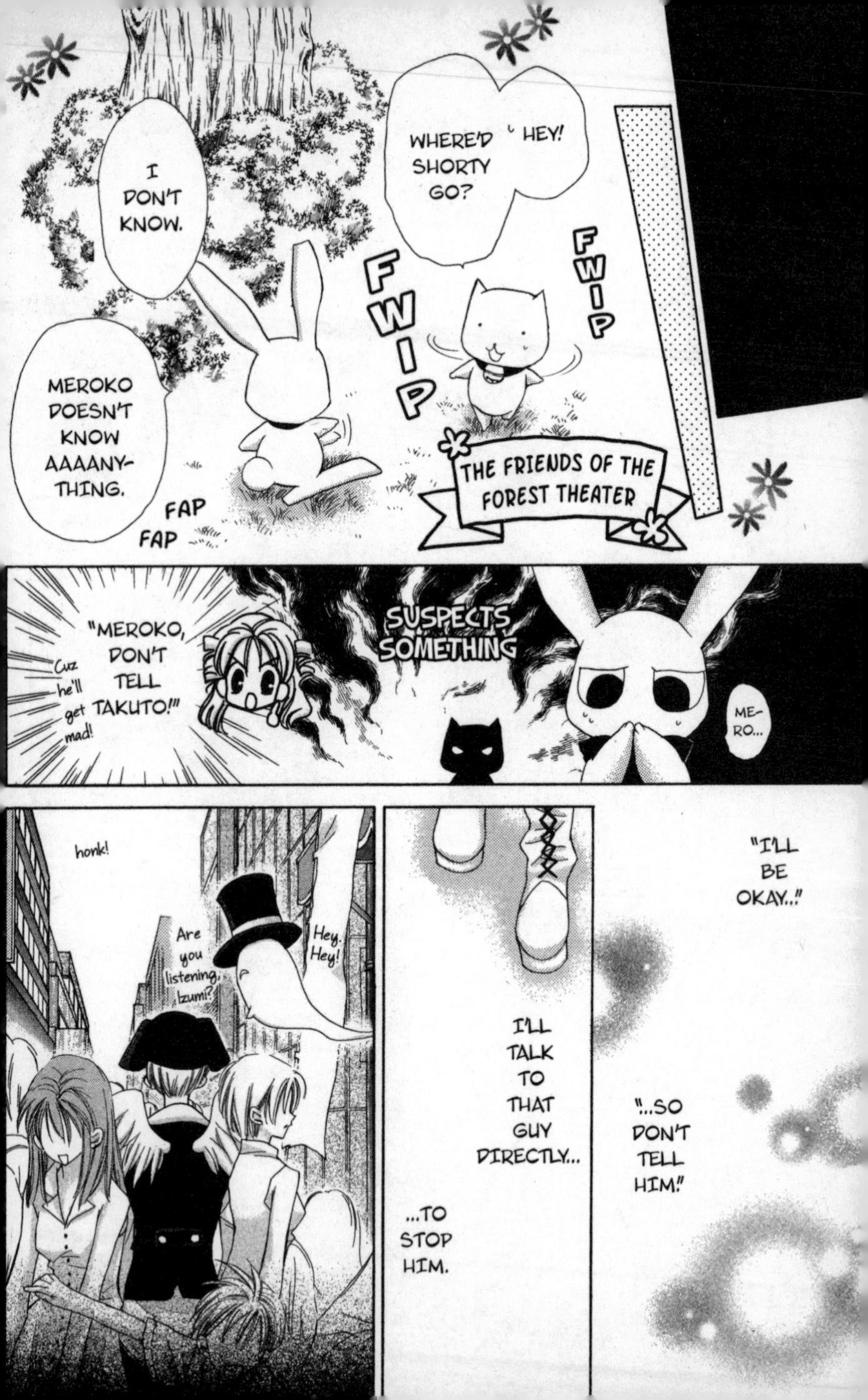
HEY! WHERE'D SHORTY GO?
FWIP
FWIP
I DON'T KNOW.
MEROKO DOESN'T KNOW AAAANY-THING.
FAP FAP
THE FRIENDS OF THE FOREST THEATER
MERO...
SUSPECTS SOMETHING
"MEROKO, DON'T TELL TAKUTO!"
Cuz he'll get mad!
"I'LL BE OKAY..."
"...SO DON'T TELL HIM."
I'LL TALK TO THAT GUY DIRECTLY...
...TO STOP HIM.
Hey. Hey!
Are you listening, Izumi?
honk!

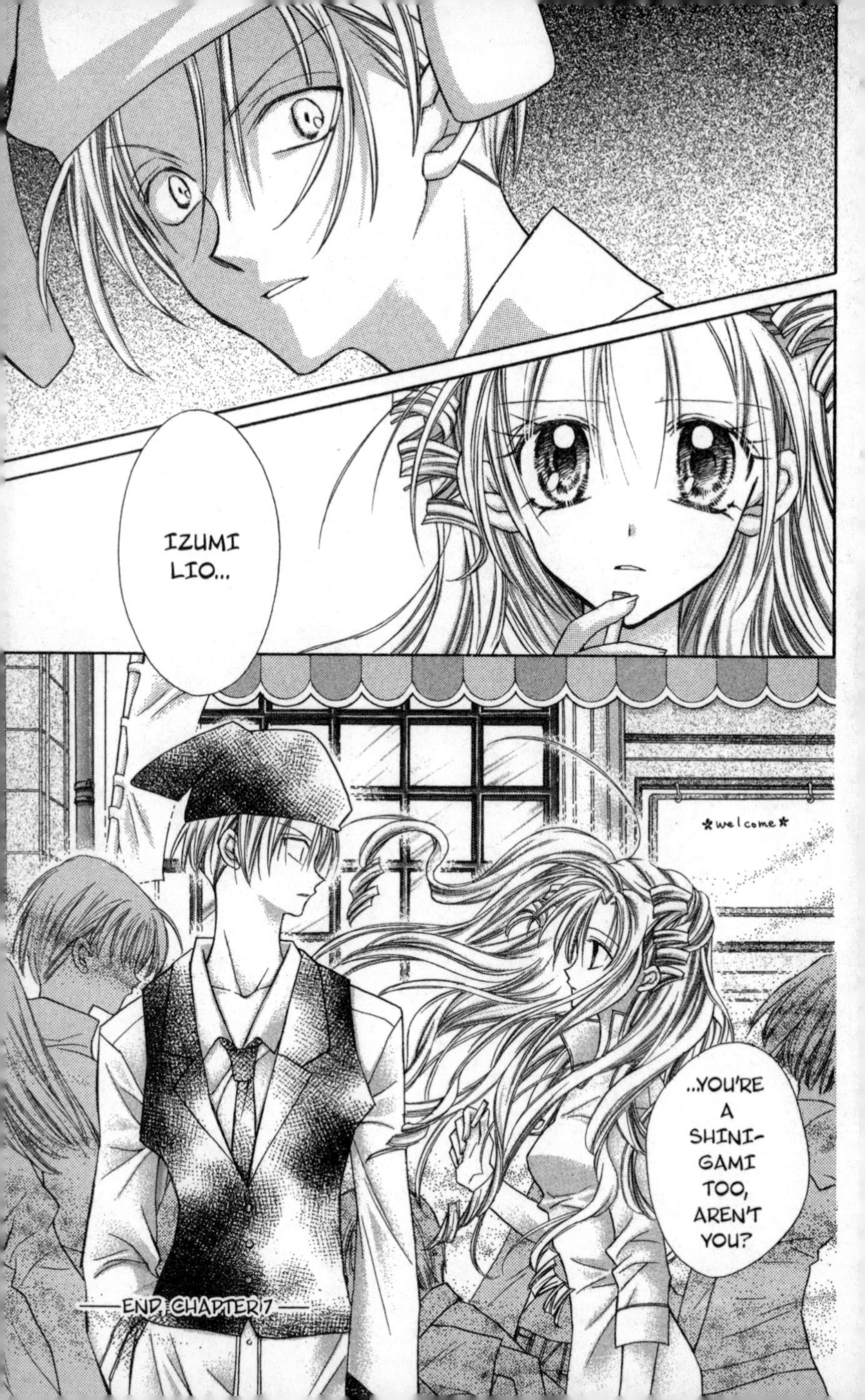
IZUMI LIO...
welcome
...YOU'RE A SHINIGAMI TOO, AREN'T YOU?
—END, CHAPTER 7—

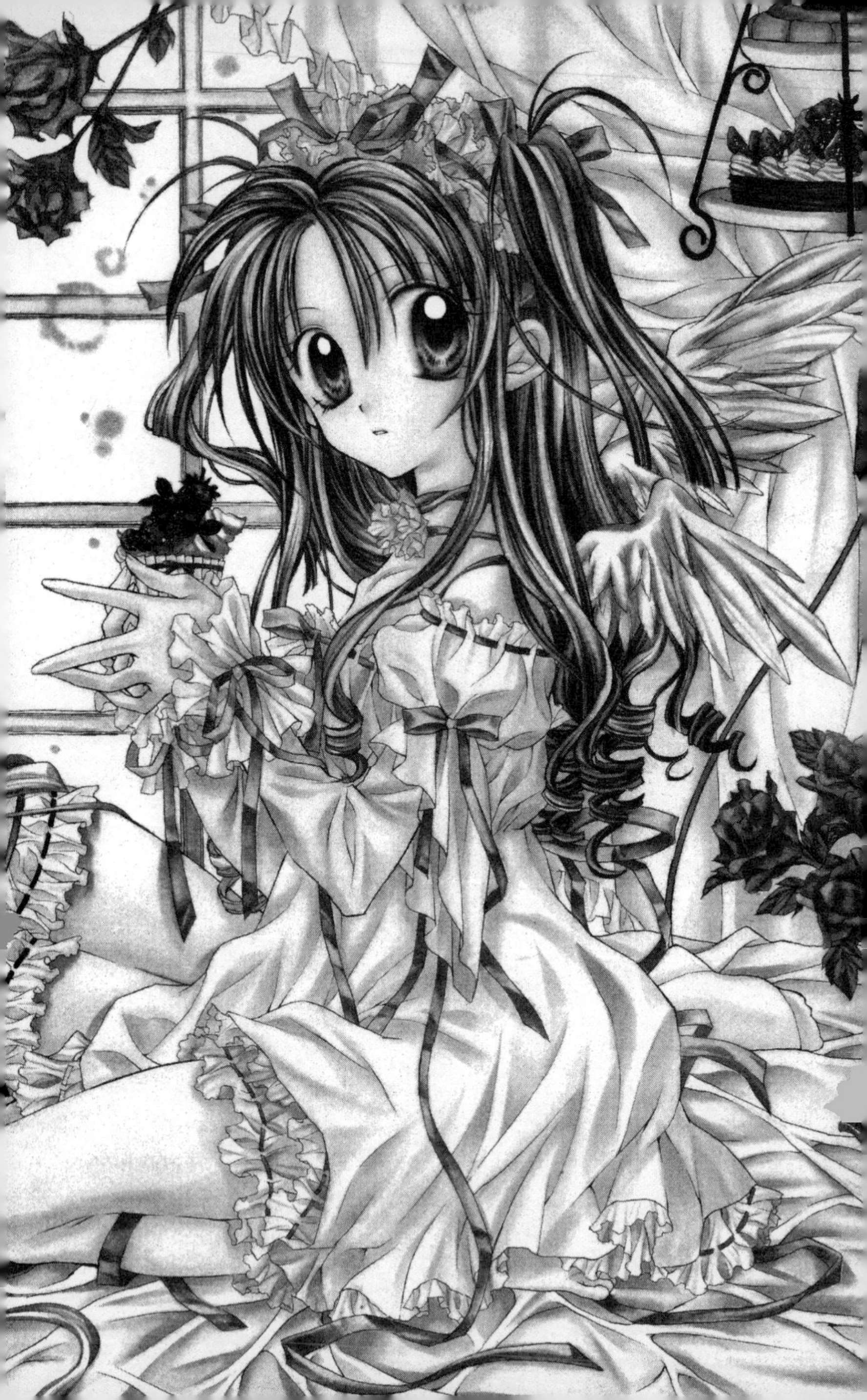

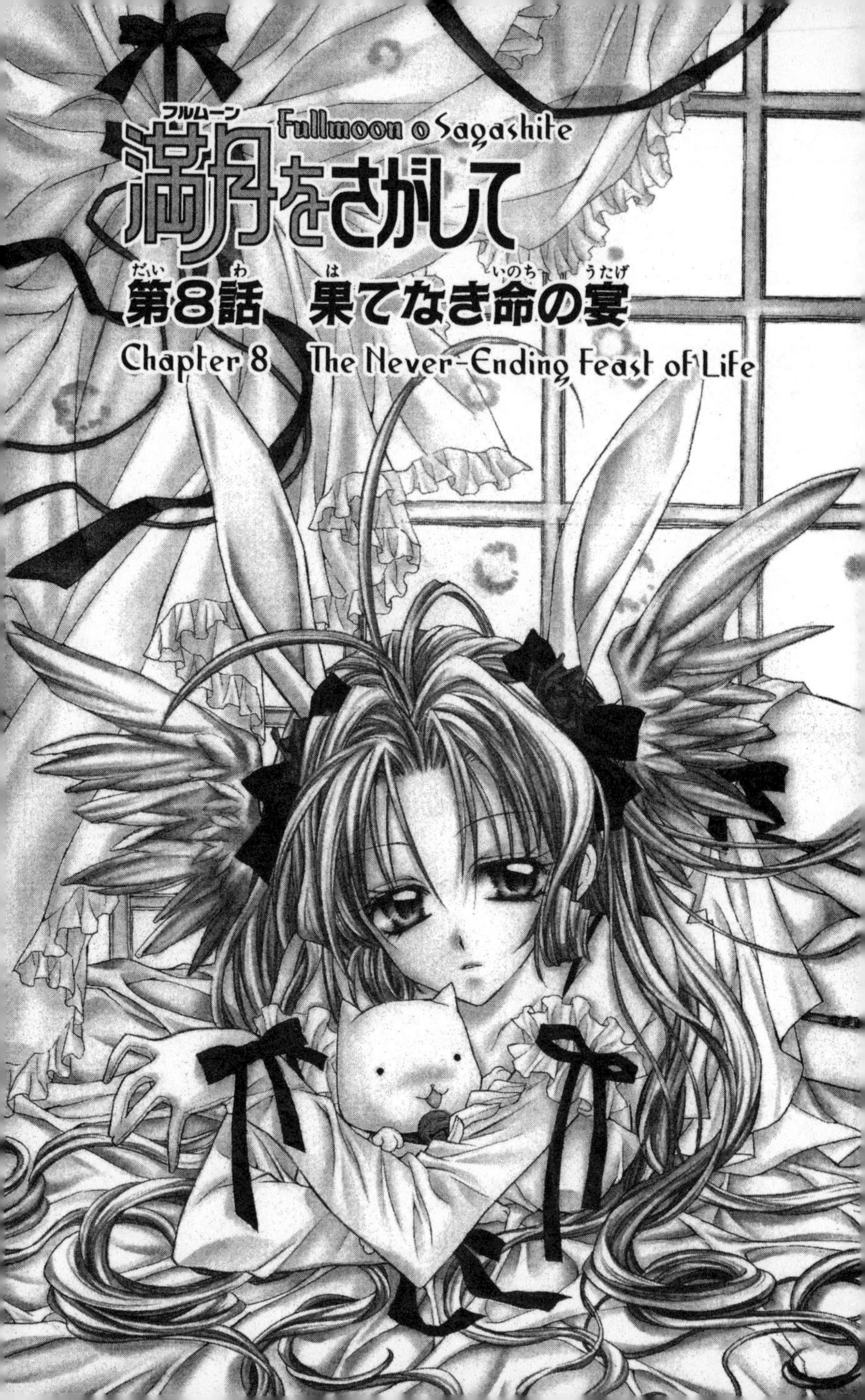
フルムーン
満月をさがして
Fullmoon o Sagashite
第8話　果てなき命の宴
Chapter 8　The Never-Ending Feast of Life

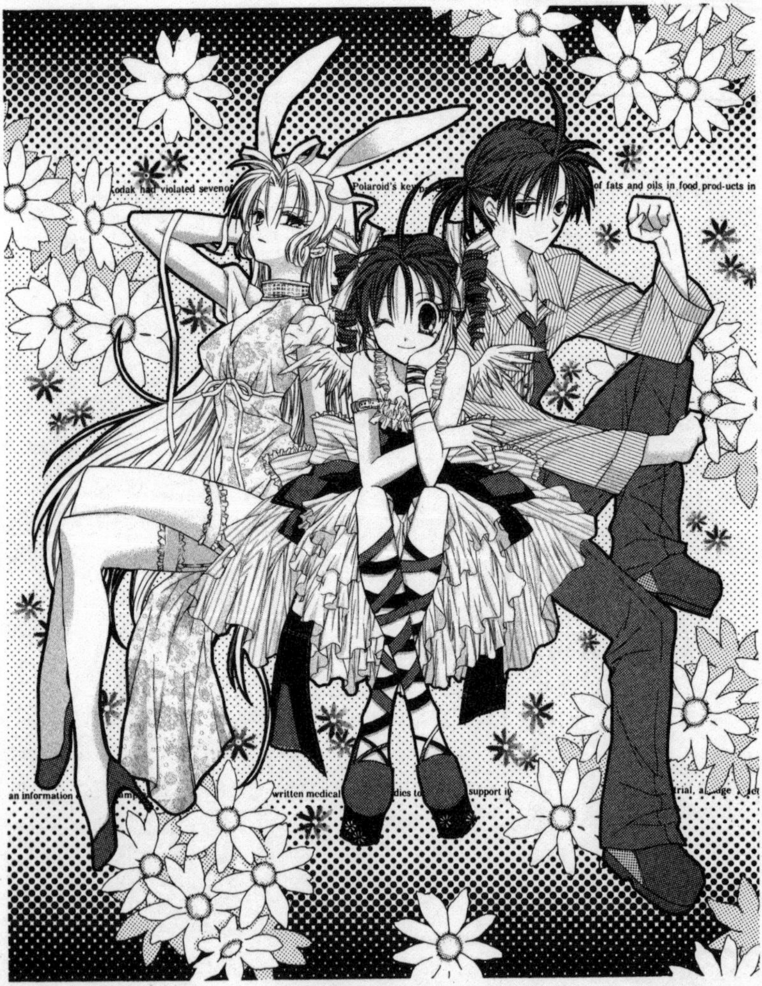
Kodak had violated seven
Polaroid's key
of fats and oils in food prod-ucts in
an information
written medical
support

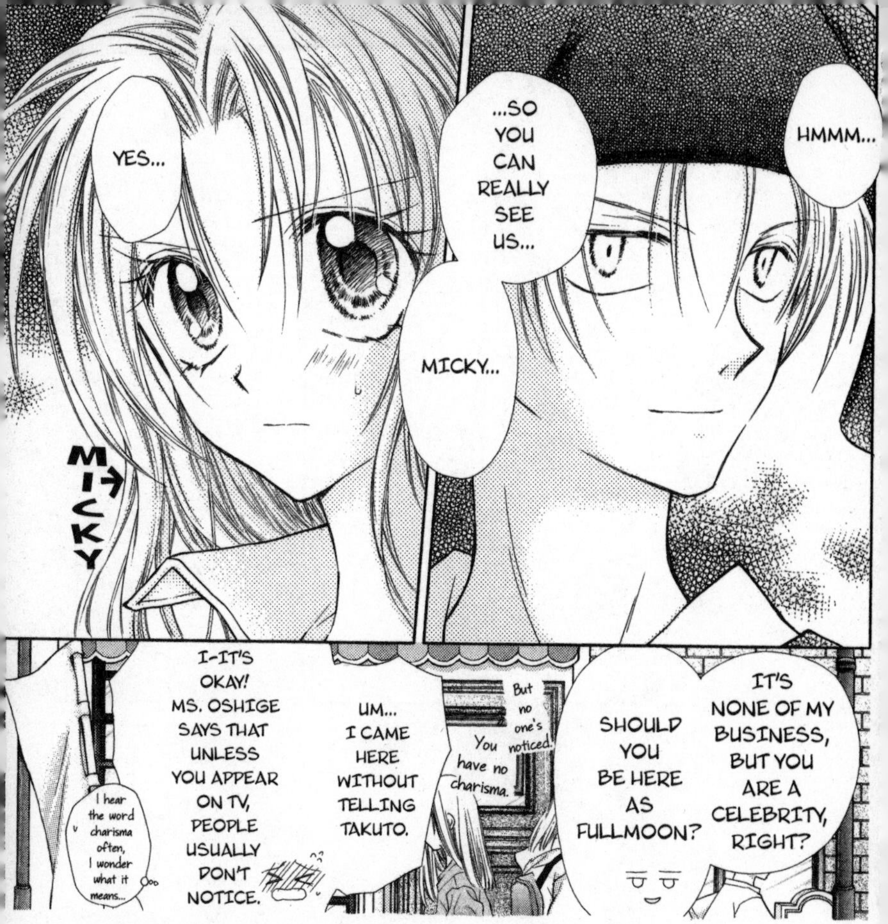
HMMM...
...SO YOU CAN REALLY SEE US...
MICKY...
YES...
MICKY
IT'S NONE OF MY BUSINESS, BUT YOU ARE A CELEBRITY, RIGHT?
SHOULD YOU BE HERE AS FULLMOON?
But no one's noticed.
You have no charisma.
UM... I CAME HERE WITHOUT TELLING TAKUTO.
I-IT'S OKAY! MS. OSHIGE SAYS THAT UNLESS YOU APPEAR ON TV, PEOPLE USUALLY DON'T NOTICE.
I hear the word charisma often, I wonder what it means...

Spoilers ahead

Chapter 8: The Never-ending Feast of Life Cover Copy Only girls can understand another girl's feelings!

Thanks to everyone, this cover illustration was very popular. When I was coloring it, I didn't have much time, and I was thinking "what should I do?" But it came out well in print, so everything turned out okay.

Based on this cover, I started a series called "Mitsuki and her Friends." (It was originally "Mitsuki and her Friend," but in Chapter 10 (which will be in Vol. 3), I drew three characters.) Although this illustration has Neko-kun in it, too.

I saw this really lovely baby-doll dress, and I drew it because I wanted to draw it, and then the illustration became a little sexy. ← Lingerie ////

The words of a person who's tired of drawing Negi-ramen's costumes.

About the story...I think I drew a lot of Izumi-kun. Izumi-kun is easy to draw and I like that. So I love him for that reason too. Love You! ♪ Megumi Ogata is doing his voice, and even more Love You! Mitsuki-chan's heart...I want someone to make it throb soon (I shouldn't be saying that.)

For the time being, since Eichi-kun is not around, I thought Takuto!...but hmmm...he has a long way to go. Anyway, let's go slow! I plan to spend time on this series. (Although I don't plan to drag it out.)

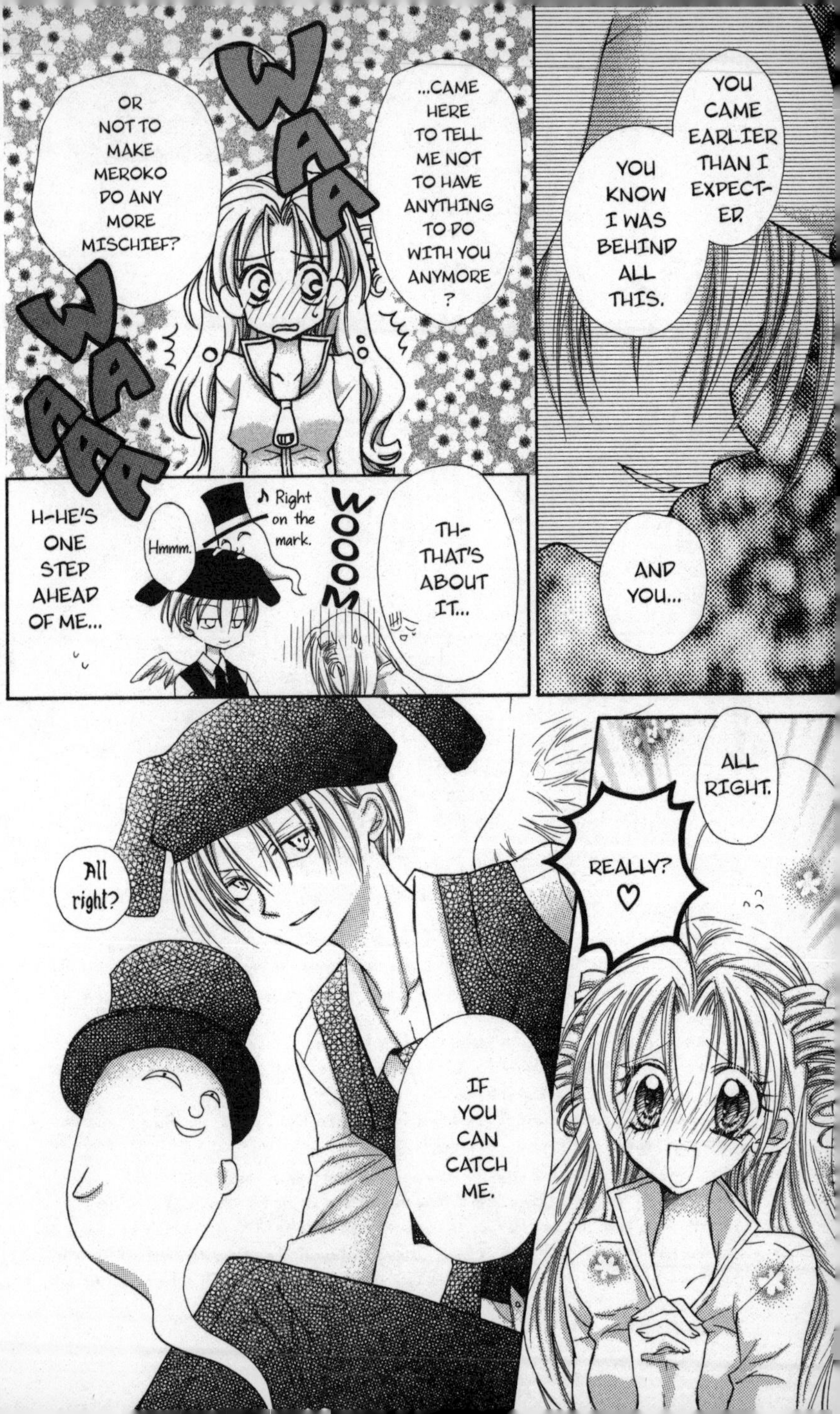
YOU CAME EARLIER THAN I EXPECTED.
YOU KNOW I WAS BEHIND ALL THIS.
AND YOU...
...CAME HERE TO TELL ME NOT TO HAVE ANYTHING TO DO WITH YOU ANYMORE?
OR NOT TO MAKE MEROKO DO ANY MORE MISCHIEF?
WAA
WAAAA
TH-THAT'S ABOUT IT...
WOOOM
♪ Right on the mark.
Hmmm.
H-HE'S ONE STEP AHEAD OF ME...
ALL RIGHT.
REALLY? ♡
All right?
IF YOU CAN CATCH ME.

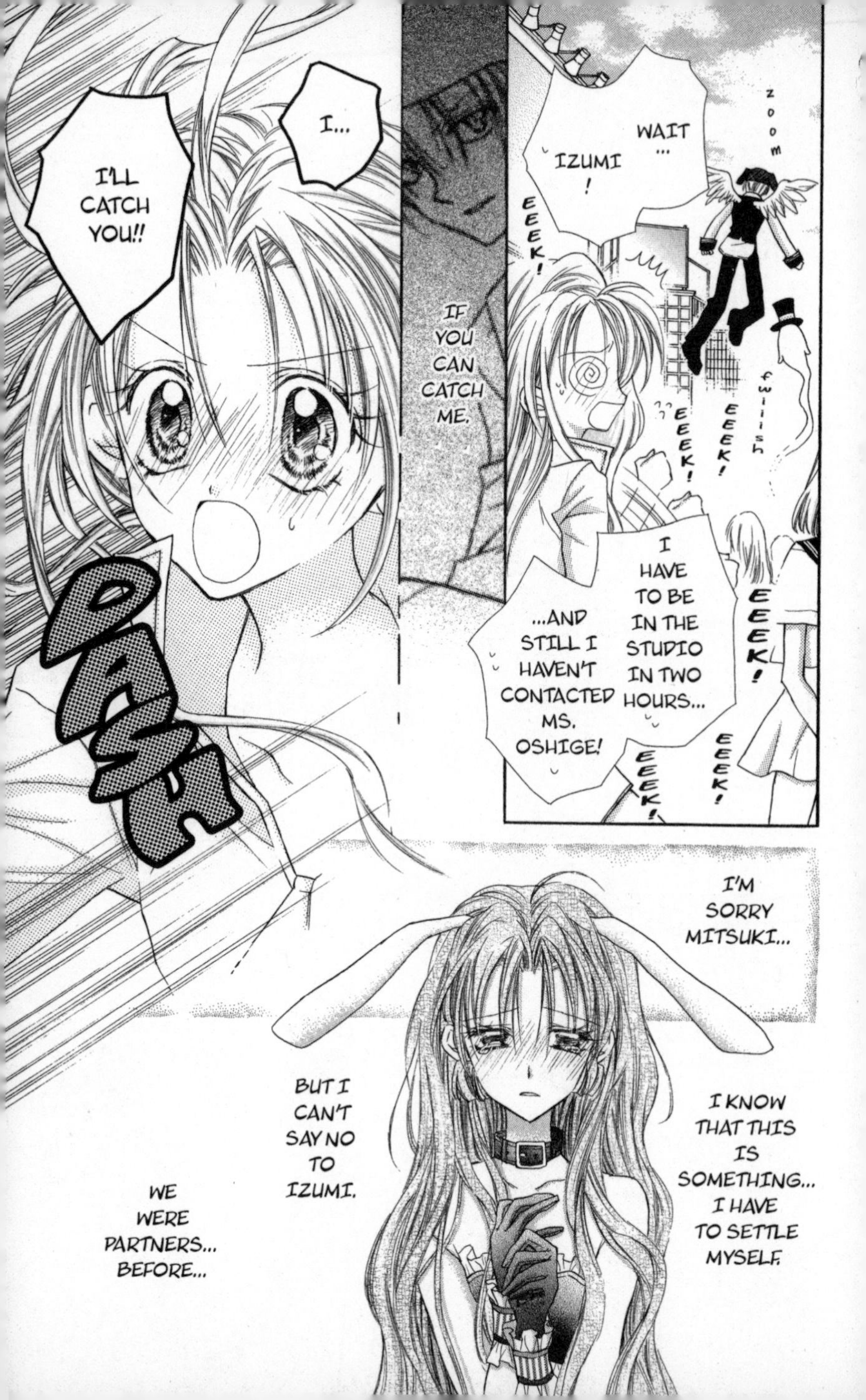
WAIT... IZUMI!
EEEK!
zoom
fwiish
EEEK!
EEEK!
EEEK!
I HAVE TO BE IN THE STUDIO IN TWO HOURS...
...AND STILL I HAVEN'T CONTACTED MS. OSHIGE!
EEEK!
EEEK!
EEEK!
IF YOU CAN CATCH ME.
I...
I'LL CATCH YOU!!
DASH
I'M SORRY MITSUKI...
I KNOW THAT THIS IS SOMETHING... I HAVE TO SETTLE MYSELF.
BUT I CAN'T SAY NO TO IZUMI.
WE WERE PARTNERS... BEFORE...

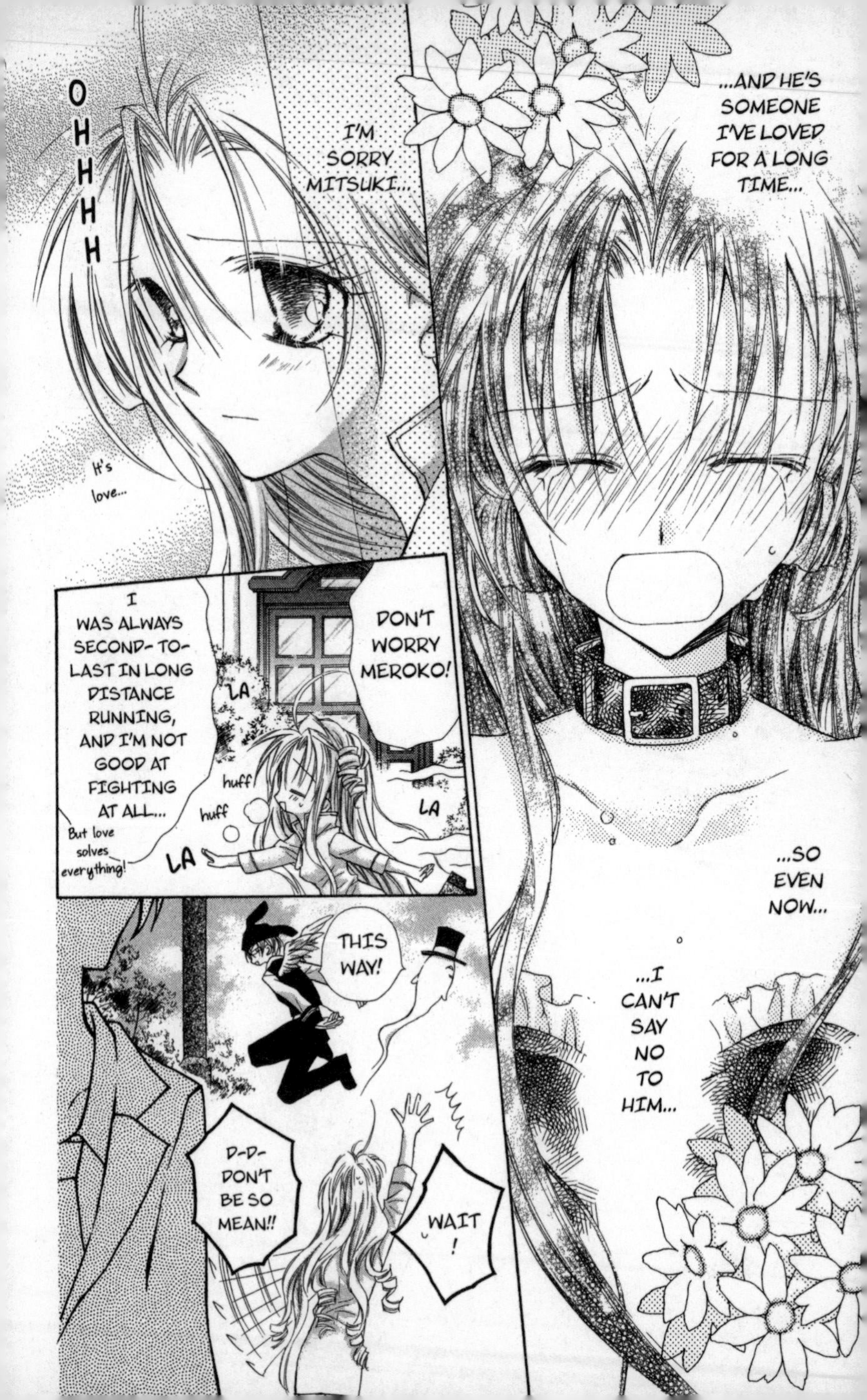
...AND HE'S SOMEONE I'VE LOVED FOR A LONG TIME...
...SO EVEN NOW...
...I CAN'T SAY NO TO HIM...
I'M SORRY MITSUKI...
OHHHH
It's love...
DON'T WORRY MEROKO!
I WAS ALWAYS SECOND-TO-LAST IN LONG DISTANCE RUNNING, AND I'M NOT GOOD AT FIGHTING AT ALL...
LA
LA
huff
huff
LA
But love solves everything!
THIS WAY!
WAIT!
D-D-DON'T BE SO MEAN!!

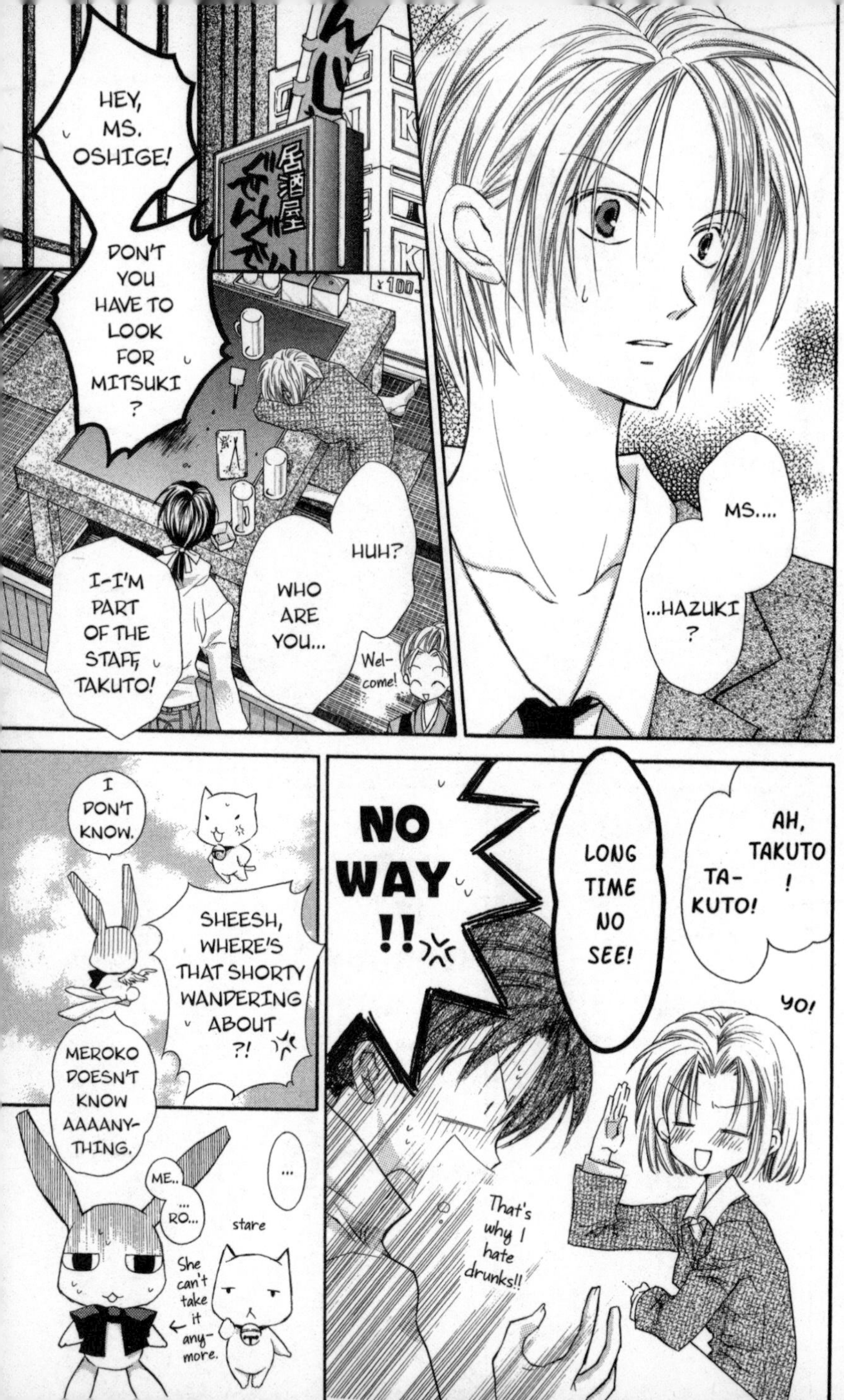
MS....
...HAZUKI ?
HEY, MS. OSHIGE!
DON'T YOU HAVE TO LOOK FOR MITSUKI ?
居酒屋
HUH?
WHO ARE YOU...
Wel-come!
I-I'M PART OF THE STAFF, TAKUTO!
AH, TAKUTO !
TA-KUTO!
YO!
LONG TIME NO SEE!
NO WAY !!
That's why I hate drunks!!
I DON'T KNOW.
SHEESH, WHERE'S THAT SHORTY WANDERING ABOUT ?!
MEROKO DOESN'T KNOW AAAANY-THING.
...
ME.. ... RO...
stare
She can't take it any-more.

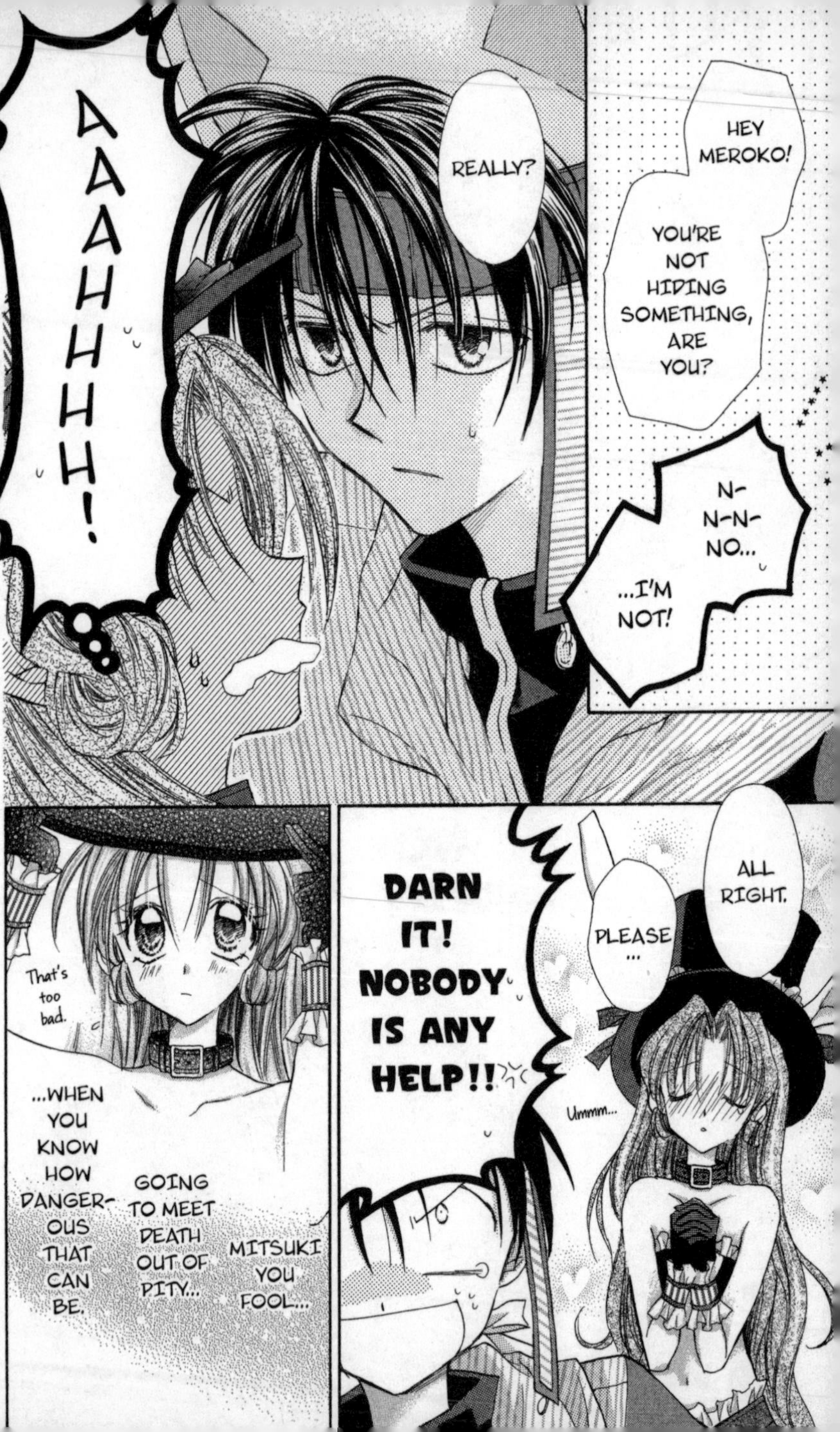
HEY MEROKO!
YOU'RE NOT HIDING SOMETHING, ARE YOU?
N-N-N-NO...
...I'M NOT!
REALLY?
AAAHHHH!
ALL RIGHT.
PLEASE ...
DARN IT! NOBODY IS ANY HELP!!
Ummmm...
That's too bad.
MITSUKI YOU FOOL...
GOING TO MEET DEATH OUT OF PITY...
...WHEN YOU KNOW HOW DANGER-OUS THAT CAN BE.

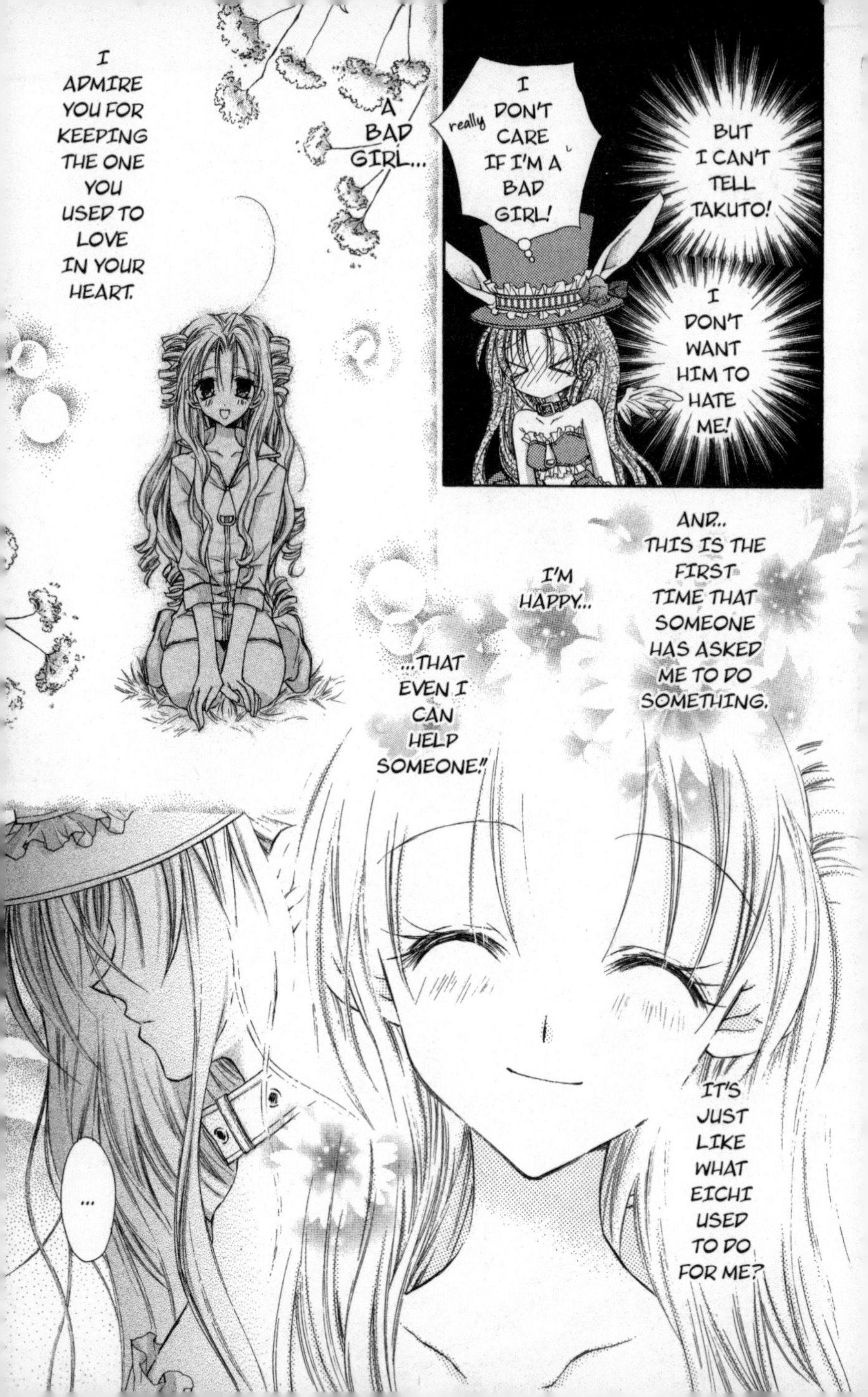

BUT I CAN'T TELL TAKUTO!
I really DON'T CARE IF I'M A BAD GIRL!
I DON'T WANT HIM TO HATE ME!
A BAD GIRL...
I ADMIRE YOU FOR KEEPING THE ONE YOU USED TO LOVE IN YOUR HEART.
AND.. THIS IS THE FIRST TIME THAT SOMEONE HAS ASKED ME TO DO SOMETHING.
I'M HAPPY...
...THAT EVEN I CAN HELP SOMEONE!!
IT'S JUST LIKE WHAT EICHI USED TO DO FOR ME?
...

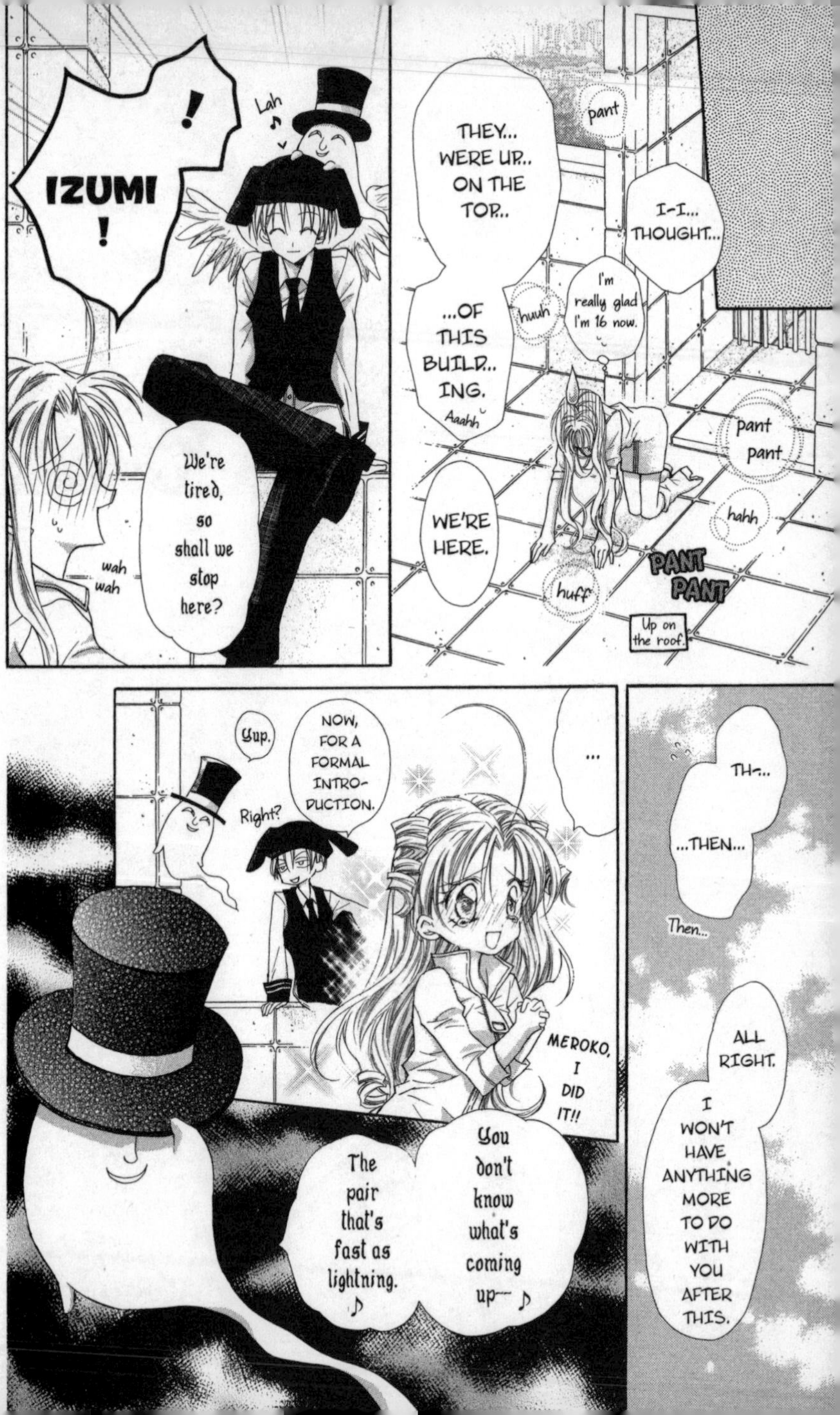
pant
I-I... THOUGHT...
THEY... WERE UP... ON THE TOP...
I'm really glad I'm 16 now.
huuh
...OF THIS BUILD... ING.
Aaahh
pant pant
hahh
WE'RE HERE.
PANT PANT
huff
Up on the roof.
!
Lah ♪
IZUMI !
We're tired, so shall we stop here?
wah wah
TH-...
...THEN...
Then...
ALL RIGHT.
I WON'T HAVE ANYTHING MORE TO DO WITH YOU AFTER THIS.
...
NOW, FOR A FORMAL INTRODUCTION.
Yup.
Right?
MEROKO, I DID IT!!
You don't know what's coming up~ ♪
The pair that's fast as lightning. ♪

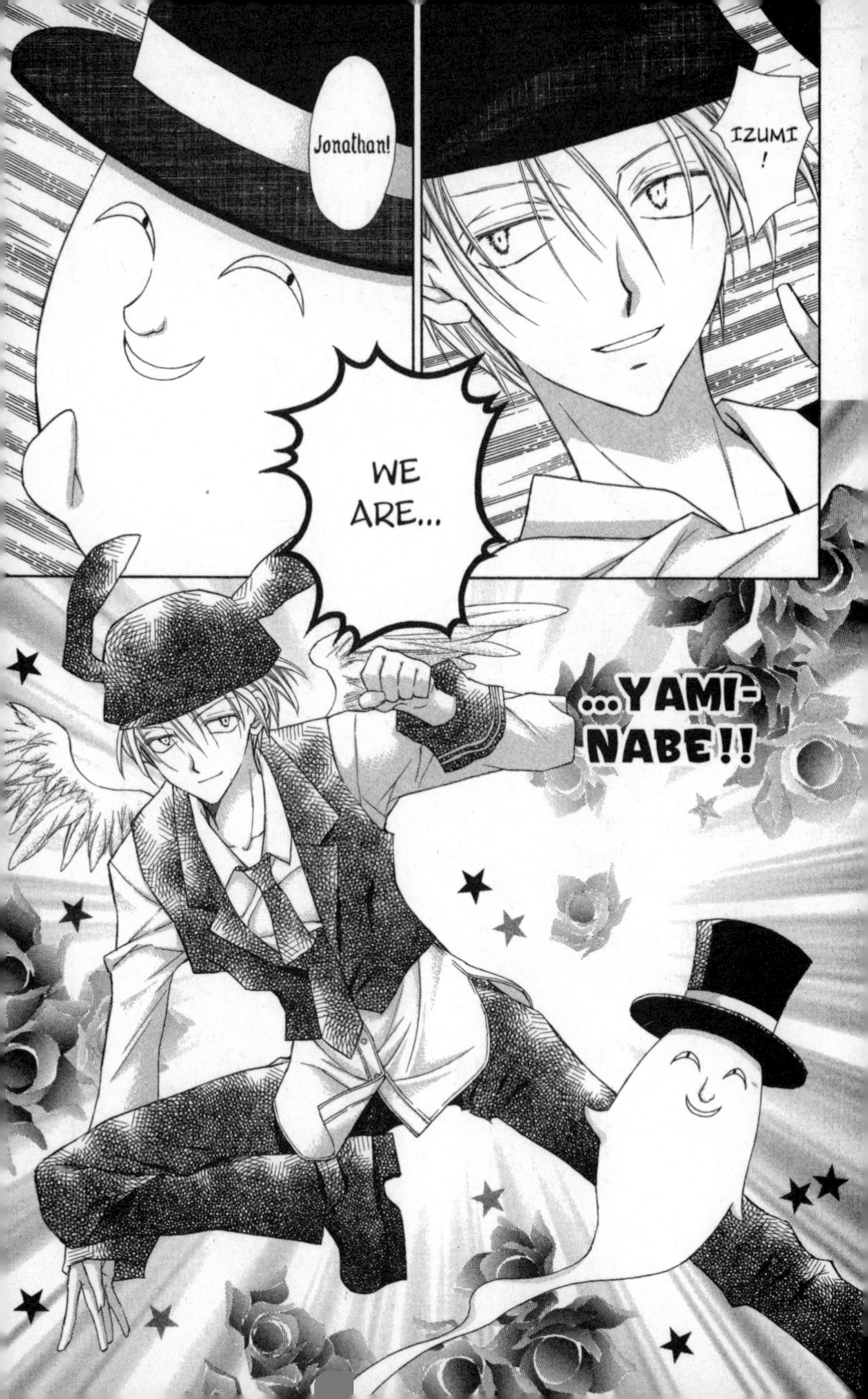
IZUMI!
Jonathan!
WE ARE...
...YAMI-NABE!!

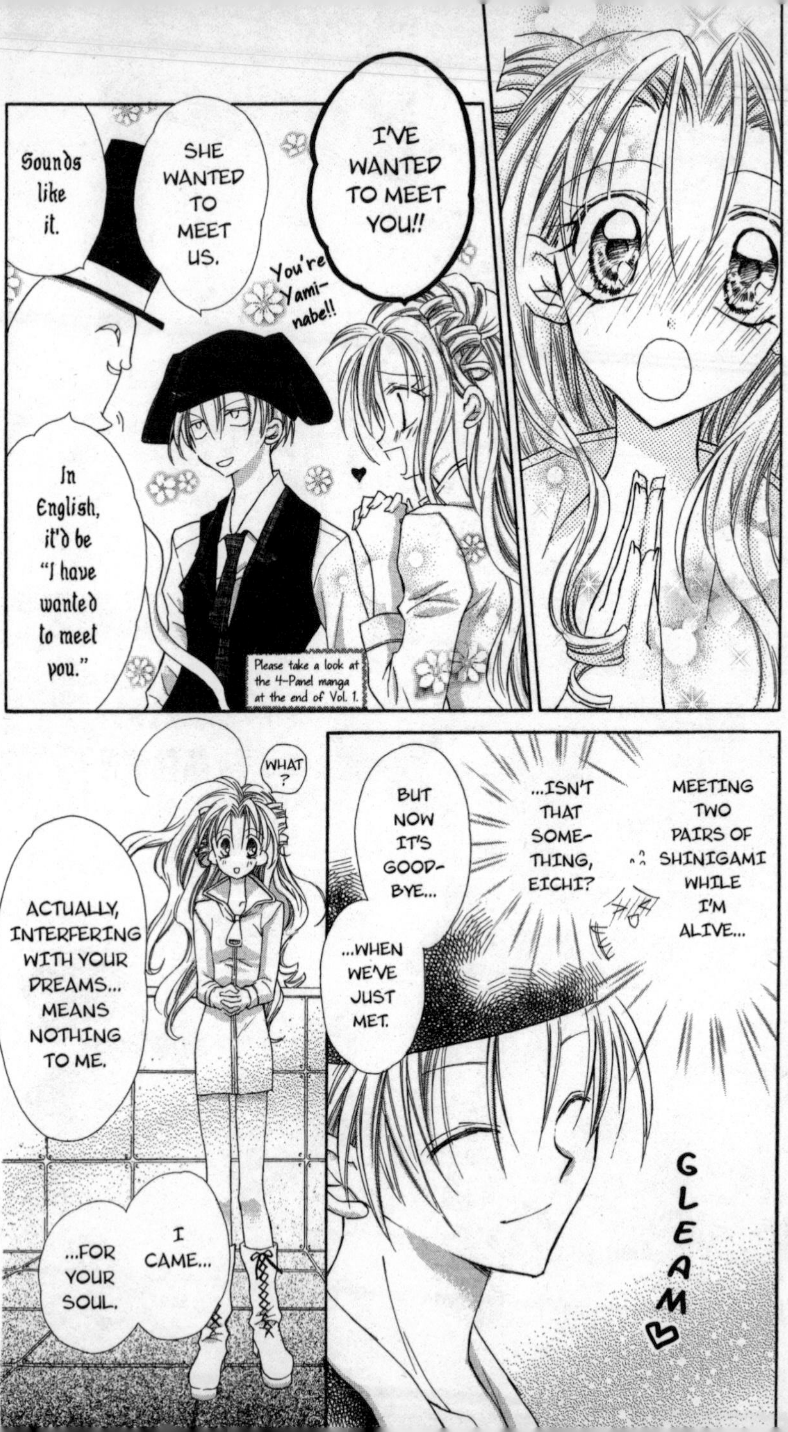
I'VE WANTED TO MEET YOU!!
You're Yami-nabe!!
SHE WANTED TO MEET US.
Sounds like it.
In English, it'd be "I have wanted to meet you."
Please take a look at the 4-Panel manga at the end of Vol. 1.
MEETING TWO PAIRS OF SHINIGAMI WHILE I'M ALIVE...
...ISN'T THAT SOMETHING, EICHI?
BUT NOW IT'S GOOD-BYE...
...WHEN WE'VE JUST MET.
GLEAM
WHAT?
ACTUALLY, INTERFERING WITH YOUR DREAMS... MEANS NOTHING TO ME.
I CAME...
...FOR YOUR SOUL.

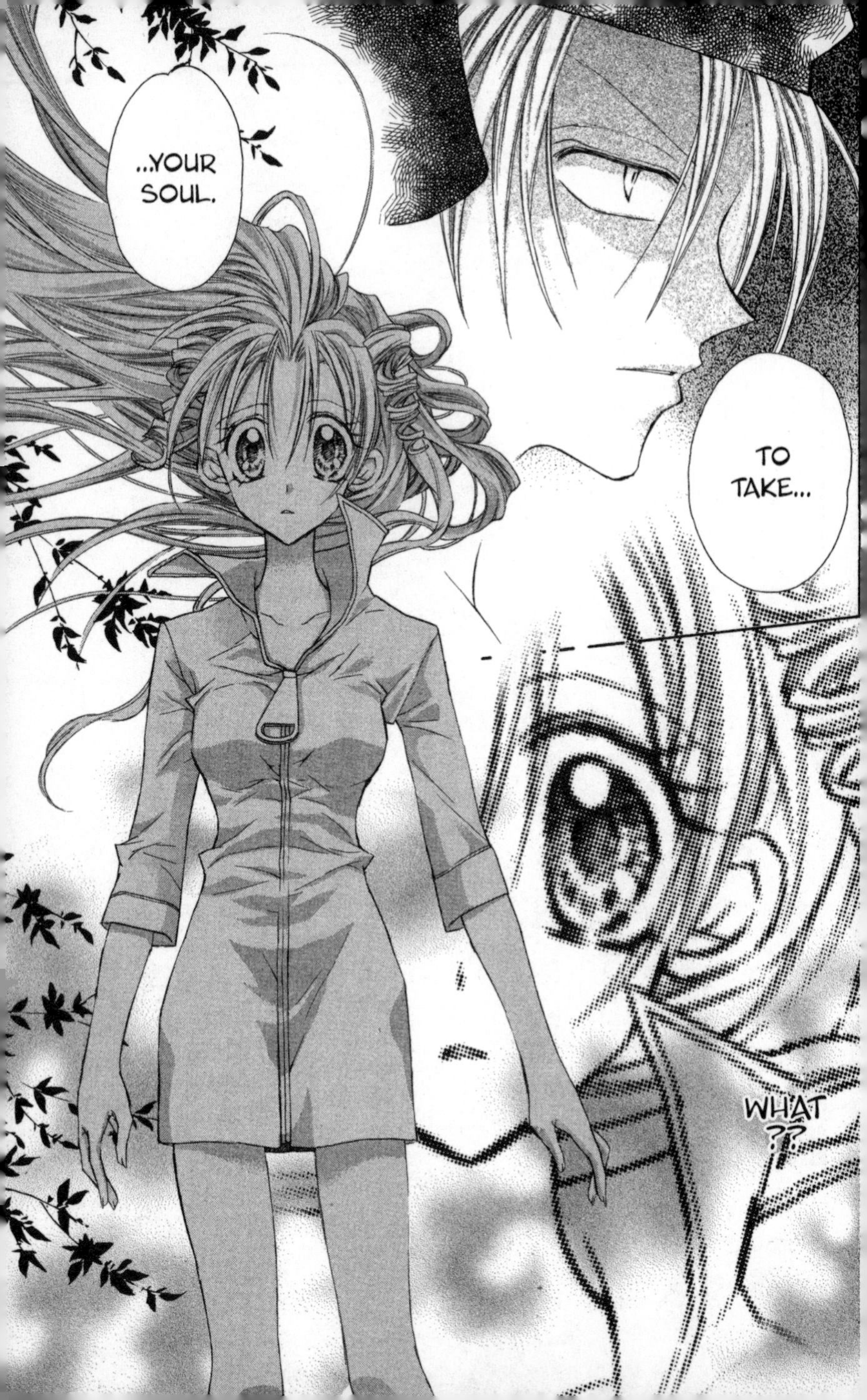
TO TAKE...
...YOUR SOUL.
WHAT ??

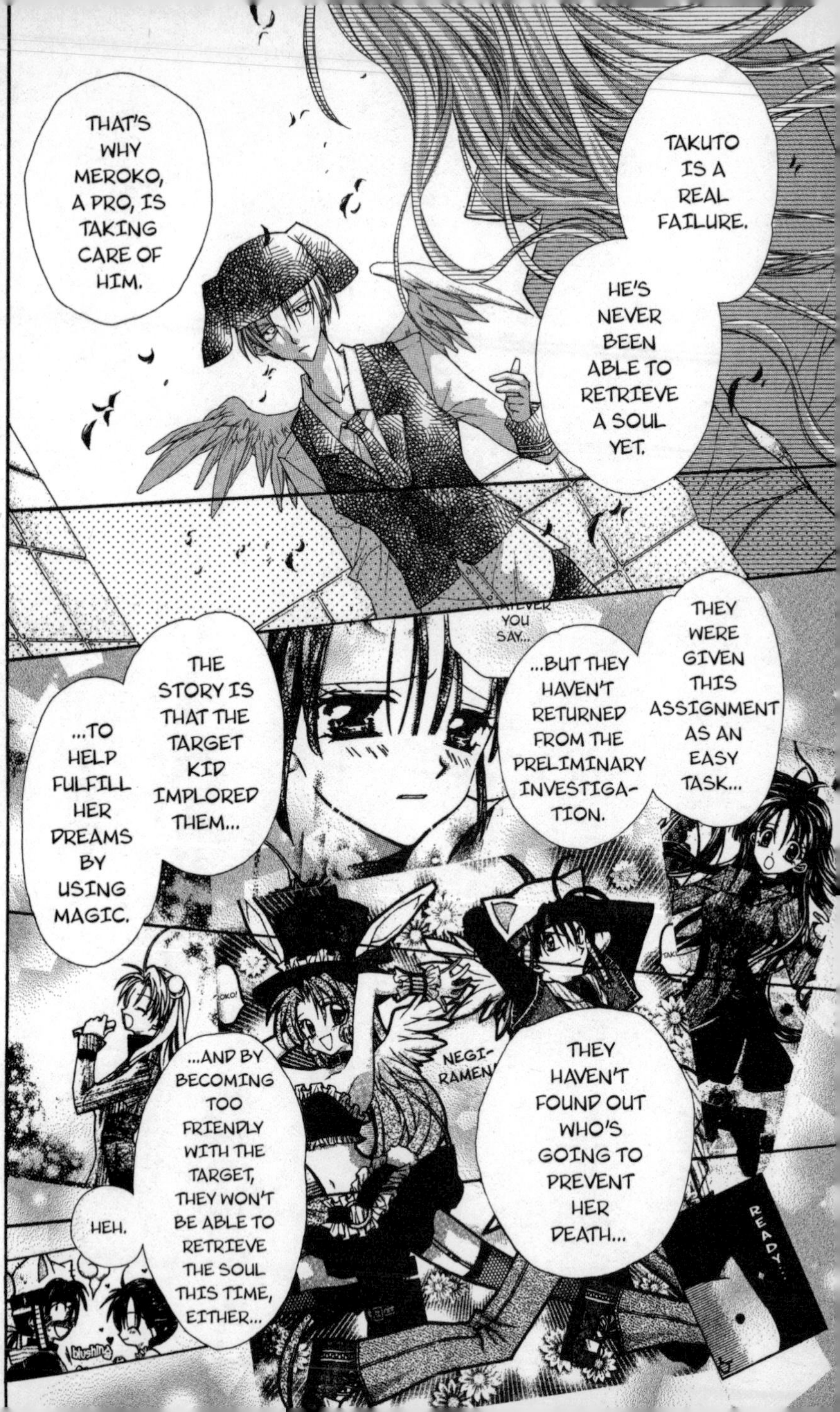
TAKUTO IS A REAL FAILURE.
HE'S NEVER BEEN ABLE TO RETRIEVE A SOUL YET.
THAT'S WHY MEROKO, A PRO, IS TAKING CARE OF HIM.
THEY WERE GIVEN THIS ASSIGNMENT AS AN EASY TASK...
YOU SAY...
...BUT THEY HAVEN'T RETURNED FROM THE PRELIMINARY INVESTIGA-TION.
THE STORY IS THAT THE TARGET KID IMPLORED THEM...
...TO HELP FULFILL HER DREAMS BY USING MAGIC.
READY...
THEY HAVEN'T FOUND OUT WHO'S GOING TO PREVENT HER DEATH...
NEGI-RAMEN
...AND BY BECOMING TOO FRIENDLY WITH THE TARGET, THEY WON'T BE ABLE TO RETRIEVE THE SOUL THIS TIME, EITHER...
HEH.
blushing

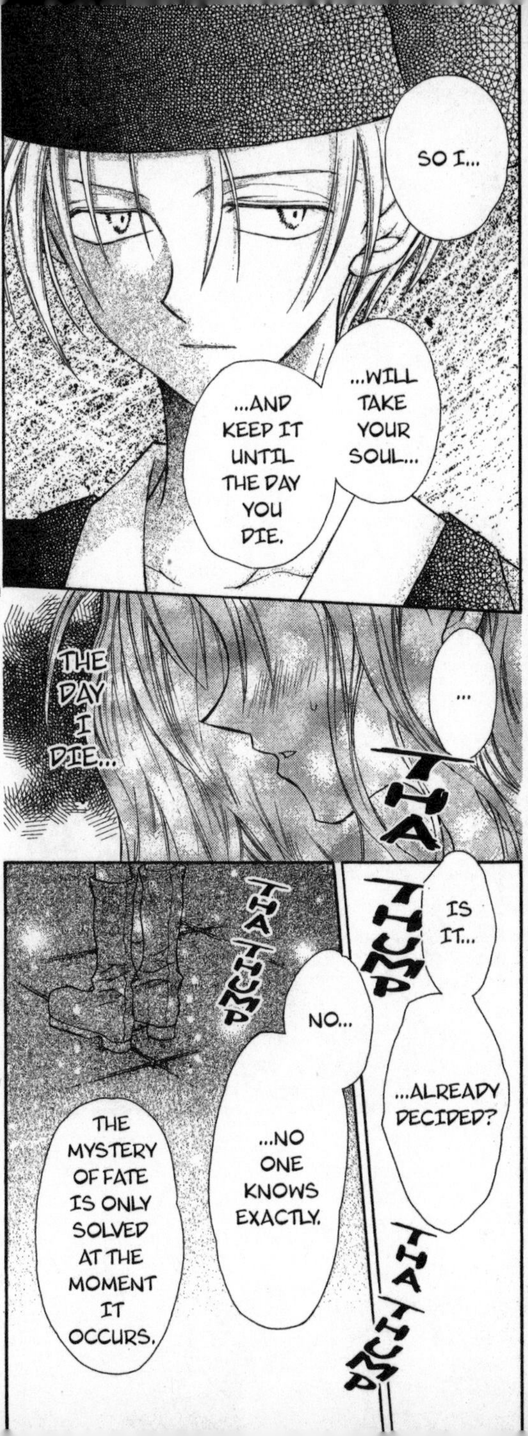
SO I...
...WILL TAKE YOUR SOUL...
...AND KEEP IT UNTIL THE DAY YOU DIE.
...
THE DAY I DIE...
THA
THUMP
IS IT...
...ALREADY DECIDED?
THA THUMP
NO...
...NO ONE KNOWS EXACTLY.
THE MYSTERY OF FATE IS ONLY SOLVED AT THE MOMENT IT OCCURS.
THA THUMP

●My Favorites, Part ③●

We Love Cats After All (drama)

I saw the DVD-BOX and bought it. (Yes, I'm poor because I buy too many DVDs.) When the drama was first broadcast, I liked Kimi-chan, but watching it now, I love Rei-chan. (T-too funny! I like big sister Kayano too.) And timely enough, in the commercial for Sapporo Nama-shibori beer, "Recommend Nama shibori to your Friends," Satomi Kobayashi (who played Kimie) was recommending Nama-shibori to Masako Motai (who played big sister Kayano), and as a fan of the drama, I was really happy.♥

Next, I'd like Motai-san to recommend it to Shigeru Muroi (who played Reiko)!! (Please)

There's still more white space...

Please enjoy the dazzling of Jonathan.

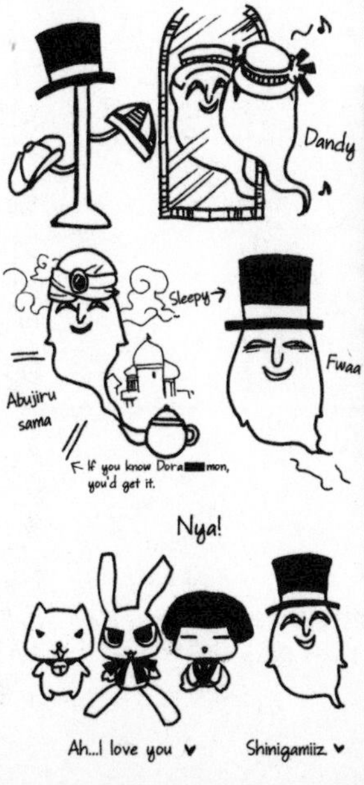
Dandy
Sleepy→
Abujiru sama
Fwaa
← If you know Dora[redacted]mon, you'd get it.
Nya!
Ah...I love you ♥
Shinigamiiz ♥

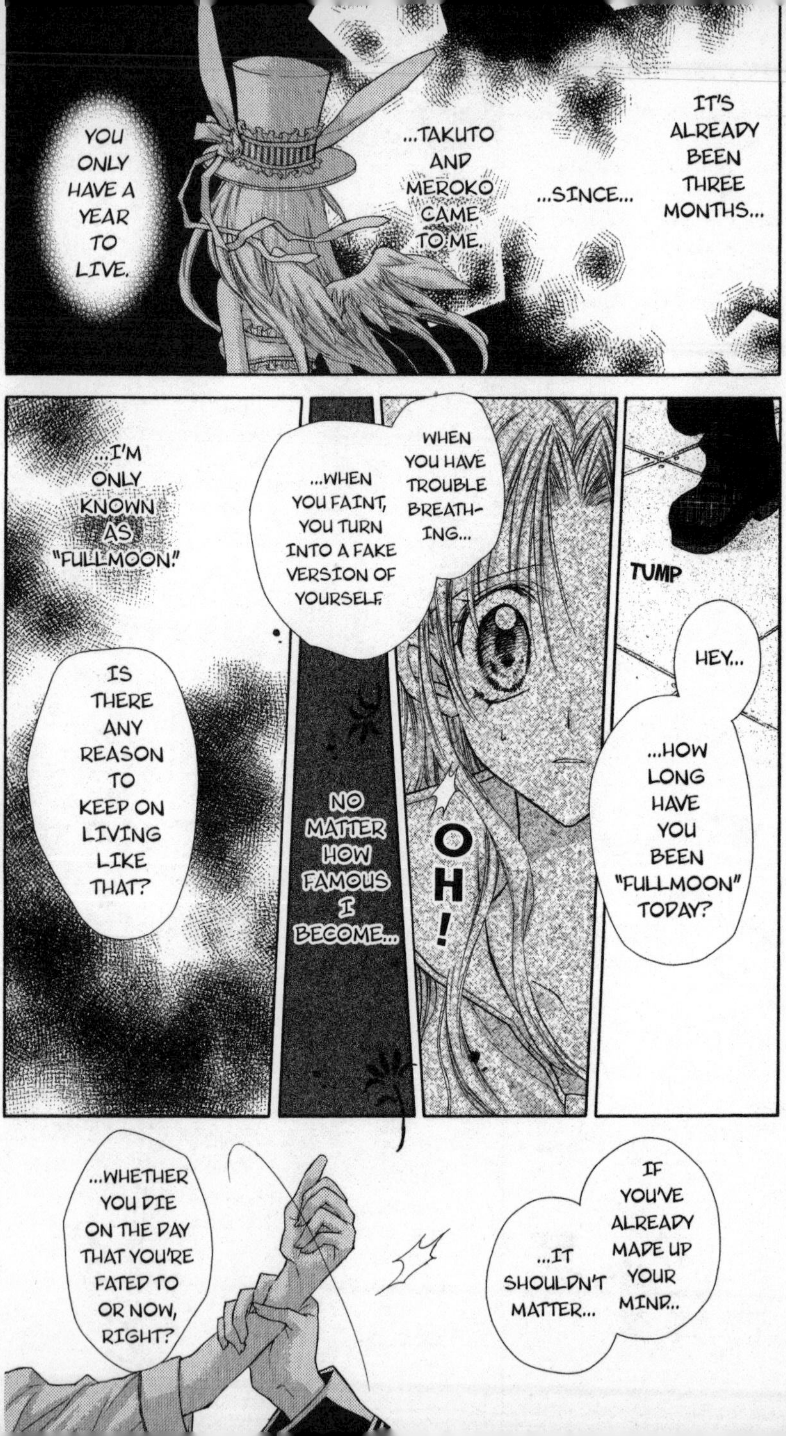
IT'S ALREADY BEEN THREE MONTHS...
...SINCE...
...TAKUTO AND MEROKO CAME TO ME.
YOU ONLY HAVE A YEAR TO LIVE.
TUMP
HEY...
...HOW LONG HAVE YOU BEEN "FULLMOON" TODAY?
WHEN YOU HAVE TROUBLE BREATH-ING...
...WHEN YOU FAINT, YOU TURN INTO A FAKE VERSION OF YOURSELF.
OH!
NO MATTER HOW FAMOUS I BECOME...
...I'M ONLY KNOWN AS "FULLMOON."
IS THERE ANY REASON TO KEEP ON LIVING LIKE THAT?
IF YOU'VE ALREADY MADE UP YOUR MIND..
...IT SHOULDN'T MATTER...
...WHETHER YOU DIE ON THE DAY THAT YOU'RE FATED TO OR NOW, RIGHT?

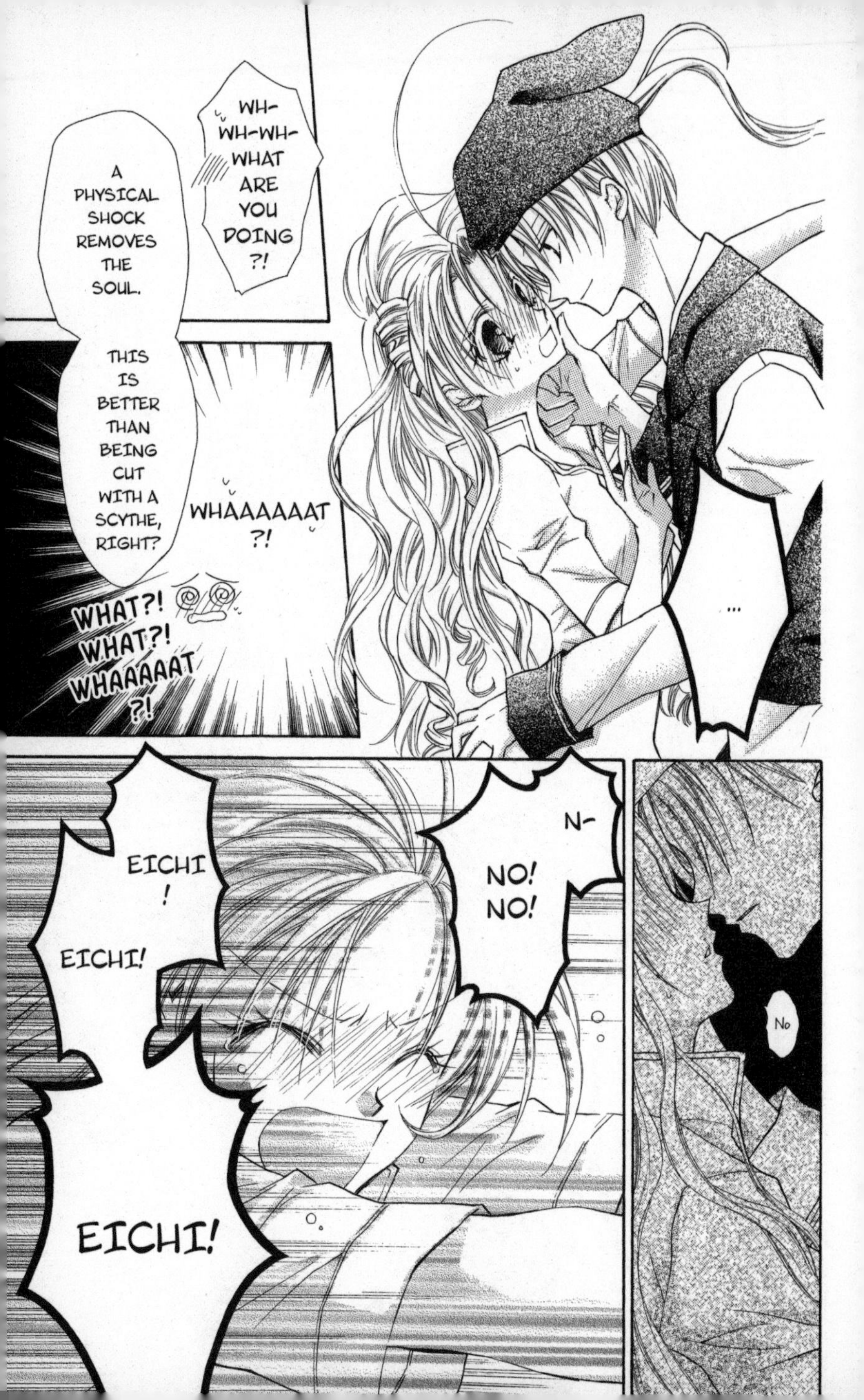
...
WH-WH-WH-WHAT ARE YOU DOING?!
A PHYSICAL SHOCK REMOVES THE SOUL.
THIS IS BETTER THAN BEING CUT WITH A SCYTHE, RIGHT?
WHAAAAAAT?!
WHAT?! WHAT?! WHAAAAAT?!
No
N- NO! NO!
EICHI!
EICHI!
EICHI!

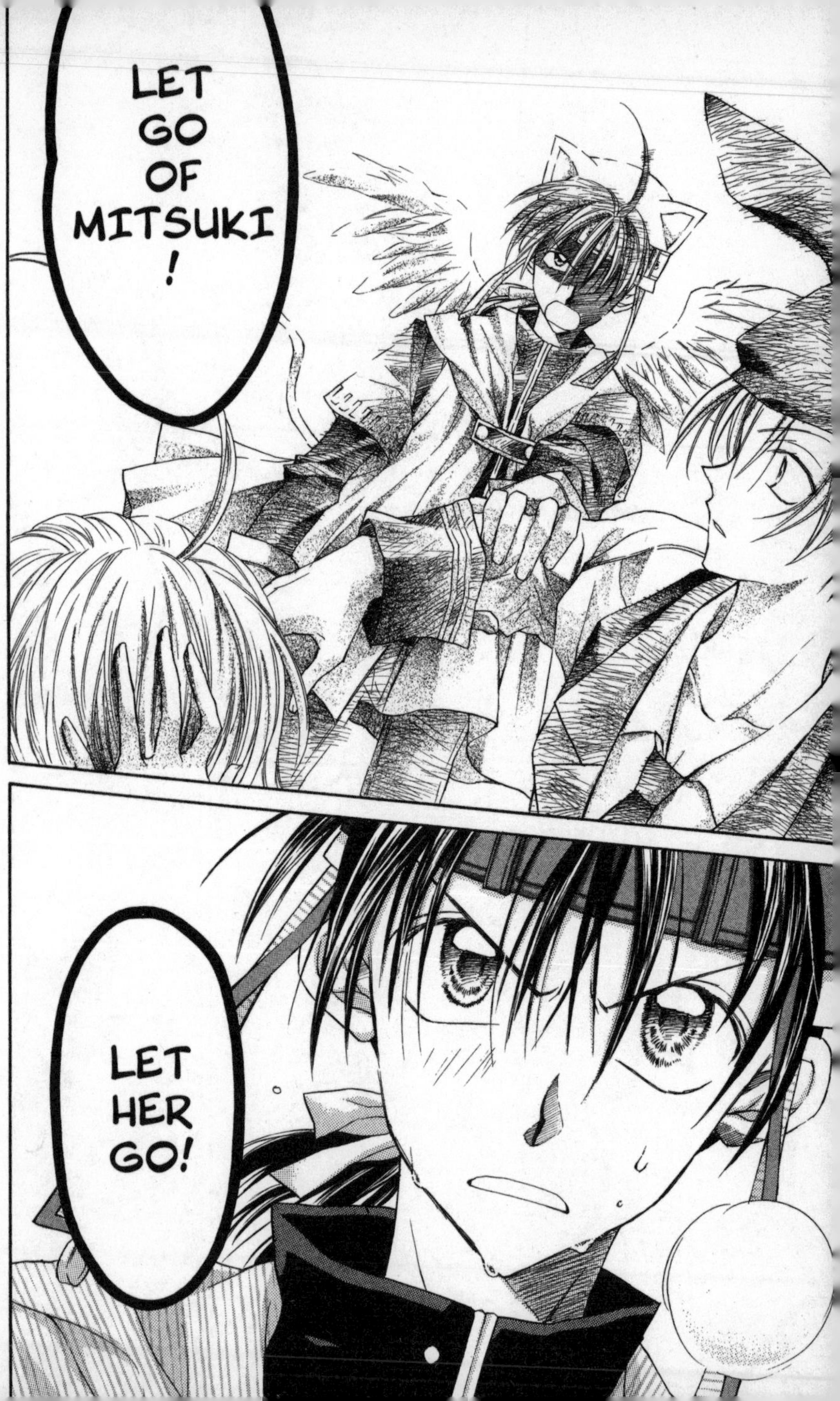
LET GO OF MITSUKI!
LET HER GO!

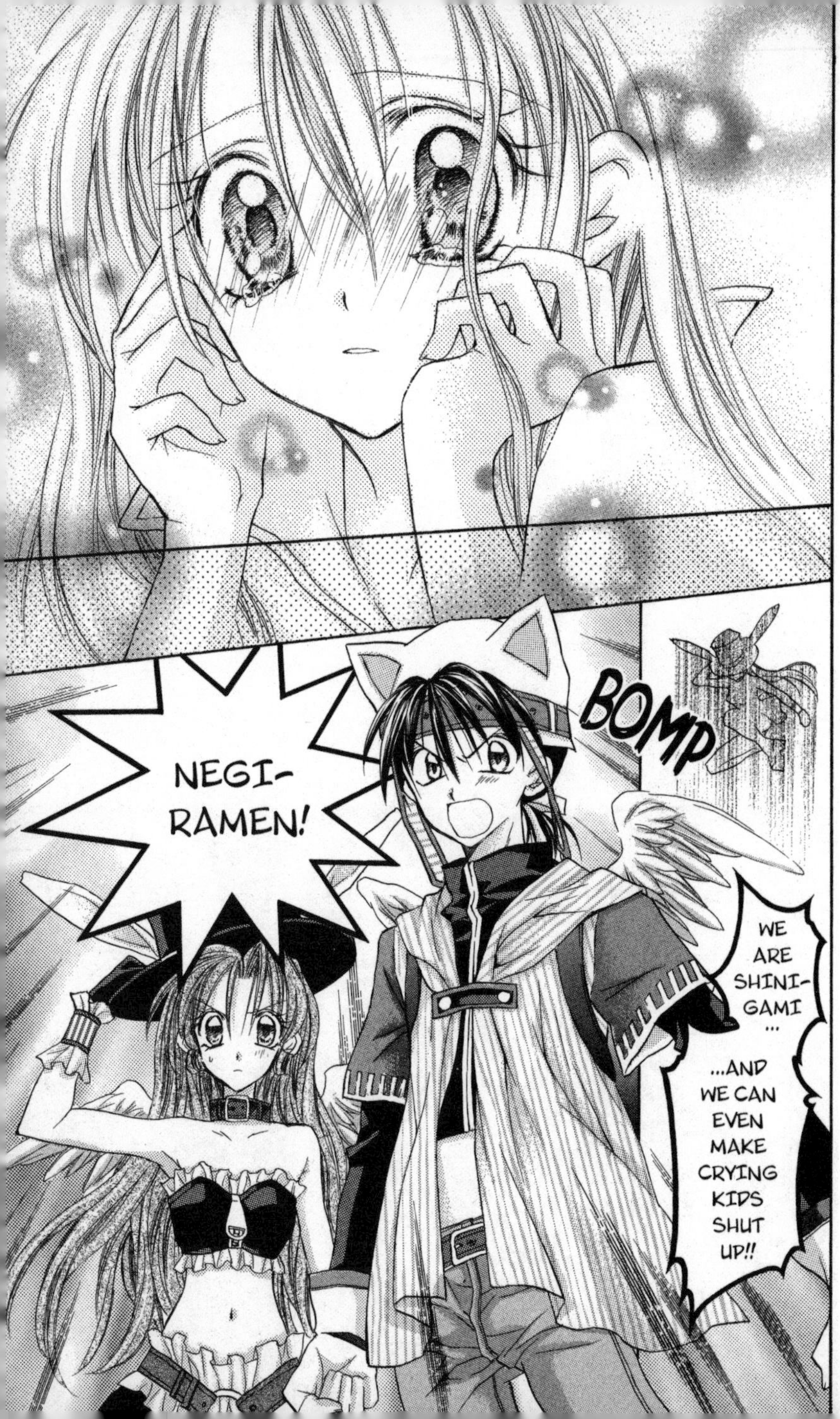
BOMP
WE ARE SHINI-GAMI ...
...AND WE CAN EVEN MAKE CRYING KIDS SHUT UP!!
NEGI-RAMEN!

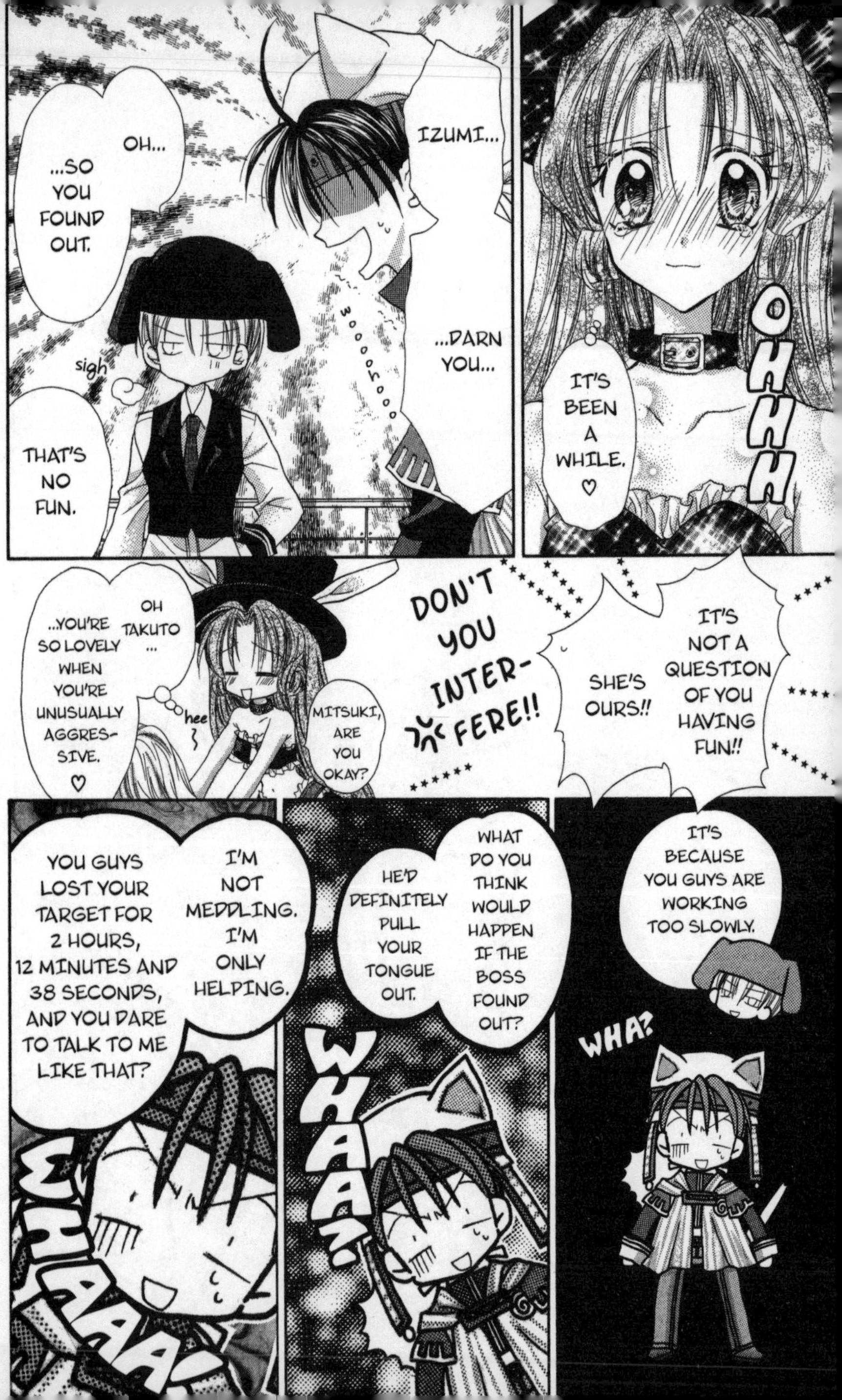
OHHHH
IT'S BEEN A WHILE. ♡
IZUMI...
...DARN YOU...
woooohoooo
OH...
...SO YOU FOUND OUT.
sigh
THAT'S NO FUN.
IT'S NOT A QUESTION OF YOU HAVING FUN!!
SHE'S OURS!!
DON'T YOU INTER-FERE!!
OH TAKUTO ...
...YOU'RE SO LOVELY WHEN YOU'RE UNUSUALLY AGGRES-SIVE. ♡
hee
MITSUKI, ARE YOU OKAY?
IT'S BECAUSE YOU GUYS ARE WORKING TOO SLOWLY.
WHA?
WHAT DO YOU THINK WOULD HAPPEN IF THE BOSS FOUND OUT?
HE'D DEFINITELY PULL YOUR TONGUE OUT.
WHAAA
I'M NOT MEDDLING. I'M ONLY HELPING.
YOU GUYS LOST YOUR TARGET FOR 2 HOURS, 12 MINUTES AND 38 SECONDS, AND YOU DARE TO TALK TO ME LIKE THAT?
WHAAAA

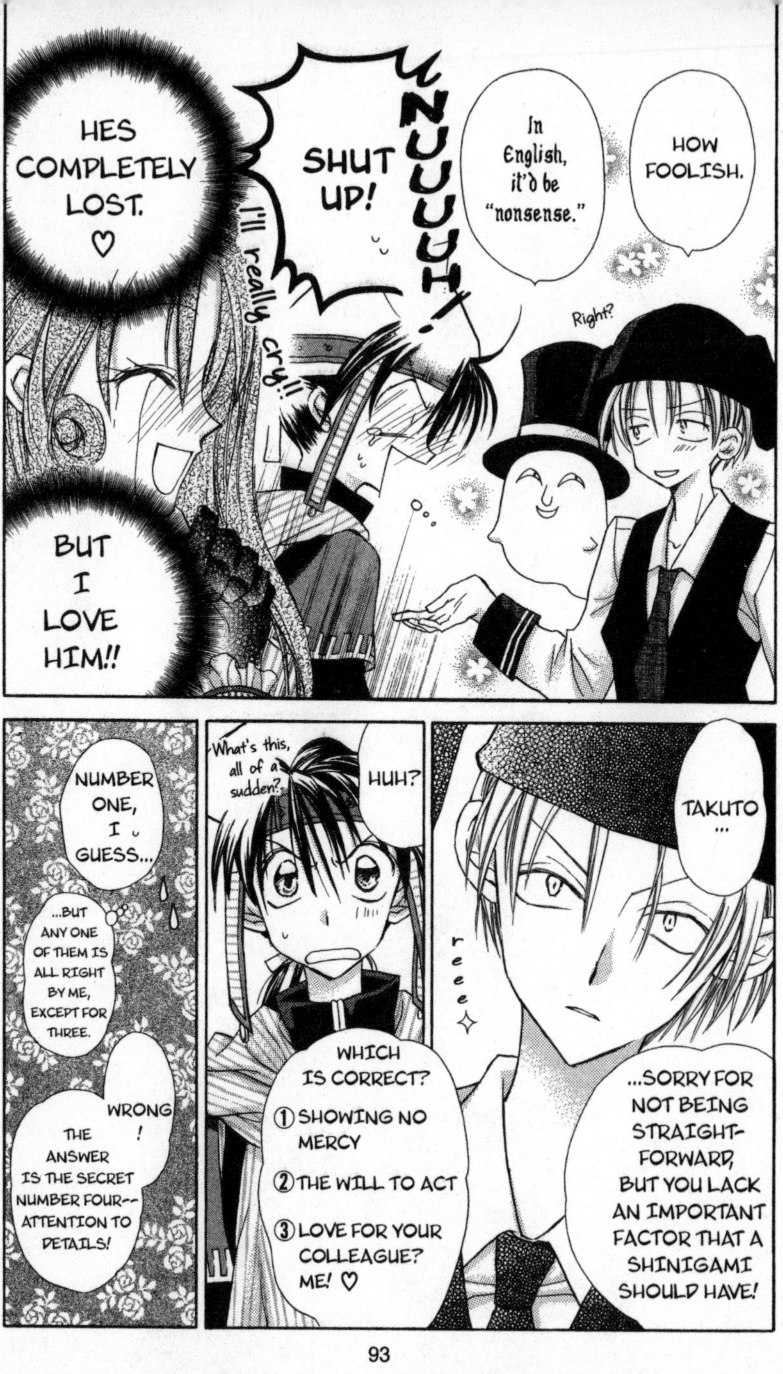
HOW FOOLISH.
In English, it'd be "nonsense."
Right?
NUUUUH!
SHUT UP!
I'll really cry!!
HES COMPLETELY LOST. ♡
BUT I LOVE HIM!!
TAKUTO ...
reee
...SORRY FOR NOT BEING STRAIGHT-FORWARD, BUT YOU LACK AN IMPORTANT FACTOR THAT A SHINIGAMI SHOULD HAVE!
HUH?
What's this, all of a sudden?
WHICH IS CORRECT?
① SHOWING NO MERCY
② THE WILL TO ACT
③ LOVE FOR YOUR COLLEAGUE? ME! ♡
NUMBER ONE, I GUESS...
...BUT ANY ONE OF THEM IS ALL RIGHT BY ME, EXCEPT FOR THREE.
WRONG!
THE ANSWER IS THE SECRET NUMBER FOUR--ATTENTION TO DETAILS!

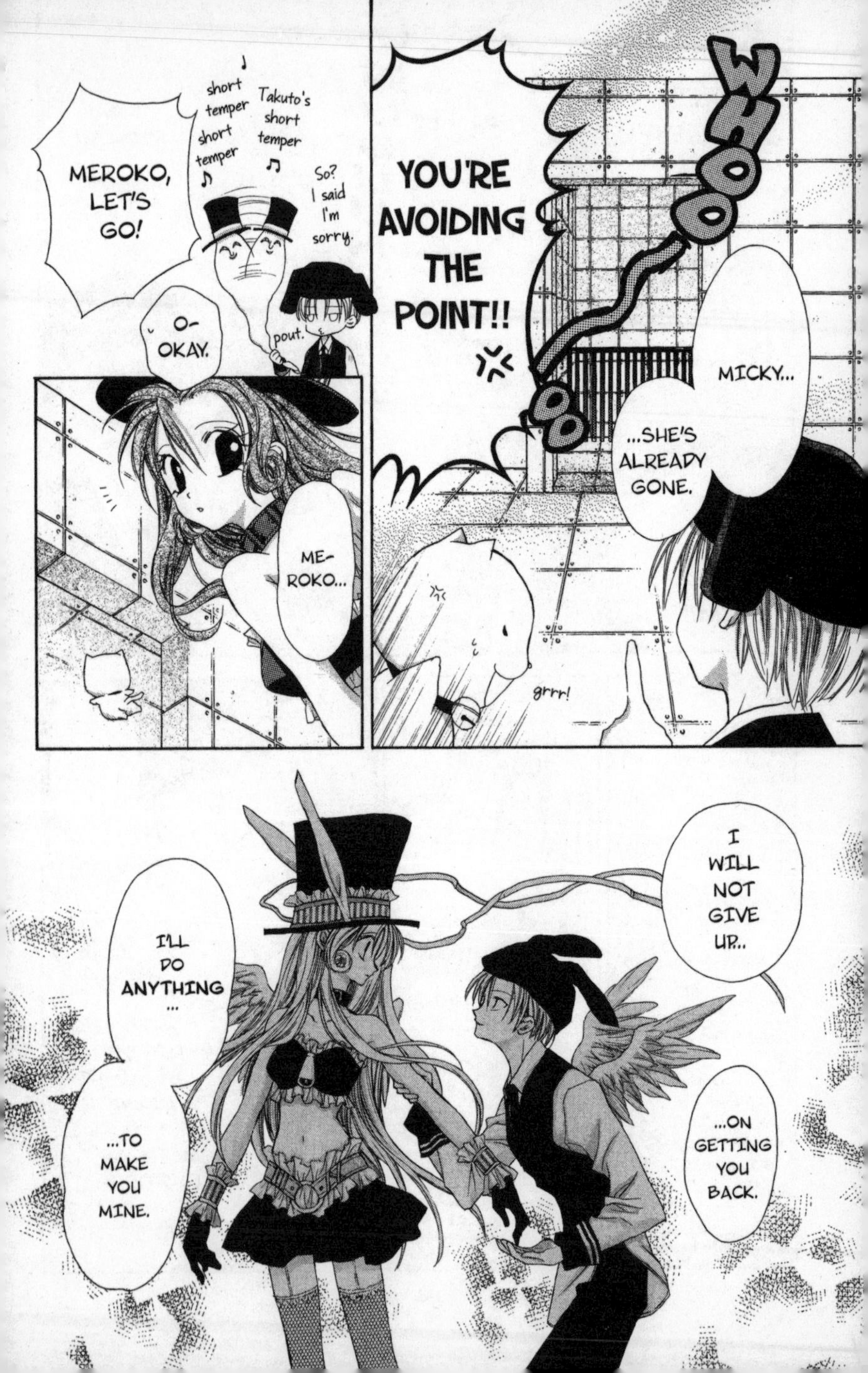
WHOOOOO
YOU'RE AVOIDING THE POINT!!
MICKY...
...SHE'S ALREADY GONE.
grrr!
MEROKO, LET'S GO!
short temper short temper Takuto's short temper
So? I said I'm sorry.
O-OKAY.
pout.
ME-ROKO...
I WILL NOT GIVE UP..
...ON GETTING YOU BACK.
I'LL DO ANYTHING...
...TO MAKE YOU MINE.

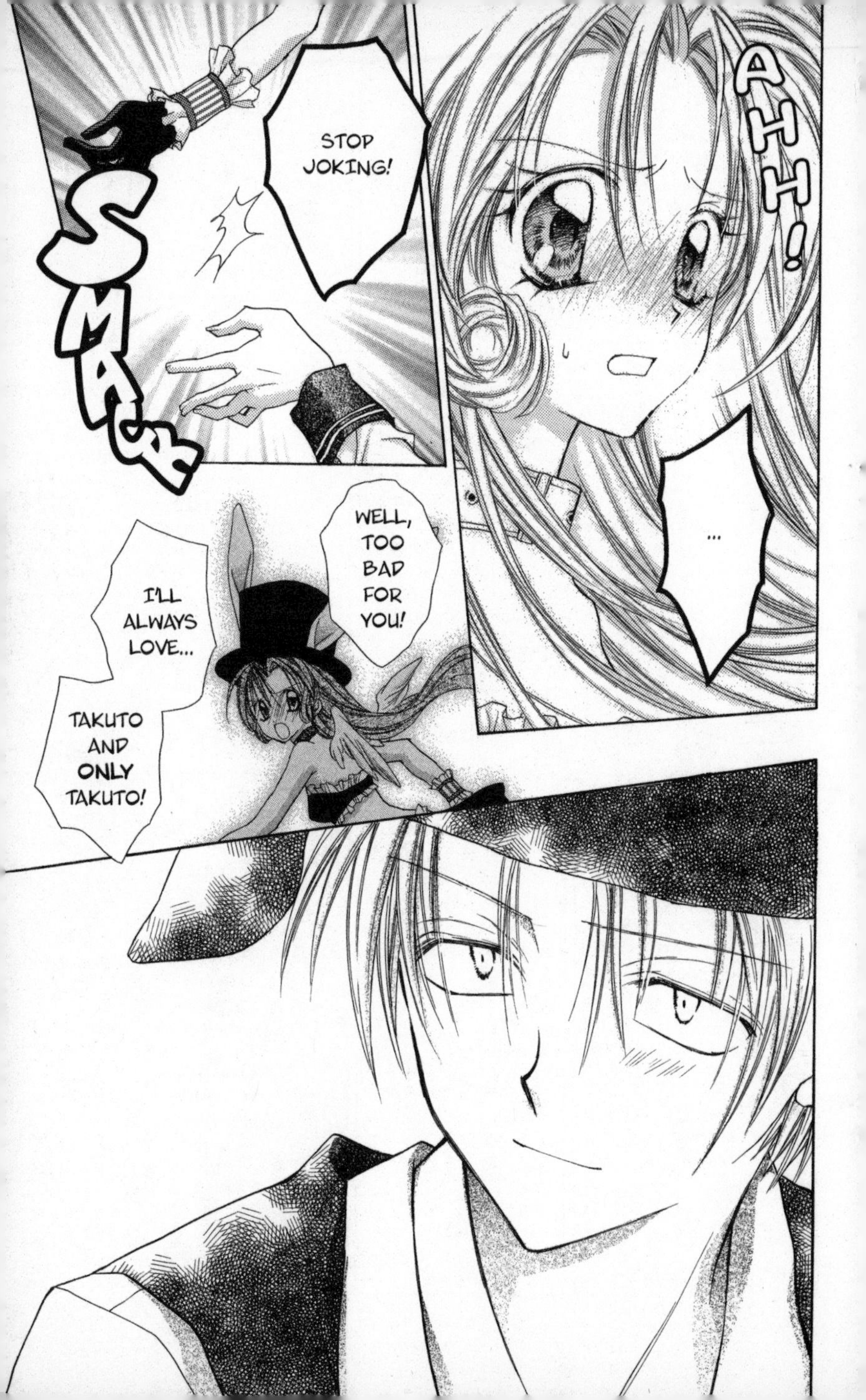
AHHH!
...
STOP JOKING!
SMACK
WELL, TOO BAD FOR YOU!
I'LL ALWAYS LOVE...
TAKUTO AND ONLY TAKUTO!

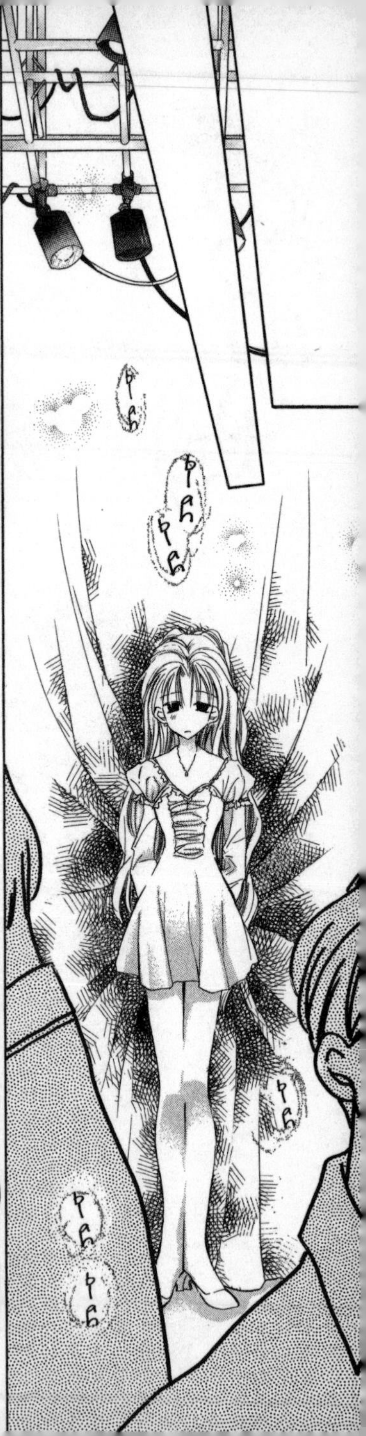

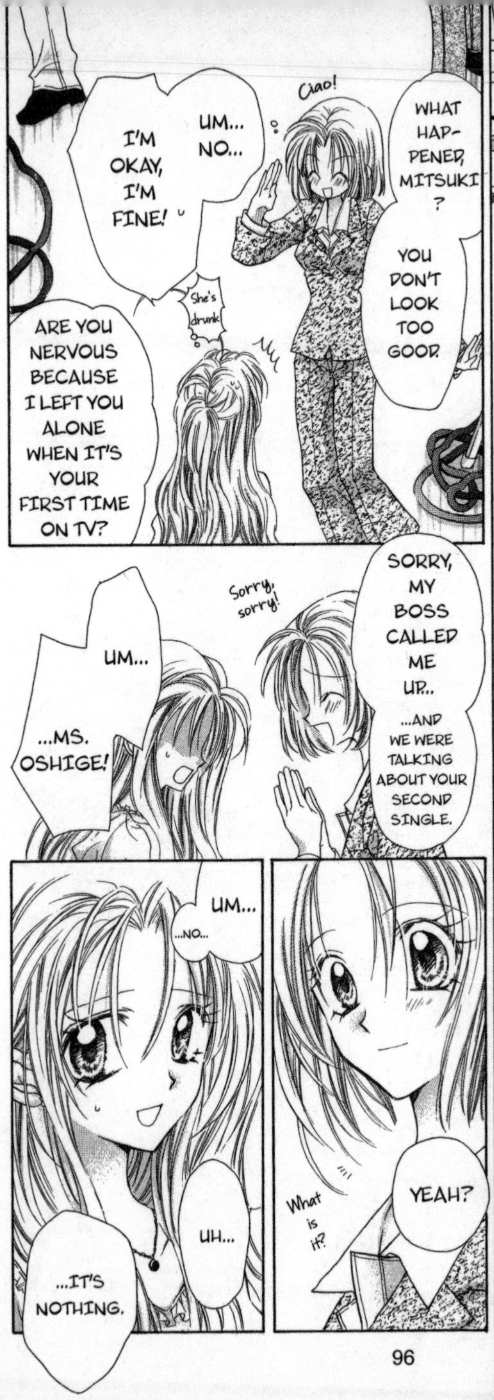
WHAT HAPPENED, MITSUKI?
YOU DON'T LOOK TOO GOOD.
Ciao!
UM... NO...
I'M OKAY, I'M FINE!
She's drunk
ARE YOU NERVOUS BECAUSE I LEFT YOU ALONE WHEN IT'S YOUR FIRST TIME ON TV?
Sorry, sorry!
SORRY, MY BOSS CALLED ME UP...
...AND WE WERE TALKING ABOUT YOUR SECOND SINGLE.
UM...
...MS. OSHIGE!
What is it?
YEAH?
UM...
...NO...
UH...
...IT'S NOTHING.

Me Nowadays

I went to a B'Z concert. A friend couldn't make it to the Nagoya concert because she had an assistant assignment, so she decided to come to the Yokohama [August 30th] concert, and I decided to go too. She reserved the tickets, and was I surprised! We were in sixth row in the arena, and we could see Inaba-san's face and Matsumoto-san's face really clearly

It's been eight years since I last went to a B'Z concert, and I was surprised that the concert was even more full of everything, but the two leads were cool like always, and I love them even more now. Some fans got invited on stage, and the two moved from the stage in front of the arena to the back (right below the stand seats) and played some acoustic numbers. They're such big artists, but they seemed so close to the fans. B'Z are the best!! When I go to their concerts, I really get that feeling.

I also went to see the voice-over being done for the anime (I did some voice acting, too.) Everyone was really friendly and serious and it was wonderful. Professionals do a fantastic job!! My very dear Izumi-kun will be played by one of my favorites, Megumi Ogata, so I would DEFINITELY love to go see them again.
(To all the staff, and Ogata-san... thank you so much for listening to my wishes♥)
I'm looking forward to it ~♪
la la la~♪

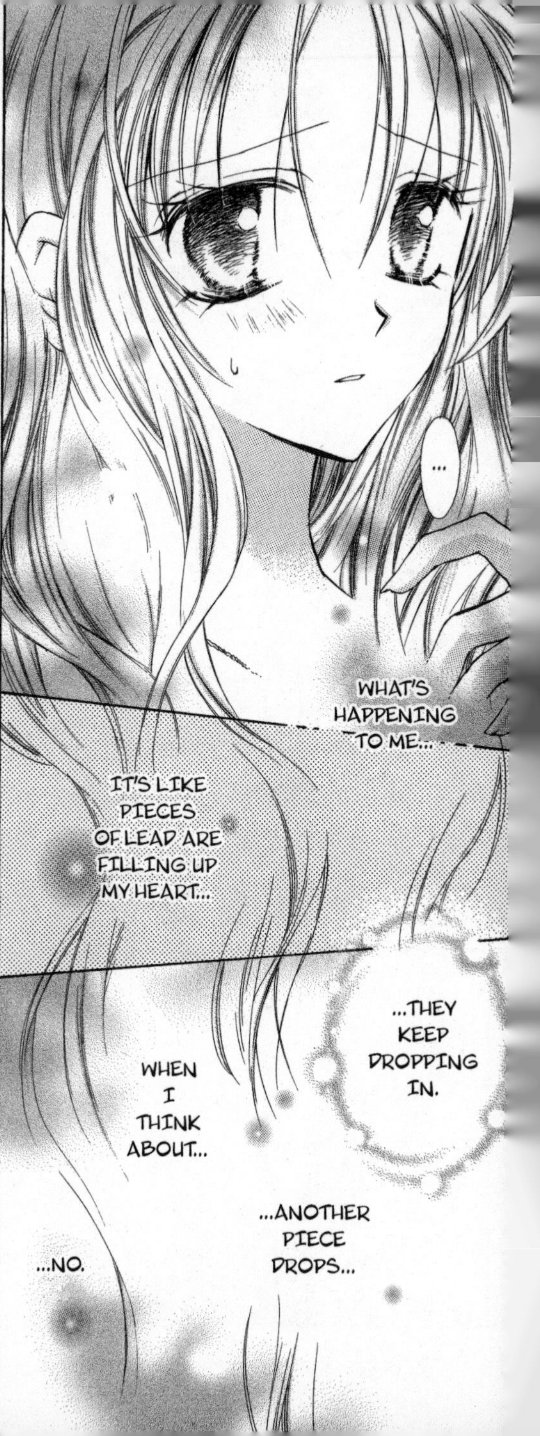
...
WHAT'S HAPPENING TO ME...
IT'S LIKE PIECES OF LEAD ARE FILLING UP MY HEART...
...THEY KEEP DROPPING IN.
WHEN I THINK ABOUT...
...ANOTHER PIECE DROPS...
...NO.

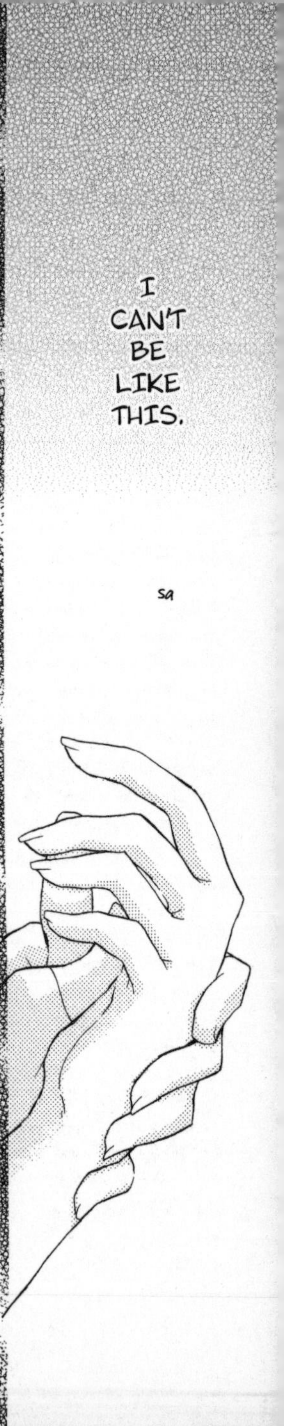
I CAN'T BE LIKE THIS.
sa

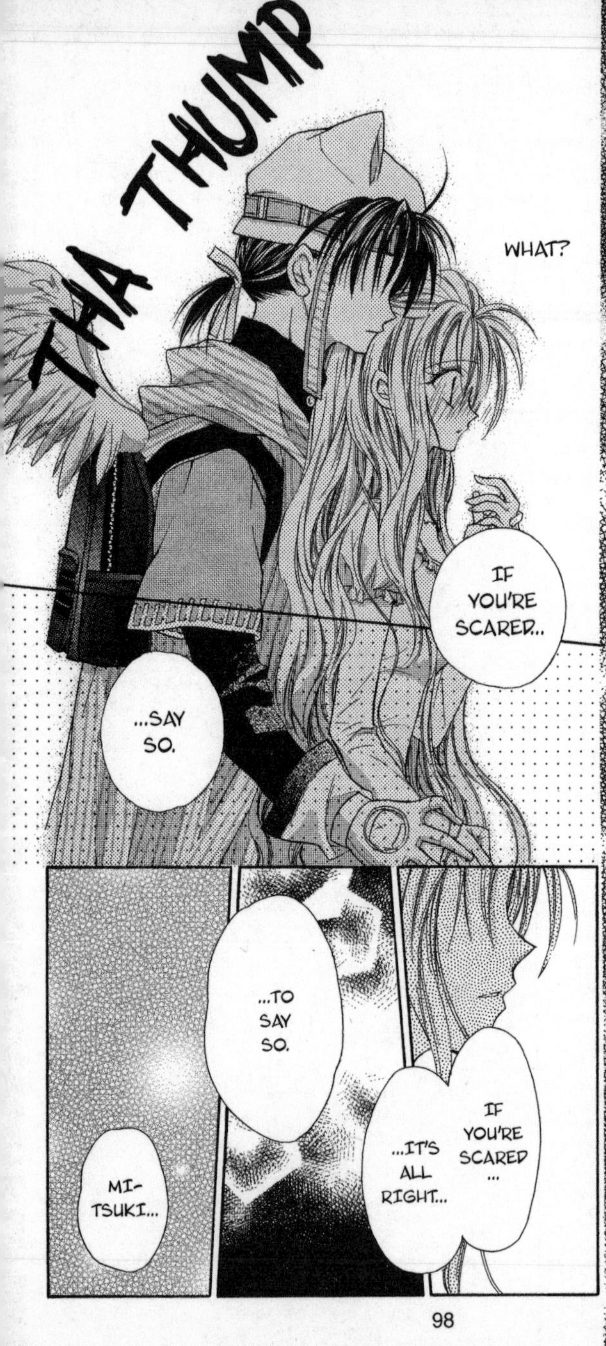
THA THUMP
WHAT?
IF YOU'RE SCARED...
...SAY SO.
IF YOU'RE SCARED ...
...IT'S ALL RIGHT...
...TO SAY SO.
MI-TSUKI...

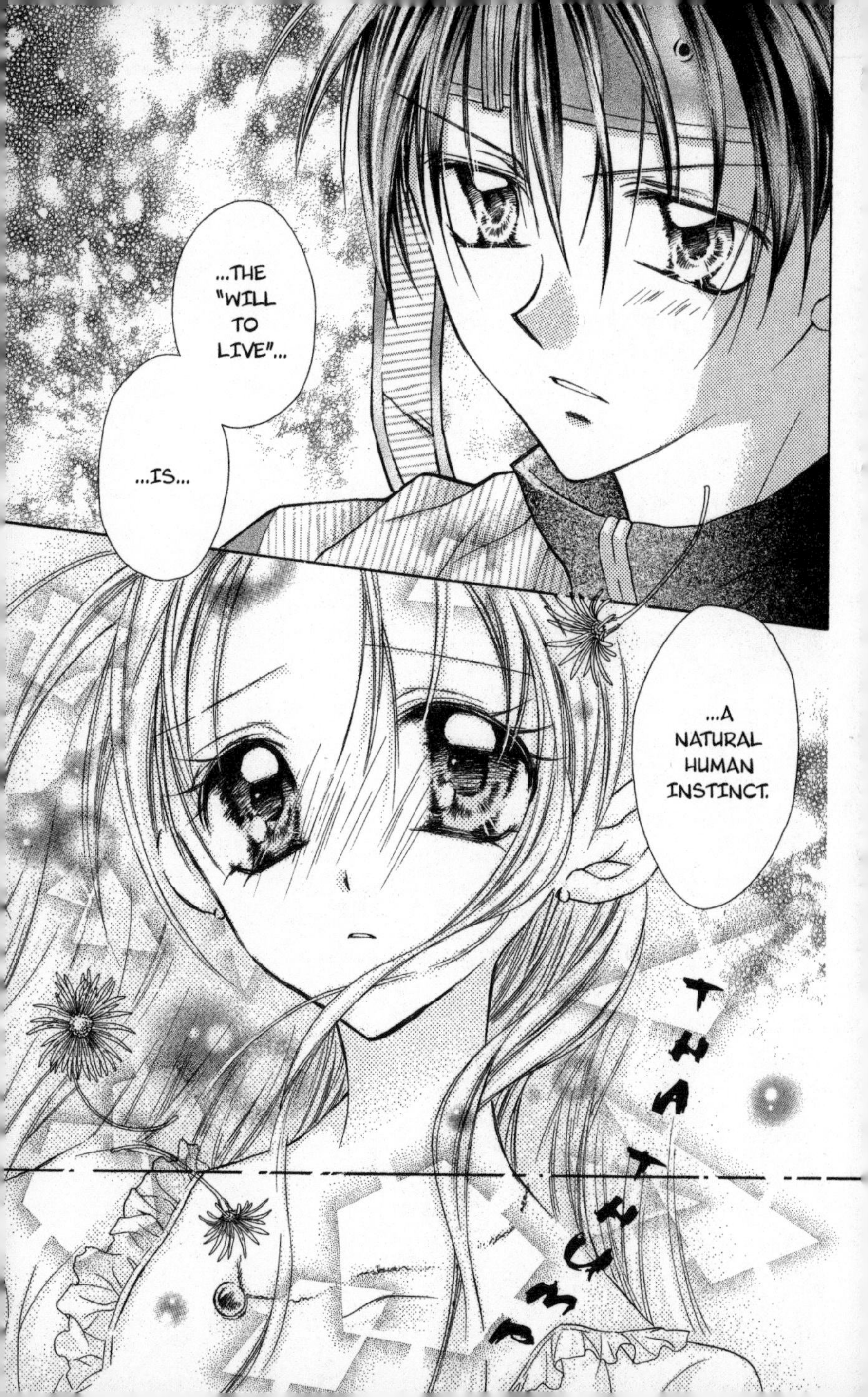
...THE "WILL TO LIVE"...
...IS...
...A NATURAL HUMAN INSTINCT.
THUMP THUMP

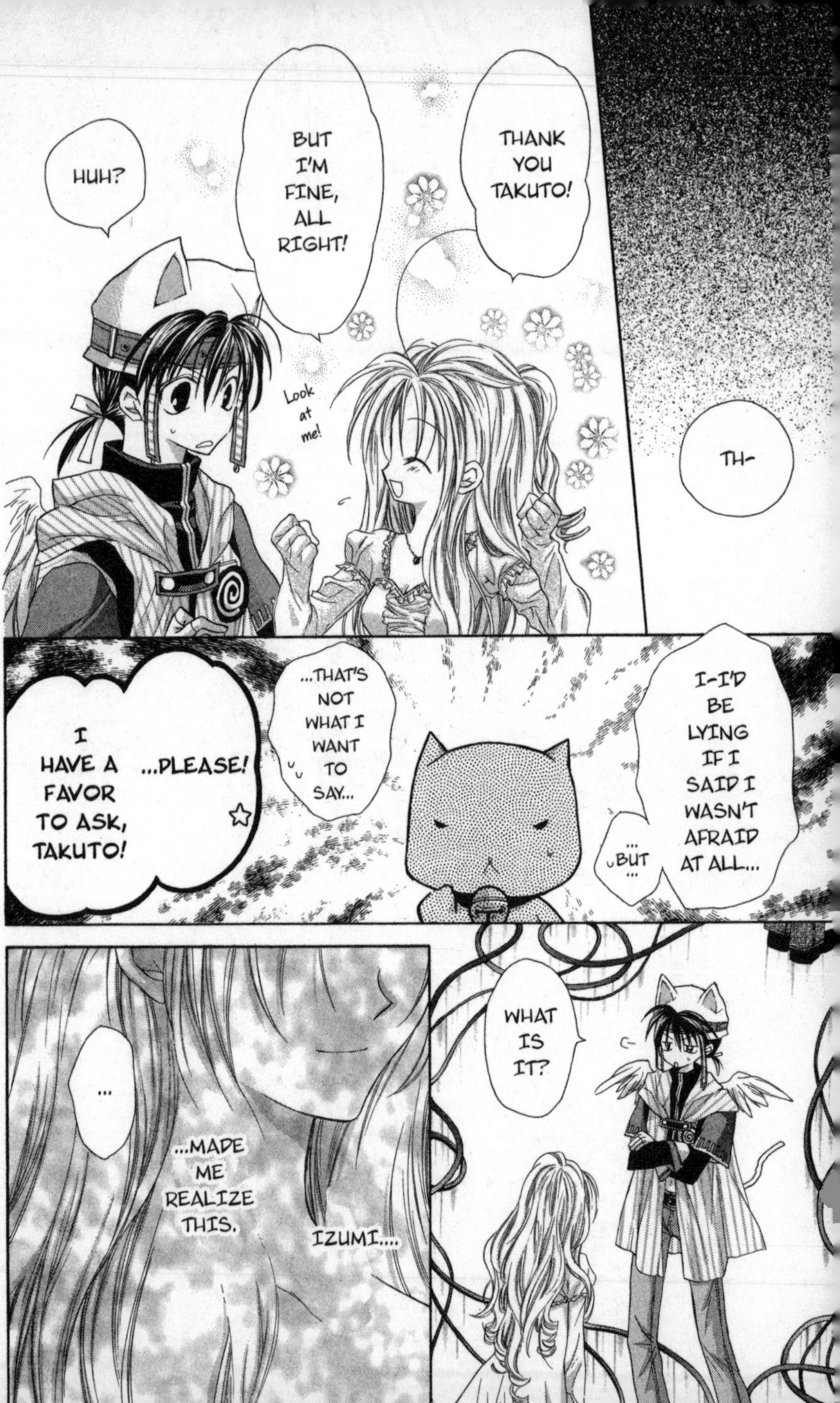
TH-
THANK YOU TAKUTO!
BUT I'M FINE, ALL RIGHT!
HUH?
Look at me!
I-I'D BE LYING IF I SAID I WASN'T AFRAID AT ALL...
...BUT...
...THAT'S NOT WHAT I WANT TO SAY...
...PLEASE!
I HAVE A FAVOR TO ASK, TAKUTO!
WHAT IS IT?
IZUMI....
...MADE ME REALIZE THIS.
...

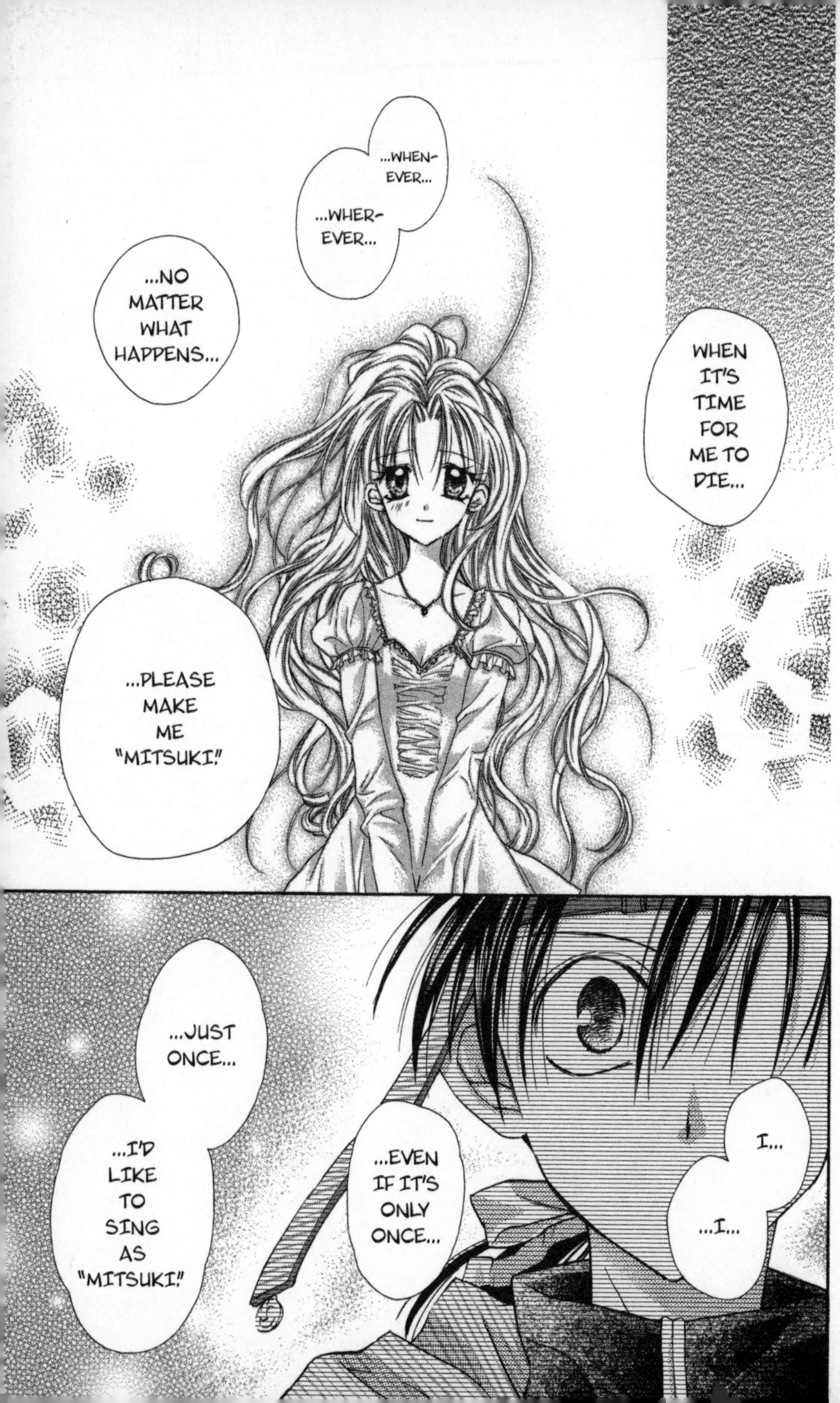
WHEN IT'S TIME FOR ME TO DIE...
...WHEN-EVER...
...WHER-EVER...
...NO MATTER WHAT HAPPENS...
...PLEASE MAKE ME "MITSUKI!"
I...
...I...
...EVEN IF IT'S ONLY ONCE...
...JUST ONCE...
...I'D LIKE TO SING AS "MITSUKI!"

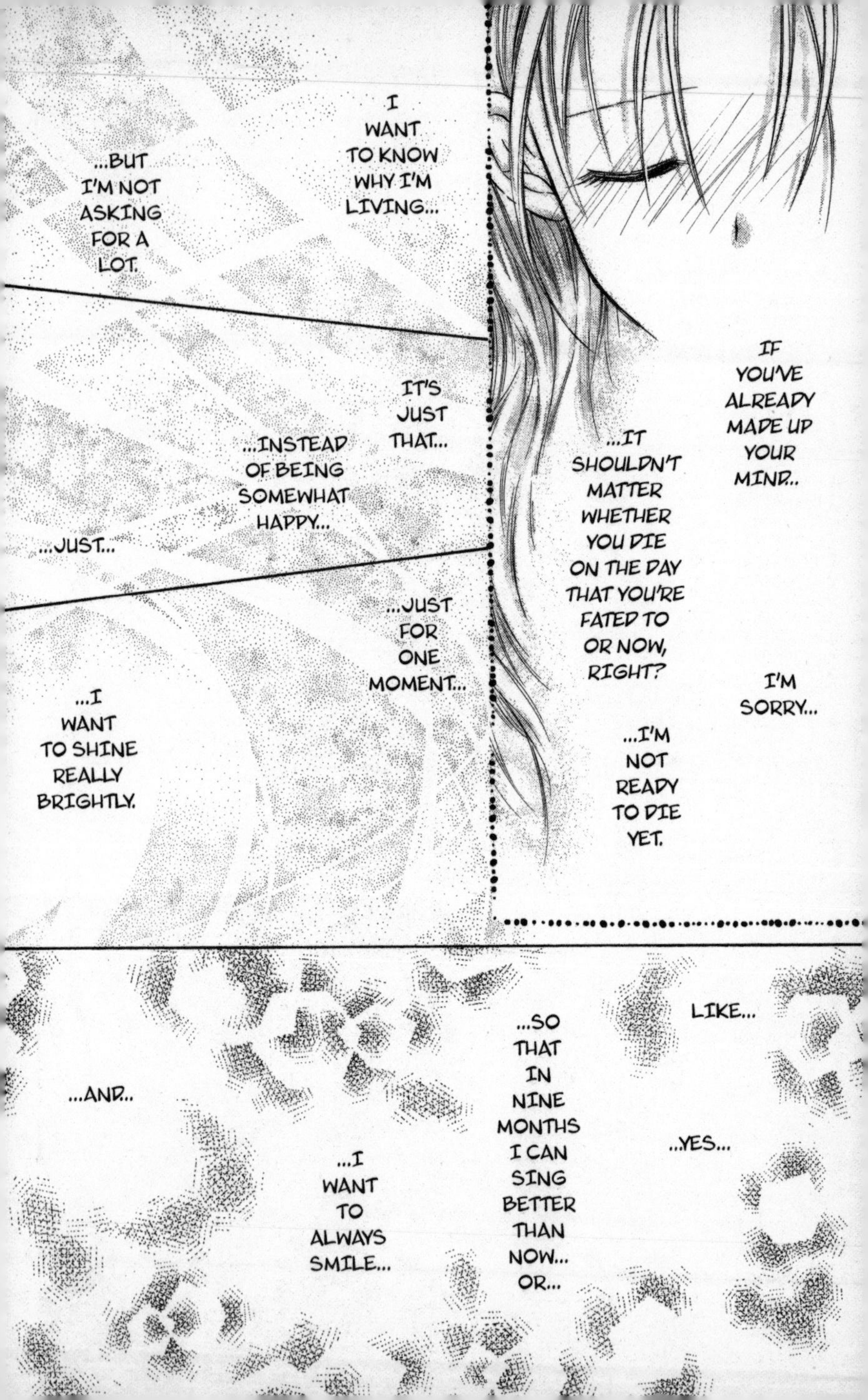
IF YOU'VE ALREADY MADE UP YOUR MIND..
...IT SHOULDN'T MATTER WHETHER YOU DIE ON THE DAY THAT YOU'RE FATED TO OR NOW, RIGHT?
I'M SORRY...
...I'M NOT READY TO DIE YET.
I WANT TO KNOW WHY I'M LIVING...
...BUT I'M NOT ASKING FOR A LOT.
IT'S JUST THAT...
...INSTEAD OF BEING SOMEWHAT HAPPY...
...JUST...
...JUST FOR ONE MOMENT...
...I WANT TO SHINE REALLY BRIGHTLY.
LIKE...
...YES...
...SO THAT IN NINE MONTHS I CAN SING BETTER THAN NOW... OR...
...I WANT TO ALWAYS SMILE...
...AND..

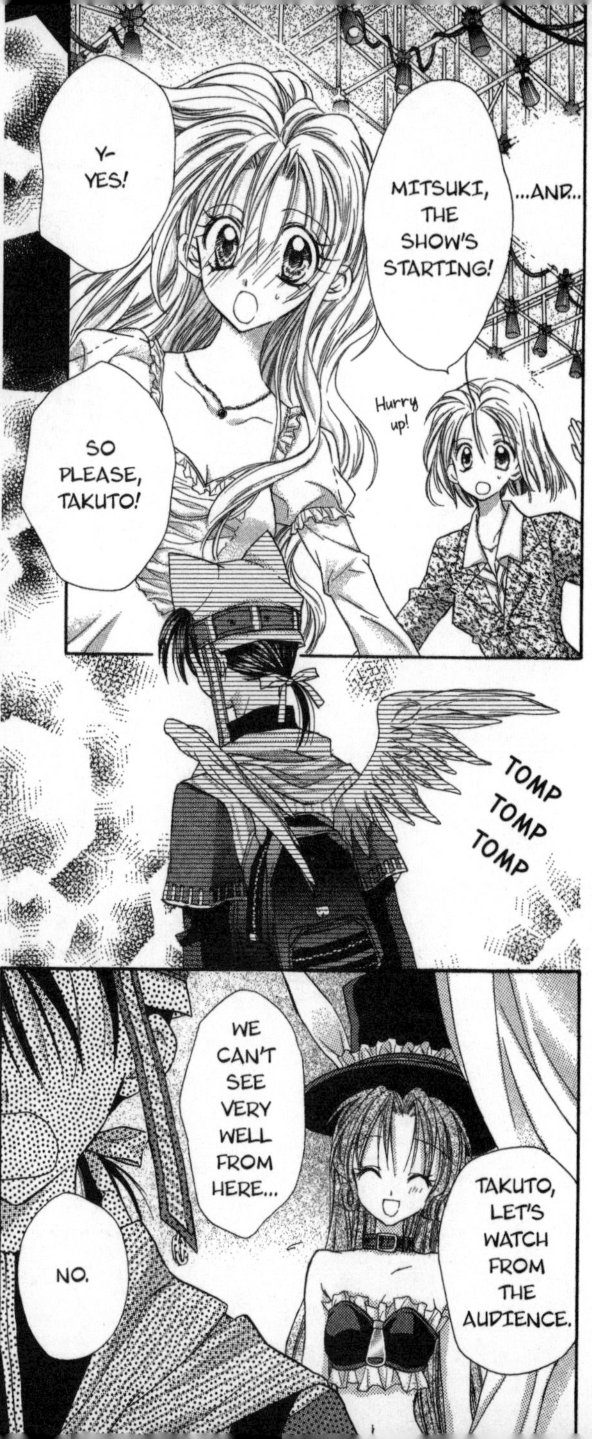
...AND...
MITSUKI, THE SHOW'S STARTING!
Hurry up!
Y-YES!
SO PLEASE, TAKUTO!
TOMP TOMP TOMP
TAKUTO, LET'S WATCH FROM THE AUDIENCE.
WE CAN'T SEE VERY WELL FROM HERE...
NO.

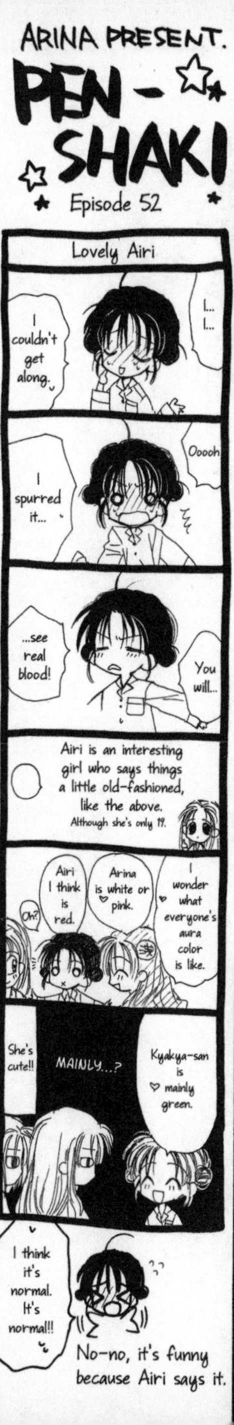
ARINA PRESENT.
PEN-SHAKI
Episode 52
Lovely Airi
I... I...
I couldn't get along.
Ooooh
I spurred it...
You will...
...see real blood!
Airi is an interesting girl who says things a little old-fashioned, like the above.
Although she's only 19.
I wonder what everyone's aura color is like.
Arina is white or pink.
Airi I think is red.
Oh?
Kyakya-san is mainly green.
MAINLY...?
She's cute!!
I think it's normal. It's normal!!
No-no, it's funny because Airi says it.

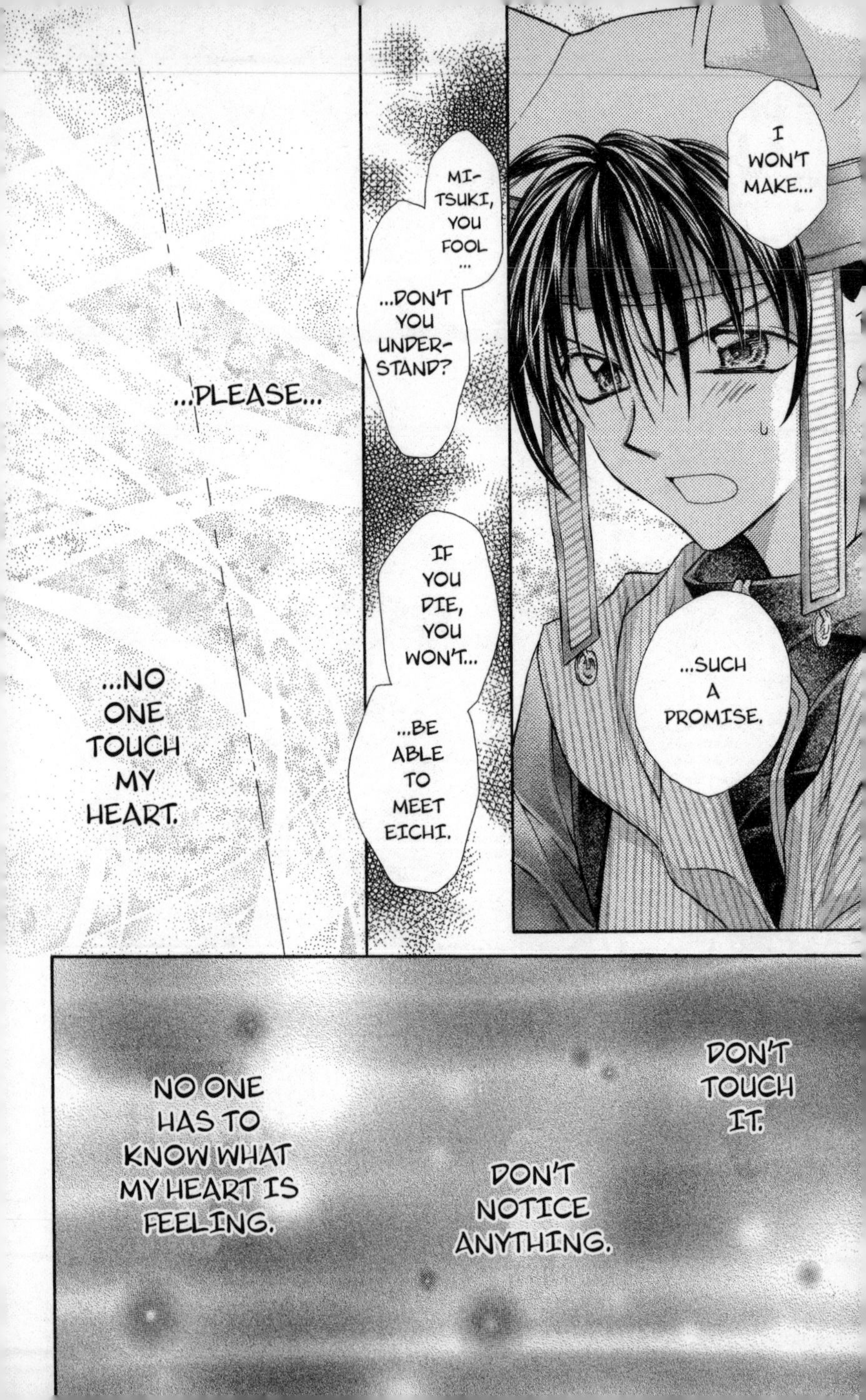
I WON'T MAKE...
...SUCH A PROMISE.
MI-TSUKI, YOU FOOL...
...DON'T YOU UNDERSTAND?
IF YOU DIE, YOU WON'T...
...BE ABLE TO MEET EICHI.
...PLEASE...
...NO ONE TOUCH MY HEART.
DON'T TOUCH IT.
DON'T NOTICE ANYTHING.
NO ONE HAS TO KNOW WHAT MY HEART IS FEELING.

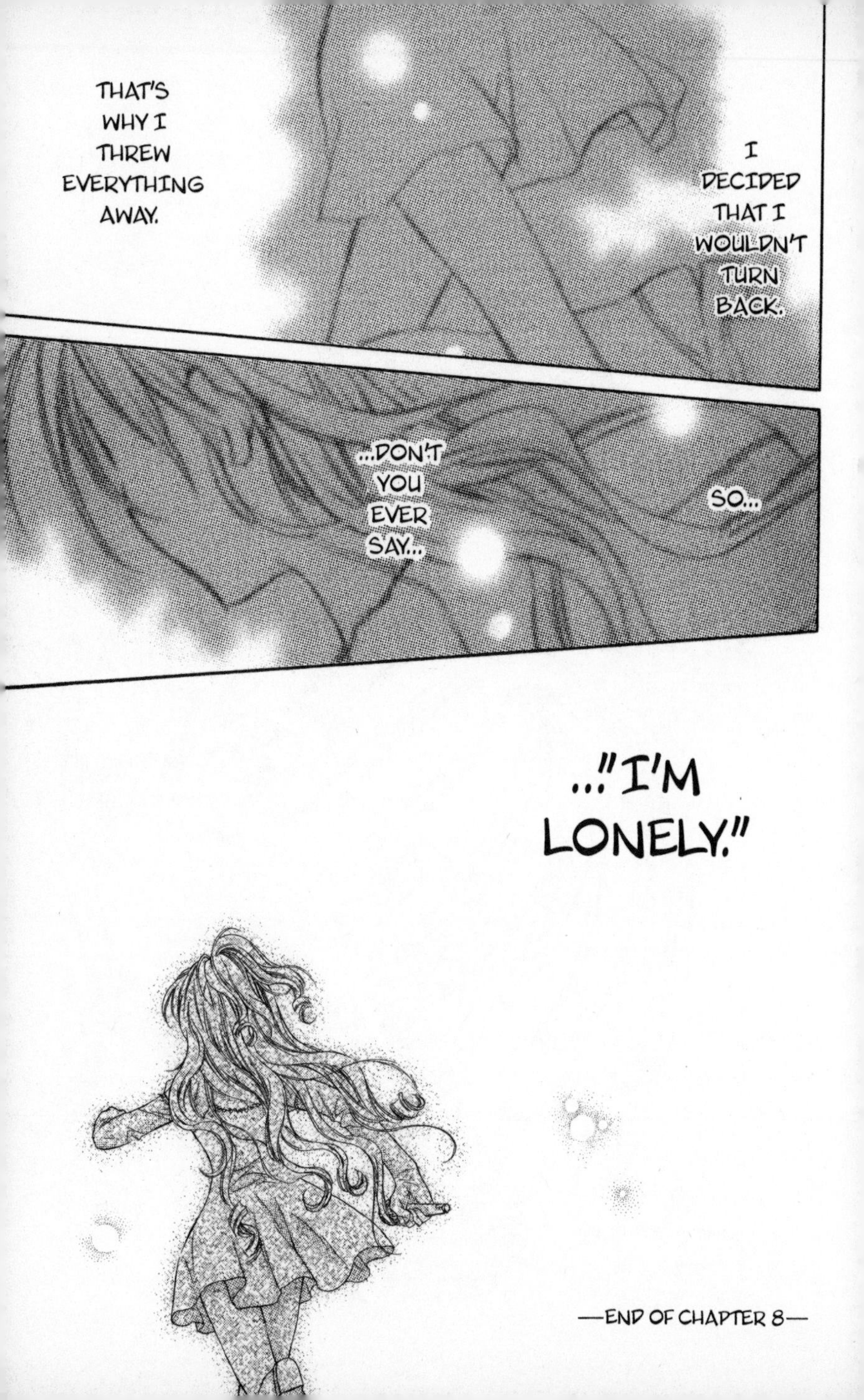
I DECIDED THAT I WOULDN'T TURN BACK.
THAT'S WHY I THREW EVERYTHING AWAY.
SO...
...DON'T YOU EVER SAY...
..."I'M LONELY."
—END OF CHAPTER 8—

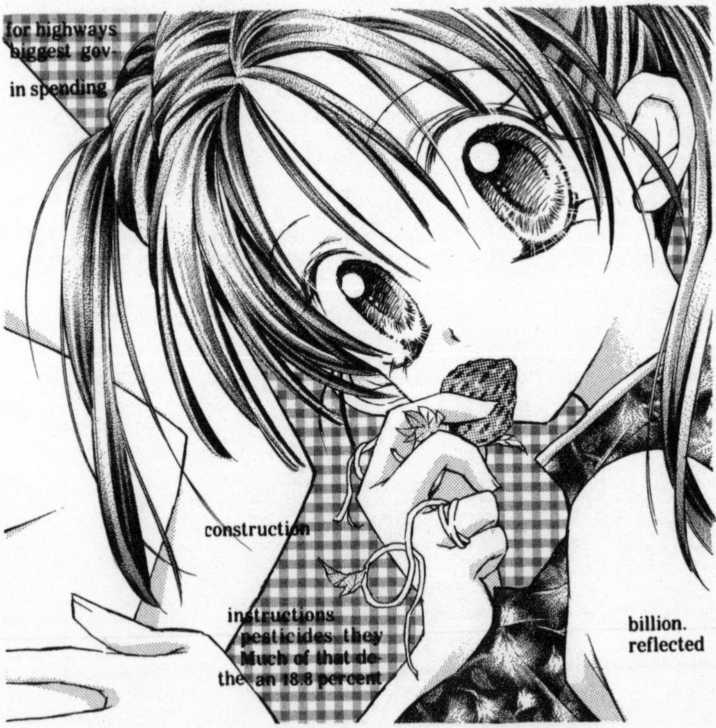
for highways
biggest gov-
in spending
construction
instructions
pesticides they
Much of that de
the an 18.8 percent
billion.
reflected

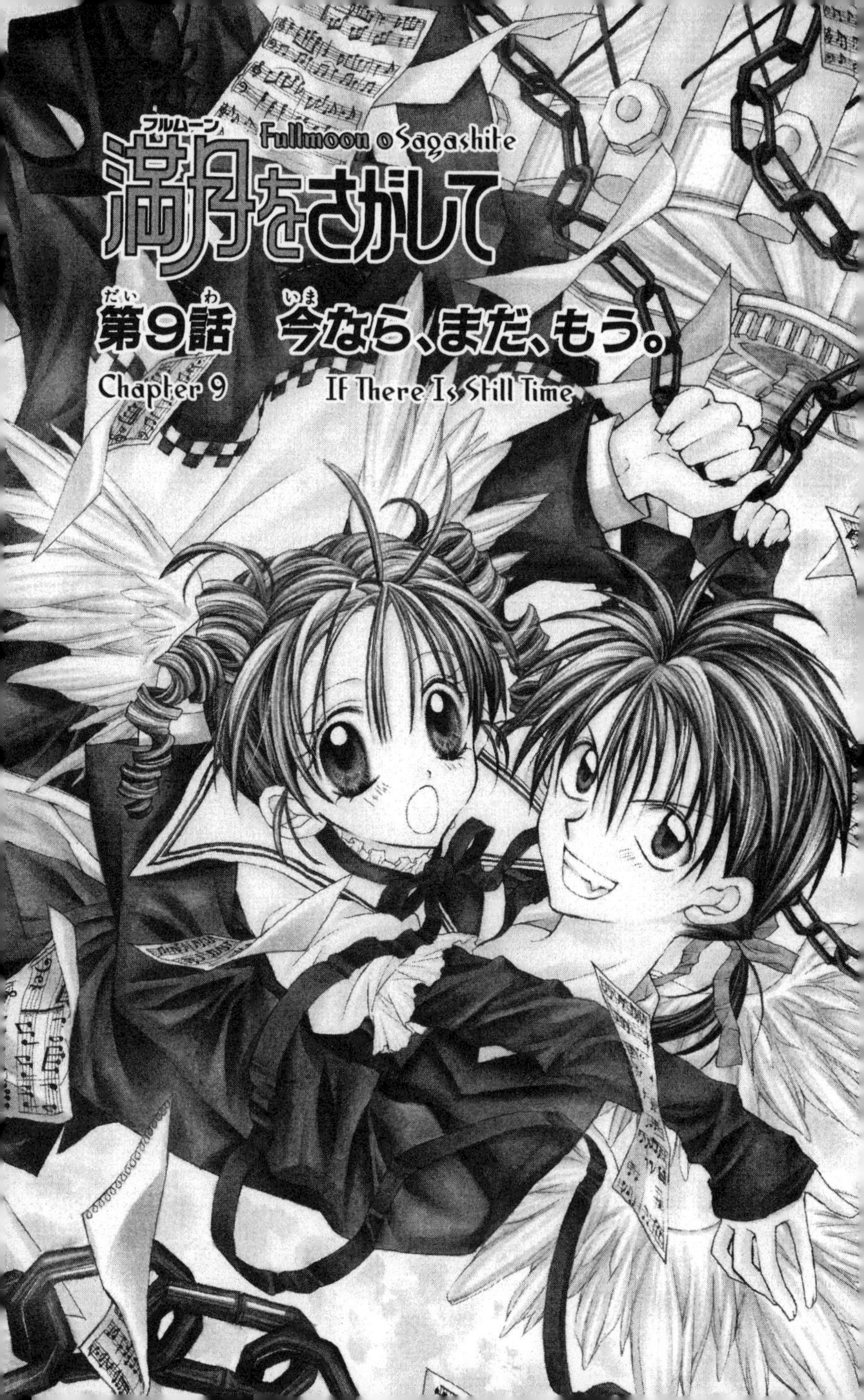
フルムーン
満月をさがして
Fullmoon o Sagashite
第9話 今なら、まだ、もう。
Chapter 9
If There Is Still Time

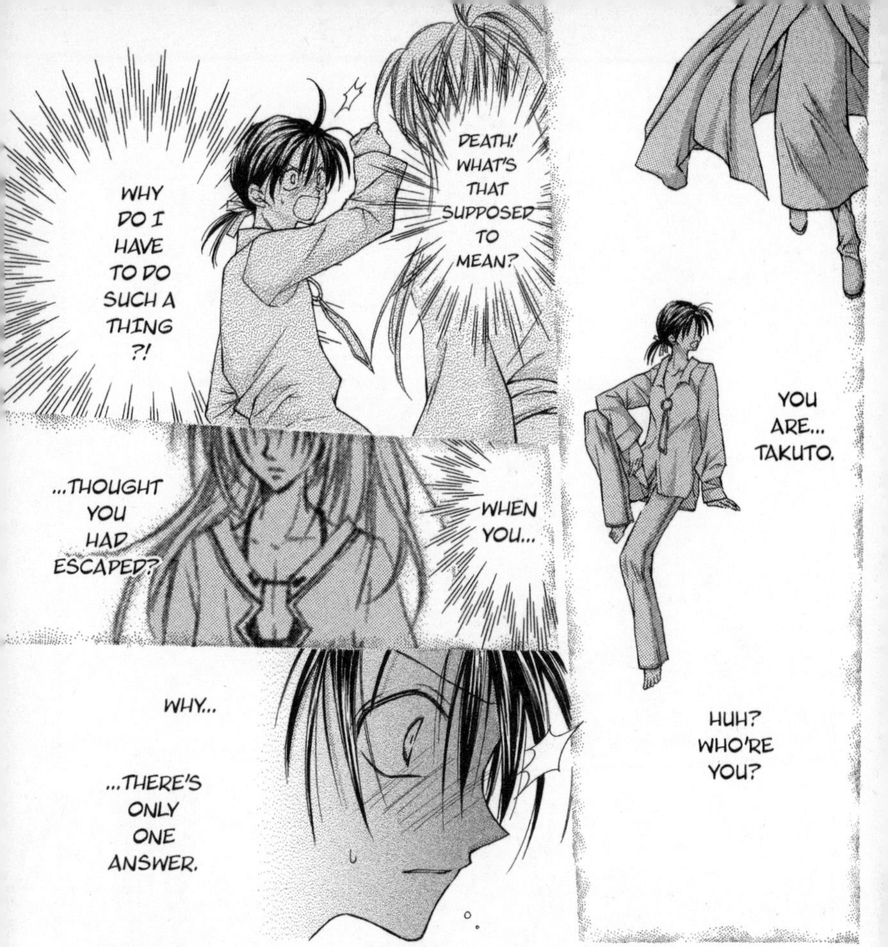
YOU ARE... TAKUTO.
HUH? WHO'RE YOU?
DEATH! WHAT'S THAT SUPPOSED TO MEAN?
WHY DO I HAVE TO DO SUCH A THING ?!
WHEN YOU...
...THOUGHT YOU HAD ESCAPED?
WHY...
...THERE'S ONLY ONE ANSWER.

Chapter 9: If There Is Still Time [Cover Copy] We two play the melody of adventure ♪

Spoilers follow

Cover Illustration.

I was told "I like this" often. I tried to put a classical feel (just the feel) to the illustration...but I wonder how it turned out. I...wanted to draw chains. Fans of the Eichi-Mitsuki coupling were angry at this, and that made me laugh.♥ (From my point of view, fans of Takuto don't mind Eichi, but fans of Eichi don't seem to like Takuto.) → not fans of Eichi, but rather people who like the Eichi♥Mitsuki coupling?

About the story, um, I secretly had fun with Jonathan. (It's all right if no one notices! Jonathan is that kind of guy.) ↑ Do-ing nee-dlework♪

Uh, other than that, I enjoyed drawing the stuff about the Shinigamiiz. The dark part. Yes. Isn't it good...

I'll do the Takuto story eventually, but I want to do a story about Izumi-kun's past. (Yes! Oh dear! With "Fullmoon..." I want to do too much about the side characters. Eichi...Oshige-san... Wakaoji-sensei...) I'm ready to take a vote. (We will do one! —Koike) I love voting contests! I love rankings of any kind!! ♥ ♥.

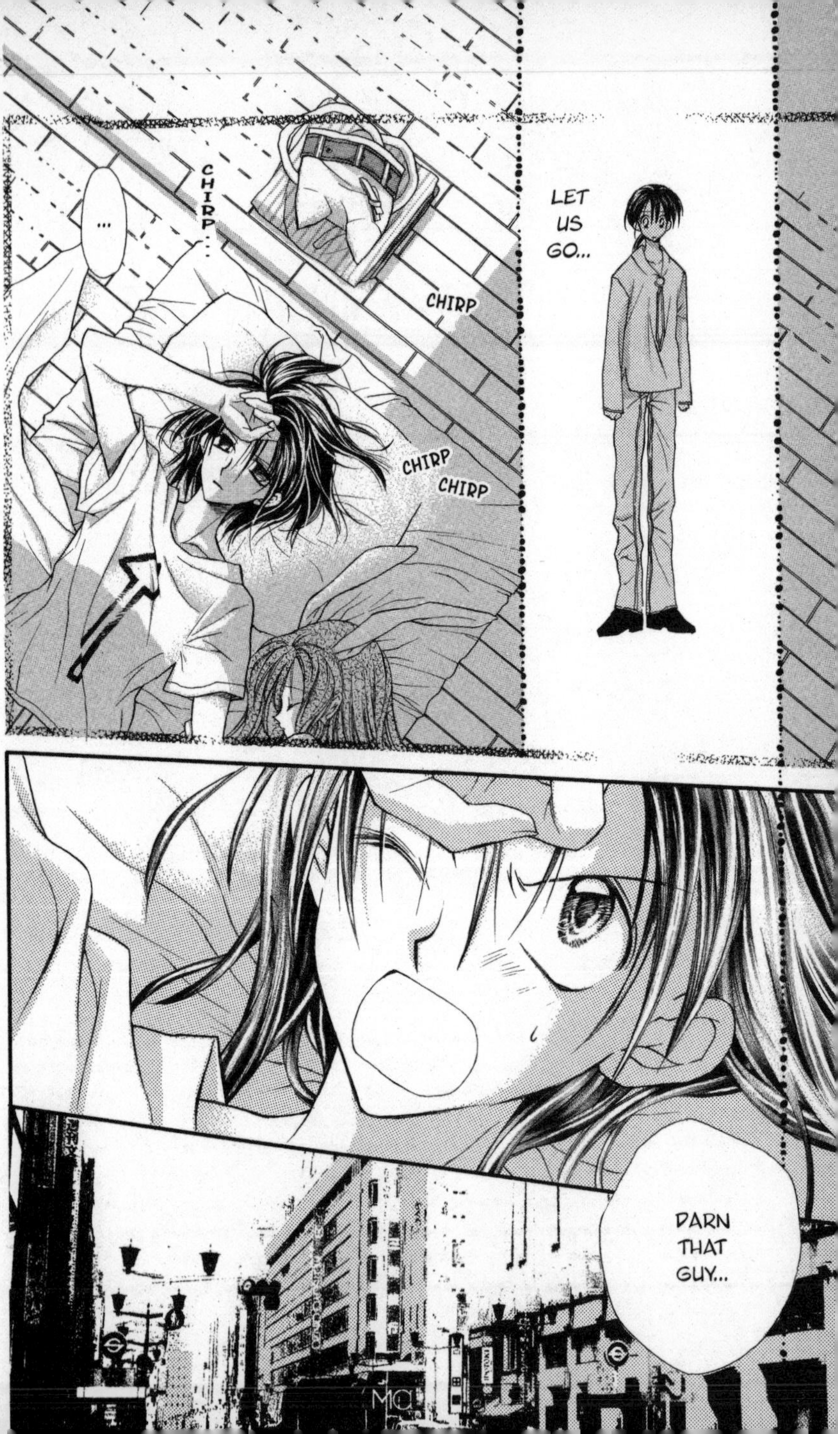
LET US GO...
...
CHIRP CHIRP...
CHIRP
CHIRP CHIRP
DARN THAT GUY...

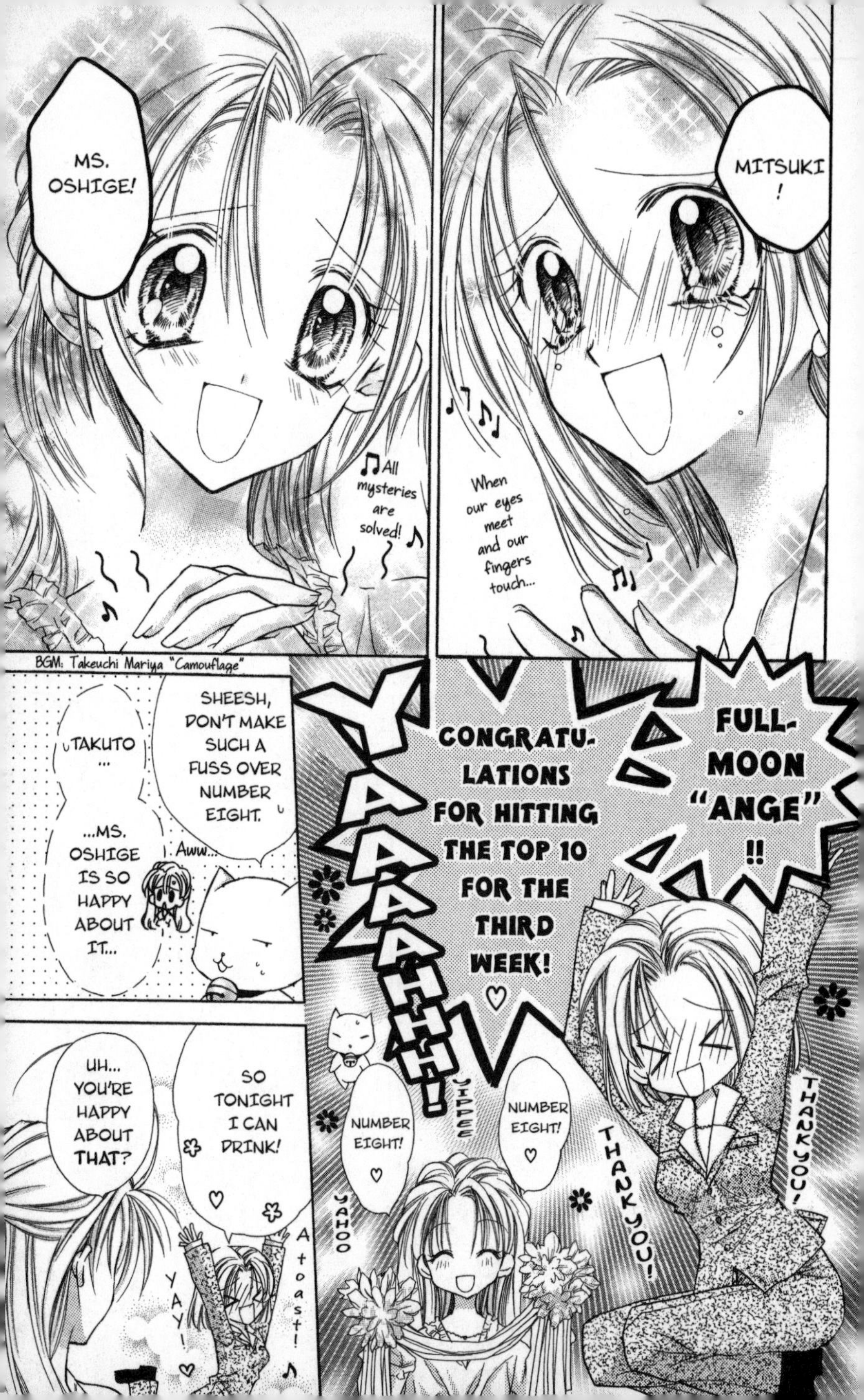
MITSUKI!
When our eyes meet and our fingers touch...
MS. OSHIGE!
All mysteries are solved!
BGM: Takeuchi Mariya "Camouflage"
YAAAAHHH!
FULL-MOON "ANGE"!!
CONGRATULATIONS FOR HITTING THE TOP 10 FOR THE THIRD WEEK!
THANK YOU!
THANK YOU!
NUMBER EIGHT!
YIPPEE
NUMBER EIGHT!
YAHOO
SHEESH, DON'T MAKE SUCH A FUSS OVER NUMBER EIGHT.
TAKUTO ...
...MS. OSHIGE IS SO HAPPY ABOUT IT...
Aww...
SO TONIGHT I CAN DRINK!
UH... YOU'RE HAPPY ABOUT THAT?
A toast!
YAY!

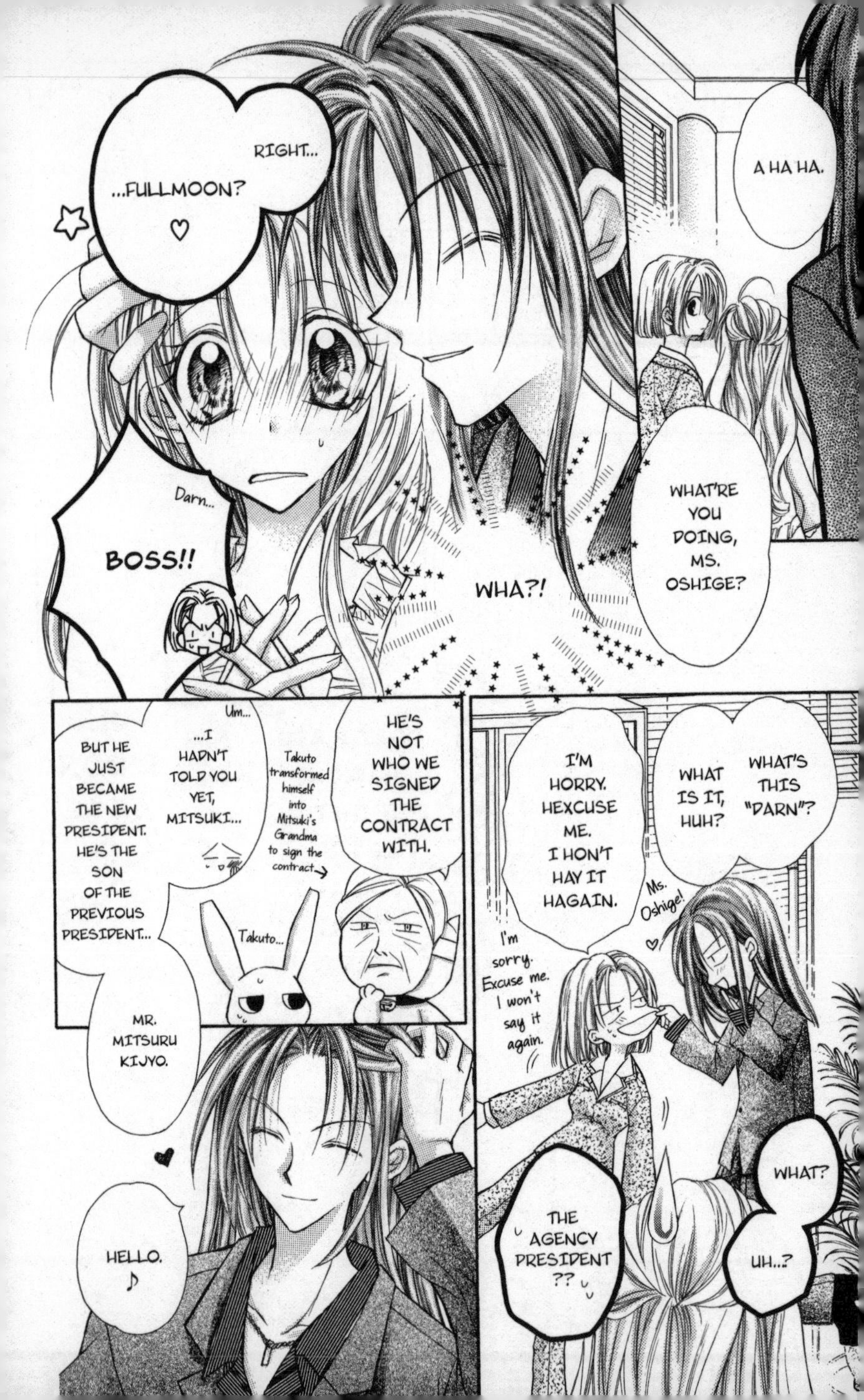
A HA HA.
WHAT'RE YOU DOING, MS. OSHIGE?
RIGHT... ...FULLMOON? ♡
WHA?!
Darn...
BOSS!!
WHAT'S THIS "DARN"?
WHAT IS IT, HUH?
I'M HORRY. HEXCUSE ME. I HON'T HAY IT HAGAIN.
Ms. Oshige! ♡
I'm sorry. Excuse me. I won't say it again.
WHAT?
UH..?
THE AGENCY PRESIDENT??
HE'S NOT WHO WE SIGNED THE CONTRACT WITH.
Takuto transformed himself into Mitsuki's Grandma to sign the contract
Um...
...I HADN'T TOLD YOU YET, MITSUKI...
BUT HE JUST BECAME THE NEW PRESIDENT. HE'S THE SON OF THE PREVIOUS PRESIDENT...
Takuto...
MR. MITSURU KIJYO.
HELLO. ♪

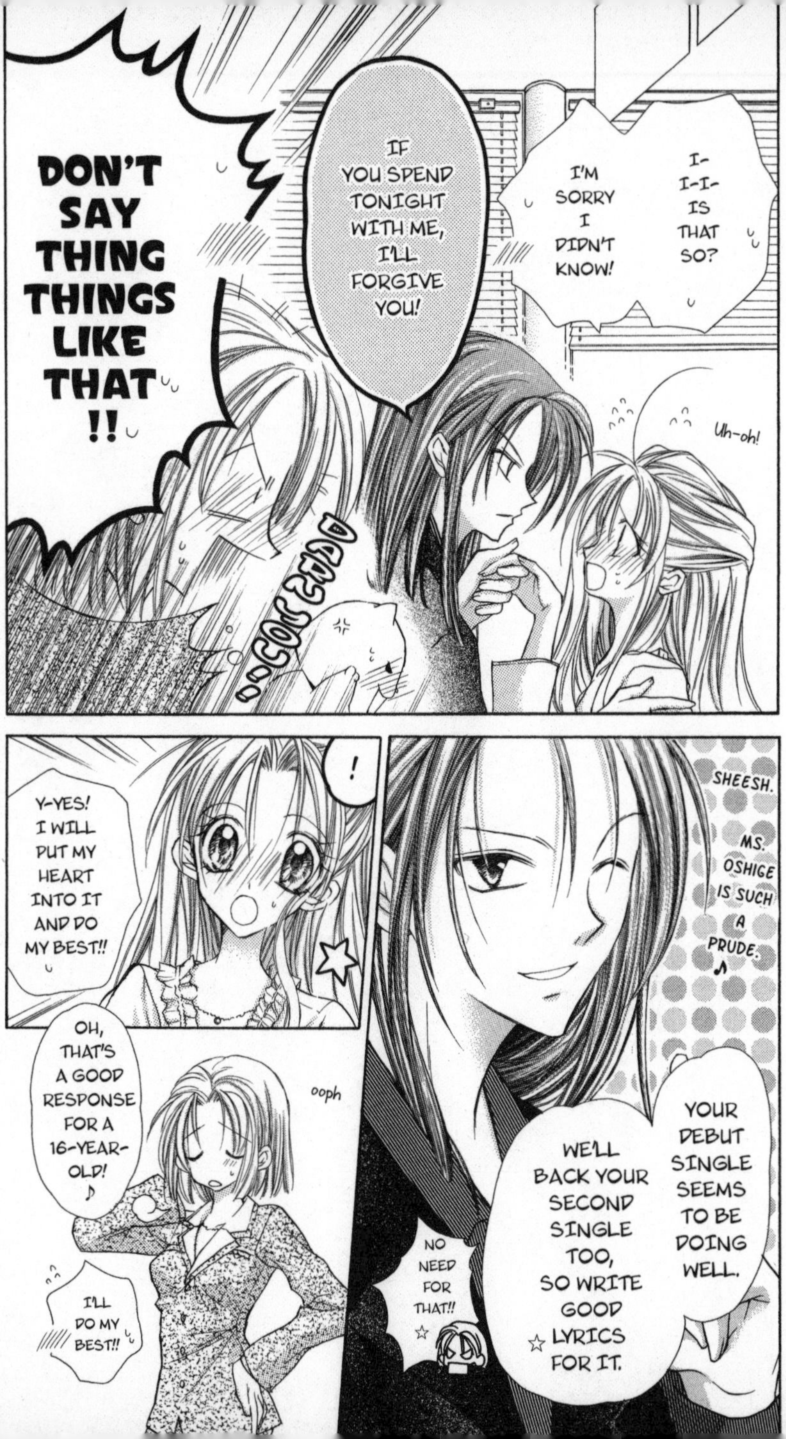
I-I-I-IS THAT SO?
I'M SORRY I DIDN'T KNOW!
IF YOU SPEND TONIGHT WITH ME, I'LL FORGIVE YOU!
DON'T SAY THING THINGS LIKE THAT!!
Uh-oh!
YOUR DEBUT SINGLE SEEMS TO BE DOING WELL.
WE'LL BACK YOUR SECOND SINGLE TOO, SO WRITE GOOD LYRICS FOR IT.
SHEESH.
MS. OSHIGE IS SUCH A PRUDE. ♪
NO NEED FOR THAT!!
!
Y-YES! I WILL PUT MY HEART INTO IT AND DO MY BEST!!
OH, THAT'S A GOOD RESPONSE FOR A 16-YEAR-OLD! ♪
ooph
I'LL DO MY BEST!!

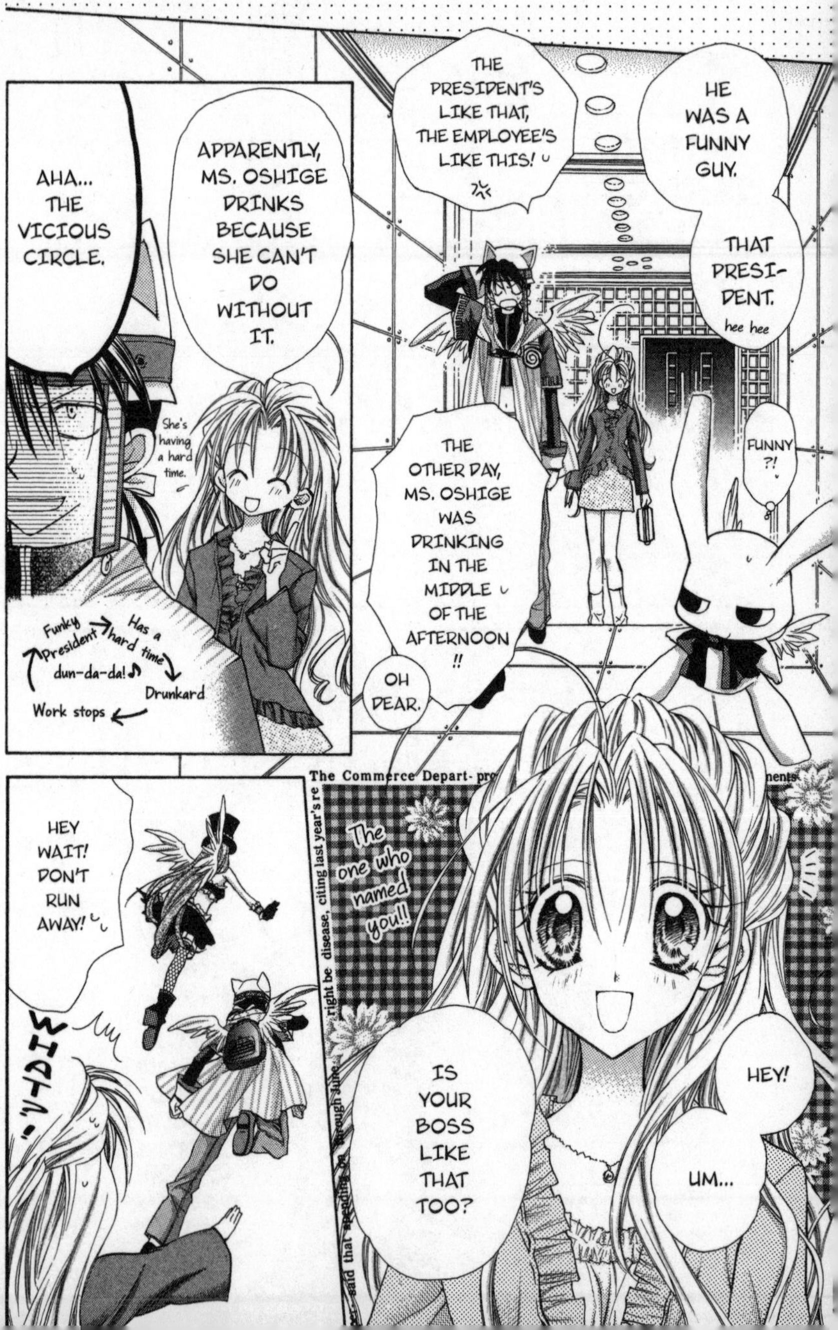
HE WAS A FUNNY GUY.
THAT PRESIDENT.
hee hee
THE PRESIDENT'S LIKE THAT, THE EMPLOYEE'S LIKE THIS!
FUNNY ?!
THE OTHER DAY, MS. OSHIGE WAS DRINKING IN THE MIDDLE OF THE AFTERNOON!!
OH DEAR.
APPARENTLY, MS. OSHIGE DRINKS BECAUSE SHE CAN'T DO WITHOUT IT.
She's having a hard time.
AHA... THE VICIOUS CIRCLE.
Funky President → Has a hard time → Drunkard → Work stops → dun-da-da!♪
The one who named you!!
HEY!
UM...
IS YOUR BOSS LIKE THAT TOO?
HEY WAIT! DON'T RUN AWAY!
WHAT-!

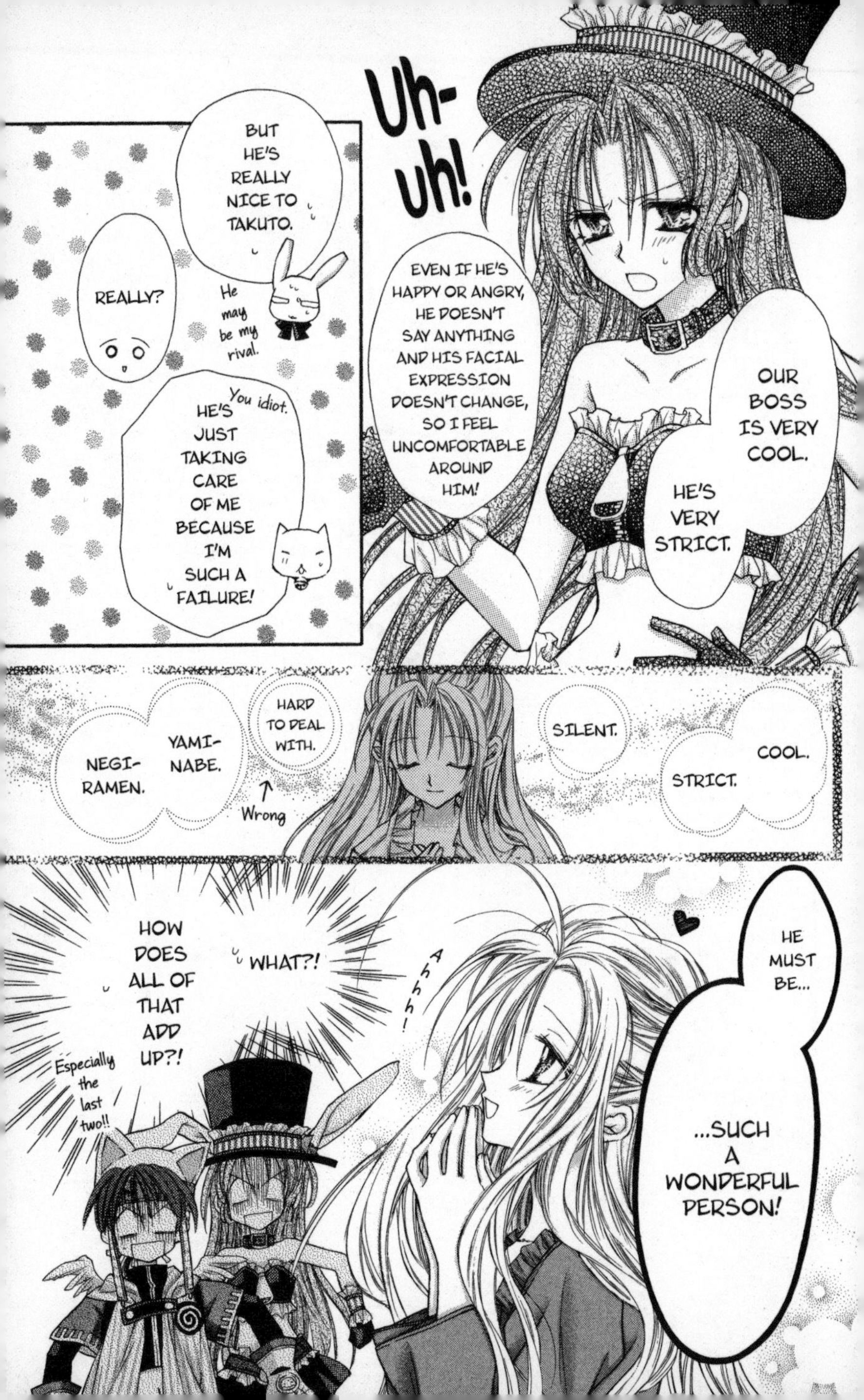
Uh-uh!
OUR BOSS IS VERY COOL.
HE'S VERY STRICT.
EVEN IF HE'S HAPPY OR ANGRY, HE DOESN'T SAY ANYTHING AND HIS FACIAL EXPRESSION DOESN'T CHANGE, SO I FEEL UNCOMFORTABLE AROUND HIM!
BUT HE'S REALLY NICE TO TAKUTO.
He may be my rival.
REALLY?
HE'S JUST TAKING CARE OF ME BECAUSE I'M SUCH A FAILURE!
You idiot.
COOL.
STRICT.
SILENT.
HARD TO DEAL WITH.
Wrong
YAMI-NABE.
NEGI-RAMEN.
HE MUST BE...
...SUCH A WONDERFUL PERSON!
Ahhh!
WHAT?!
HOW DOES ALL OF THAT ADD UP?!
Especially the last two!!

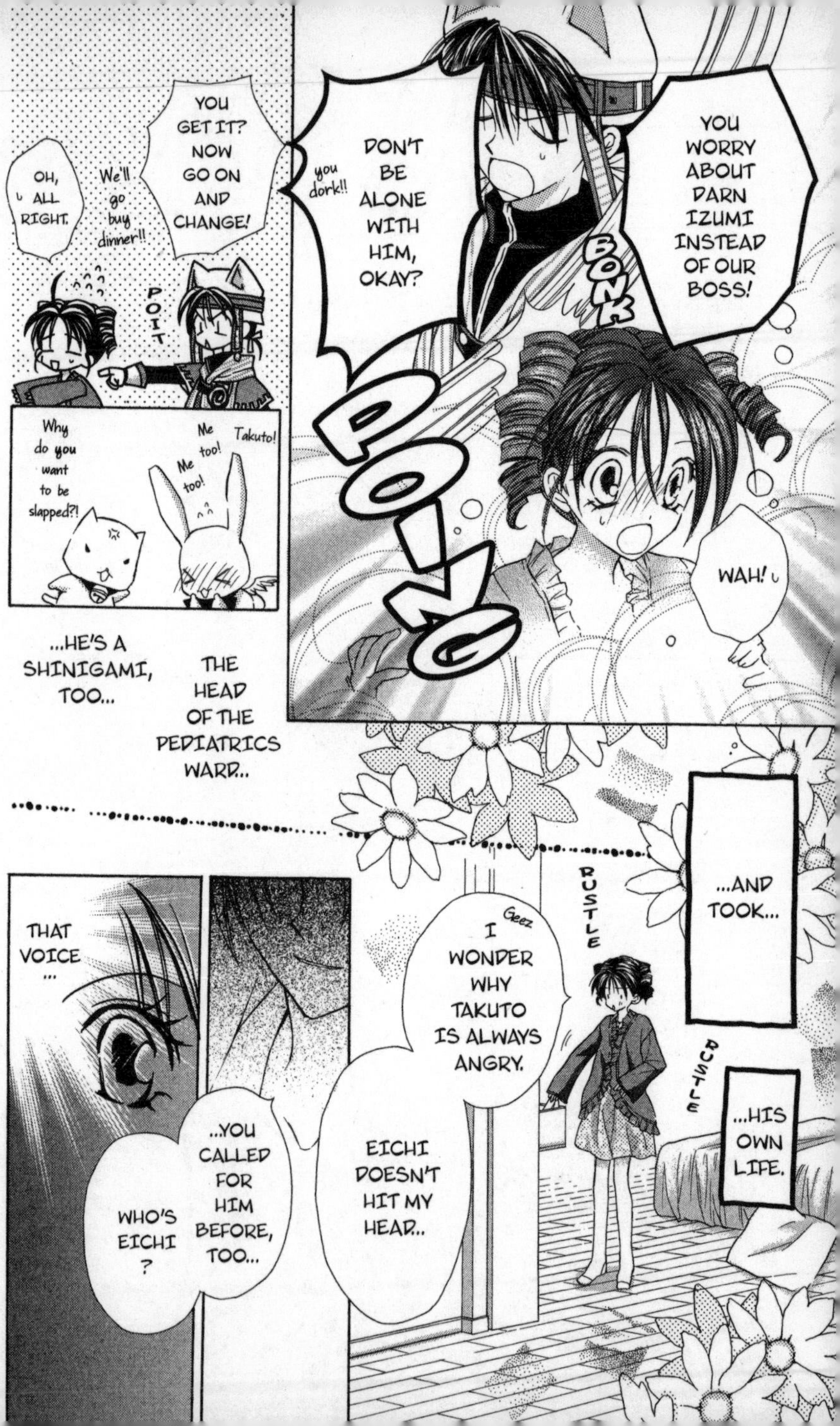
YOU WORRY ABOUT DARN IZUMI INSTEAD OF OUR BOSS!
BONK
DON'T BE ALONE WITH HIM, OKAY?
you dork!!
POING
WAH!
YOU GET IT? NOW GO ON AND CHANGE!
We'll go buy dinner!!
OH, ALL RIGHT.
POIT
Takuto!
Me too!
Me too!
Why do you want to be slapped?!
THE HEAD OF THE PEDIATRICS WARD...
...HE'S A SHINIGAMI, TOO...
...AND TOOK...
...HIS OWN LIFE.
RUSTLE
RUSTLE
Geez
I WONDER WHY TAKUTO IS ALWAYS ANGRY.
EICHI DOESN'T HIT MY HEAD...
...YOU CALLED FOR HIM BEFORE, TOO...
WHO'S EICHI?
THAT VOICE ...

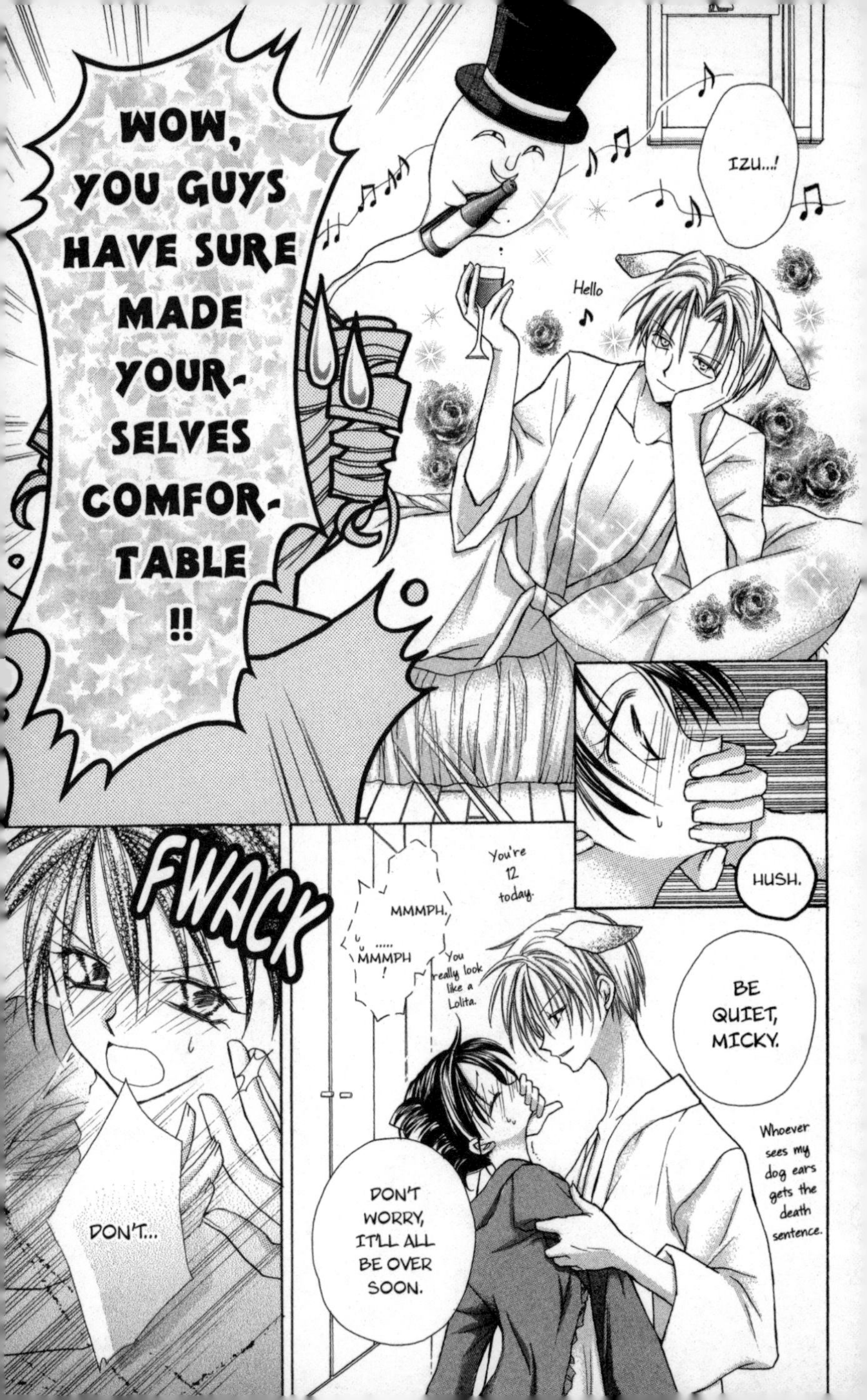
IZU...!
Hello
WOW, YOU GUYS HAVE SURE MADE YOURSELVES COMFORTABLE!!
HUSH.
BE QUIET, MICKY.
You're 12 today.
MMMPH. ..... MMMPH!
You really look like a Lolita.
Whoever sees my dog ears gets the death sentence.
DON'T WORRY, IT'LL ALL BE OVER SOON.
FWACK
DON'T...

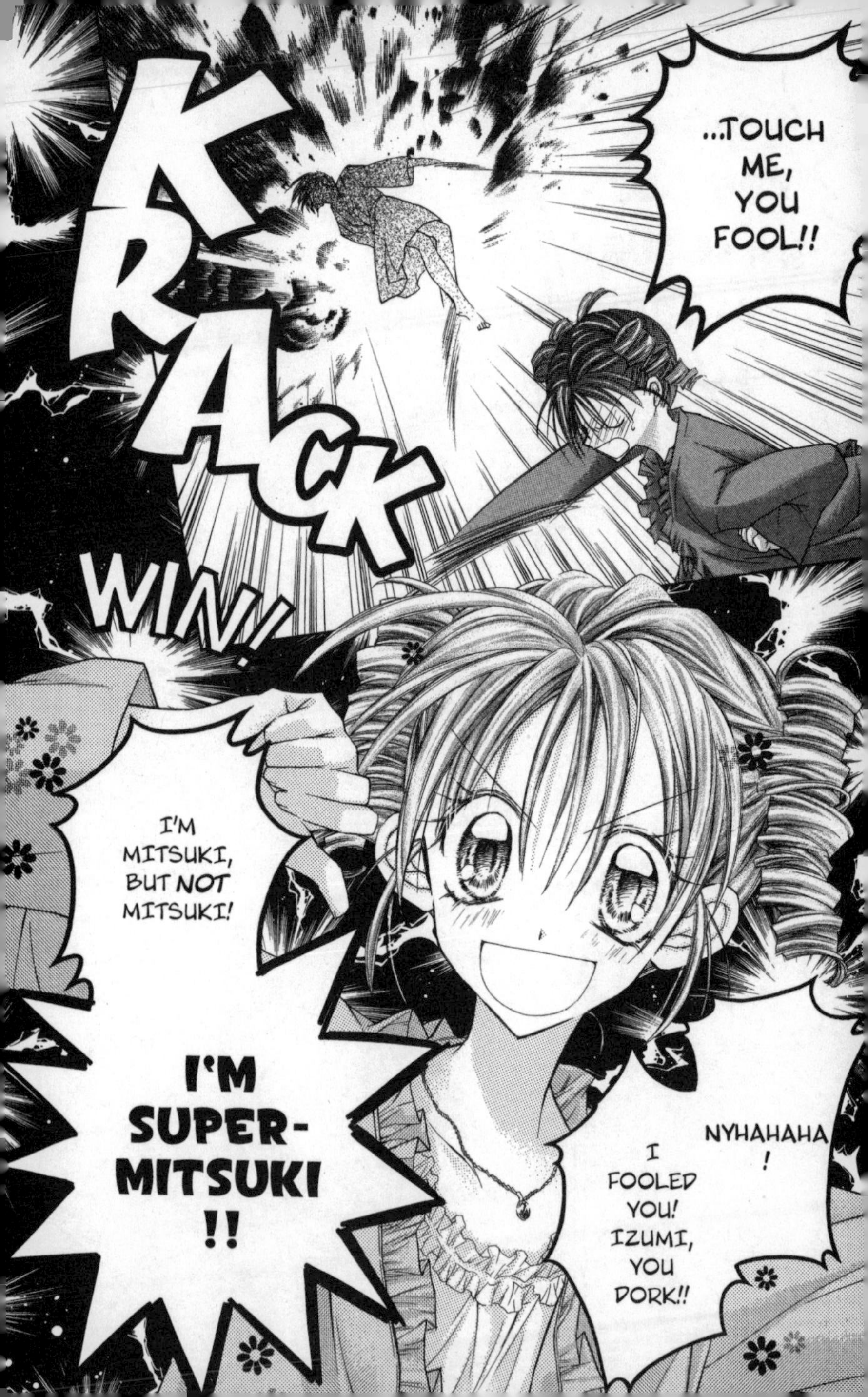
...TOUCH ME, YOU FOOL!!
KRACK
WIN!!
NYHAHAHA!
I FOOLED YOU! IZUMI, YOU DORK!!
I'M MITSUKI, BUT NOT MITSUKI!
I'M SUPER-MITSUKI!!

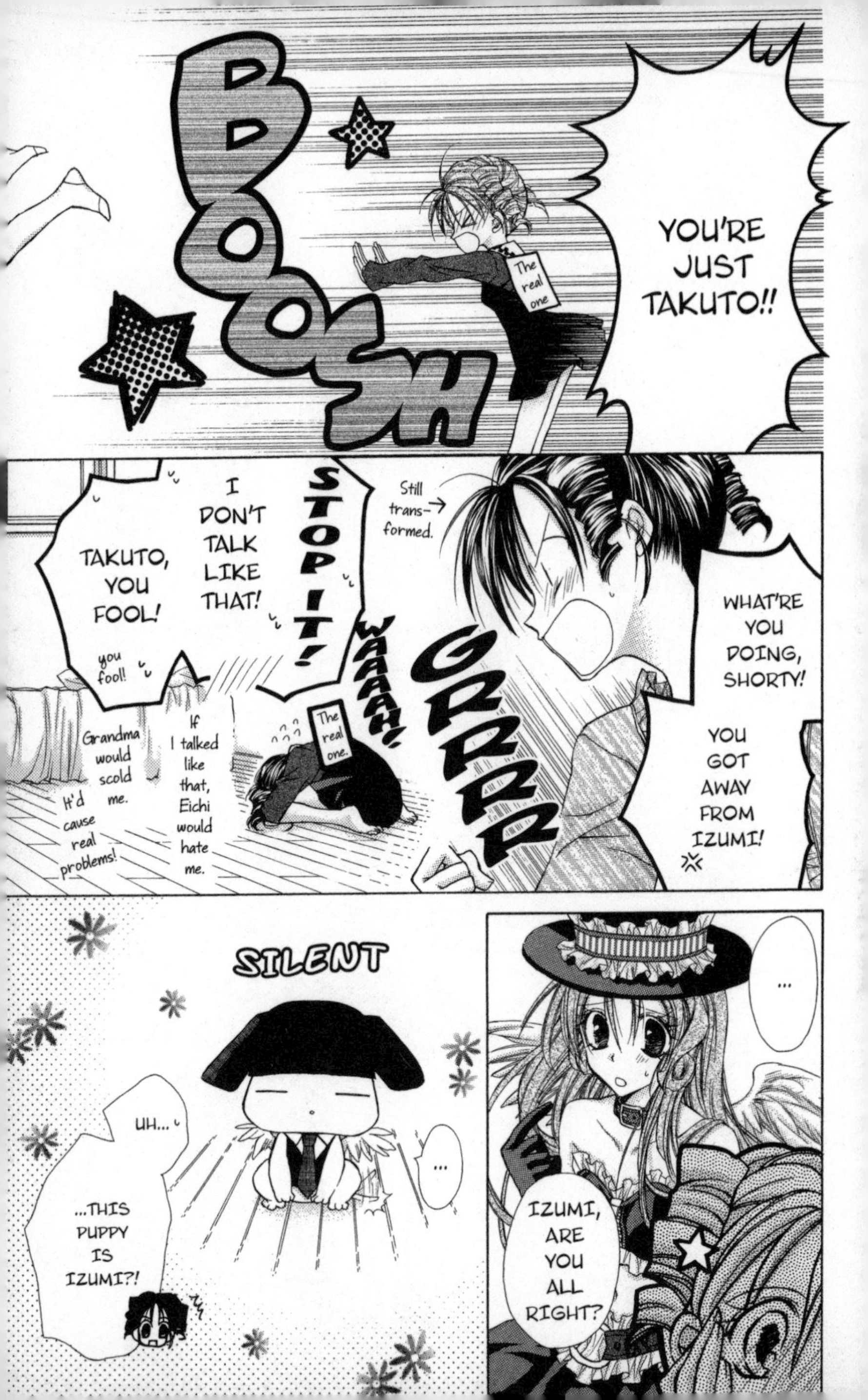
BOOOSH
YOU'RE JUST TAKUTO!!
The real one
WHAT'RE YOU DOING, SHORTY!
YOU GOT AWAY FROM IZUMI!
GRRRR
Still trans-formed.
WAAAAH!
The real one.
STOP IT!
I DON'T TALK LIKE THAT!
TAKUTO, YOU FOOL!
you fool!
If I talked like that, Eichi would hate me.
Grandma would scold me.
It'd cause real problems!
...
IZUMI, ARE YOU ALL RIGHT?
SILENT
...
UH...
...THIS PUPPY IS IZUMI?!

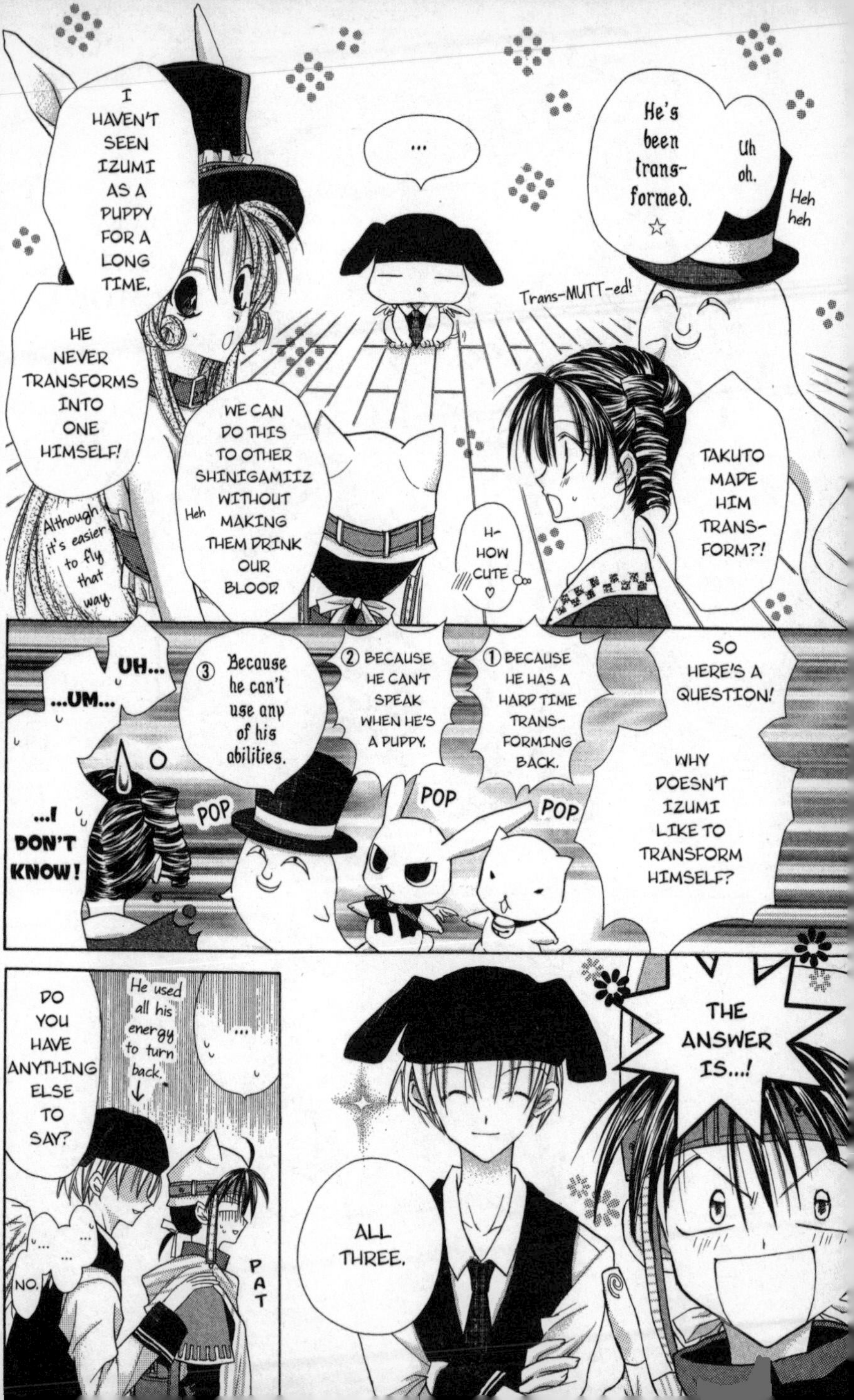

He's been transformed. ☆
Uh oh.
Heh heh
...
I HAVEN'T SEEN IZUMI AS A PUPPY FOR A LONG TIME.
Trans-MUTT-ed!
TAKUTO MADE HIM TRANSFORM?!
H-HOW CUTE ♡
HE NEVER TRANSFORMS INTO ONE HIMSELF!
WE CAN DO THIS TO OTHER SHINIGAMIIZ WITHOUT MAKING THEM DRINK OUR BLOOD.
Heh
Although it's easier to fly that way.
SO HERE'S A QUESTION!
WHY DOESN'T IZUMI LIKE TO TRANSFORM HIMSELF?
① BECAUSE HE HAS A HARD TIME TRANSFORMING BACK.
② BECAUSE HE CAN'T SPEAK WHEN HE'S A PUPPY.
③ Because he can't use any of his abilities.
POP
POP
POP
UH...
...UM...
O
...I DON'T KNOW!
THE ANSWER IS...!
ALL THREE.
DO YOU HAVE ANYTHING ELSE TO SAY?
...
He used all his energy to turn back.
... ...
NO.
PAT

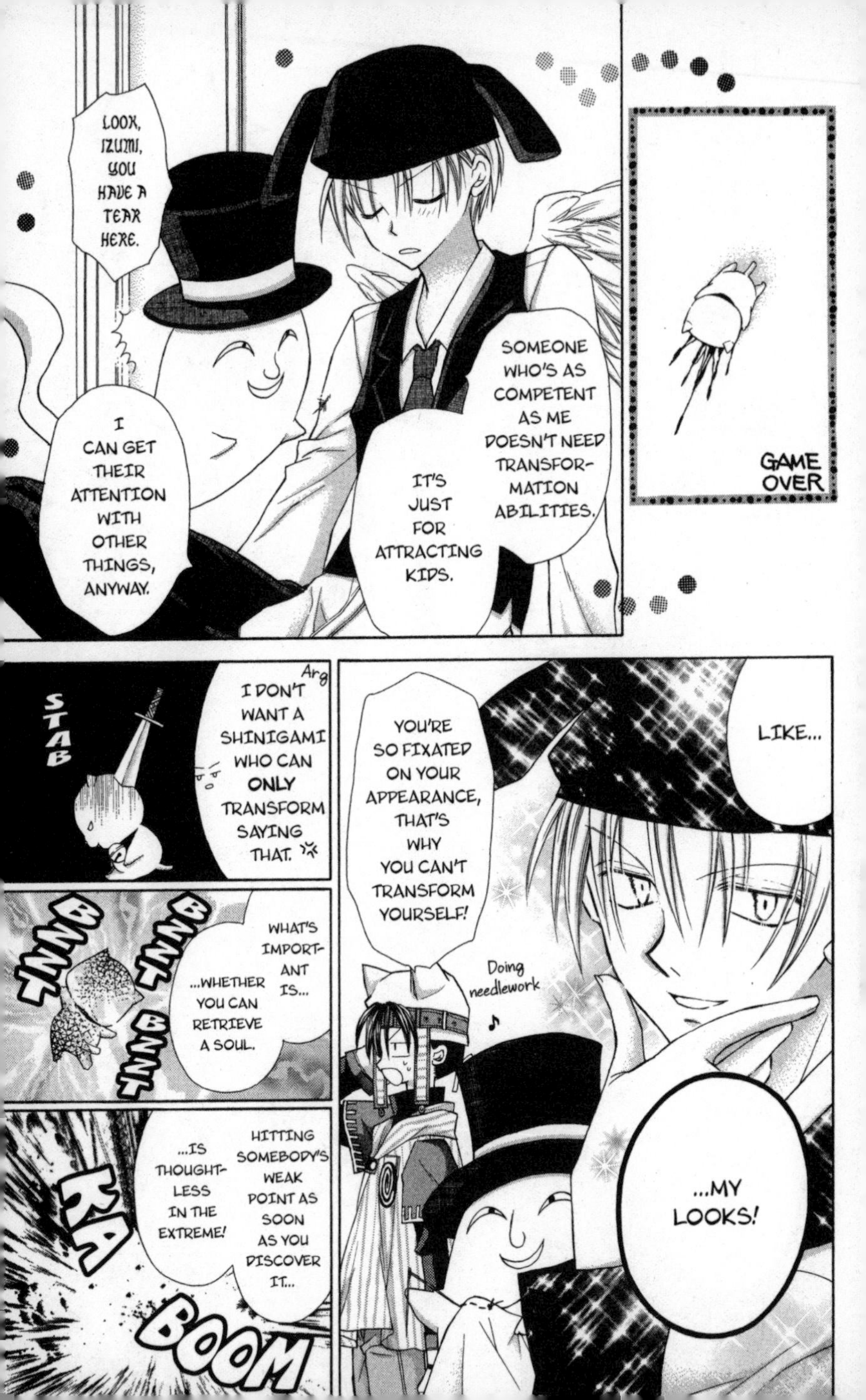
GAME OVER
SOMEONE WHO'S AS COMPETENT AS ME DOESN'T NEED TRANSFORMATION ABILITIES.
IT'S JUST FOR ATTRACTING KIDS.
LOOK, IZUMI, YOU HAVE A TEAR HERE.
I CAN GET THEIR ATTENTION WITH OTHER THINGS, ANYWAY.
LIKE...
...MY LOOKS!
YOU'RE SO FIXATED ON YOUR APPEARANCE, THAT'S WHY YOU CAN'T TRANSFORM YOURSELF!
Doing needlework ♪
Arg
I DON'T WANT A SHINIGAMI WHO CAN **ONLY** TRANSFORM SAYING THAT.
STAB
WHAT'S IMPORTANT IS...
...WHETHER YOU CAN RETRIEVE A SOUL.
BNNT BNNT BNNT
HITTING SOMEBODY'S WEAK POINT AS SOON AS YOU DISCOVER IT...
...IS THOUGHTLESS IN THE EXTREME!
KA BOOM

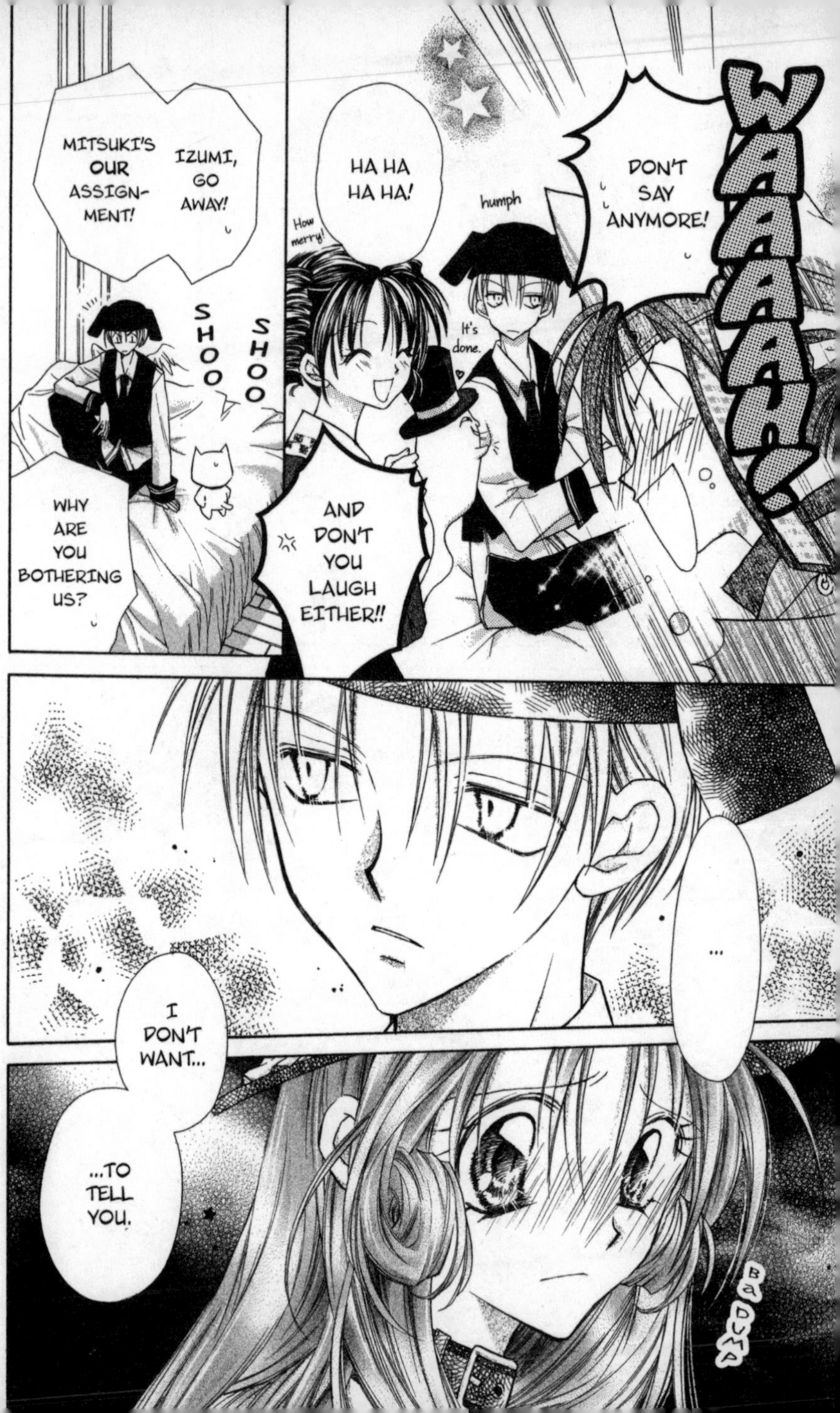
WAAAAH!
DON'T SAY ANYMORE!
humph
HA HA HA HA!
How merry!
It's done.
AND DON'T YOU LAUGH EITHER!!
IZUMI, GO AWAY!
MITSUKI'S OUR ASSIGNMENT!
SHOO
SHOO
WHY ARE YOU BOTHERING US?
...
I DON'T WANT...
...TO TELL YOU.
BADUMP

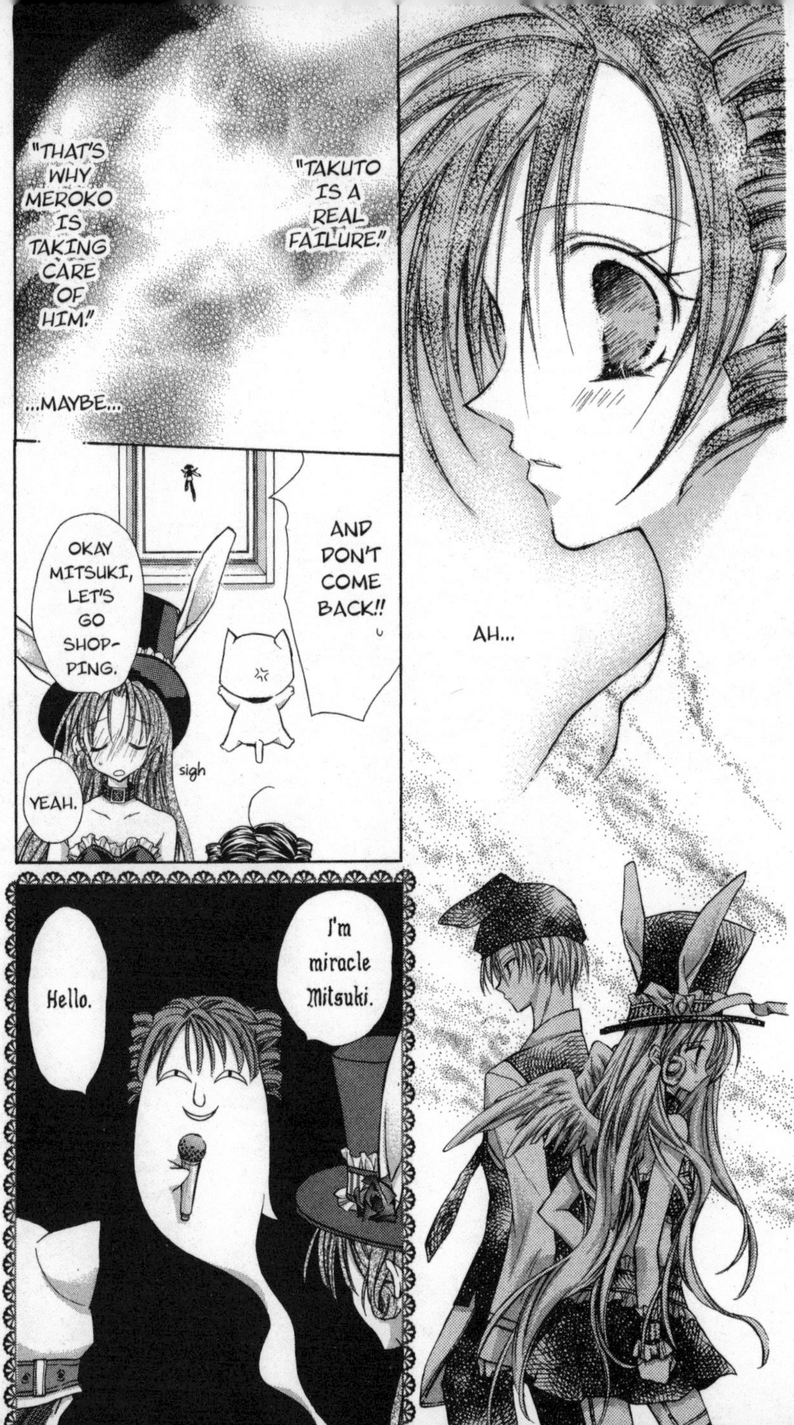
AH...
"TAKUTO IS A REAL FAILURE."
"THAT'S WHY MEROKO IS TAKING CARE OF HIM."
...MAYBE...
AND DON'T COME BACK!!
OKAY MITSUKI, LET'S GO SHOP-PING.
sigh
YEAH.
I'm miracle Mitsuki.
Hello.

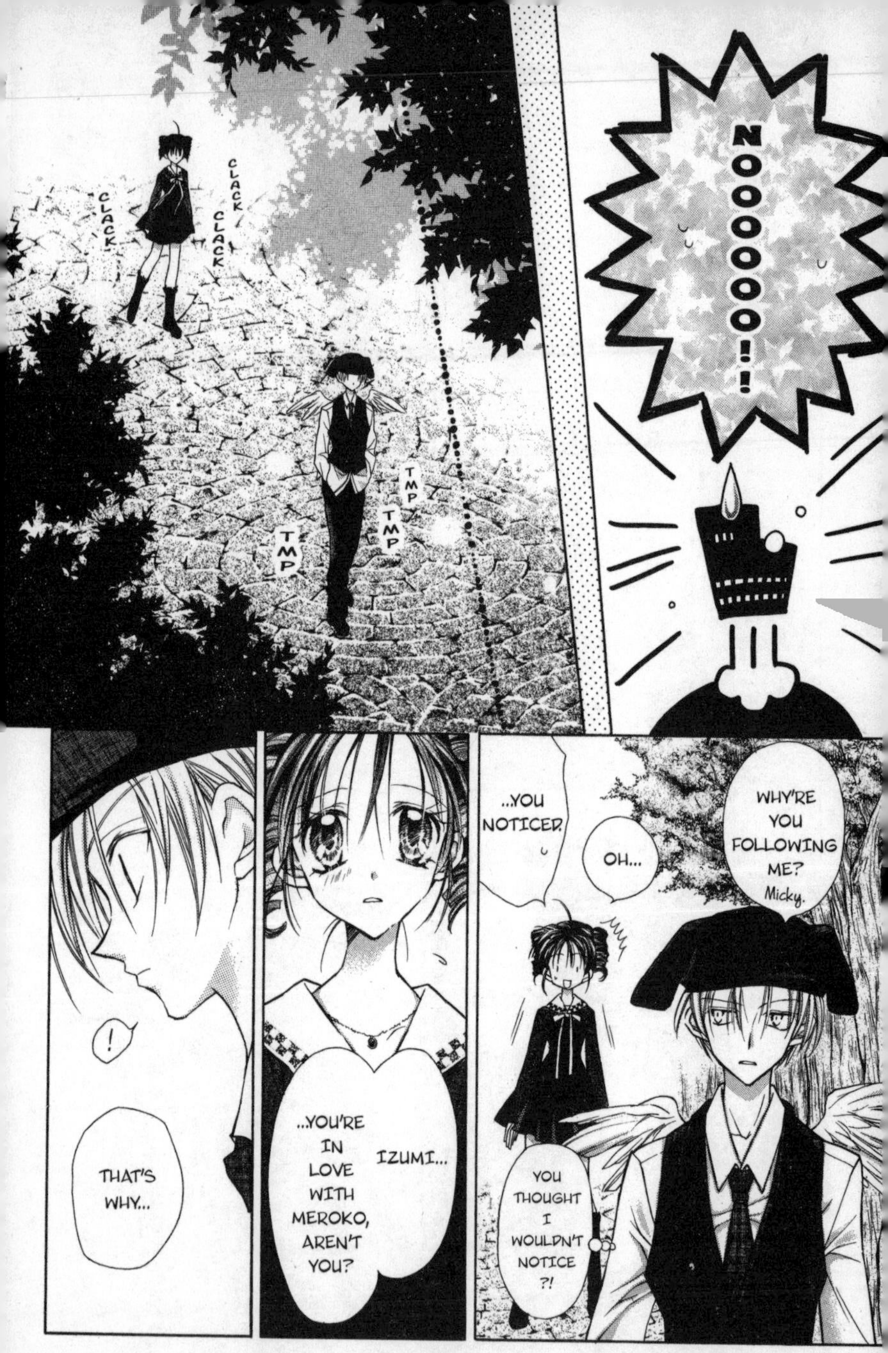
NOOOOOOO!!
CLACK CLACK
CLACK
TMP
TMP
TMP
WHY'RE YOU FOLLOWING ME? Micky.
OH...
...YOU NOTICED.
YOU THOUGHT I WOULDN'T NOTICE?!
IZUMI...
...YOU'RE IN LOVE WITH MEROKO, AREN'T YOU?
!
THAT'S WHY...

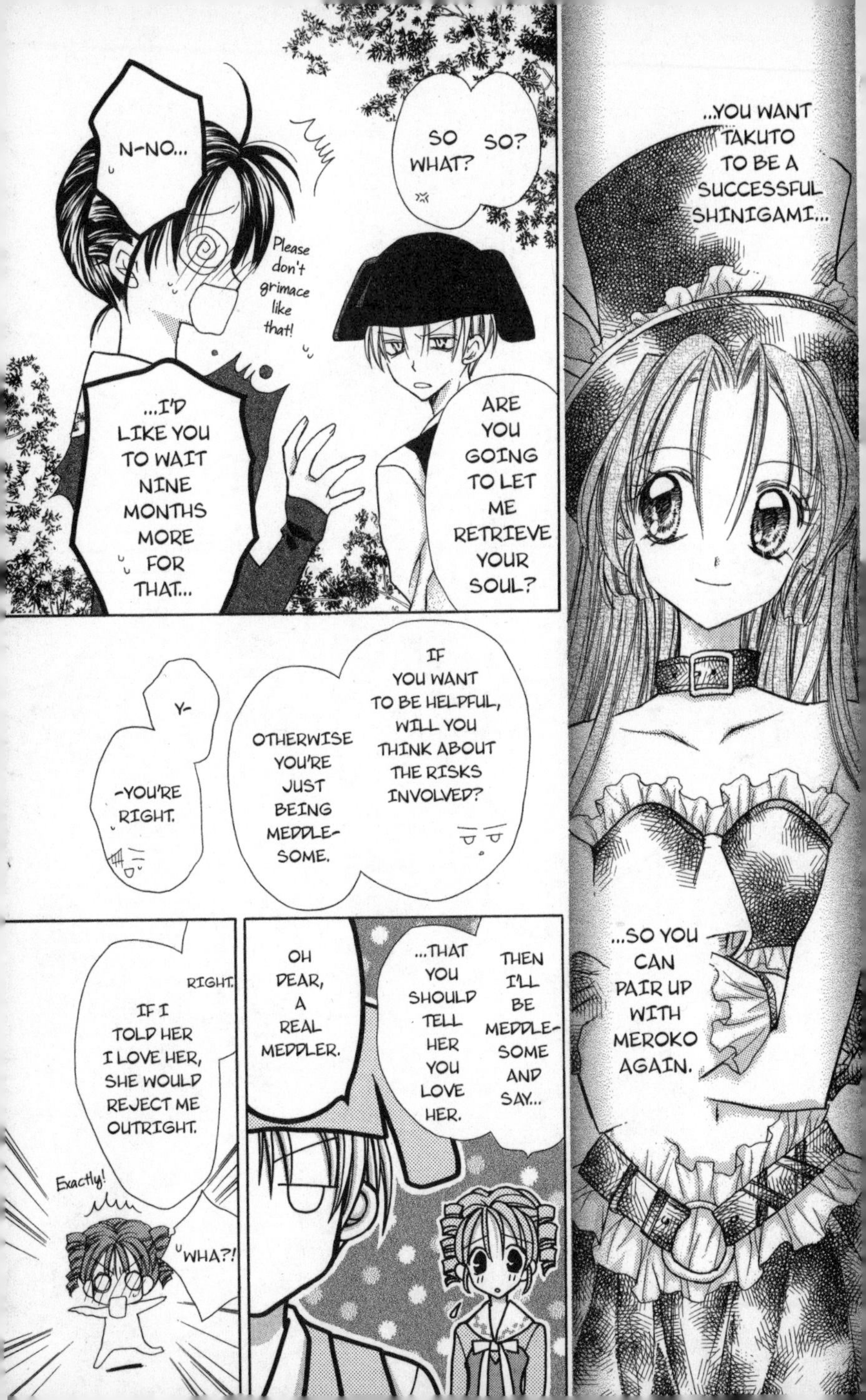
...YOU WANT TAKUTO TO BE A SUCCESSFUL SHINIGAMI...
...SO YOU CAN PAIR UP WITH MEROKO AGAIN.
SO? SO WHAT?
ARE YOU GOING TO LET ME RETRIEVE YOUR SOUL?
Please don't grimace like that!
N-NO...
...I'D LIKE YOU TO WAIT NINE MONTHS MORE FOR THAT...
IF YOU WANT TO BE HELPFUL, WILL YOU THINK ABOUT THE RISKS INVOLVED?
OTHERWISE YOU'RE JUST BEING MEDDLESOME.
Y-
-YOU'RE RIGHT.
THEN I'LL BE MEDDLESOME AND SAY...
...THAT YOU SHOULD TELL HER YOU LOVE HER.
OH DEAR, A REAL MEDDLER.
RIGHT.
IF I TOLD HER I LOVE HER, SHE WOULD REJECT ME OUTRIGHT.
WHA?!
Exactly!

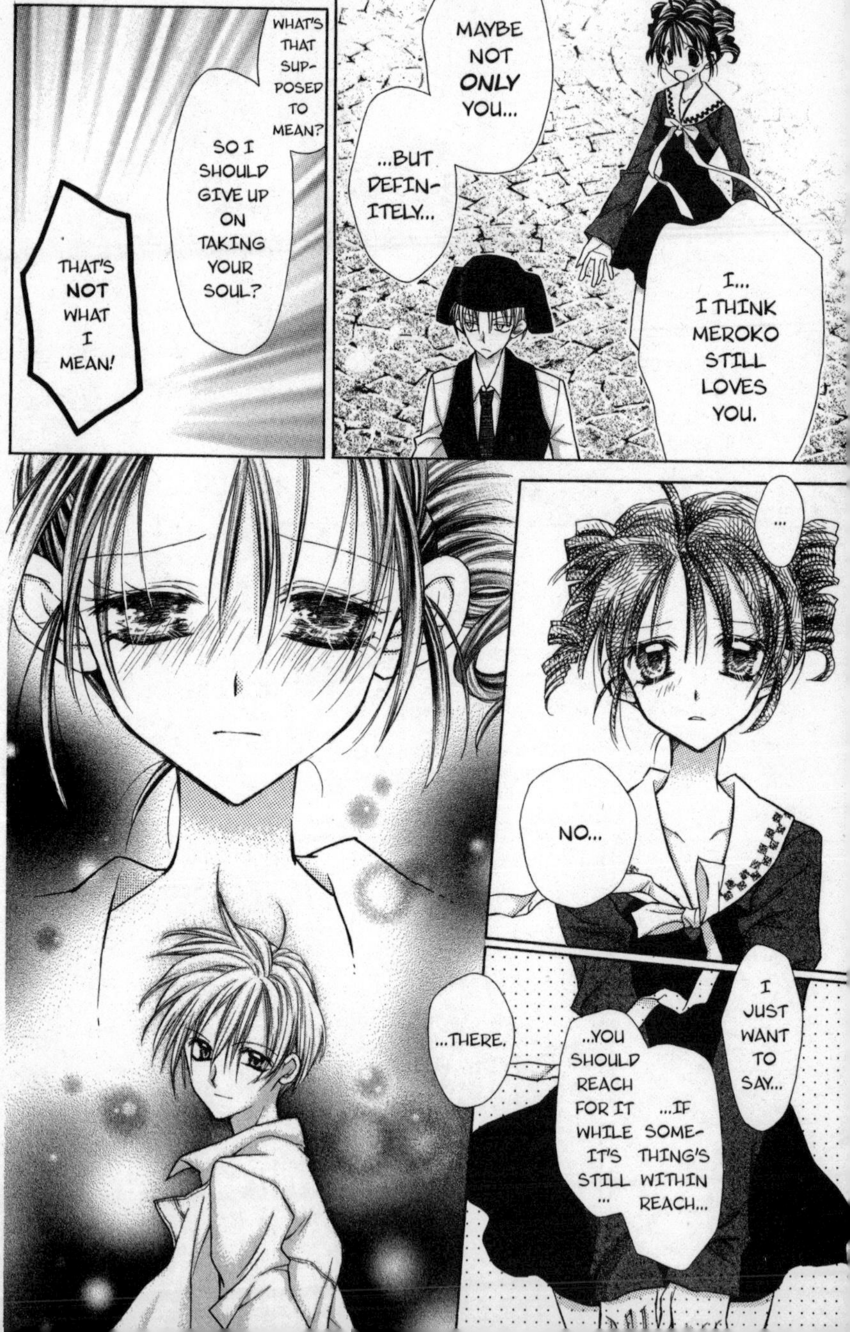
I... I THINK MEROKO STILL LOVES YOU.
MAYBE NOT ONLY YOU...
...BUT DEFINITELY...
WHAT'S THAT SUPPOSED TO MEAN?
SO I SHOULD GIVE UP ON TAKING YOUR SOUL?
THAT'S NOT WHAT I MEAN!
...
NO...
I JUST WANT TO SAY...
...IF SOMETHING'S WITHIN REACH...
...YOU SHOULD REACH FOR IT WHILE IT'S STILL ...
...THERE.

Me Nowadays, Part 2

I went to Houko Kuwashima's "Roudokuya." (She's the voice actress who played Jeanne & Maron in "Kamikaze Kaito Jeanne.") I listened to the fairy tale "Ginga Testsudo no Yoru" at the Planetarium "Starhall" on top of the Tokyu department store in Machida city. I've always wanted to go a planetarium since I was little, but I didn't have many chances to go (or maybe I went when I was little, but I don't have any memories of it). So I was very happy I could go to one.
Underneath all those stars, Hou-chan's recitation was wonderful! To explain how it was, it was like a radio drama, but she did the narration, played Giovanni and Campanella, and more than ten other characters all by herself. It was...all her voices were soooooo different in tone and really...how to say, were totally those characters' voices and even the pauses were just right, and you could really see the acting ability of voice actress Houko Kuwashima. Wow. The story was great too (I knew the rough plot, and I'd heard a bit on Hou-chan's radio "Club db," but I'd never read the book ^^), and of course because of the planetarium, my feelings rose to a great high, and I was really moved. Thank you!
http://www2.m-st.co.jp/roudokuya/

↑ the Roudokuya site.

Please take a look at it if you're interested!!

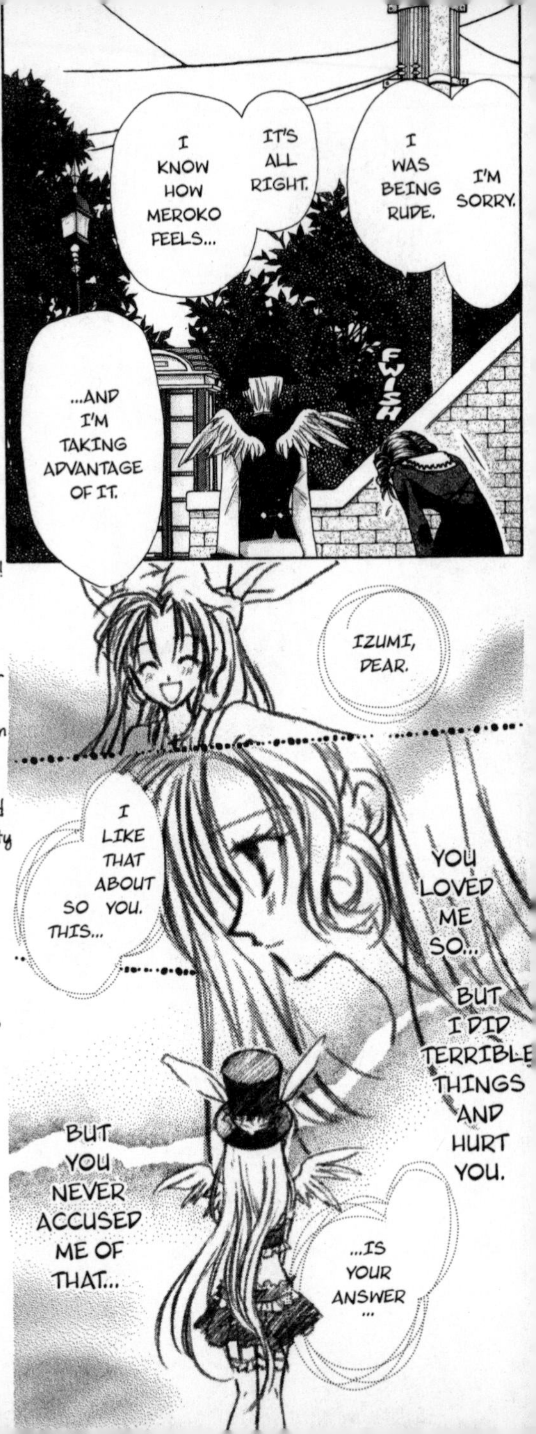
I'M SORRY.
I WAS BEING RUDE.
IT'S ALL RIGHT.
I KNOW HOW MEROKO FEELS...
FWISH
...AND I'M TAKING ADVANTAGE OF IT.
IZUMI, DEAR.
YOU LOVED ME SO...
BUT I DID TERRIBLE THINGS AND HURT YOU.
I LIKE THAT ABOUT YOU.
SO THIS...
...IS YOUR ANSWER ...
BUT YOU NEVER ACCUSED ME OF THAT...

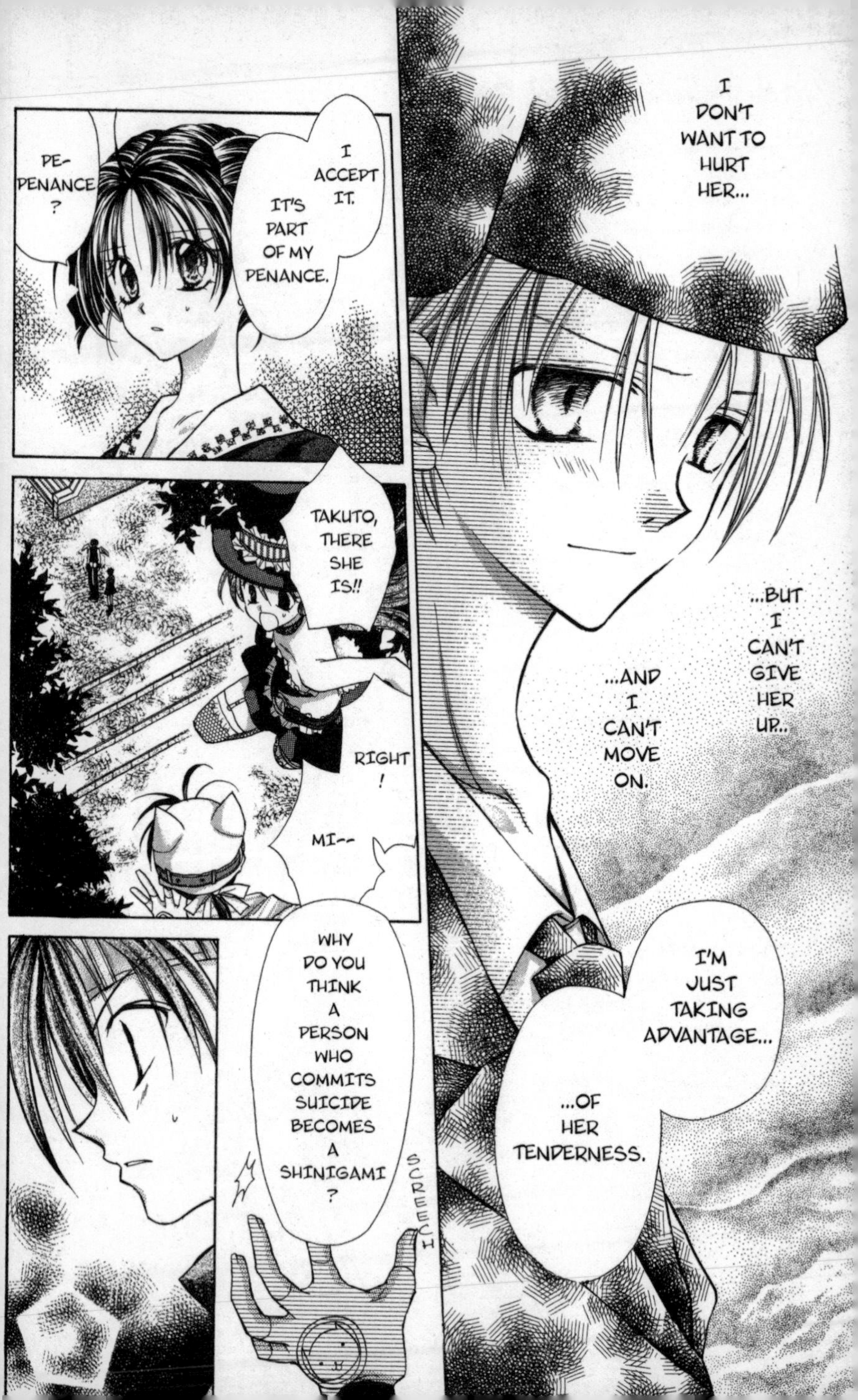
I DON'T WANT TO HURT HER...
...BUT I CAN'T GIVE HER UP...
...AND I CAN'T MOVE ON.
I'M JUST TAKING ADVANTAGE...
...OF HER TENDERNESS.
I ACCEPT IT.
IT'S PART OF MY PENANCE.
PE-PENANCE?
TAKUTO, THERE SHE IS!!
RIGHT!
MI--
WHY DO YOU THINK A PERSON WHO COMMITS SUICIDE BECOMES A SHINIGAMI?
SCREECH

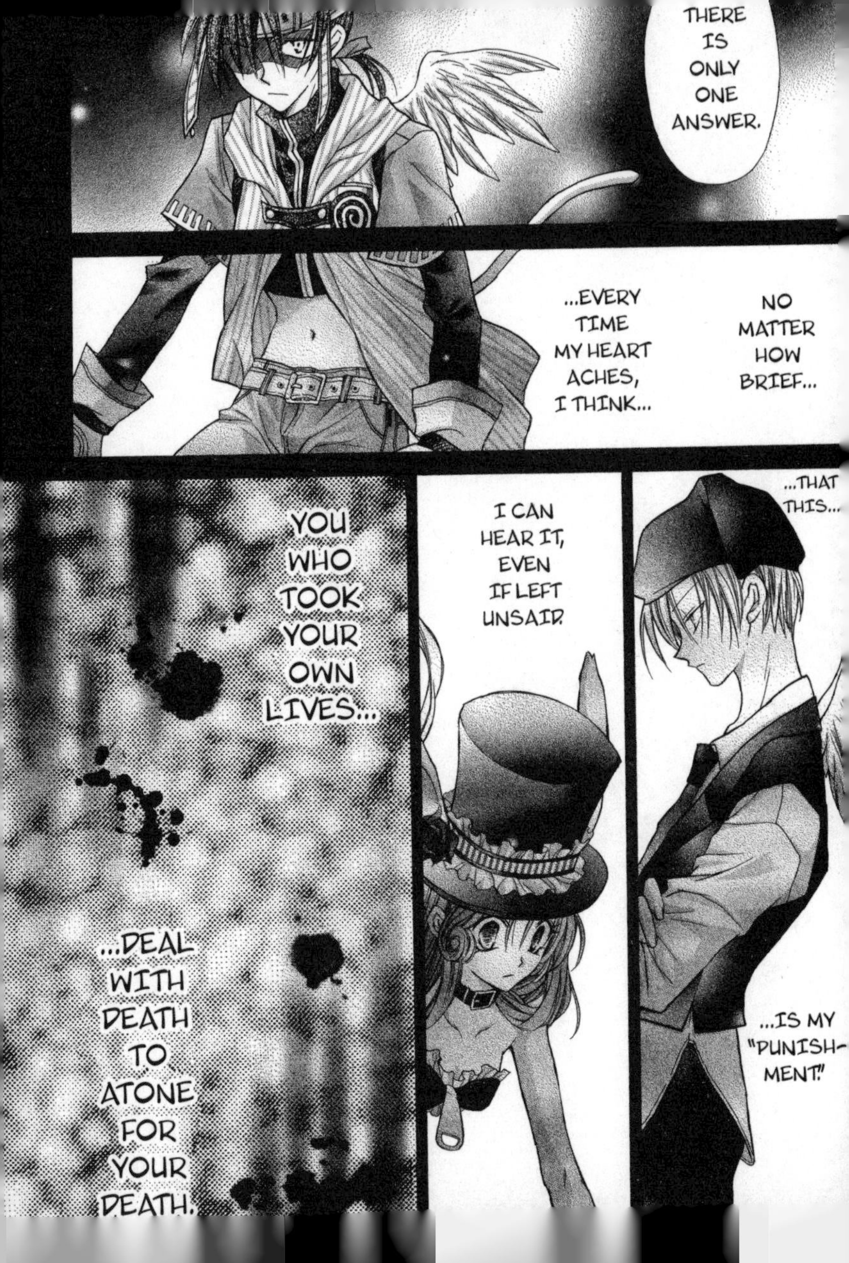
THERE IS ONLY ONE ANSWER.
NO MATTER HOW BRIEF...
...EVERY TIME MY HEART ACHES, I THINK...
...THAT THIS...
...IS MY "PUNISHMENT."
I CAN HEAR IT, EVEN IF LEFT UNSAID.
YOU WHO TOOK YOUR OWN LIVES...
...DEAL WITH DEATH TO ATONE FOR YOUR DEATH.

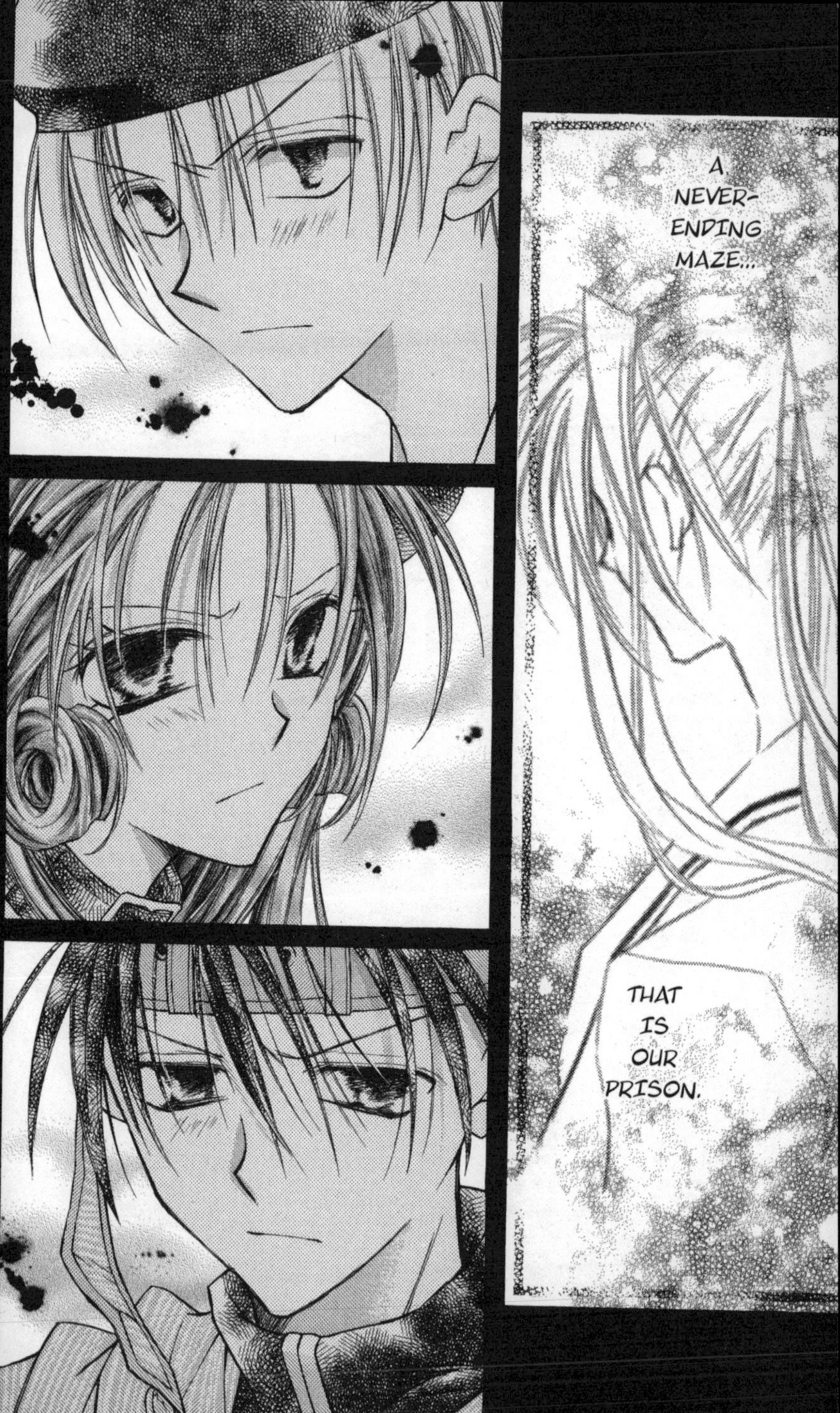
A NEVER-ENDING MAZE...
THAT IS OUR PRISON.

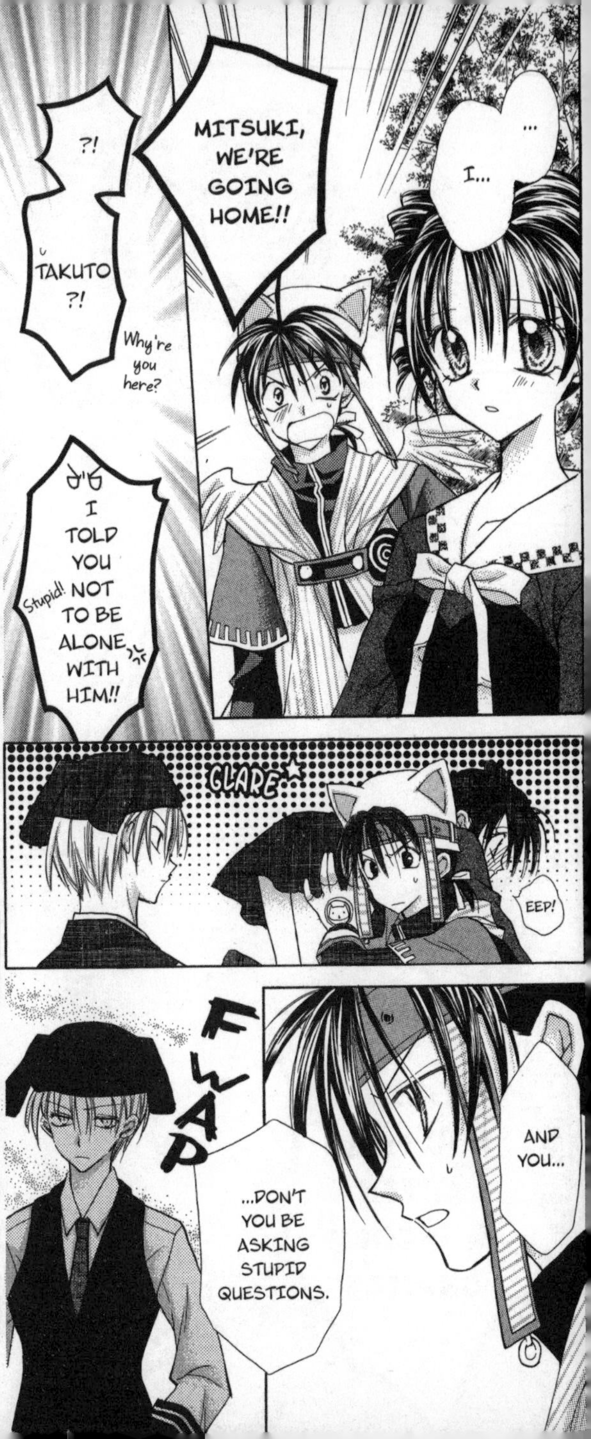
...
I...
MITSUKI, WE'RE GOING HOME!!
?!
TAKUTO ?!
Why're you here?
I TOLD YOU NOT TO BE ALONE WITH HIM!!
Stupid!
GLARE
EEP!
AND YOU...
...DON'T YOU BE ASKING STUPID QUESTIONS.
FWAP

ARINA TANEMURA'S

"PENCHI DE SHAKIN!"

Episode 53

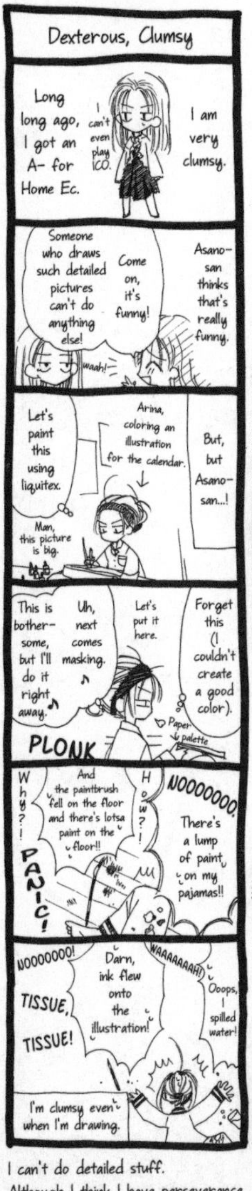
Dexterous, Clumsy
I am very clumsy.
I can't even play ICO.
Long long ago, I got an A- for Home Ec.
Asano-san thinks that's really funny.
Come on, it's funny!
Someone who draws such detailed pictures can't do anything else!
waah!
But, but Asano-san...!
Arina, coloring an illustration for the calendar.
Let's paint this using liquitex.
Man, this picture is big.
Forget this (I couldn't create a good color).
Let's put it here.
Uh, next comes masking.
This is bother-some, but I'll do it right away.
Paper palette
PLONK
NOOOOOOO.
There's a lump of paint on my pajamas!!
How?!
And the paintbrush fell on the floor and there's lotsa paint on the floor!!
Why?!
PANIC!
Ooops, I spilled water!
WAAAAAAAH!
Darn, ink flew onto the illustration!
NOOOOOOO!
TISSUE, TISSUE!
I'm clumsy even when I'm drawing.

I can't do detailed stuff.
Although I think I have perseverance.

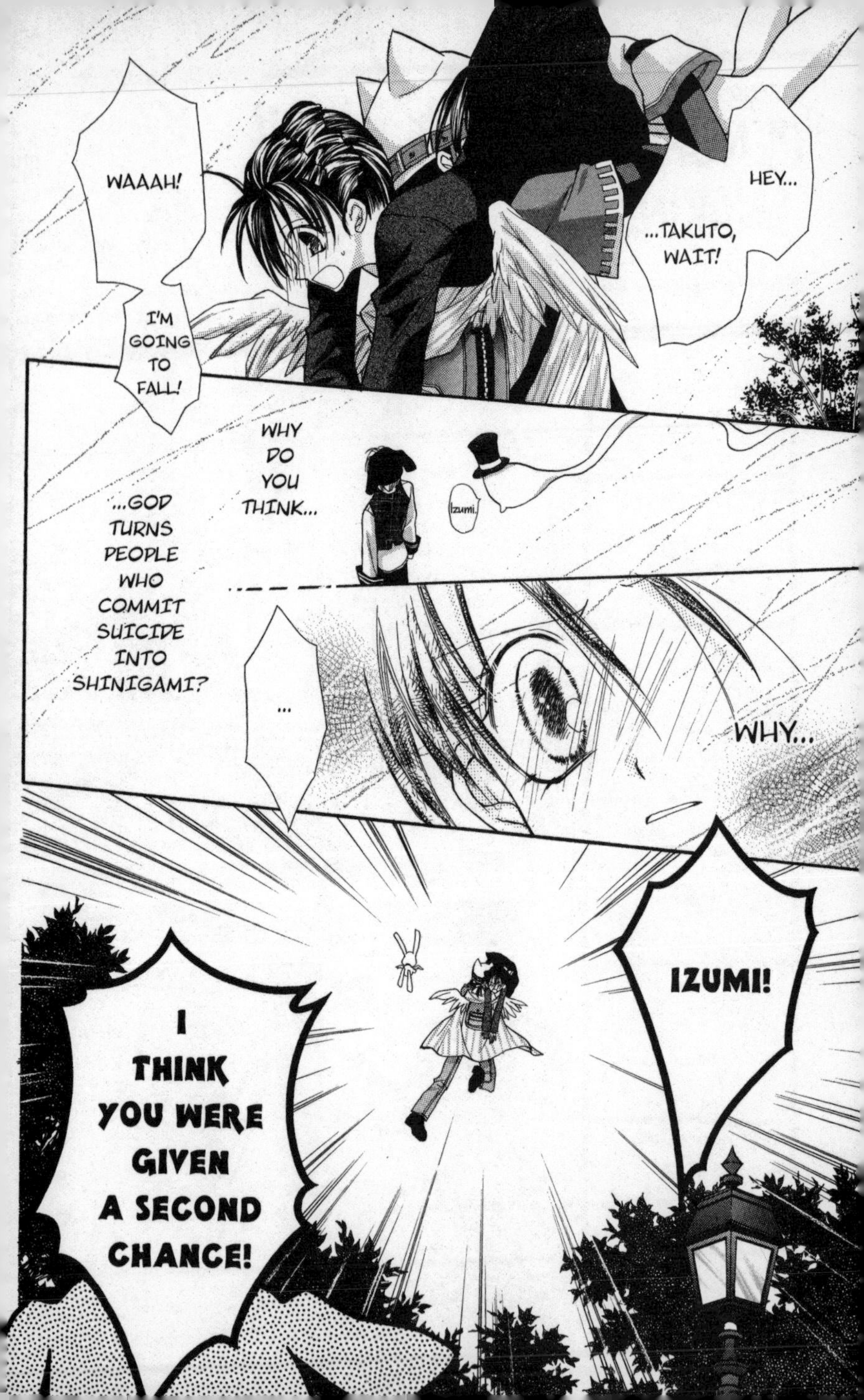
HEY...
...TAKUTO, WAIT!
WAAAH!
I'M GOING TO FALL!
Izumi.
WHY DO YOU THINK...
...GOD TURNS PEOPLE WHO COMMIT SUICIDE INTO SHINIGAMI?
WHY...
...
IZUMI!
I THINK YOU WERE GIVEN A SECOND CHANCE!

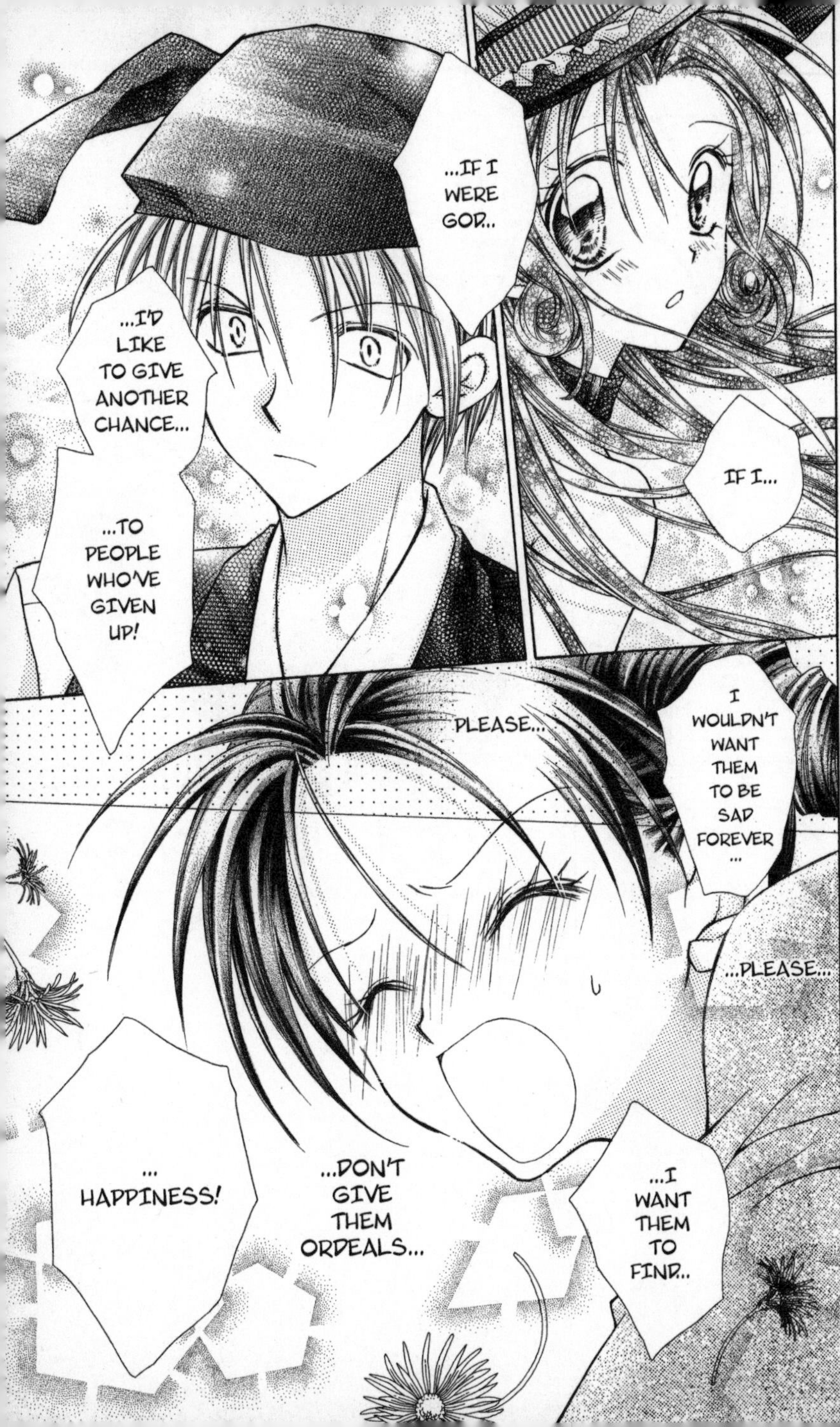
IF I...
...IF I WERE GOD...
...I'D LIKE TO GIVE ANOTHER CHANCE...
...TO PEOPLE WHO'VE GIVEN UP!
I WOULDN'T WANT THEM TO BE SAD FOREVER...
PLEASE...
...PLEASE...
...I WANT THEM TO FIND..
...DON'T GIVE THEM ORDEALS...
...HAPPINESS!

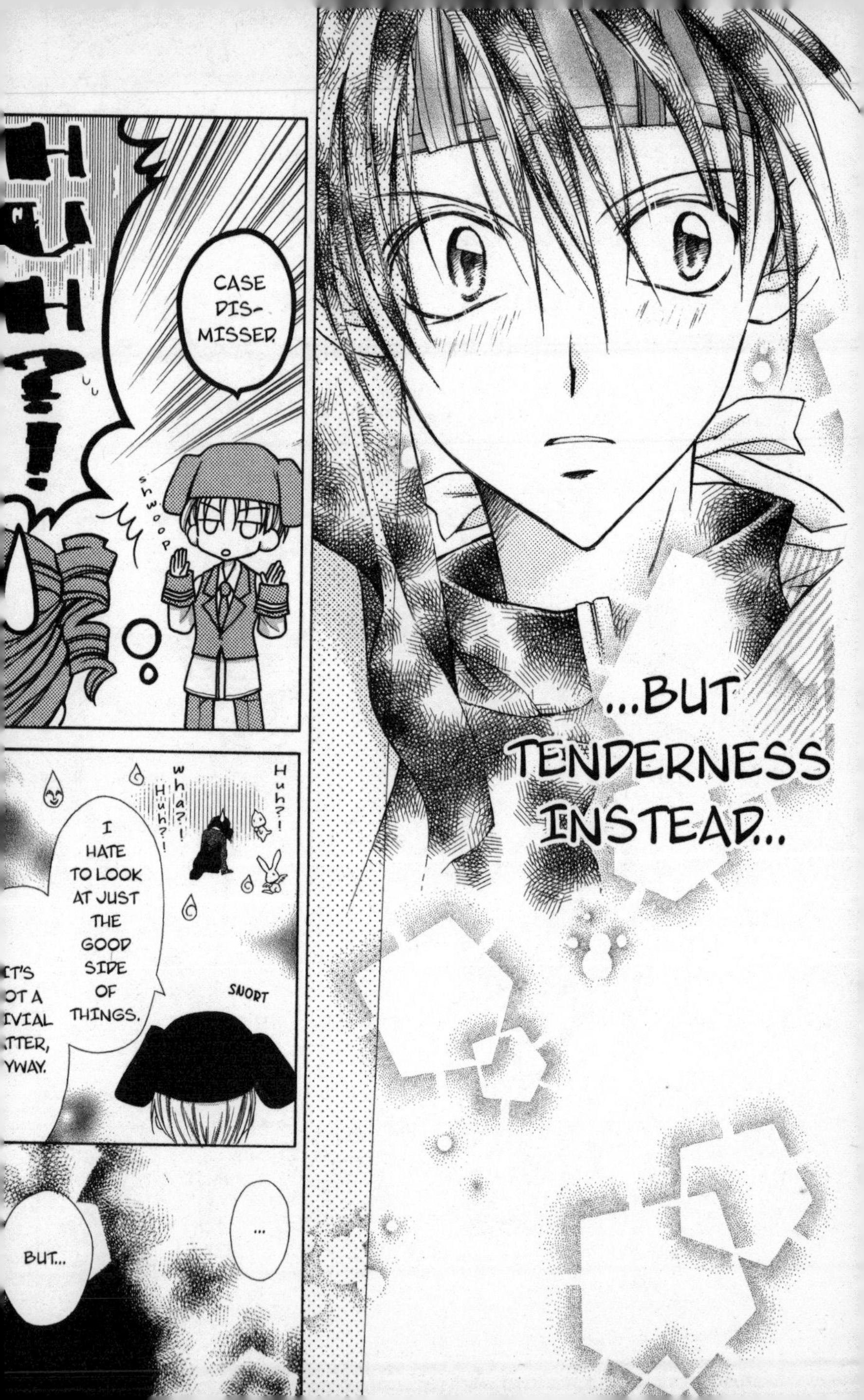
...BUT TENDERNESS INSTEAD...
CASE DISMISSED.
HUH?!
SHWOOP
Huh?!
Wha?!
Huh?!
I HATE TO LOOK AT JUST THE GOOD SIDE OF THINGS.
SNORT
...
BUT...

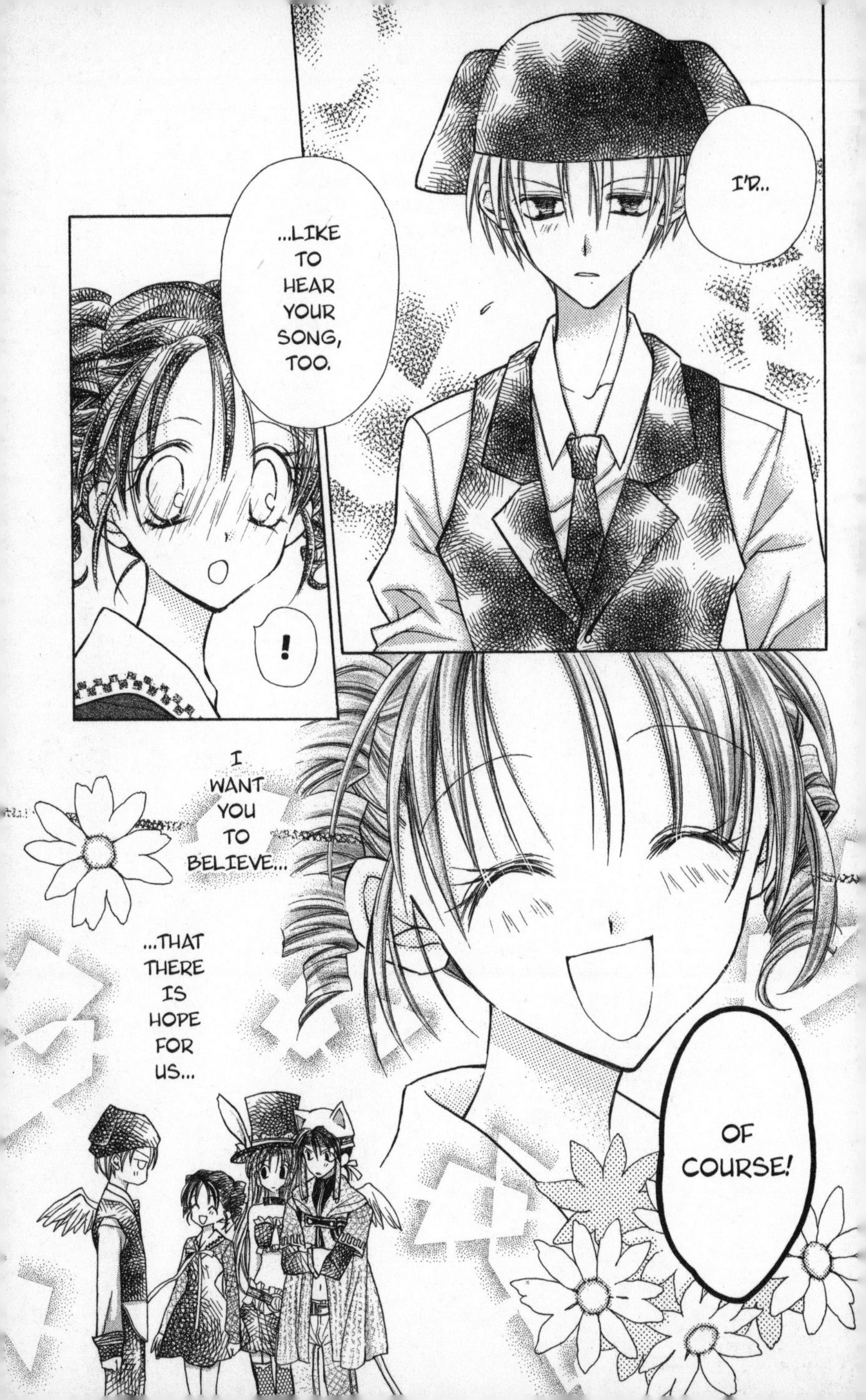
I'D...
...LIKE TO HEAR YOUR SONG, TOO.
!
OF COURSE!
I WANT YOU TO BELIEVE...
...THAT THERE IS HOPE FOR US...

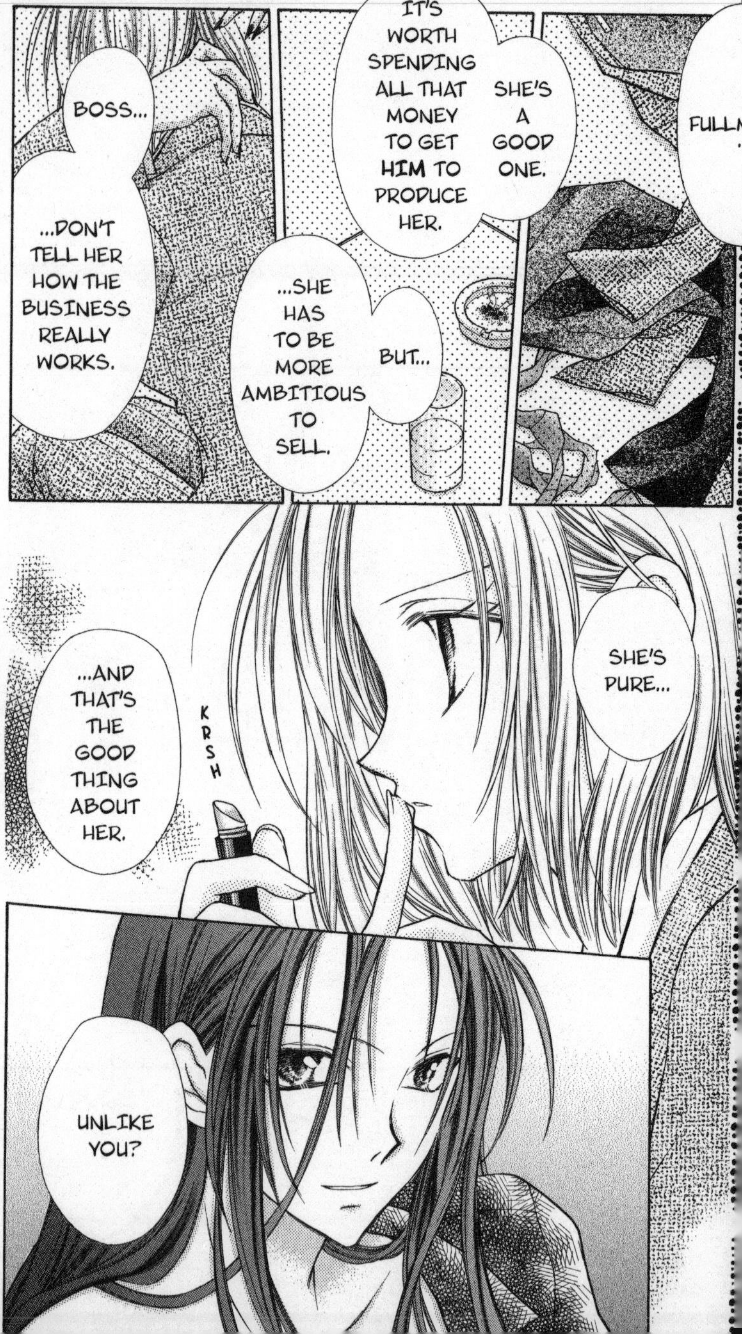
SHE'S A GOOD ONE.
IT'S WORTH SPENDING ALL THAT MONEY TO GET HIM TO PRODUCE HER.
BUT...
...SHE HAS TO BE MORE AMBITIOUS TO SELL.
BOSS...
...DON'T TELL HER HOW THE BUSINESS REALLY WORKS.
SHE'S PURE...
KRSH
...AND THAT'S THE GOOD THING ABOUT HER.
UNLIKE YOU?

Well. ⌄

(There's still the sidebar for Gin-yu Meika)

Did you enjoy "Fullmoon o Sagashite" Vol. ② ? Vol. ③ ...may have a happening. (I guess the readers are making various predictions, but once it's made clear, it may come as a shock...)

For me...too.

Um, there was a fan letter asking whether it's true that I said terrible things to my fans on the Internet. That is simply not true. (Although I have made insolent remarks in the past.) Now, unless it's at a site of a very good friend, I don't write anything. Moreover, no matter how severe a remark someone may make, I will not call a person I've never met a fool. (There seems to be a great misunderstanding, but I think I like reading critiques ← I receive them via fan letters. I don't look for them on the net myself. made about my work. Criticisms that make sense, I use to improve my work, and those that don't, I use them to understand that "Things could be taken this way.")

In any case, I've never said terrible things to my fans, so please believe me.

Send fan letters to ⌄

Full Moon c/o Shojo Beat
VIZ Media, LLC
P.O. Box 77010
San Francisco, CA 94107

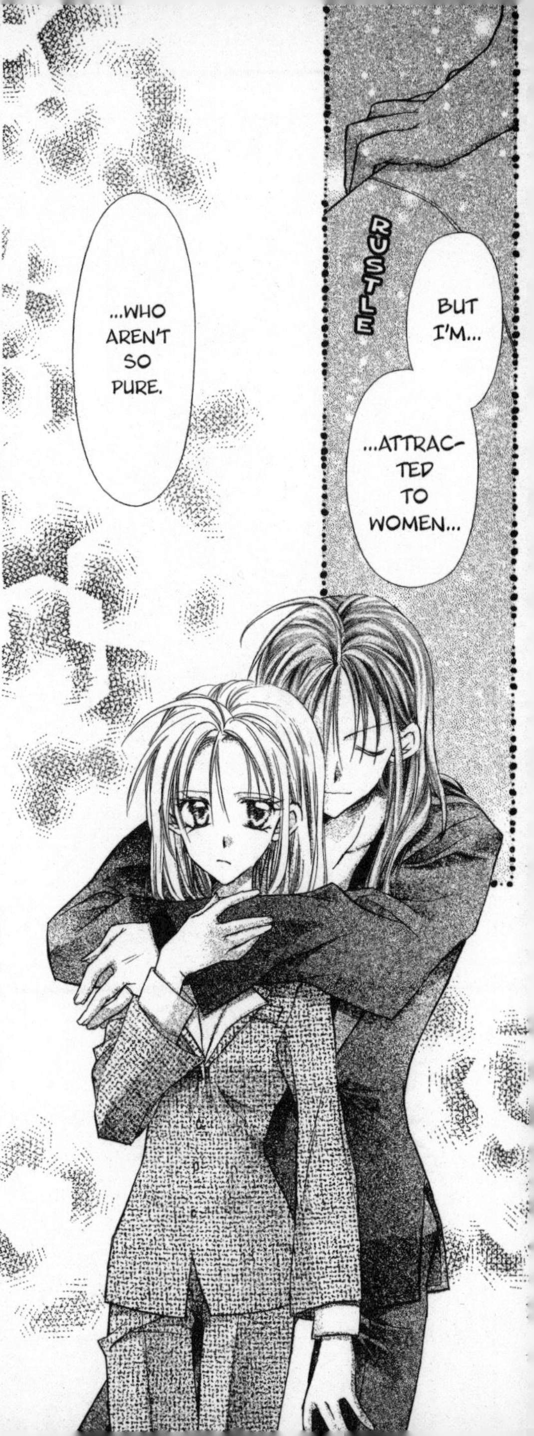

BUT I'M...
...ATTRACTED TO WOMEN...
RUSTLE
...WHO AREN'T SO PURE.

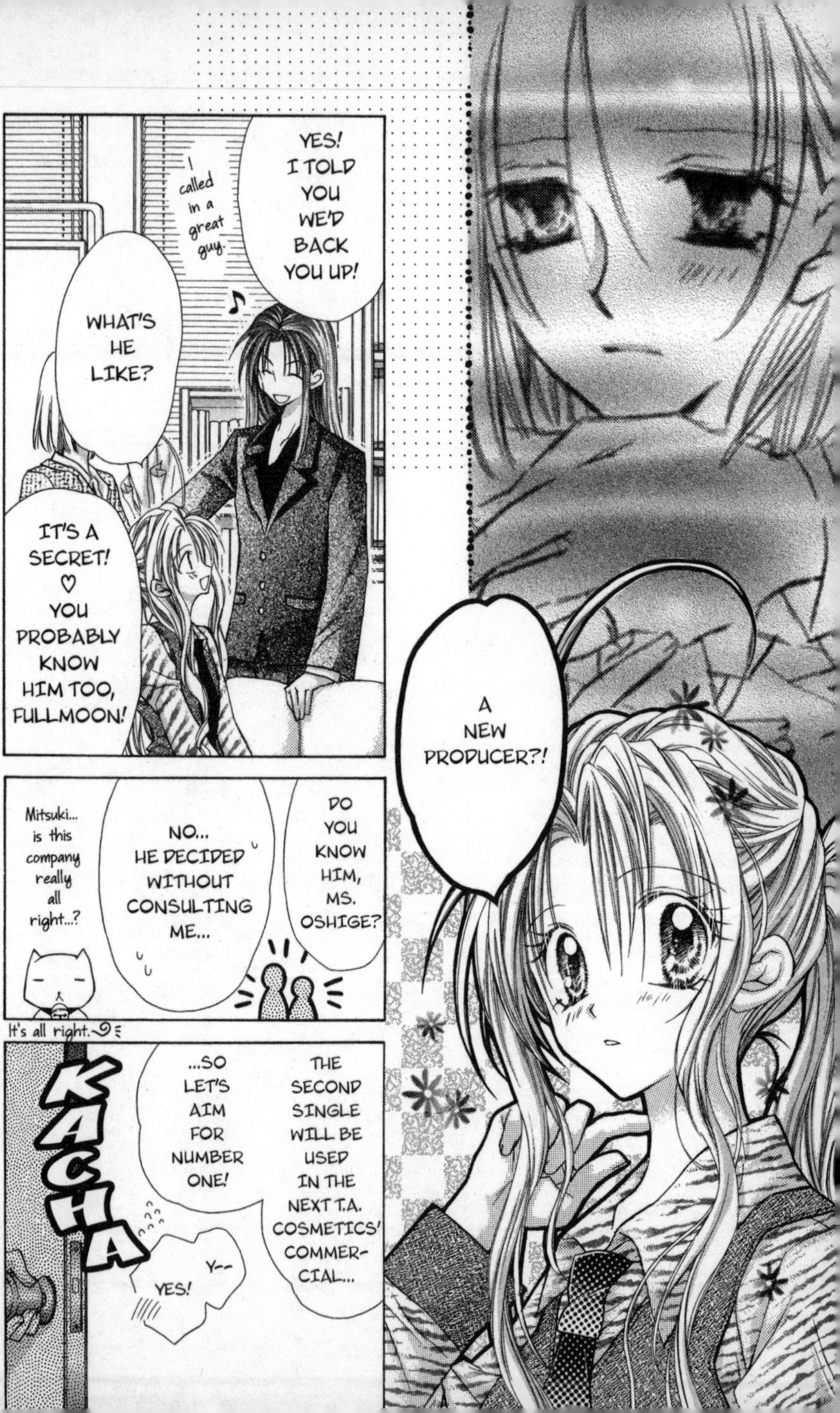
A NEW PRODUCER?!
YES! I TOLD YOU WE'D BACK YOU UP!
I called in a great guy.
WHAT'S HE LIKE?
IT'S A SECRET! ♡ YOU PROBABLY KNOW HIM TOO, FULLMOON!
DO YOU KNOW HIM, MS. OSHIGE?
NO... HE DECIDED WITHOUT CONSULTING ME...
Mitsuki... is this company really all right...?
It's all right.
THE SECOND SINGLE WILL BE USED IN THE NEXT T.A. COSMETICS' COMMERCIAL...
...SO LET'S AIM FOR NUMBER ONE!
Y-- YES!
KACHA

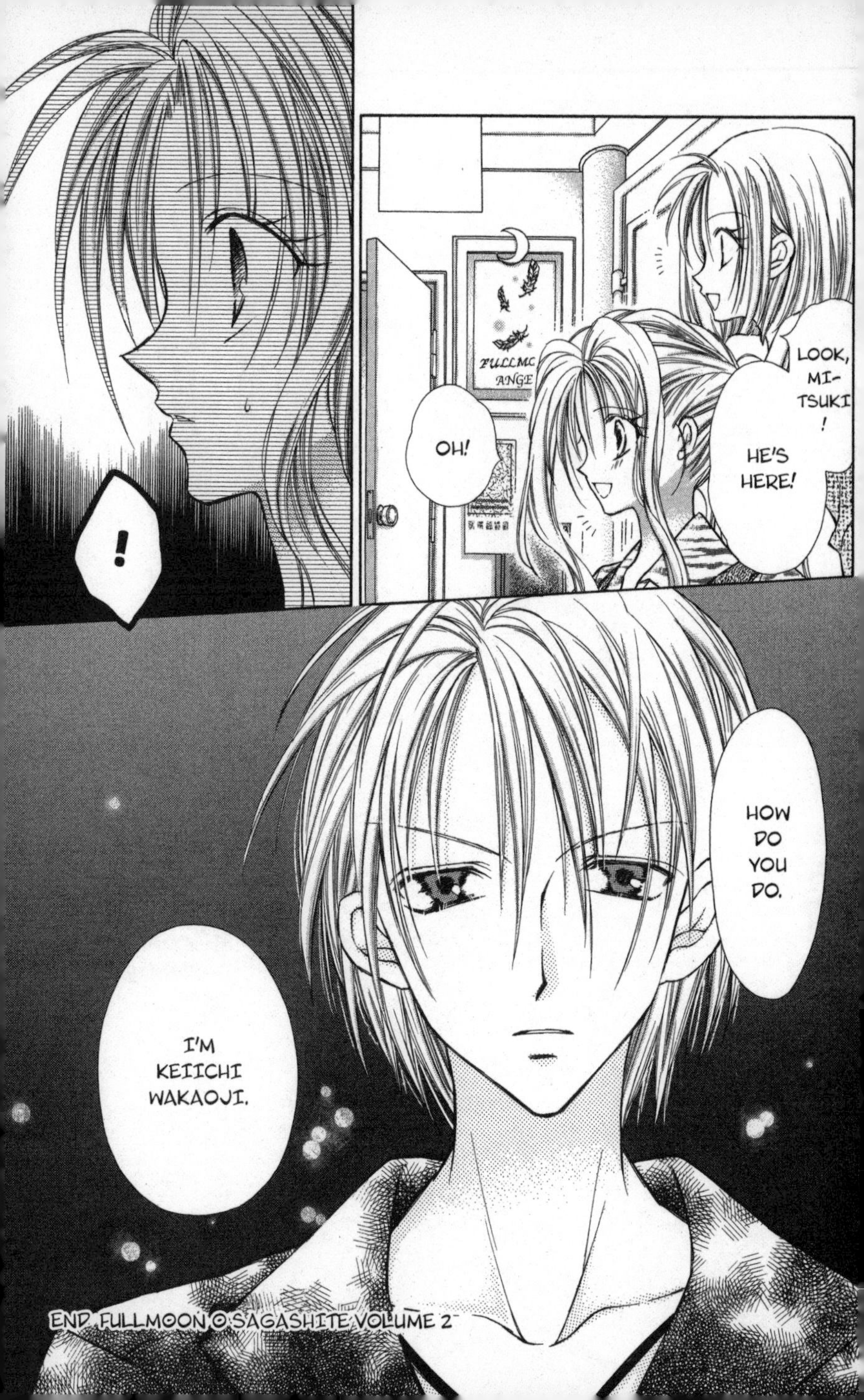
LOOK, MI-TSUKI! HE'S HERE!
OH!
!
HOW DO YOU DO.
I'M KEIICHI WAKAOJI.
END FULLMOON O SAGASHITE VOLUME 2

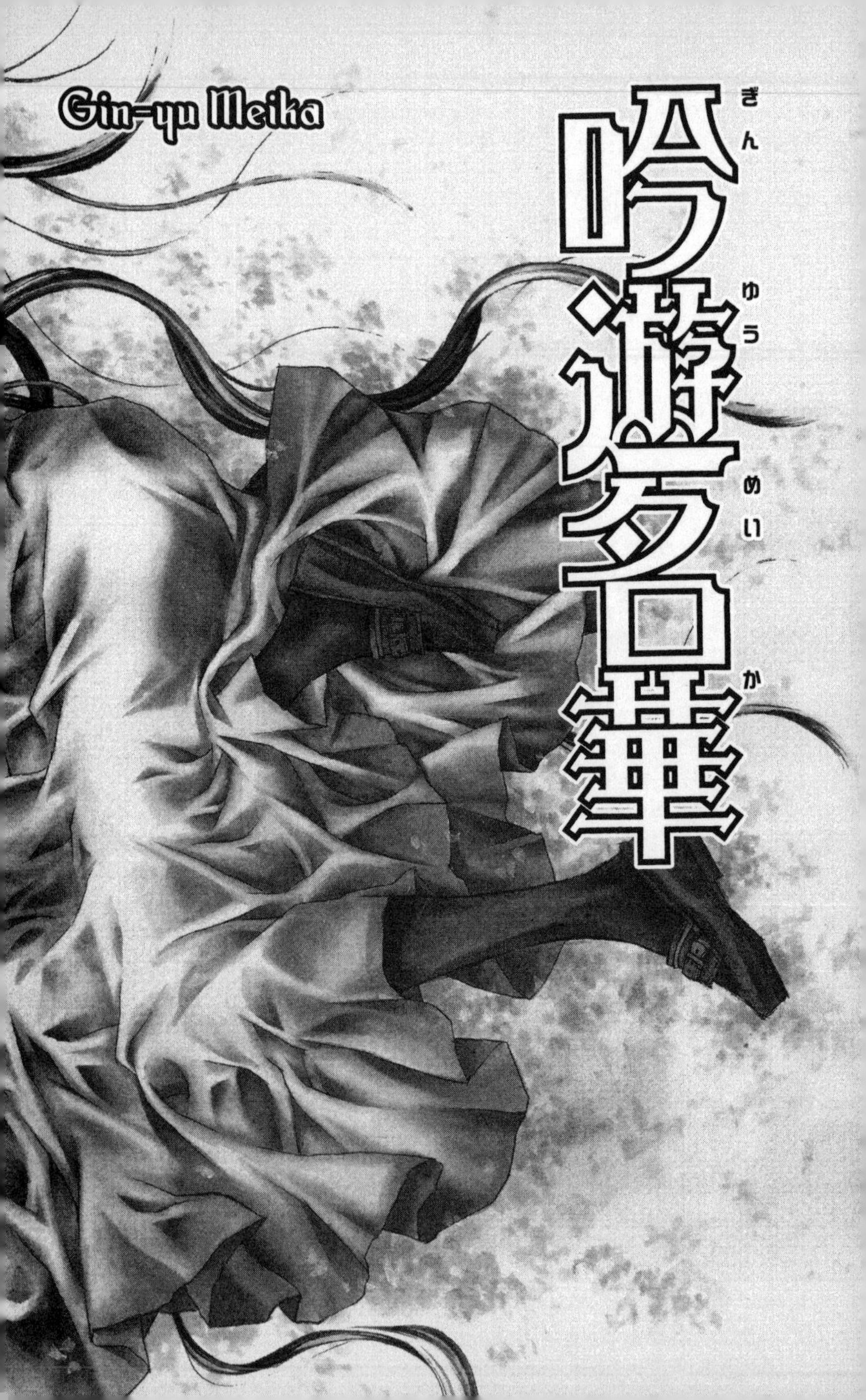
吟遊名華
ぎんゆうめいか
Gin-yu Meika

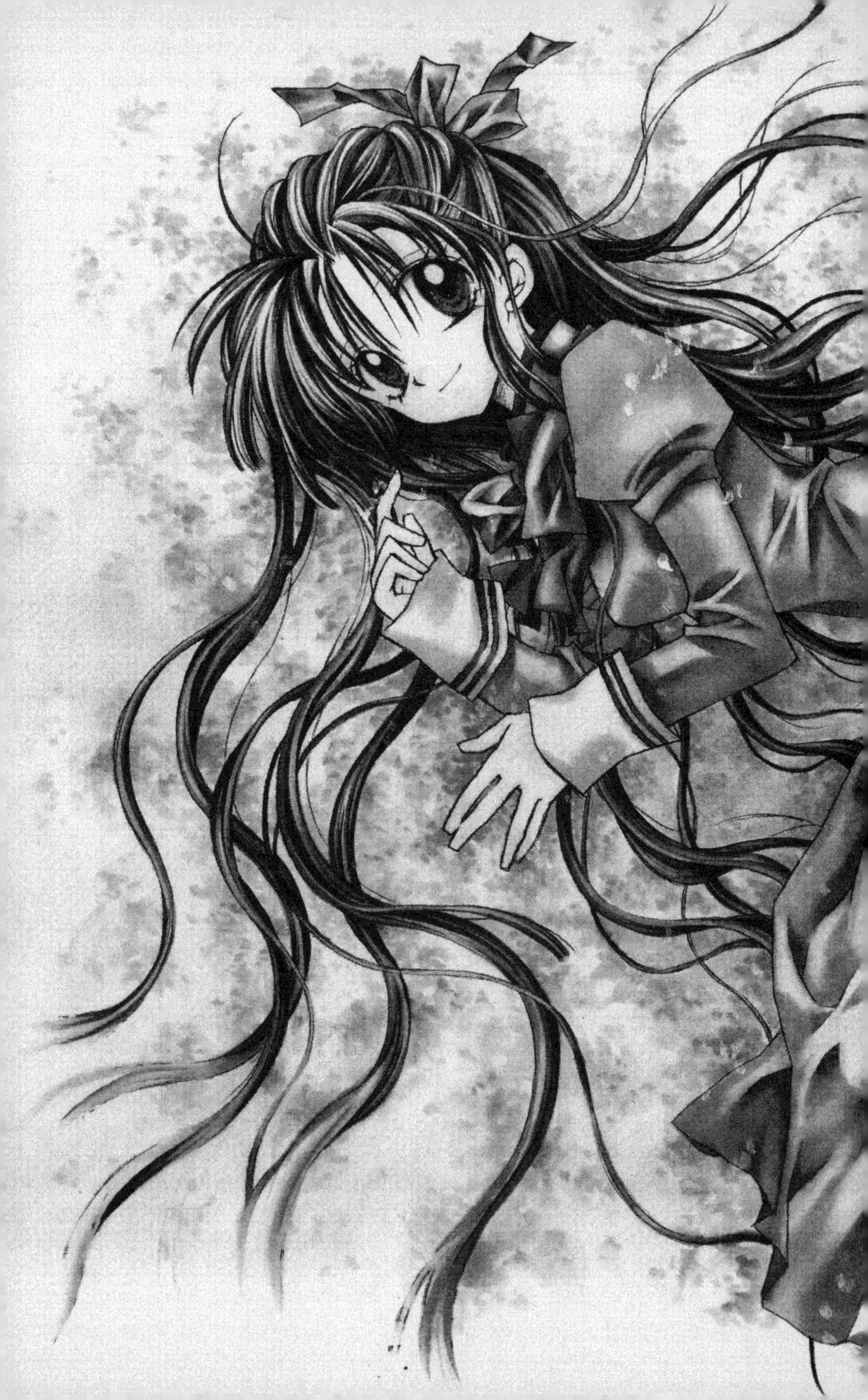

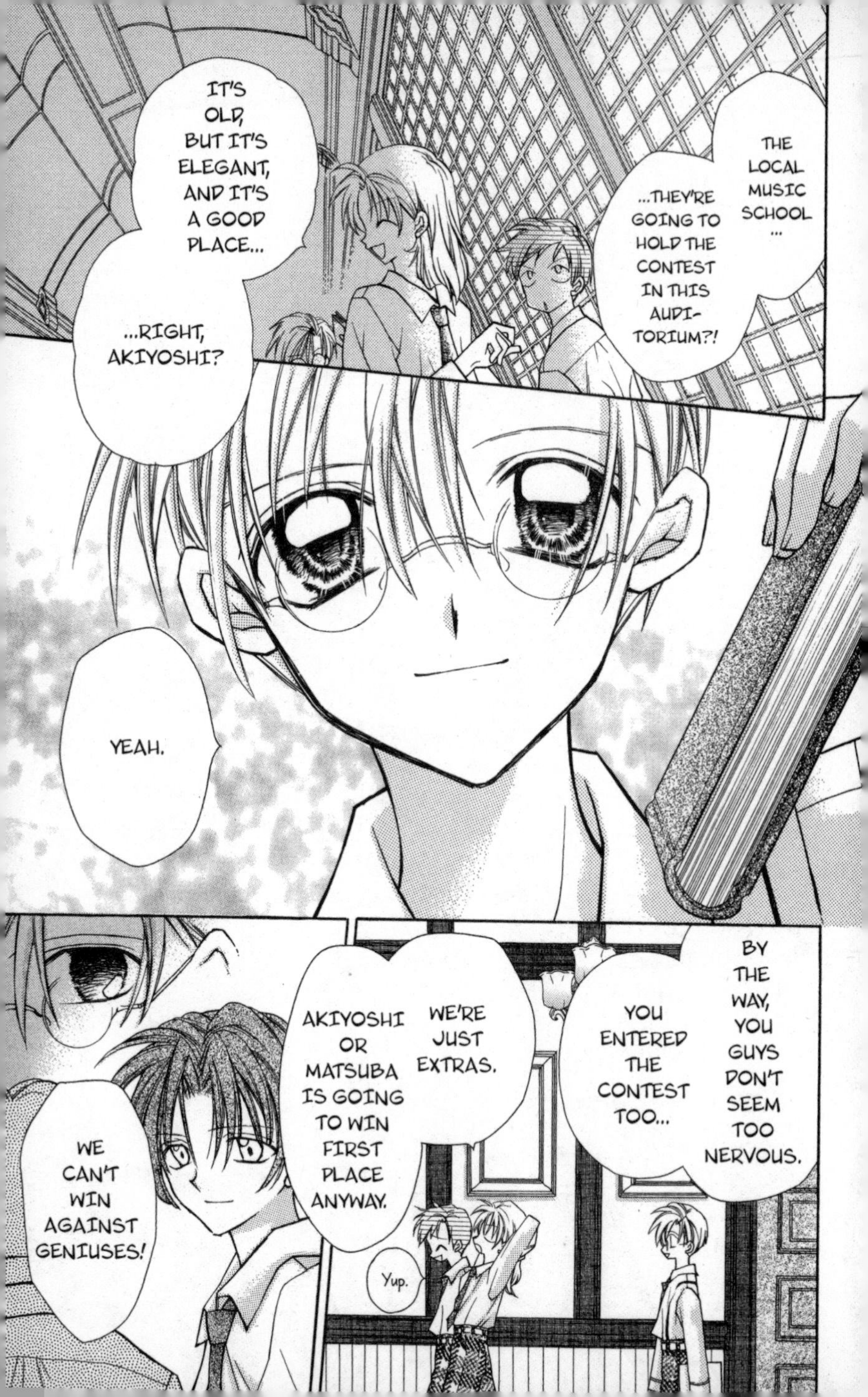
THE LOCAL MUSIC SCHOOL ...
...THEY'RE GOING TO HOLD THE CONTEST IN THIS AUDITORIUM?!
IT'S OLD, BUT IT'S ELEGANT, AND IT'S A GOOD PLACE...
...RIGHT, AKIYOSHI?
YEAH.
BY THE WAY, YOU GUYS DON'T SEEM TOO NERVOUS.
YOU ENTERED THE CONTEST TOO...
WE'RE JUST EXTRAS.
AKIYOSHI OR MATSUBA IS GOING TO WIN FIRST PLACE ANYWAY.
Yup.
WE CAN'T WIN AGAINST GENIUSES!

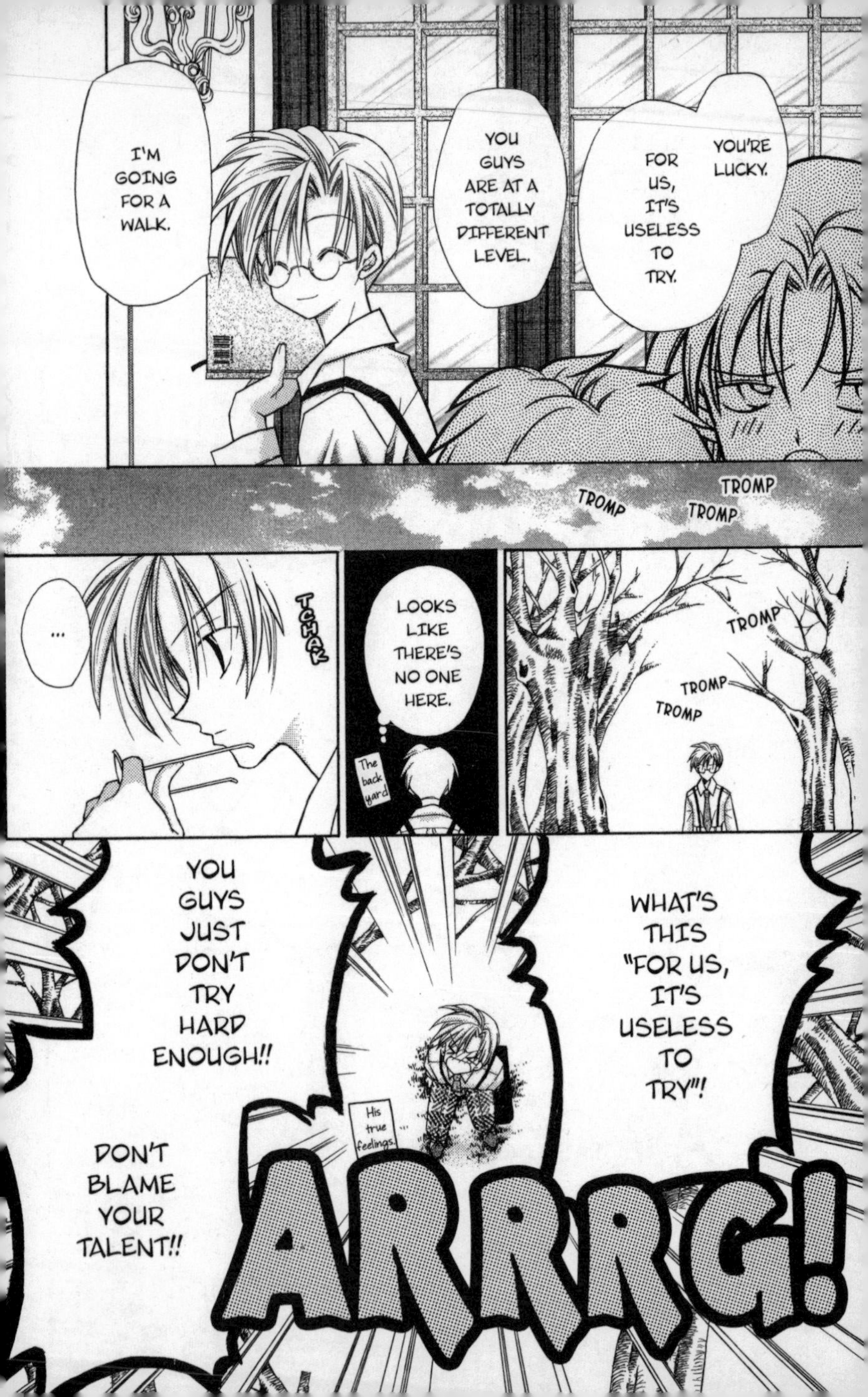
YOU'RE LUCKY.
FOR US, IT'S USELESS TO TRY.
YOU GUYS ARE AT A TOTALLY DIFFERENT LEVEL.
I'M GOING FOR A WALK.
TROMP
TROMP
TROMP
TROMP
TROMP
TROMP
The back yard
LOOKS LIKE THERE'S NO ONE HERE.
TCHAK
...
WHAT'S THIS "FOR US, IT'S USELESS TO TRY"!!
YOU GUYS JUST DON'T TRY HARD ENOUGH!!
His true feelings...
DON'T BLAME YOUR TALENT!!
ARRRG!

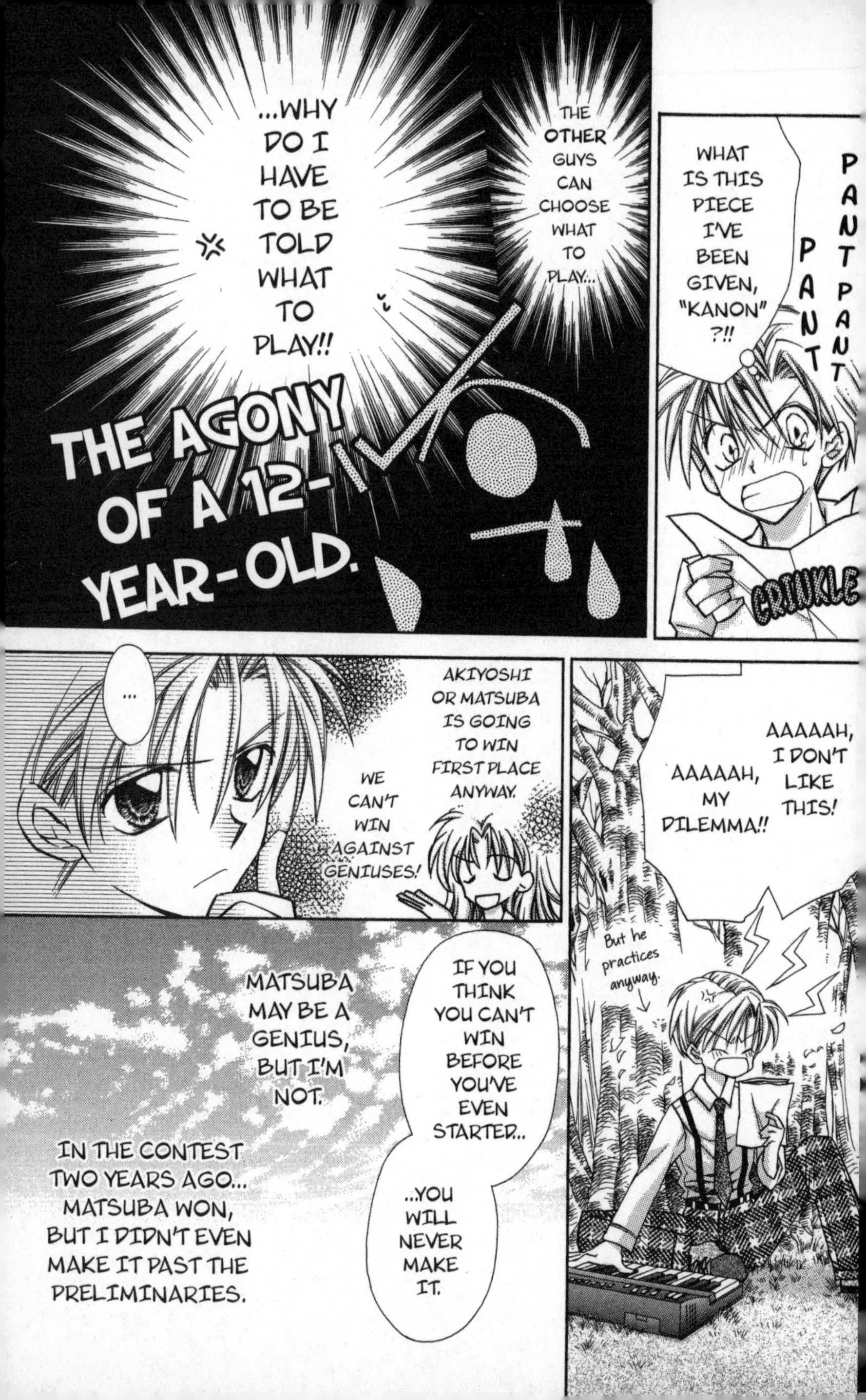
WHAT IS THIS PIECE I'VE BEEN GIVEN, "KANON" ?!!
PANT PANT
PANT PANT
CRINKLE
THE OTHER GUYS CAN CHOOSE WHAT TO PLAY...
...WHY DO I HAVE TO BE TOLD WHAT TO PLAY!!
THE AGONY OF A 12-YEAR-OLD.
AAAAAH, I DON'T LIKE THIS!
AAAAAH, MY DILEMMA!!
But he practices anyway.
AKIYOSHI OR MATSUBA IS GOING TO WIN FIRST PLACE ANYWAY.
WE CAN'T WIN AGAINST GENIUSES!
...
IF YOU THINK YOU CAN'T WIN BEFORE YOU'VE EVEN STARTED...
...YOU WILL NEVER MAKE IT.
MATSUBA MAY BE A GENIUS, BUT I'M NOT.
IN THE CONTEST TWO YEARS AGO... MATSUBA WON, BUT I DIDN'T EVEN MAKE IT PAST THE PRELIMINARIES.

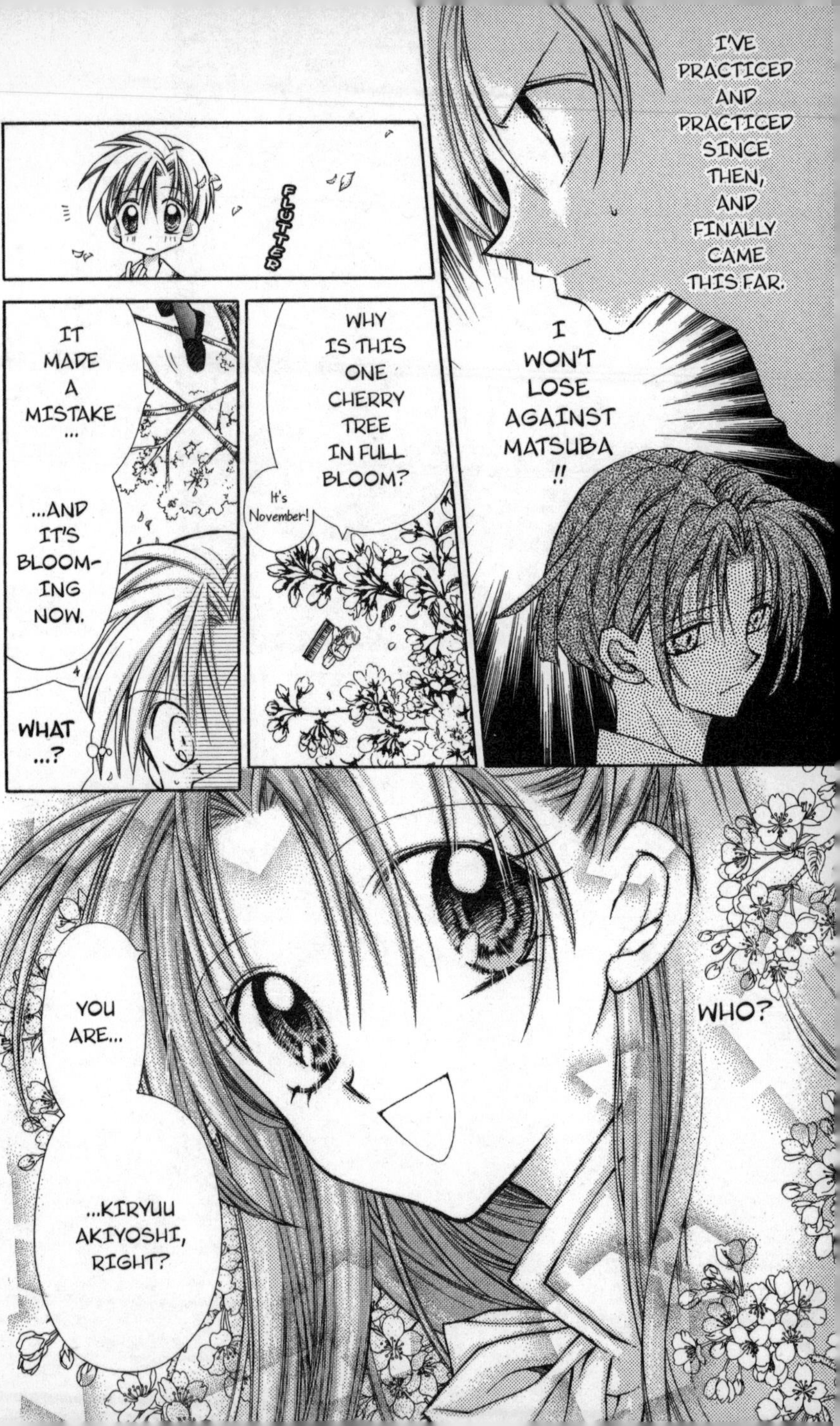
I'VE PRACTICED AND PRACTICED SINCE THEN, AND FINALLY CAME THIS FAR.
I WON'T LOSE AGAINST MATSUBA!!
FLUTTER
WHY IS THIS ONE CHERRY TREE IN FULL BLOOM?
It's November!
IT MADE A MISTAKE...
...AND IT'S BLOOMING NOW.
WHAT...?
WHO?
YOU ARE...
...KIRYUU AKIYOSHI, RIGHT?

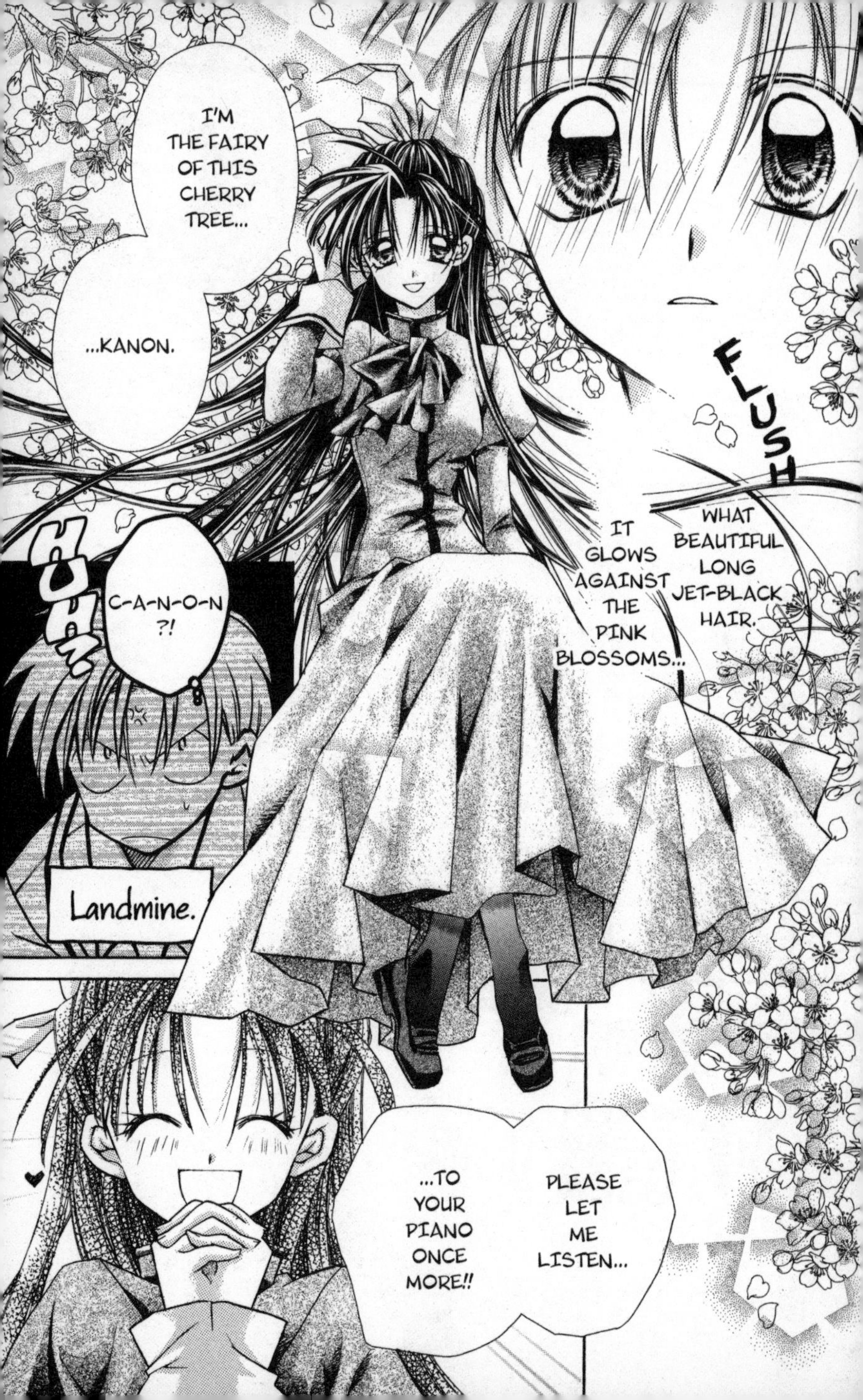
FLUSH
WHAT BEAUTIFUL LONG JET-BLACK HAIR.
IT GLOWS AGAINST THE PINK BLOSSOMS...
I'M THE FAIRY OF THIS CHERRY TREE...
...KANON.
HUH?!
C-A-N-O-N ?!
Landmine.
PLEASE LET ME LISTEN...
...TO YOUR PIANO ONCE MORE!!

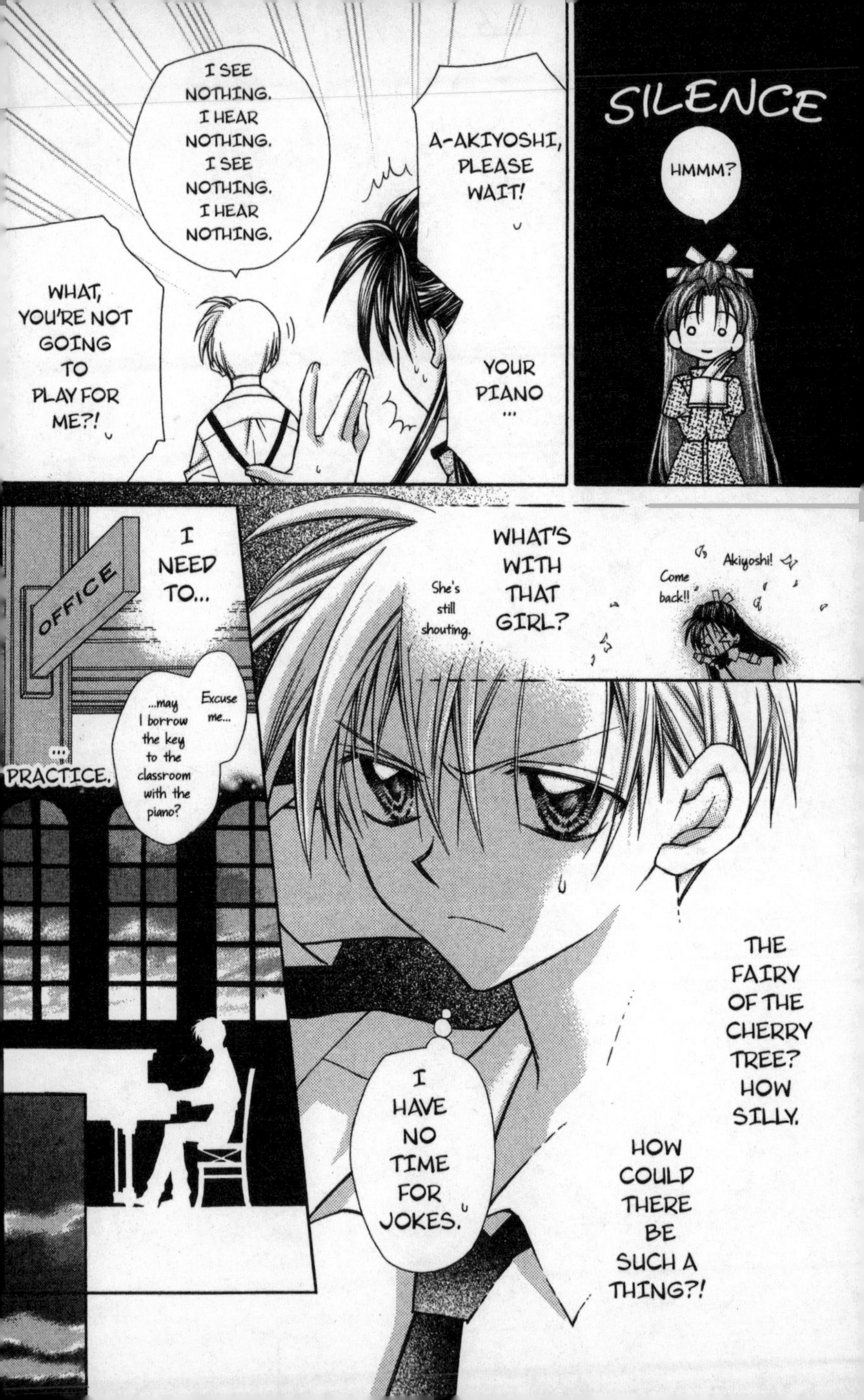
SILENCE
HMMM?
A-AKIYOSHI, PLEASE WAIT!
I SEE NOTHING. I HEAR NOTHING. I SEE NOTHING. I HEAR NOTHING.
YOUR PIANO ...
WHAT, YOU'RE NOT GOING TO PLAY FOR ME?!
Akiyoshi!
Come back!!
WHAT'S WITH THAT GIRL?
She's still shouting.
THE FAIRY OF THE CHERRY TREE? HOW SILLY.
HOW COULD THERE BE SUCH A THING?!
I HAVE NO TIME FOR JOKES.
I NEED TO...
OFFICE
Excuse me...
...may I borrow the key to the classroom with the piano?
... PRACTICE.

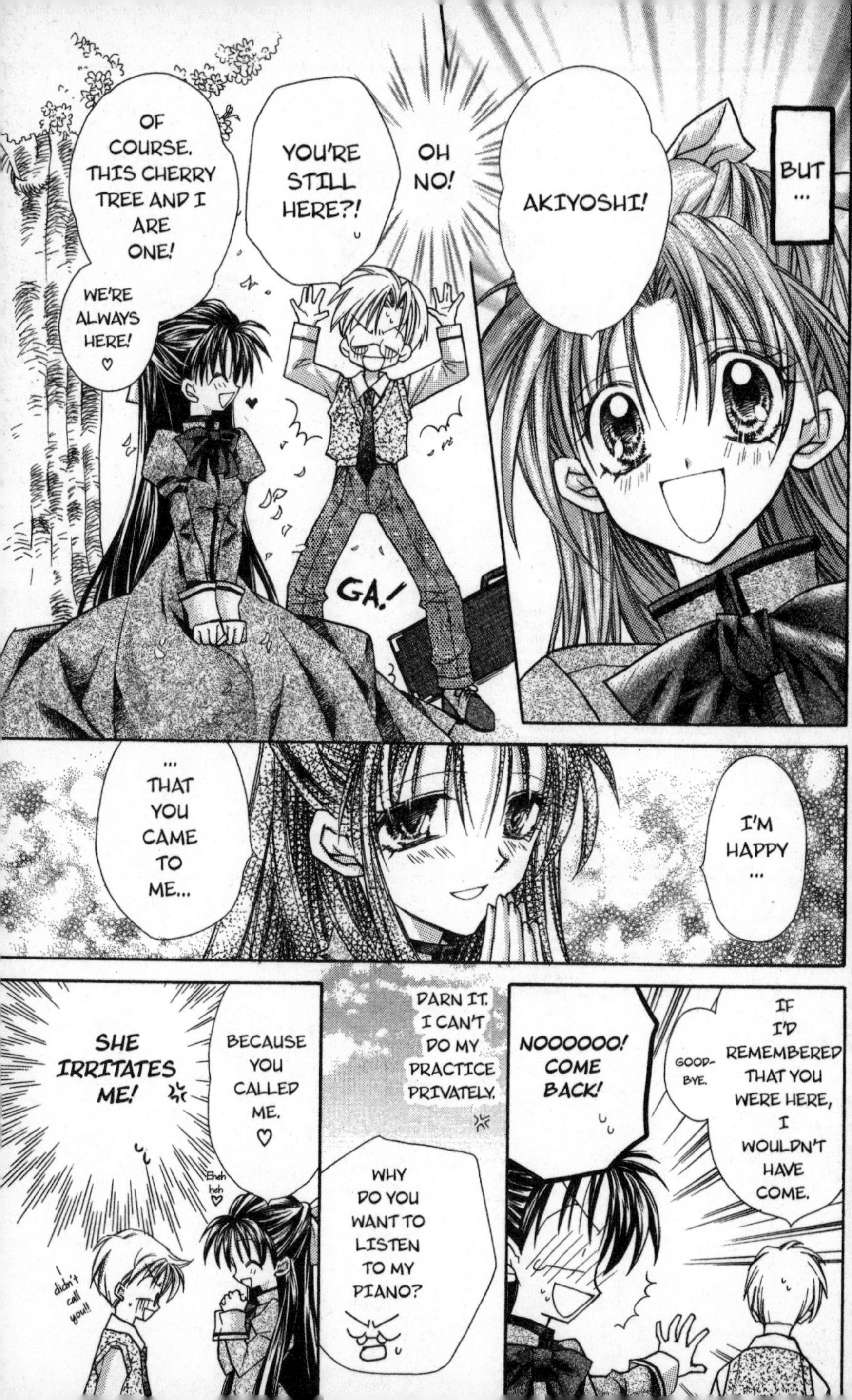
BUT ...
AKIYOSHI!
OH NO!
YOU'RE STILL HERE?!
OF COURSE. THIS CHERRY TREE AND I ARE ONE!
WE'RE ALWAYS HERE! ♡
GA!
I'M HAPPY ...
... THAT YOU CAME TO ME...
IF I'D REMEMBERED THAT YOU WERE HERE, I WOULDN'T HAVE COME.
GOOD-BYE.
NOOOOOO! COME BACK!
DARN IT. I CAN'T DO MY PRACTICE PRIVATELY.
WHY DO YOU WANT TO LISTEN TO MY PIANO?
BECAUSE YOU CALLED ME. ♡
SHE IRRITATES ME!
Eheh heh ♡
I didn't call you!!

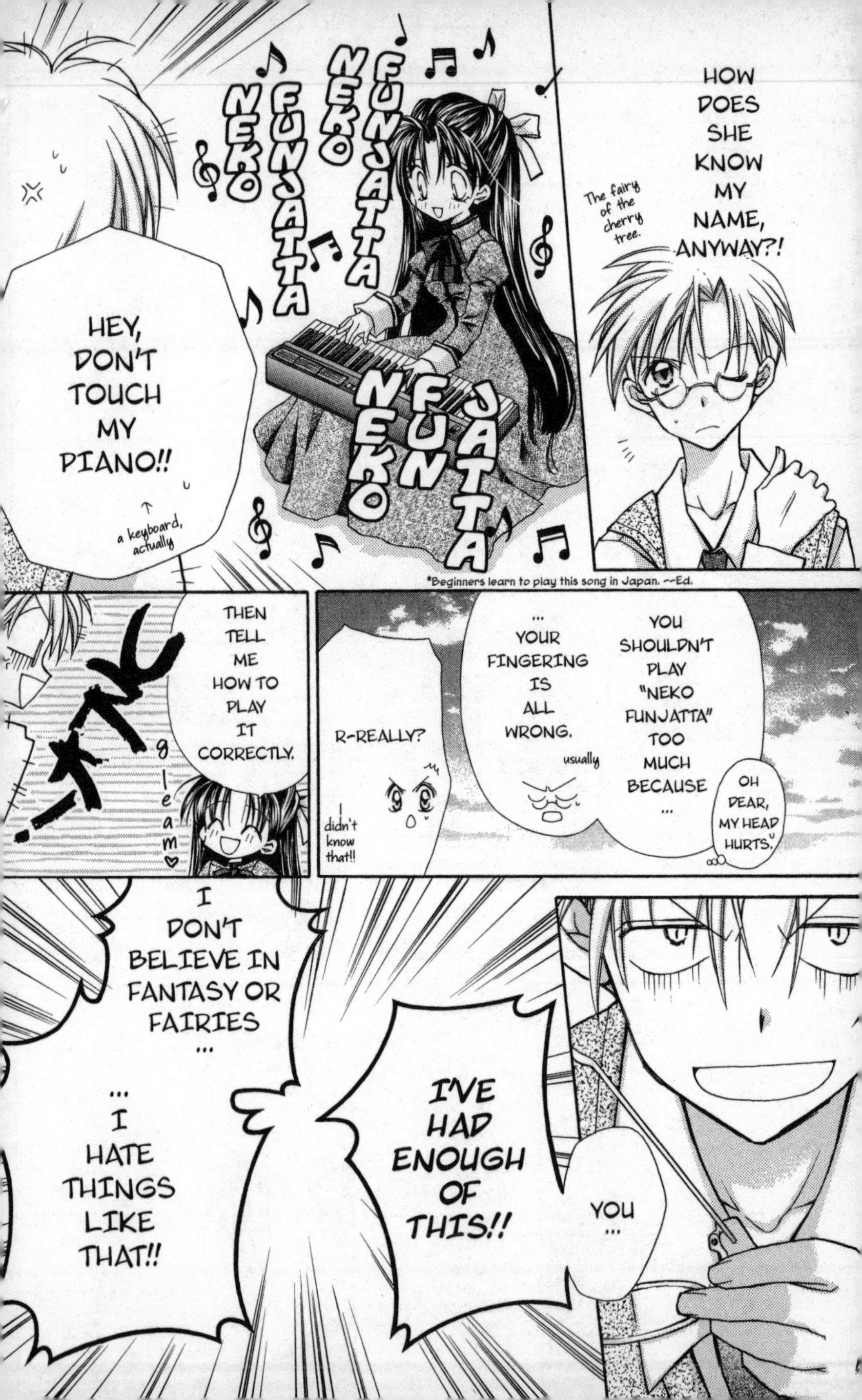
HOW DOES SHE KNOW MY NAME, ANYWAY?!
The fairy of the cherry tree.
NEKO FUNJATTA NEKO FUNJATTA
NEKO FUNJATTA
HEY, DON'T TOUCH MY PIANO!!
a keyboard, actually
YOU SHOULDN'T PLAY "NEKO FUNJATTA" TOO MUCH BECAUSE ...
... YOUR FINGERING IS ALL WRONG.
usually
OH DEAR, MY HEAD HURTS.
R-REALLY?
I didn't know that!!
THEN TELL ME HOW TO PLAY IT CORRECTLY.
gleam
YOU ...
I'VE HAD ENOUGH OF THIS!!
I DON'T BELIEVE IN FANTASY OR FAIRIES ...
... I HATE THINGS LIKE THAT!!

*Beginners learn to play this song in Japan. --Ed.

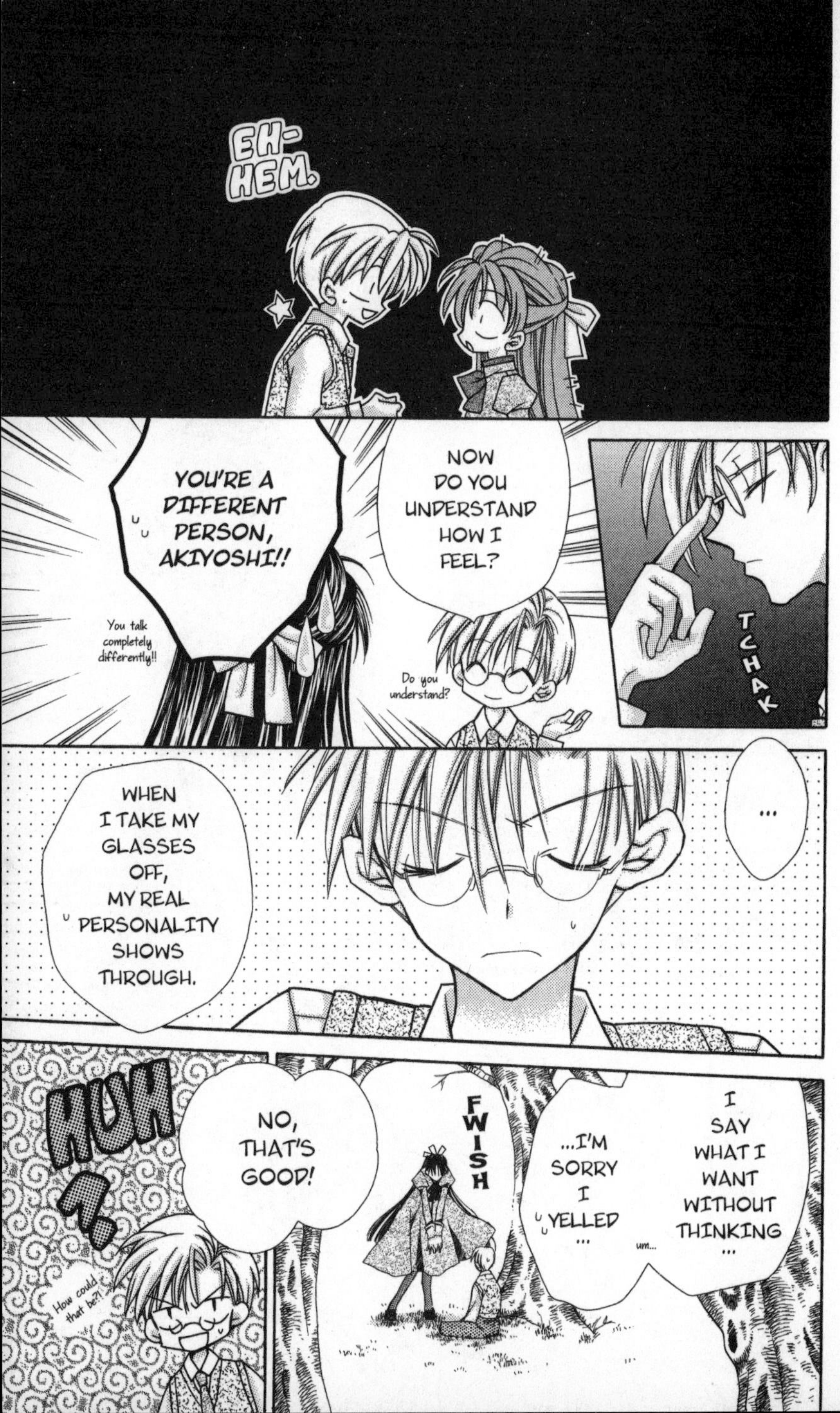
EH-HEM.
TCHAK
NOW DO YOU UNDERSTAND HOW I FEEL?
YOU'RE A DIFFERENT PERSON, AKIYOSHI!!
Do you understand?
You talk completely differently!!
...
WHEN I TAKE MY GLASSES OFF, MY REAL PERSONALITY SHOWS THROUGH.
I SAY WHAT I WANT WITHOUT THINKING...
...I'M SORRY I YELLED...
um...
FWISH
NO, THAT'S GOOD!
HUH?
How could that be?!

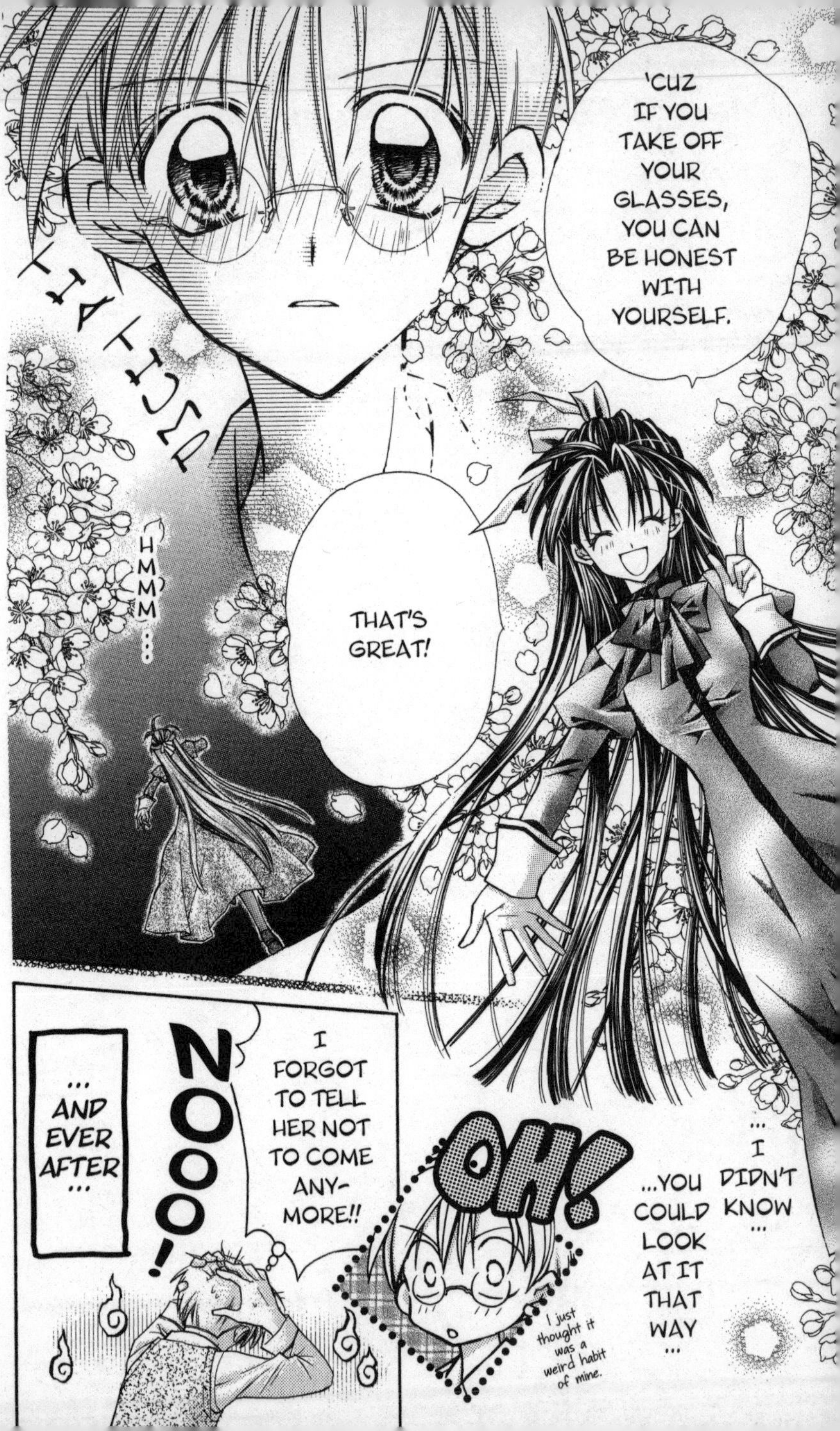
'CUZ IF YOU TAKE OFF YOUR GLASSES, YOU CAN BE HONEST WITH YOURSELF.
THAT'S GREAT!
HMMM...
... I DIDN'T KNOW ...
...YOU COULD LOOK AT IT THAT WAY ...
OH!
I just thought it was a weird habit of mine.
I FORGOT TO TELL HER NOT TO COME ANY-MORE!!
NOOOO!
... AND EVER AFTER ...

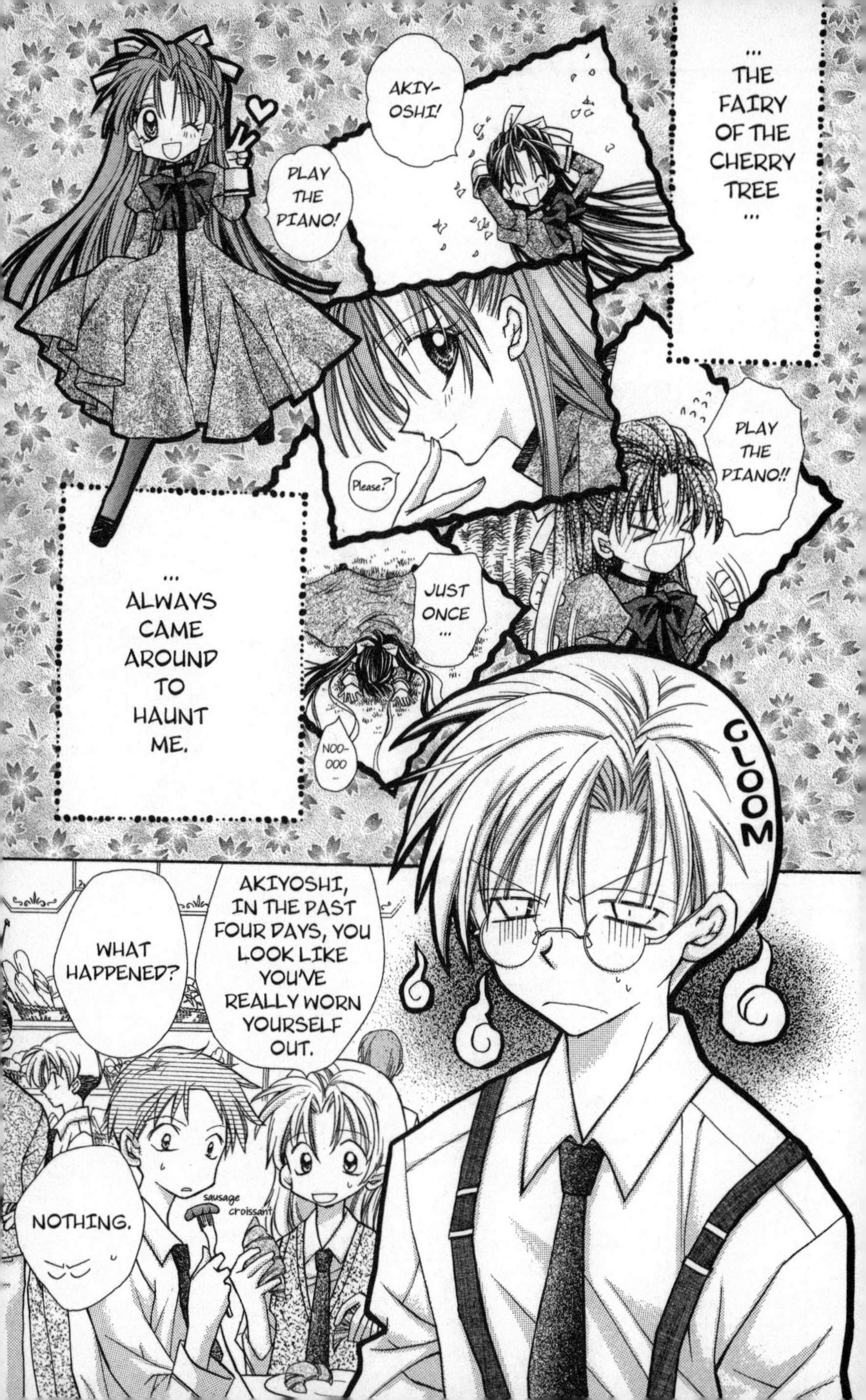
... THE FAIRY OF THE CHERRY TREE ...
AKIY-OSHI!
PLAY THE PIANO!
Please?
PLAY THE PIANO!!
JUST ONCE ...
NOO-OOO ...
... ALWAYS CAME AROUND TO HAUNT ME.
GLOOM
AKIYOSHI, IN THE PAST FOUR DAYS, YOU LOOK LIKE YOU'VE REALLY WORN YOURSELF OUT.
WHAT HAPPENED?
sausage
croissant
NOTHING.

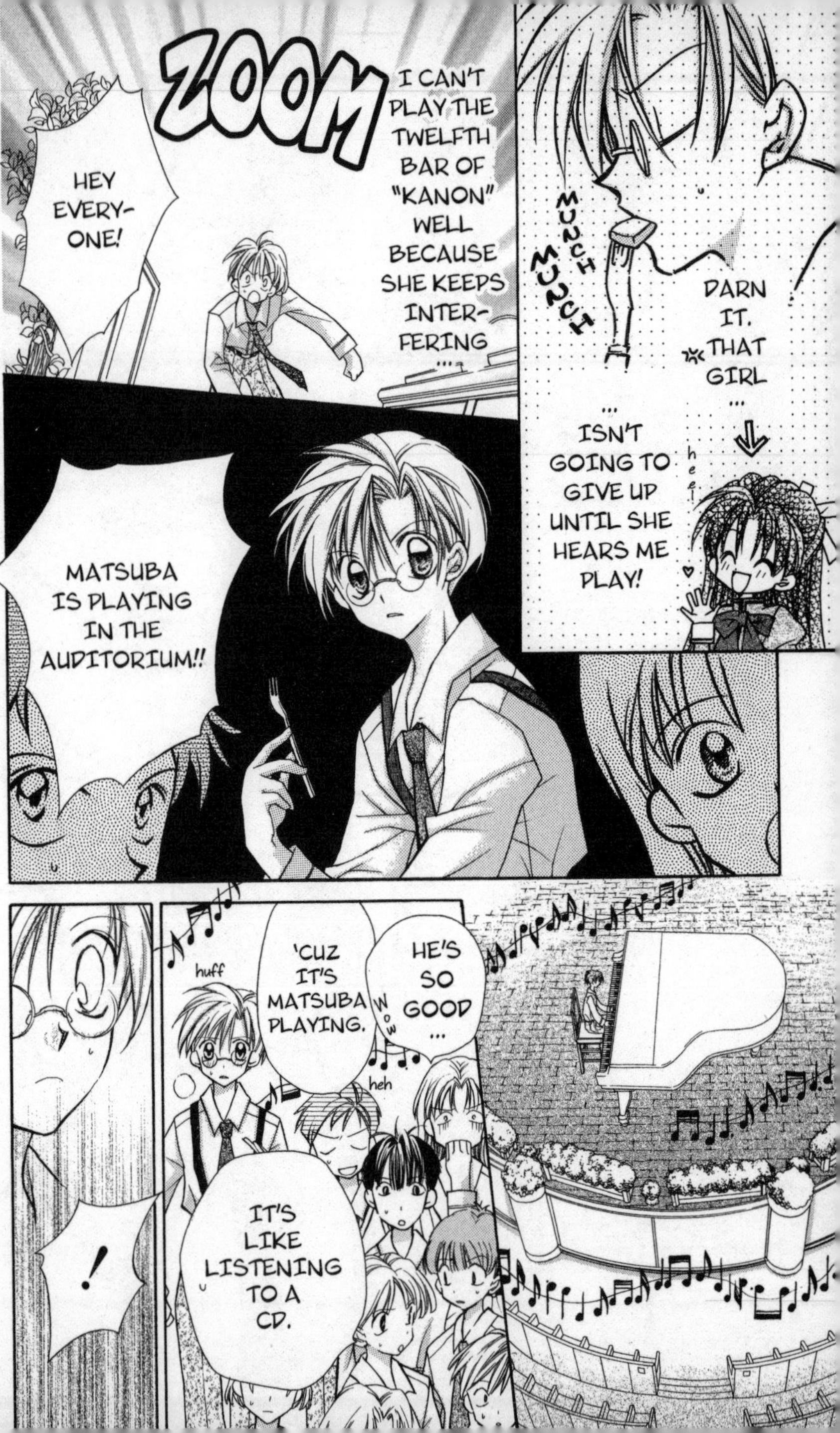
MUNCH MUNCH
DARN IT. THAT GIRL...
...ISN'T GOING TO GIVE UP UNTIL SHE HEARS ME PLAY!
heel
I CAN'T PLAY THE TWELFTH BAR OF "KANON" WELL BECAUSE SHE KEEPS INTERFERING...
ZOOM
HEY EVERYONE!
MATSUBA IS PLAYING IN THE AUDITORIUM!!
HE'S SO GOOD...
wow
'CUZ IT'S MATSUBA PLAYING.
huff
heh
IT'S LIKE LISTENING TO A CD.
!

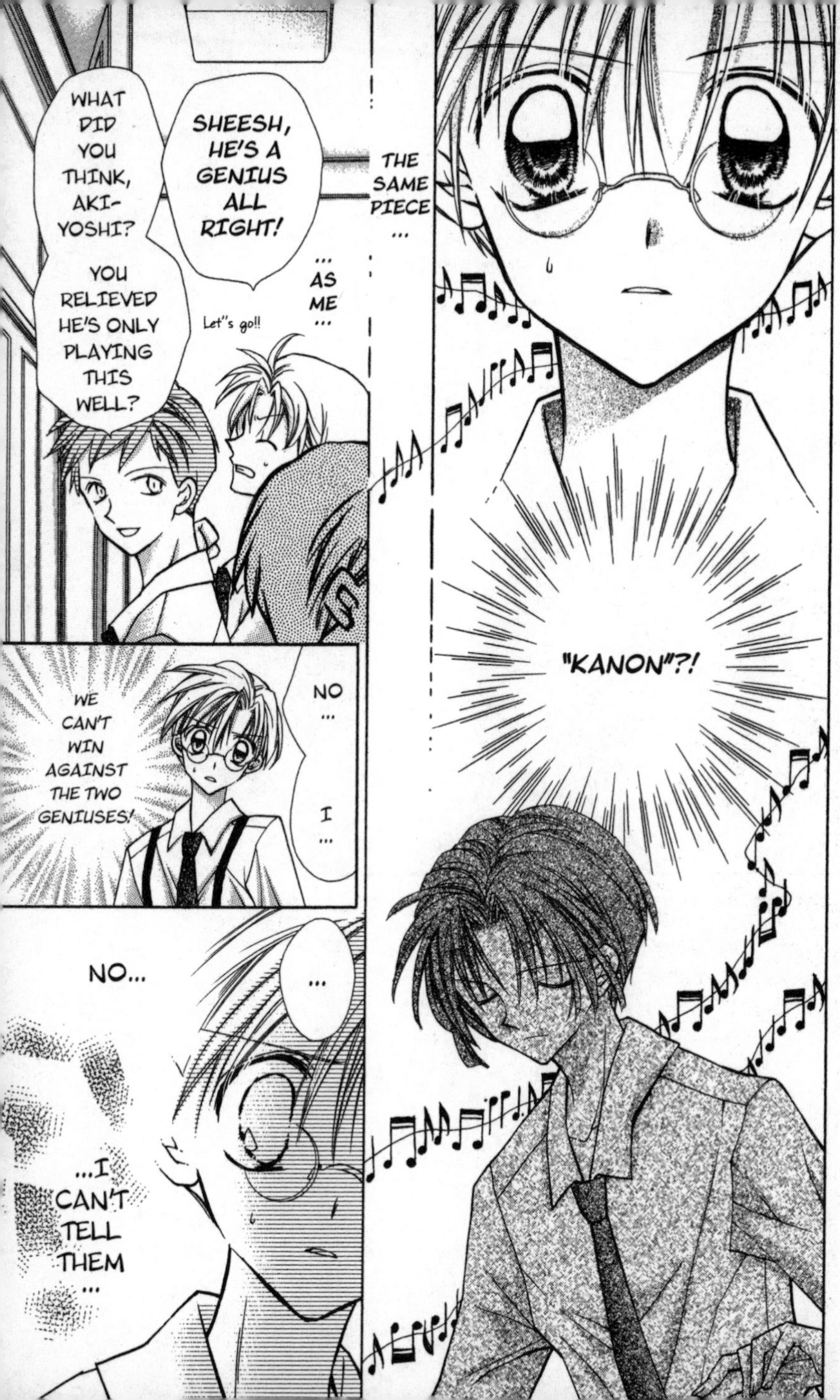
THE SAME PIECE ...
... AS ME ...
"KANON"?!
SHEESH, HE'S A GENIUS ALL RIGHT!
WHAT DID YOU THINK, AKI-YOSHI?
YOU RELIEVED HE'S ONLY PLAYING THIS WELL?
Let''s go!!
NO ...
I ...
WE CAN'T WIN AGAINST THE TWO GENIUSES!
...
NO...
...I CAN'T TELL THEM ...

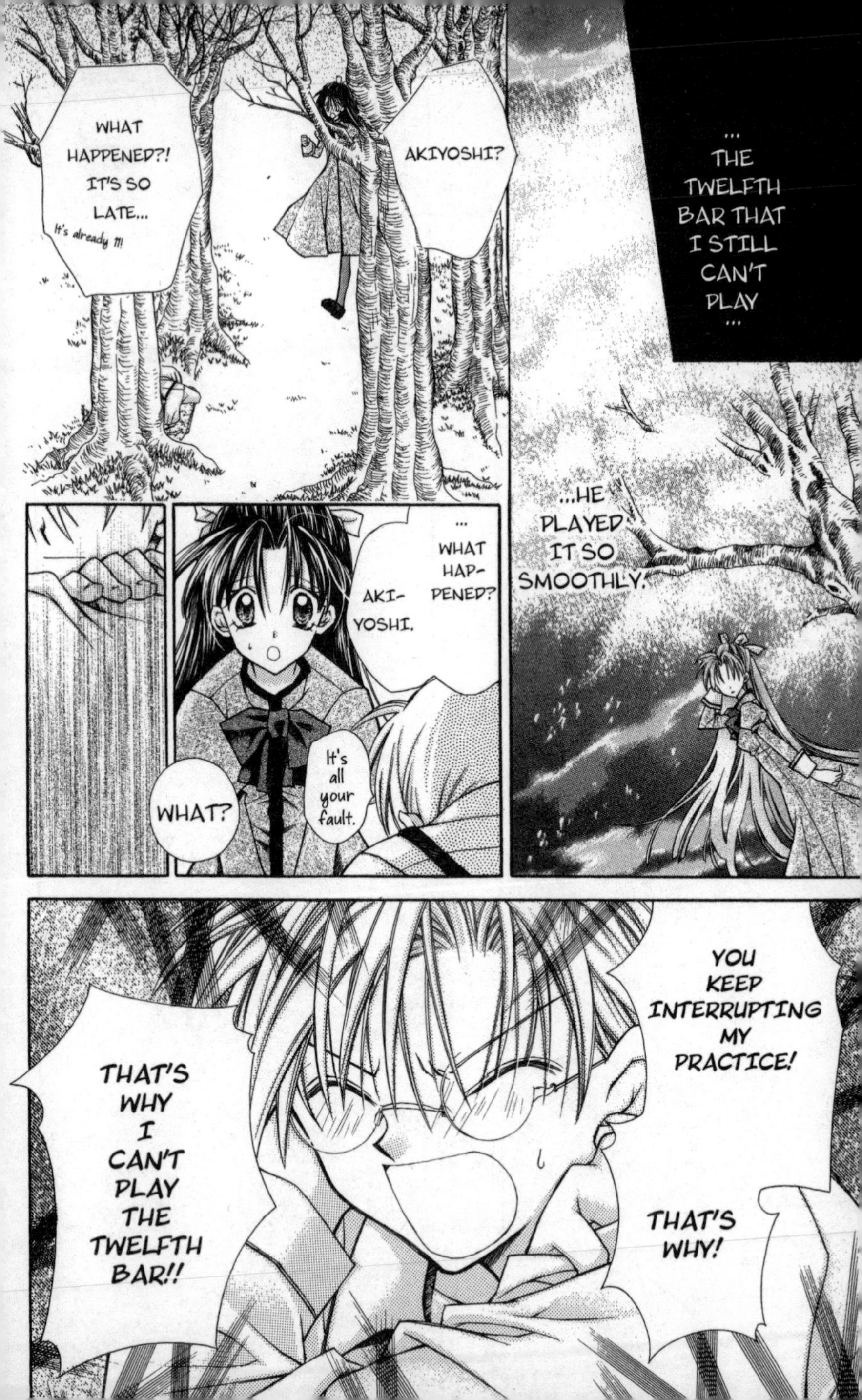
... THE TWELFTH BAR THAT I STILL CAN'T PLAY ...
...HE PLAYED IT SO SMOOTHLY.
AKIYOSHI?
WHAT HAPPENED?! IT'S SO LATE...
It's already 11!
... WHAT HAPPENED?
AKIYOSHI.
It's all your fault.
WHAT?
YOU KEEP INTERRUPTING MY PRACTICE!
THAT'S WHY!
THAT'S WHY I CAN'T PLAY THE TWELFTH BAR!!

●Gin-yu Meika●

I put many things that I love into this work. Cherry trees, a girl with long hair, a boy who's a bit sensitive (an artist!) Even now it's an important work and I love it. When the work first appeared in the magazine, there were some problems with it, so I was thinking about giving up putting the work out in book form. But due to the warm encouragement(?) of my assistants and the Ribon editorial staff (J), I re-drew parts of the work and now it's out in book form. I'm very happy about this.

I made up the title, so there is no four-kanji word that's like this. Meika has the meanings "beautiful flower" and "beautiful woman." Gin-yu...I couldn't find out the formal meaning, so I'll pass on that. I used it...to put it in a roundabout way, as "sing" or "put it in melody."

The story is about two very opposite persons meeting, and growing closer together by admiring the other person, a simple one. It was four and a half years since I last drew a one-shot manga, and I was determined to show my skills, but when I draw like that, I can't draw well. So I drew it thinking it's okay even if I haven't gotten better, I'll just draw what I want to draw! The cover illustration is simple, but I like it. I put my heart into drawing the creases of the skirt. I drew the main lines using a mechanical pencil. It was only one work, but I love Kanon-chan.

And Akiyoshi-kun.

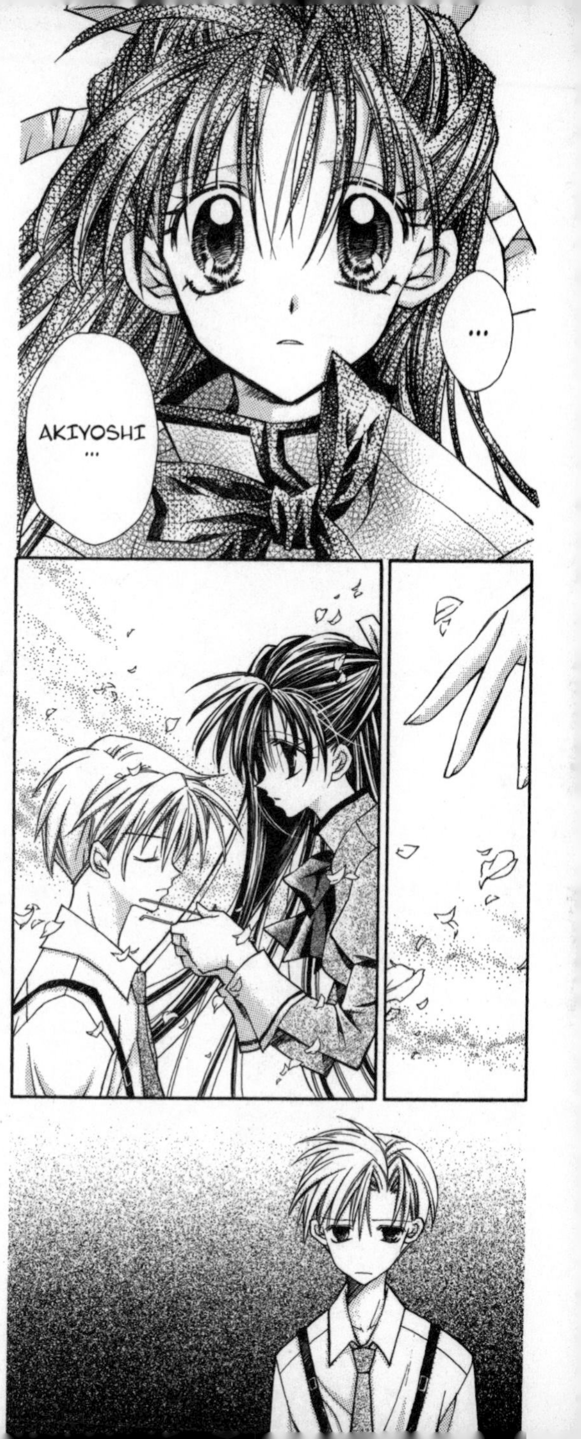
...
AKIYOSHI ...

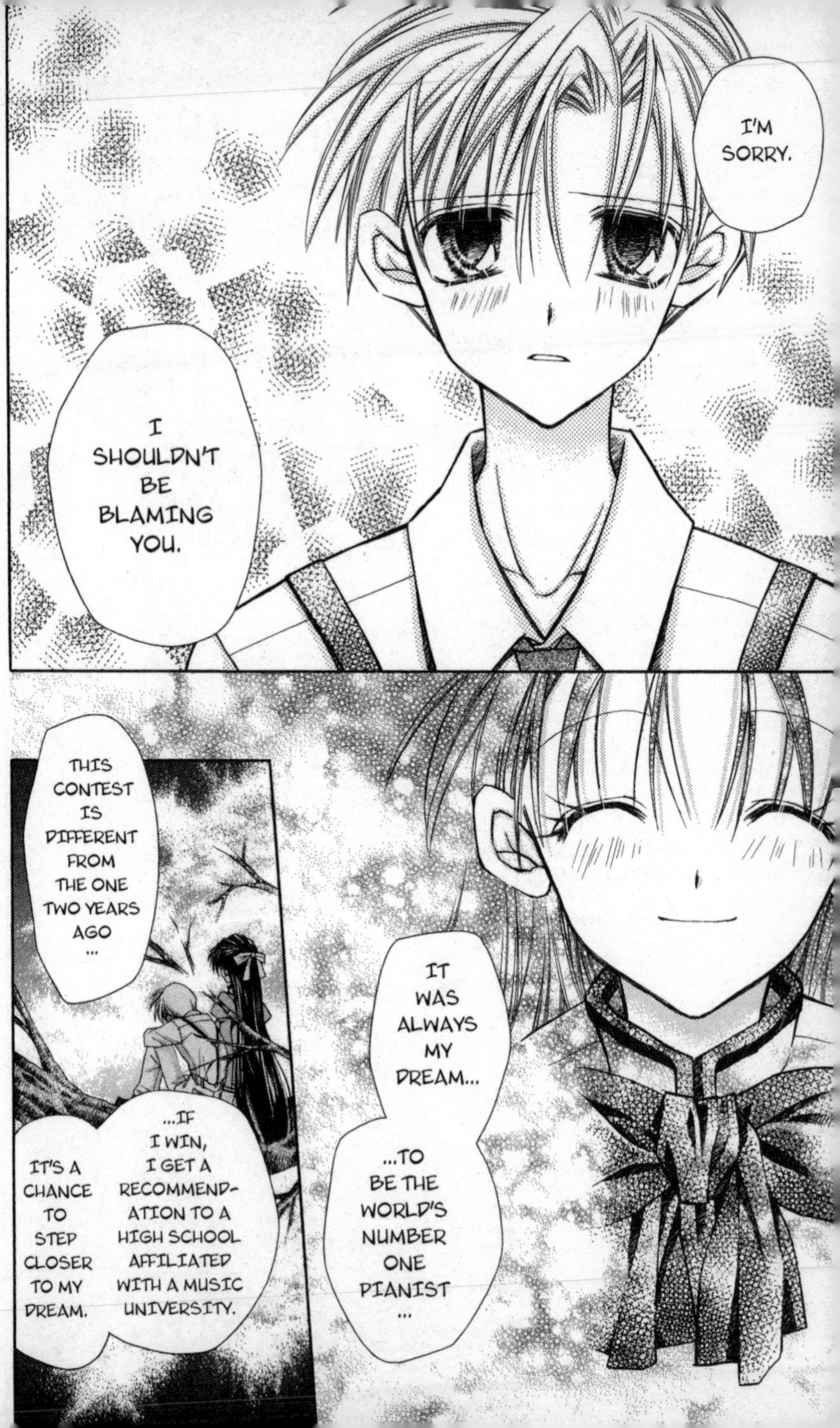
I'M SORRY.
I SHOULDN'T BE BLAMING YOU.
IT WAS ALWAYS MY DREAM...
...TO BE THE WORLD'S NUMBER ONE PIANIST ...
THIS CONTEST IS DIFFERENT FROM THE ONE TWO YEARS AGO ...
...IF I WIN, I GET A RECOMMEND-ATION TO A HIGH SCHOOL AFFILIATED WITH A MUSIC UNIVERSITY.
IT'S A CHANCE TO STEP CLOSER TO MY DREAM.

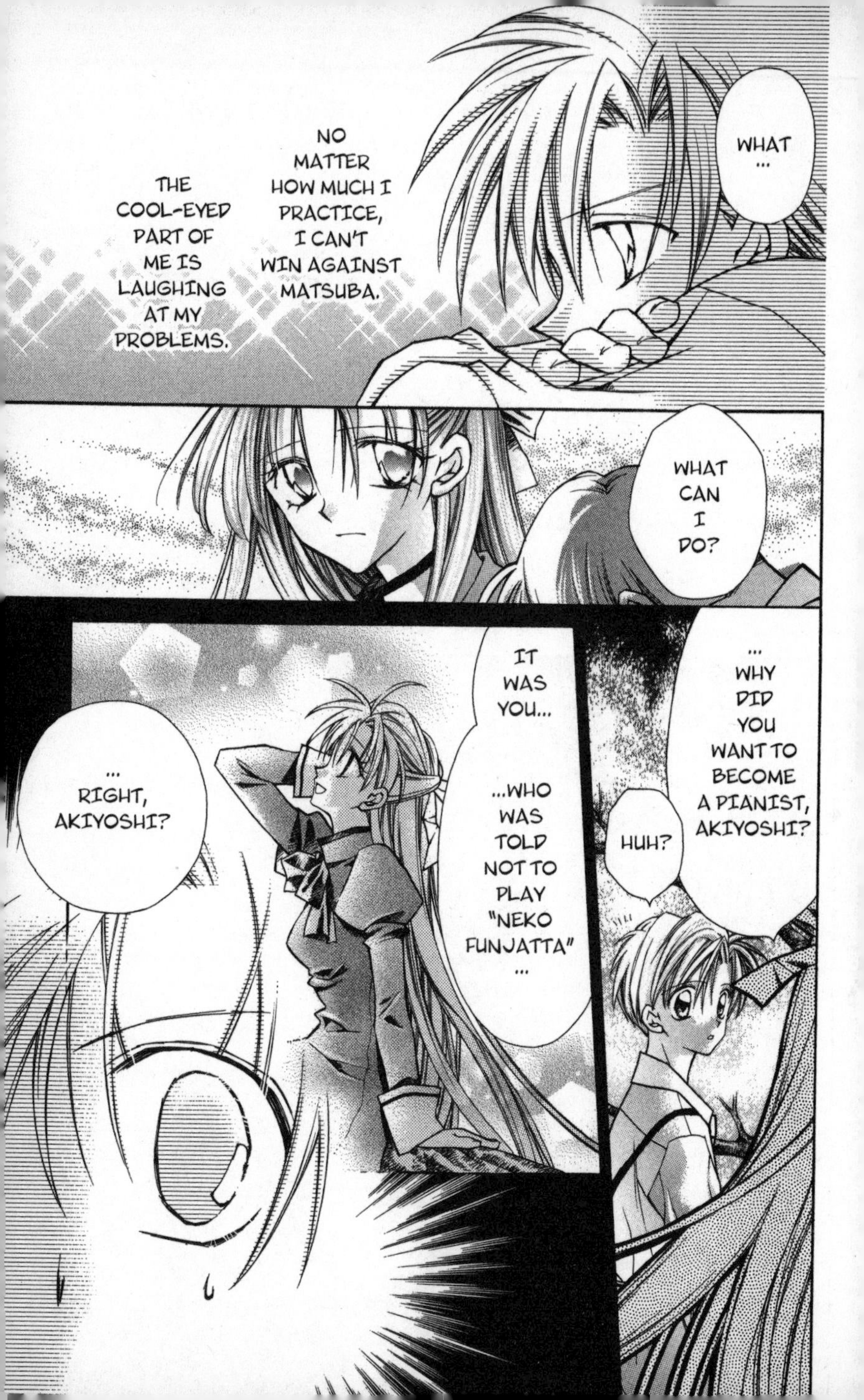
WHAT ...
NO MATTER HOW MUCH I PRACTICE, I CAN'T WIN AGAINST MATSUBA.
THE COOL-EYED PART OF ME IS LAUGHING AT MY PROBLEMS.
WHAT CAN I DO?
... WHY DID YOU WANT TO BECOME A PIANIST, AKIYOSHI?
HUH?
IT WAS YOU...
...WHO WAS TOLD NOT TO PLAY "NEKO FUNJATTA" ...
... RIGHT, AKIYOSHI?

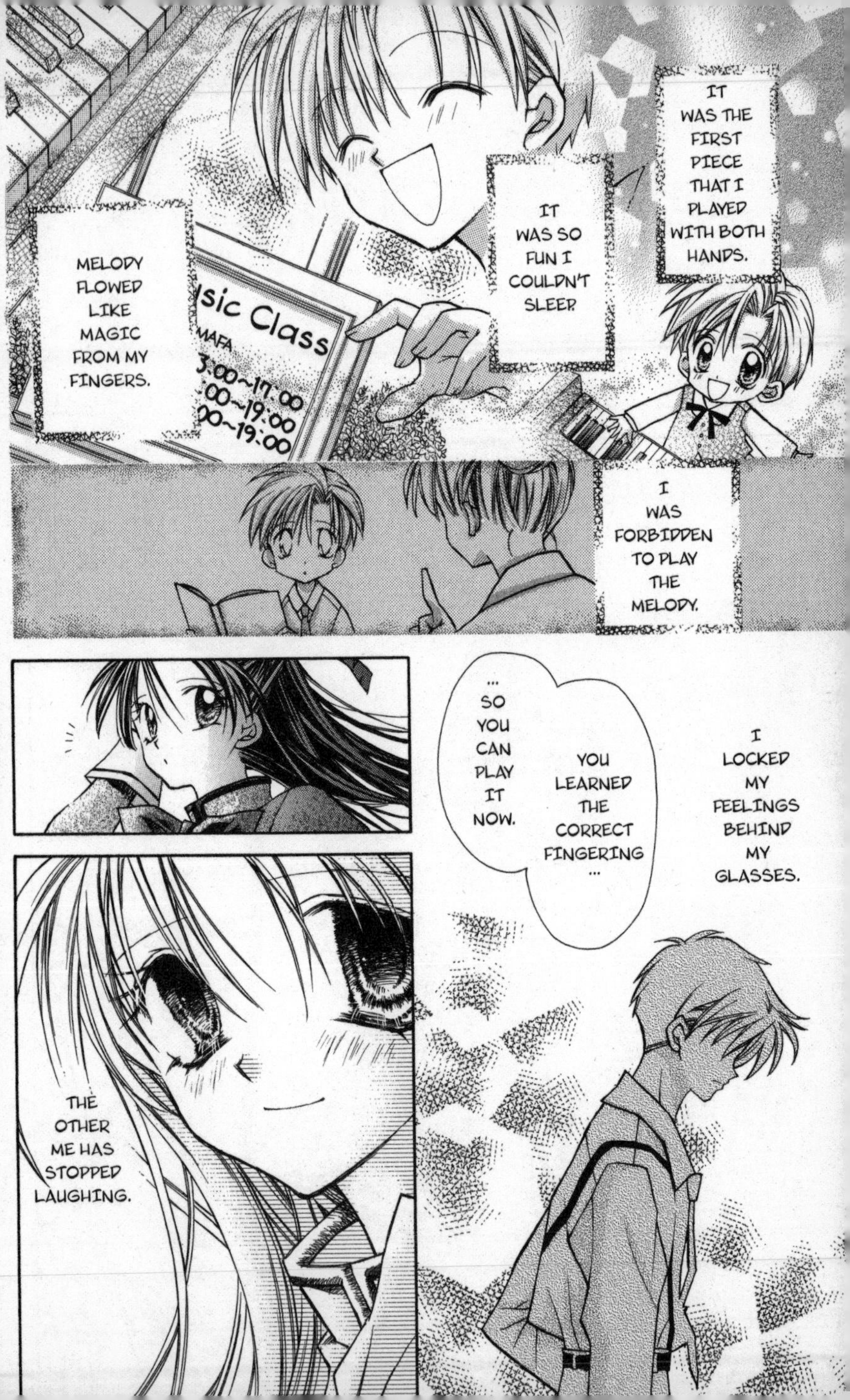
IT WAS THE FIRST PIECE THAT I PLAYED WITH BOTH HANDS.
IT WAS SO FUN I COULDN'T SLEEP.
MELODY FLOWED LIKE MAGIC FROM MY FINGERS.
I WAS FORBIDDEN TO PLAY THE MELODY.
I LOCKED MY FEELINGS BEHIND MY GLASSES.
YOU LEARNED THE CORRECT FINGERING ...
... SO YOU CAN PLAY IT NOW.
THE OTHER ME HAS STOPPED LAUGHING.

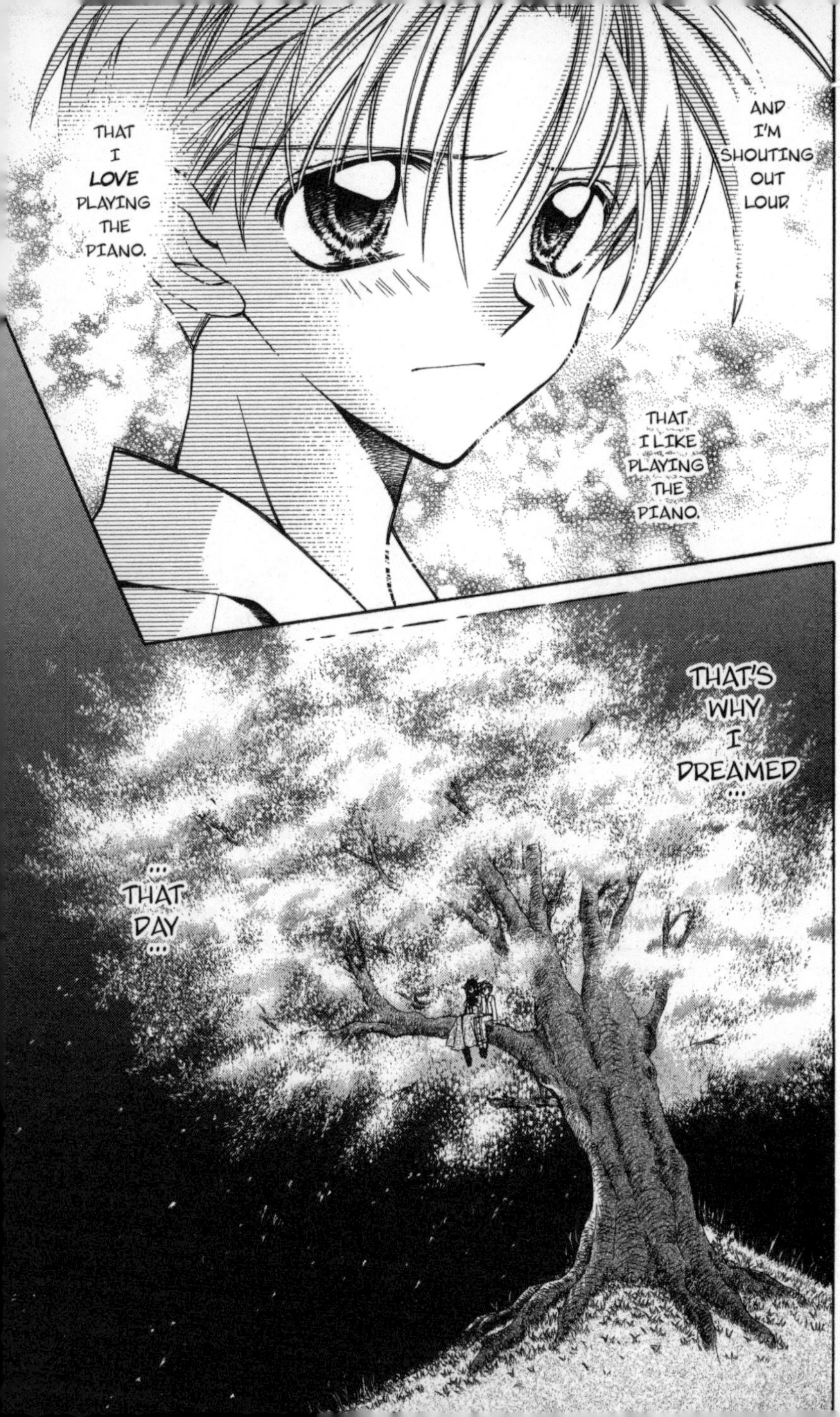
AND I'M SHOUTING OUT LOUD
THAT I LIKE PLAYING THE PIANO.
THAT I **LOVE** PLAYING THE PIANO.
THAT'S WHY I DREAMED...
...THAT DAY...

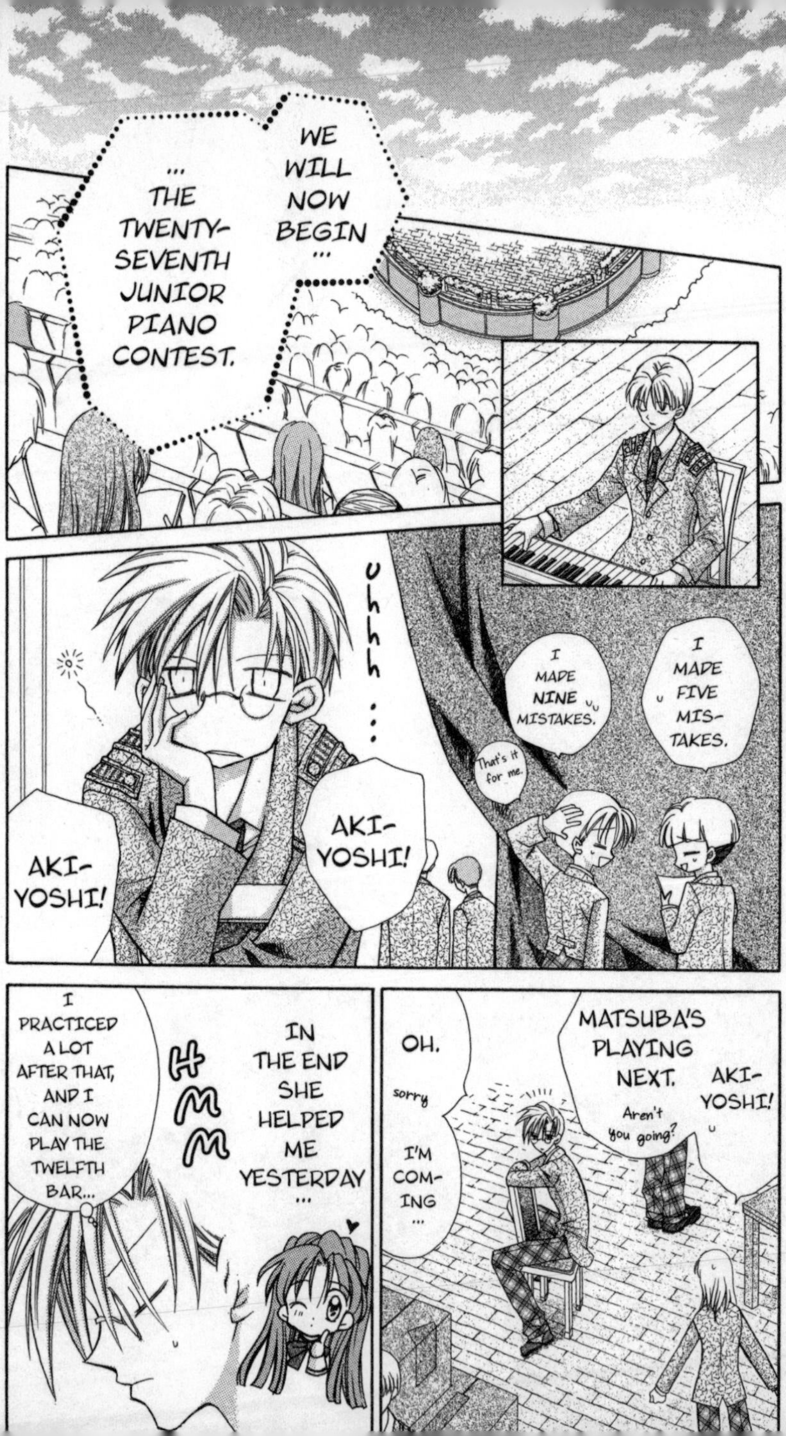
WE WILL NOW BEGIN ...
... THE TWENTY-SEVENTH JUNIOR PIANO CONTEST.
I MADE FIVE MIS-TAKES.
I MADE NINE MISTAKES.
That's it for me.
Uhhh ...
AKI-YOSHI!
AKI-YOSHI!
AKI-YOSHI!
MATSUBA'S PLAYING NEXT.
Aren't you going?
OH.
sorry
I'M COM-ING ...
IN THE END SHE HELPED ME YESTERDAY ...
HMM
I PRACTICED A LOT AFTER THAT, AND I CAN NOW PLAY THE TWELFTH BAR...

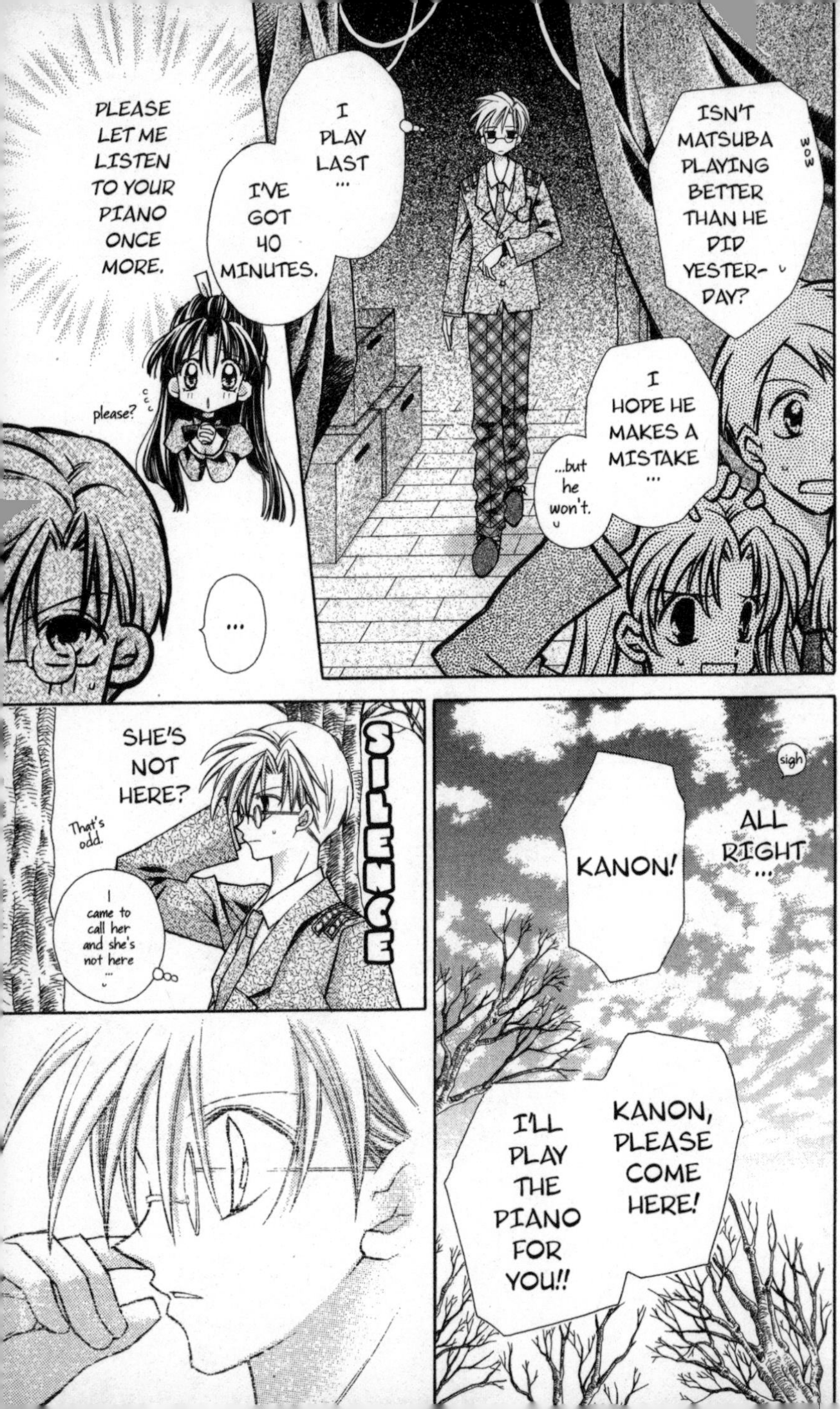
ISN'T MATSUBA PLAYING BETTER THAN HE DID YESTERDAY?
WOW
I PLAY LAST...
I'VE GOT 40 MINUTES.
I HOPE HE MAKES A MISTAKE...
...but he won't.
PLEASE LET ME LISTEN TO YOUR PIANO ONCE MORE.
please?
...
sigh
ALL RIGHT...
KANON!
KANON, PLEASE COME HERE!
I'LL PLAY THE PIANO FOR YOU!!
SHE'S NOT HERE?
That's odd.
SILENCE
I came to call her and she's not here...

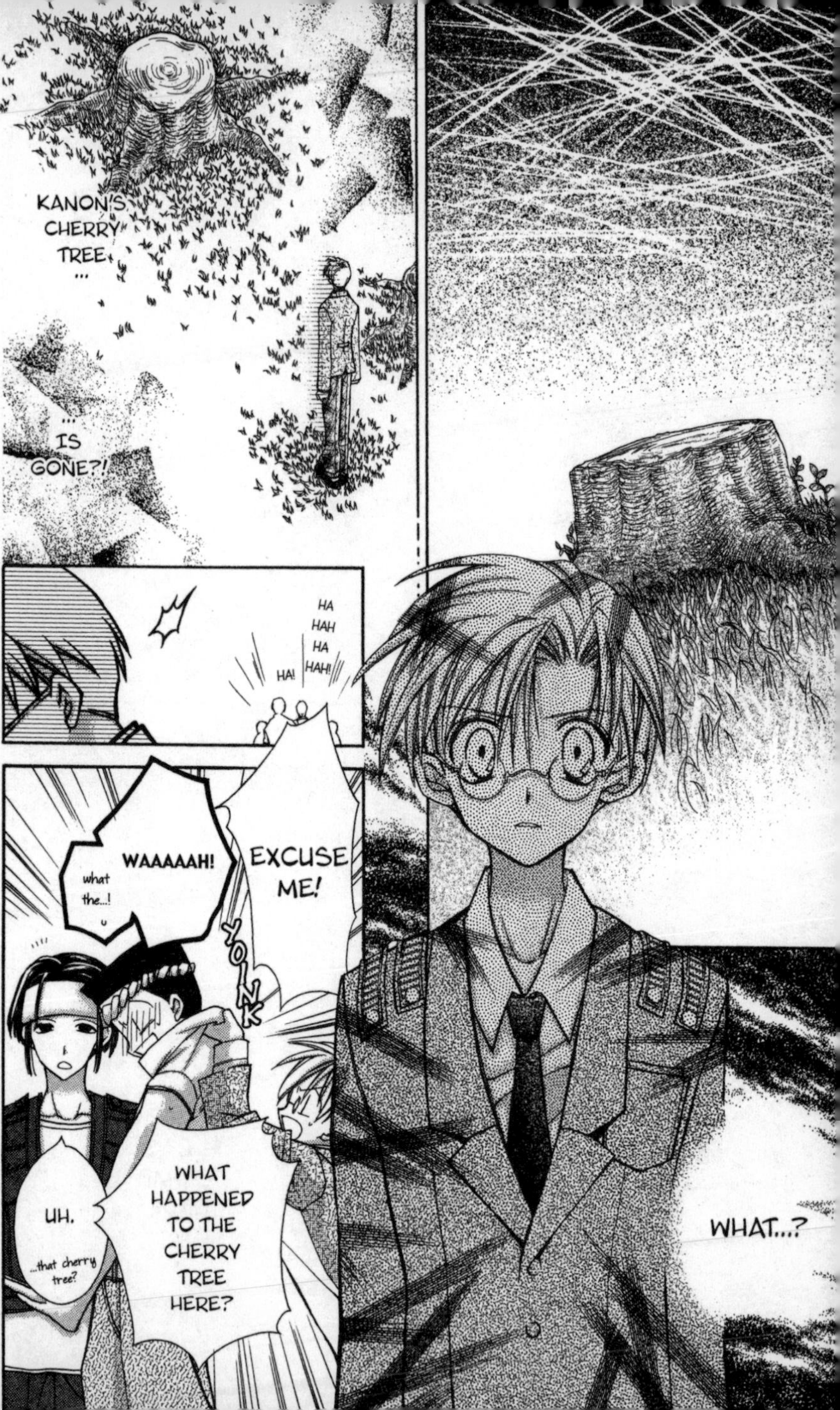
WHAT...?
KANON'S CHERRY TREE ...
... IS GONE?!
HA HAH HA HAH!
HA!
EXCUSE ME!
WAAAAAH!
what the...!
YOINK
WHAT HAPPENED TO THE CHERRY TREE HERE?
UH.
...that cherry tree?

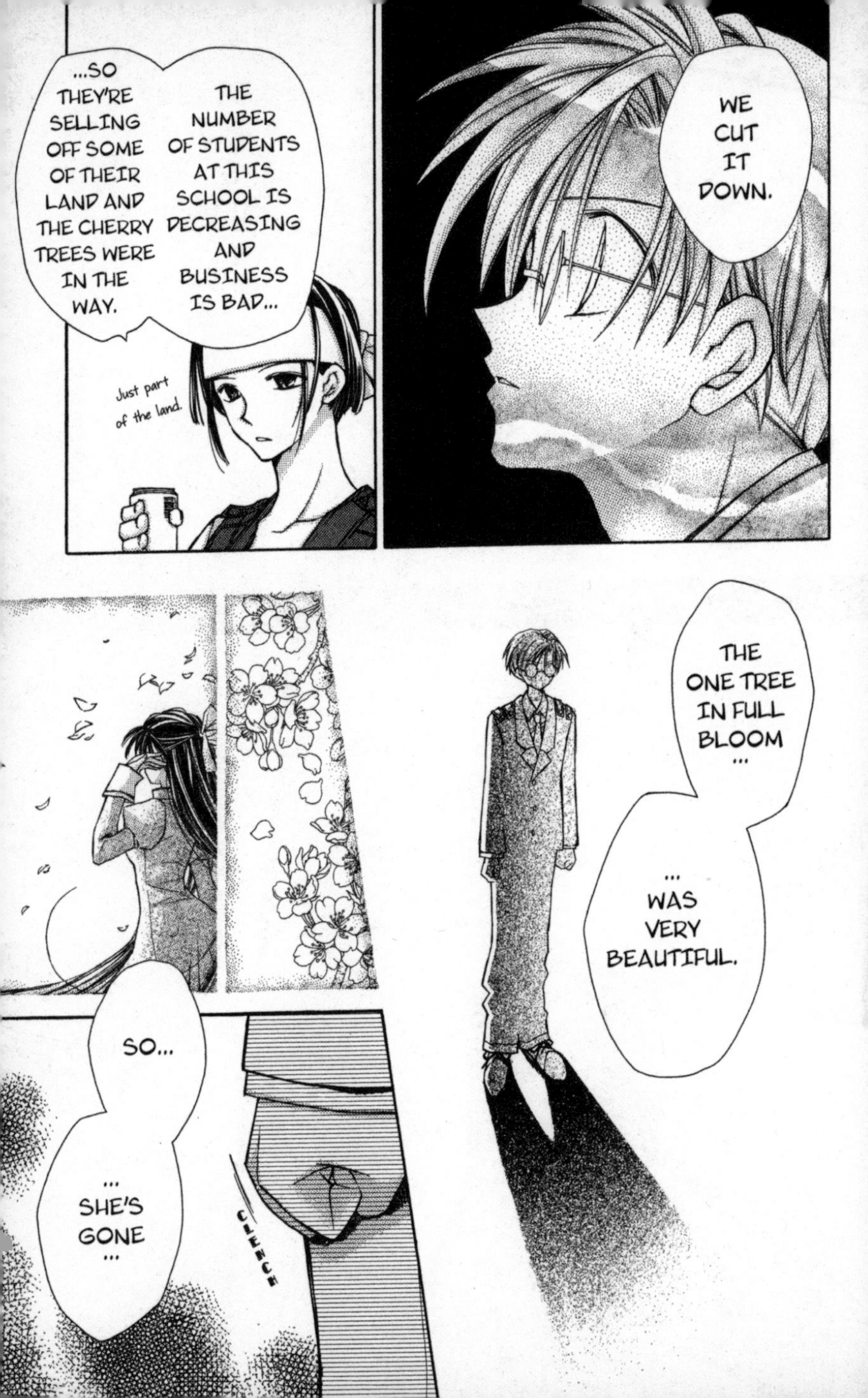
WE CUT IT DOWN.
THE NUMBER OF STUDENTS AT THIS SCHOOL IS DECREASING AND BUSINESS IS BAD...
...SO THEY'RE SELLING OFF SOME OF THEIR LAND AND THE CHERRY TREES WERE IN THE WAY.
Just part of the land.
THE ONE TREE IN FULL BLOOM ...
... WAS VERY BEAUTIFUL.
SO...
... SHE'S GONE ...
CLENCH

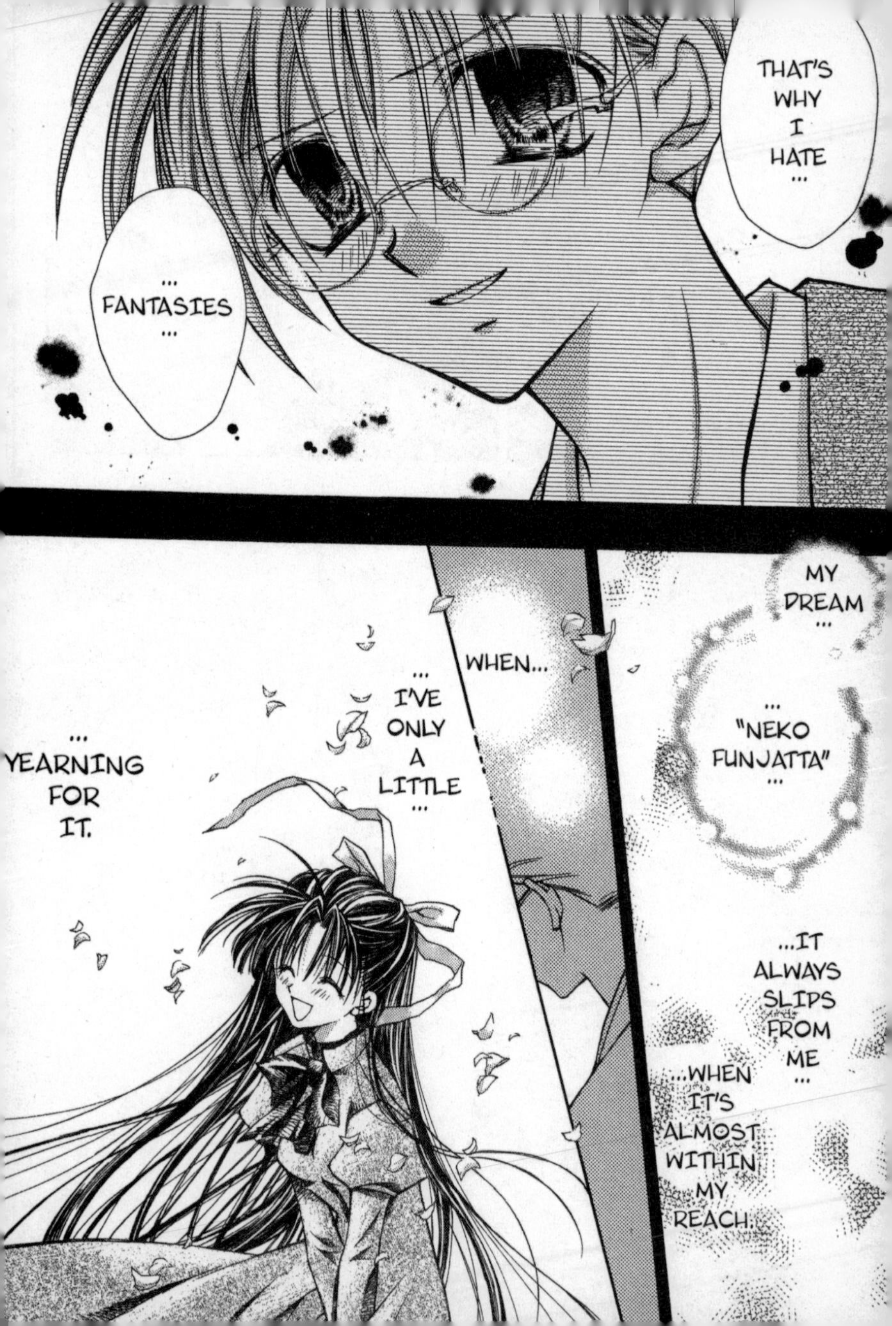
THAT'S WHY I HATE ...
... FANTASIES ...
MY DREAM ...
... "NEKO FUNJATTA" ...
...IT ALWAYS SLIPS FROM ME ...
...WHEN IT'S ALMOST WITHIN MY REACH.
WHEN...
... I'VE ONLY A LITTLE ...
... YEARNING FOR IT.

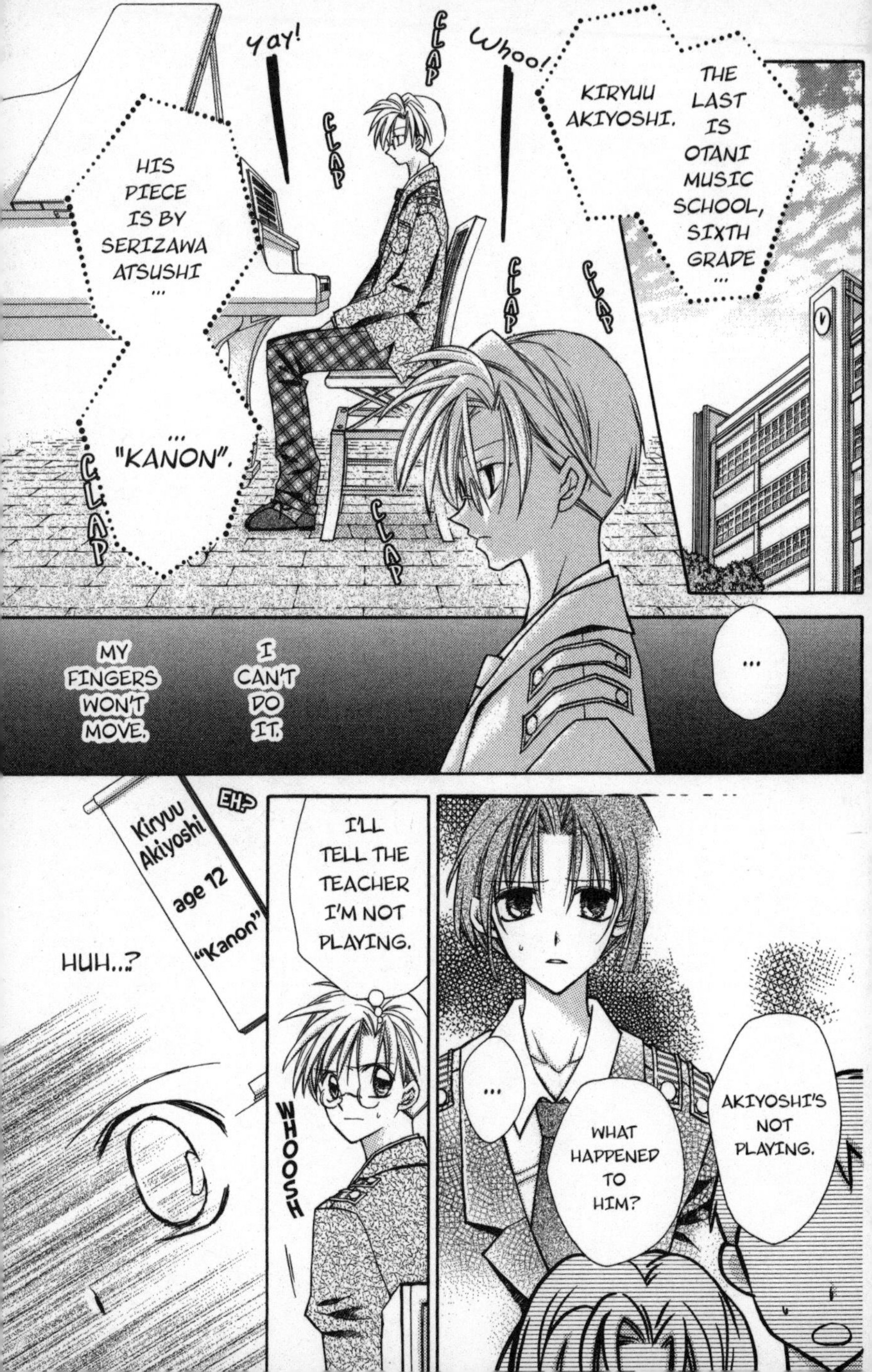
THE LAST IS OTANI MUSIC SCHOOL, SIXTH GRADE ...
KIRYUU AKIYOSHI.
Whoo!
CLAP
yay!
CLAP
HIS PIECE IS BY SERIZAWA ATSUSHI ...
... "KANON".
CLAP
CLAP
CLAP
CLAP
...
I CAN'T DO IT.
MY FINGERS WON'T MOVE.
AKIYOSHI'S NOT PLAYING.
WHAT HAPPENED TO HIM?
...
I'LL TELL THE TEACHER I'M NOT PLAYING.
WHOOSH
EH?
Kiryuu Akiyoshi age 12 "Kanon"
HUH..?

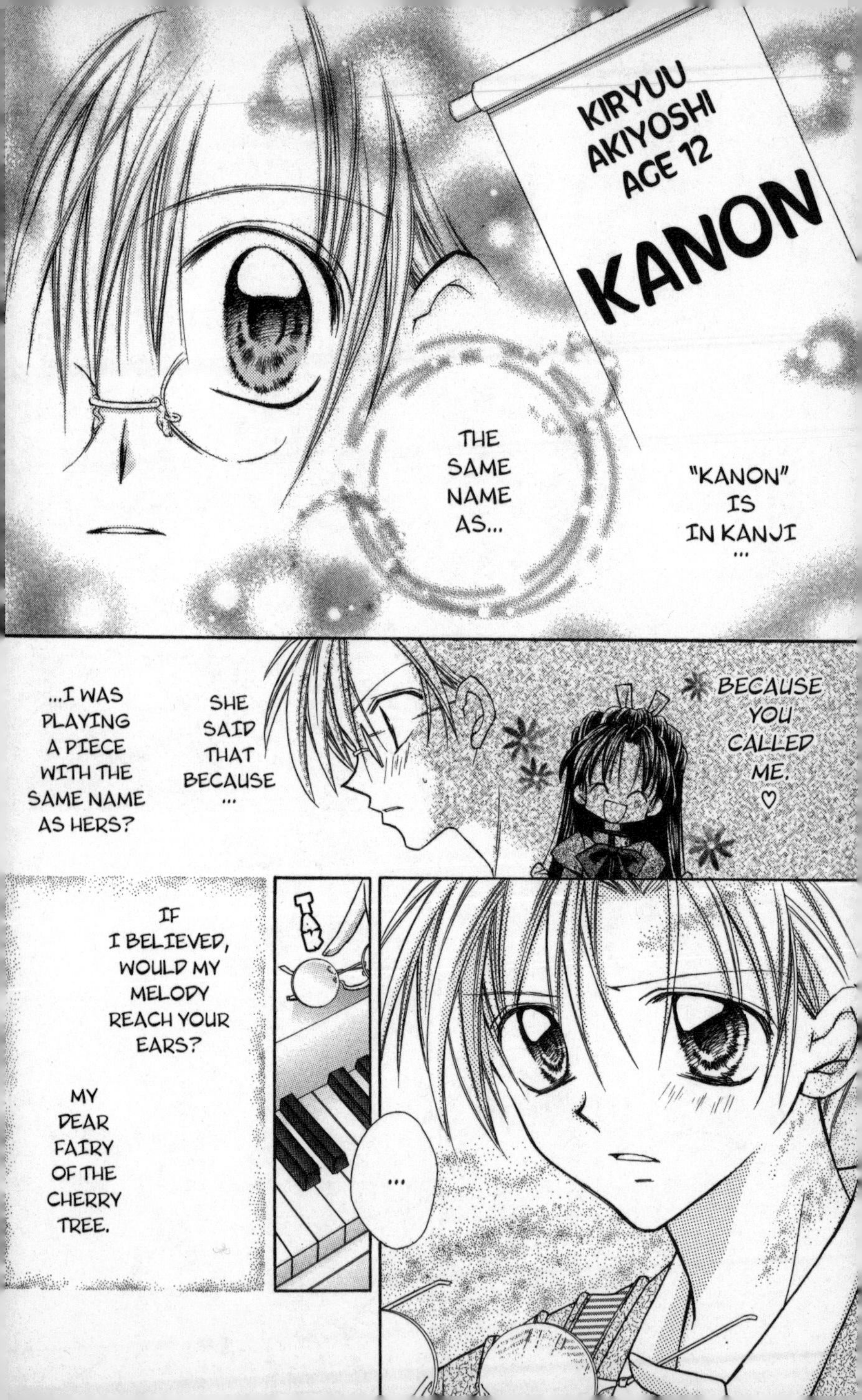
KIRYUU AKIYOSHI AGE 12
KANON
"KANON" IS IN KANJI ...
THE SAME NAME AS...
BECAUSE YOU CALLED ME. ♡
SHE SAID THAT BECAUSE ...
...I WAS PLAYING A PIECE WITH THE SAME NAME AS HERS?
...
TAK
IF I BELIEVED, WOULD MY MELODY REACH YOUR EARS?
MY DEAR FAIRY OF THE CHERRY TREE.

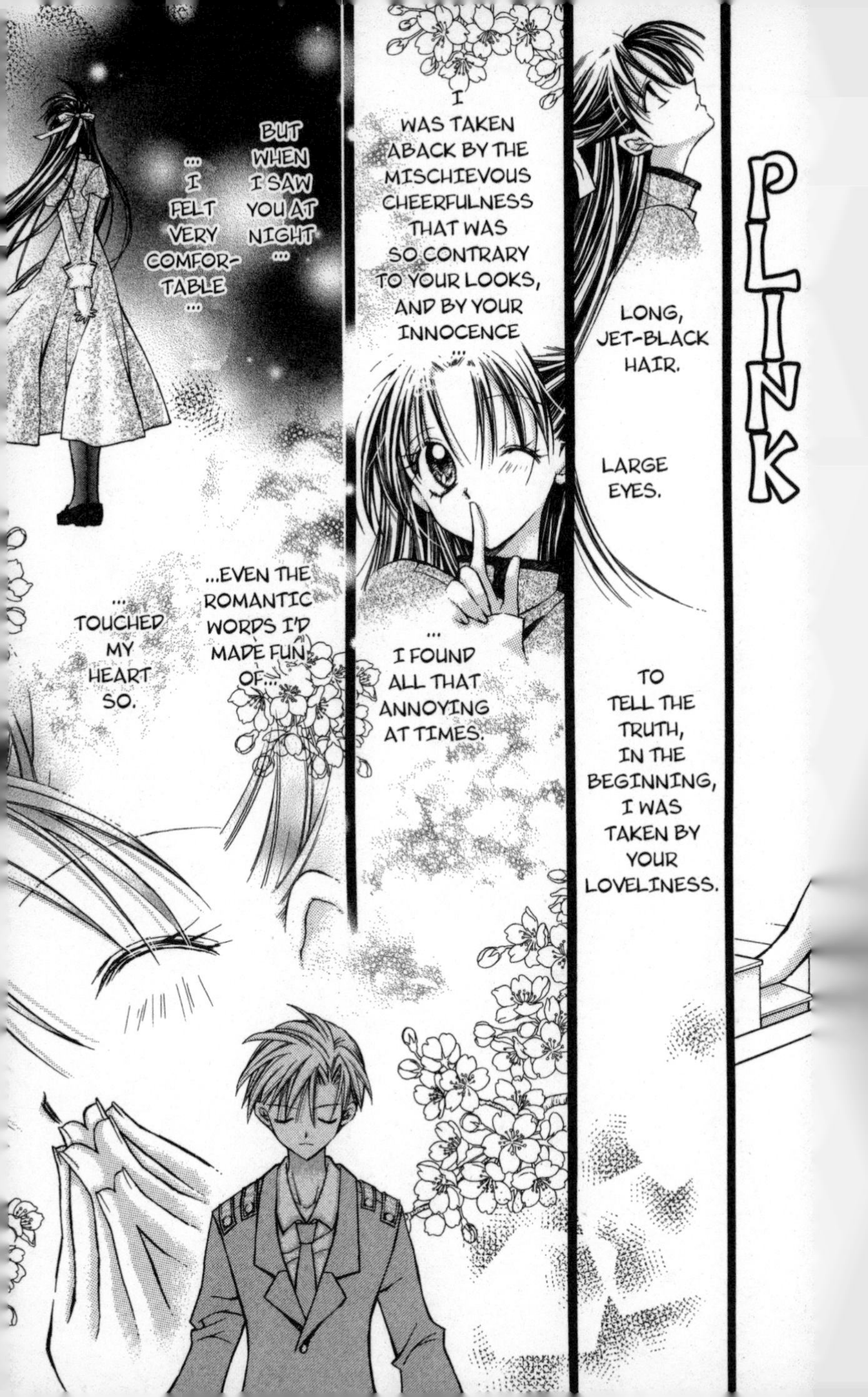
PLINK
LONG, JET-BLACK HAIR.
LARGE EYES.
TO TELL THE TRUTH, IN THE BEGINNING, I WAS TAKEN BY YOUR LOVELINESS.
I WAS TAKEN ABACK BY THE MISCHIEVOUS CHEERFULNESS THAT WAS SO CONTRARY TO YOUR LOOKS, AND BY YOUR INNOCENCE ...
... I FOUND ALL THAT ANNOYING AT TIMES.
BUT WHEN I SAW YOU AT NIGHT ...
... I FELT VERY COMFORTABLE ...
...EVEN THE ROMANTIC WORDS I'D MADE FUN OF...
... TOUCHED MY HEART SO.

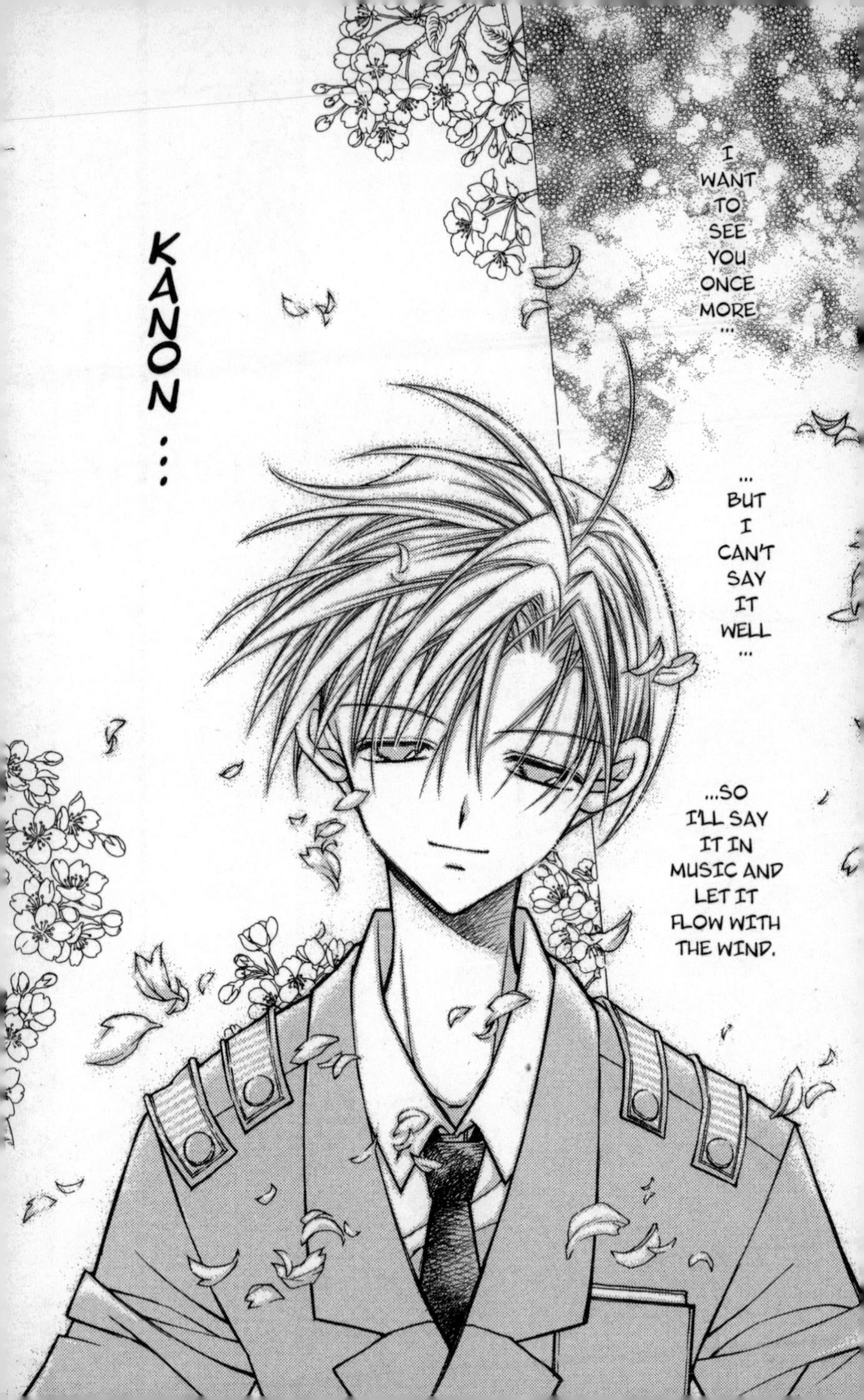
I WANT TO SEE YOU ONCE MORE...
...BUT I CAN'T SAY IT WELL...
...SO I'LL SAY IT IN MUSIC AND LET IT FLOW WITH THE WIND.
KANON...

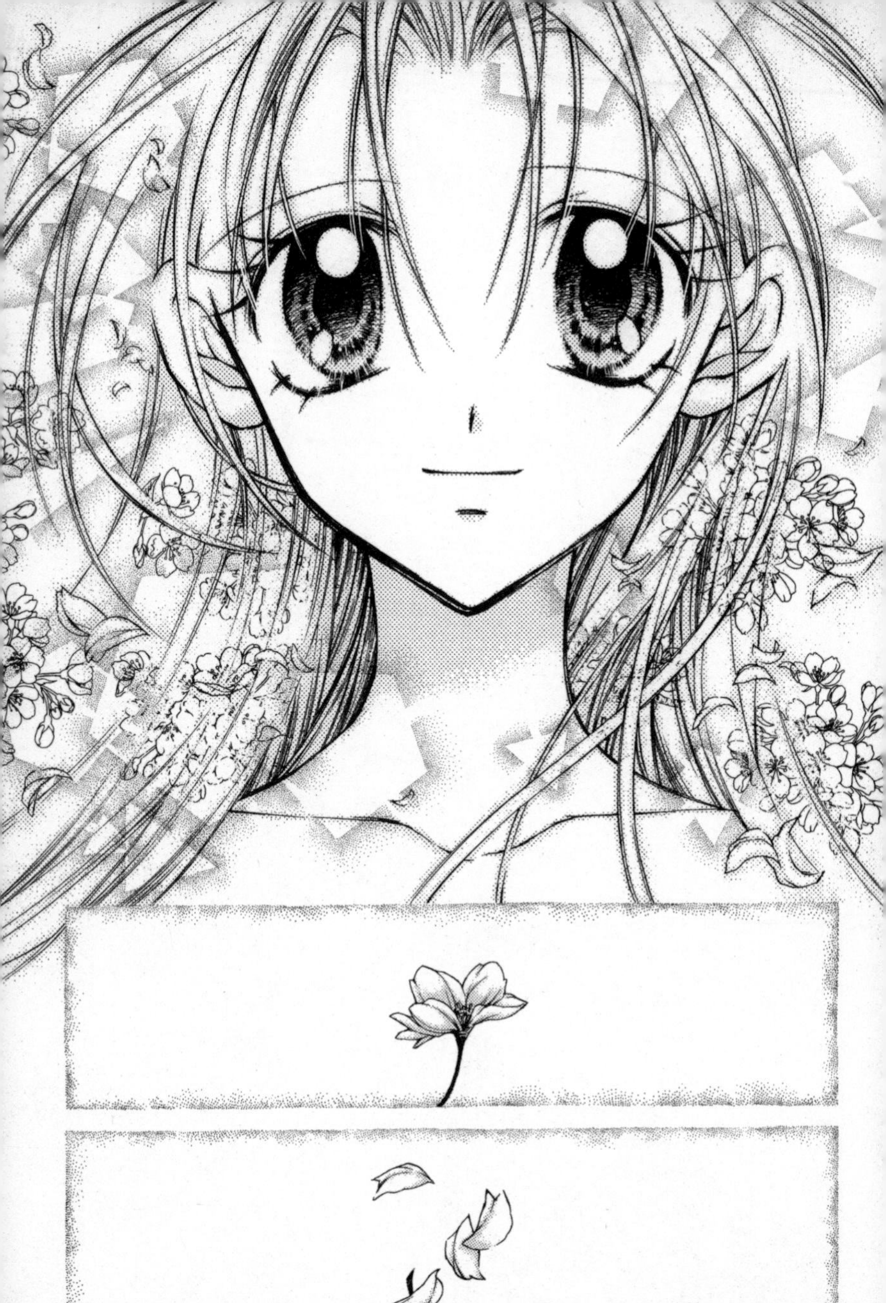

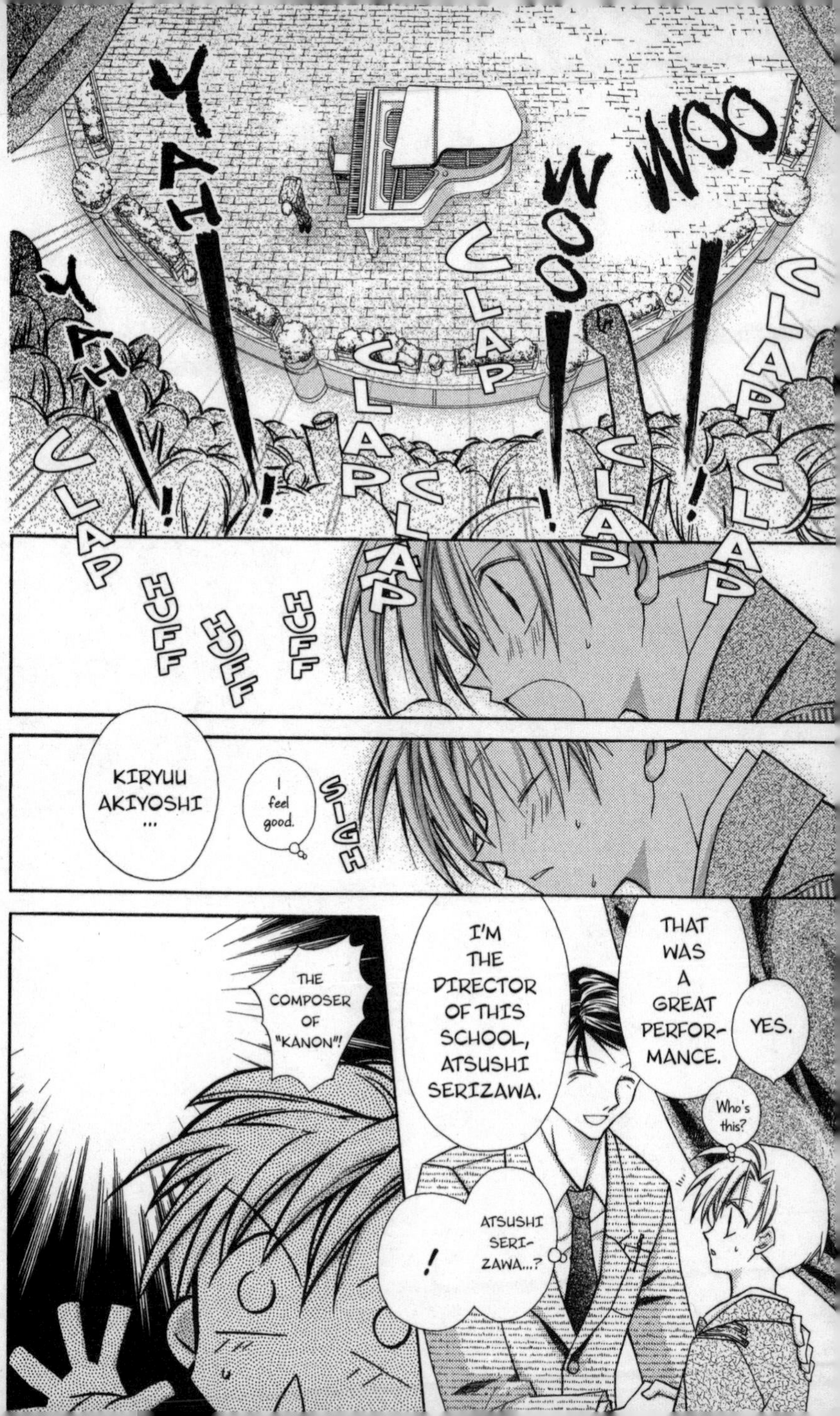
CLAP CLAP
WOO!
CLAP CLAP
WOO!
CLAP CLAP
CLAP CLAP
YAH!
YAH!
CLAP
HUFF
HUFF
HUFF
SIGH
I feel good.
KIRYUU AKIYOSHI...
THAT WAS A GREAT PERFORMANCE.
YES.
I'M THE DIRECTOR OF THIS SCHOOL, ATSUSHI SERIZAWA.
Who's this?
THE COMPOSER OF "KANON"!
ATSUSHI SERIZAWA...?
!

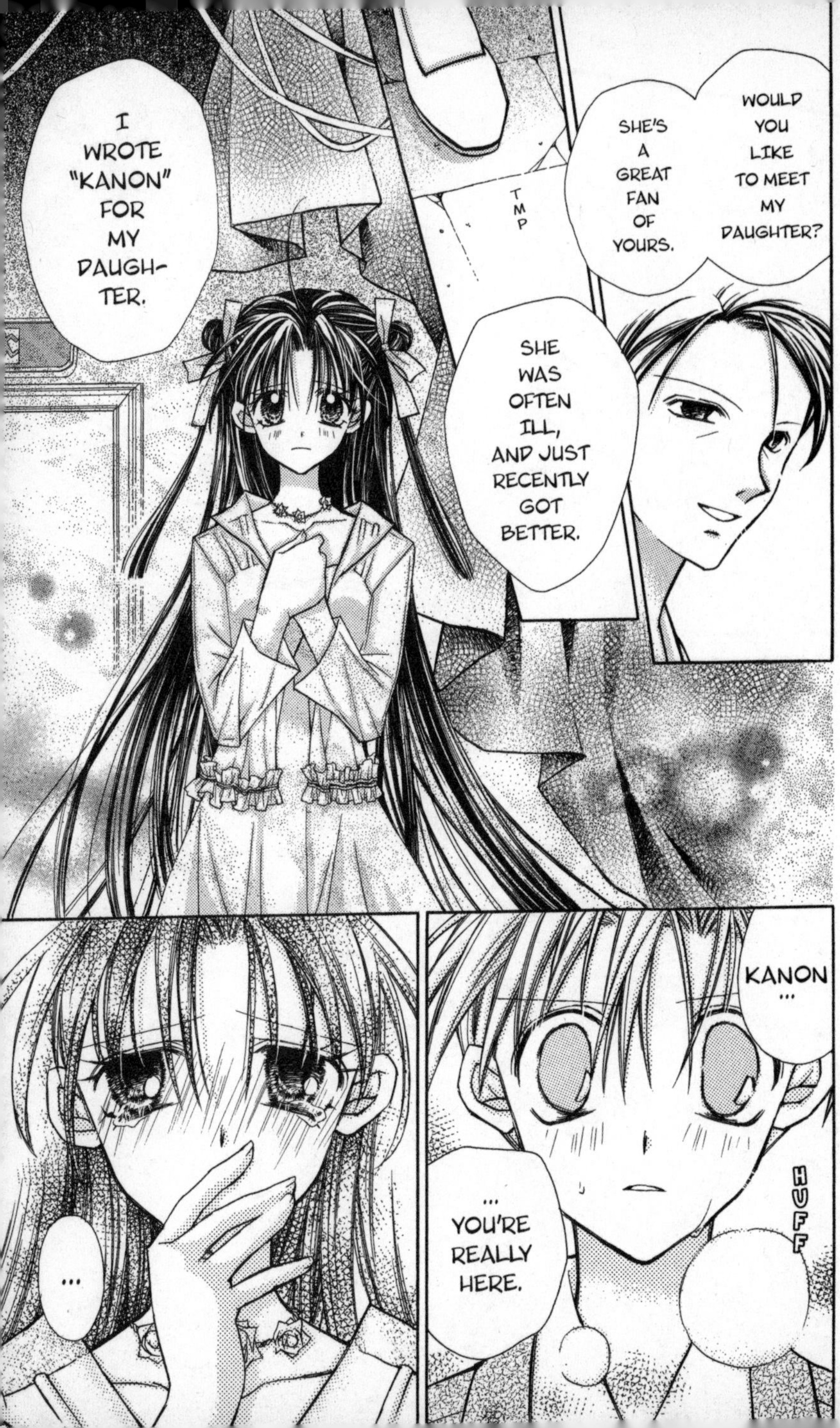
WOULD YOU LIKE TO MEET MY DAUGHTER?
SHE'S A GREAT FAN OF YOURS.
TMP
SHE WAS OFTEN ILL, AND JUST RECENTLY GOT BETTER.
I WROTE "KANON" FOR MY DAUGHTER.
KANON ...
HUFF
... YOU'RE REALLY HERE.
...

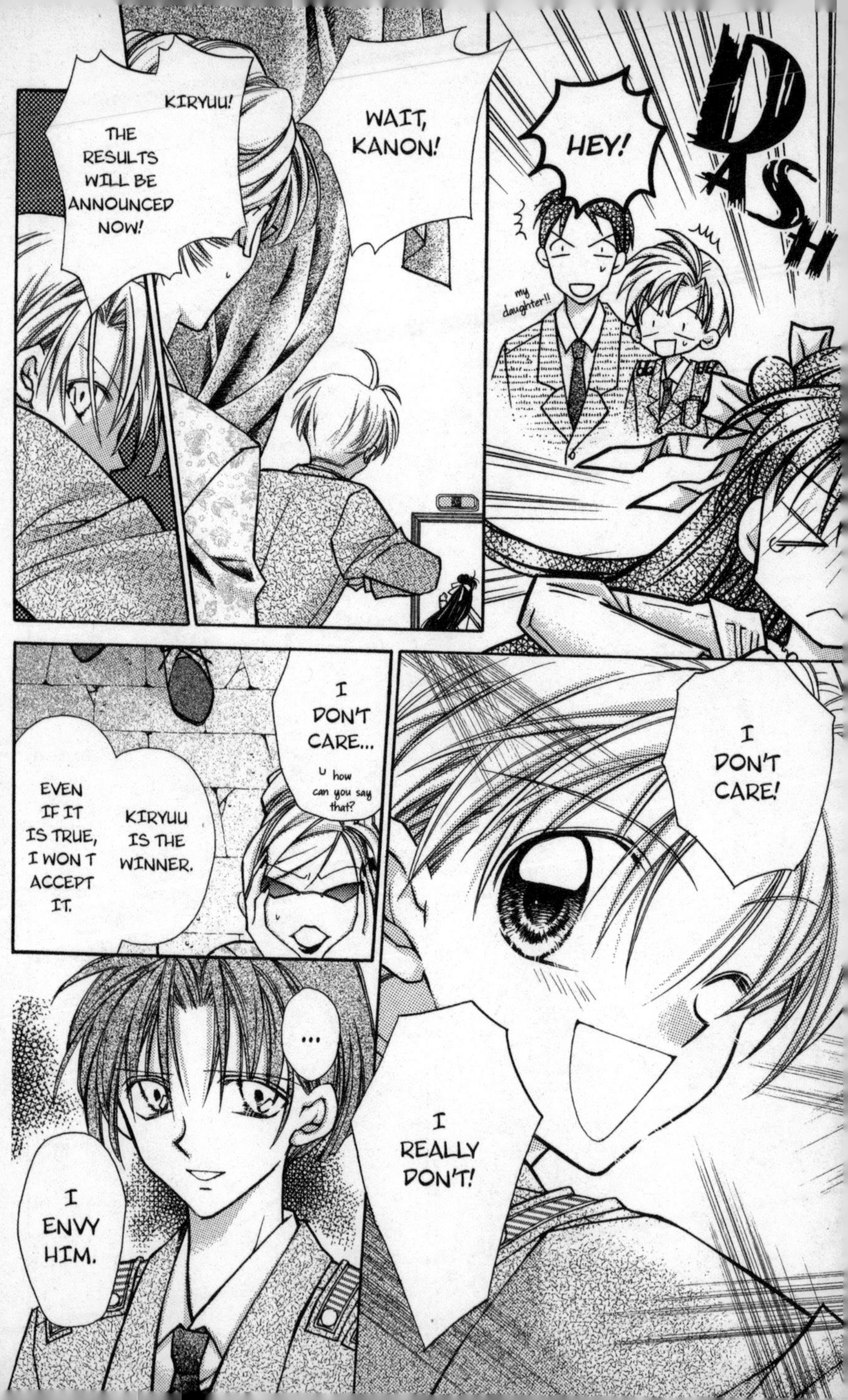
DASH
HEY!
my daughter!!
WAIT, KANON!
KIRYUU! THE RESULTS WILL BE ANNOUNCED NOW!
I DON'T CARE!
I REALLY DON'T!
I DON'T CARE...
how can you say that?
KIRYUU IS THE WINNER.
EVEN IF IT IS TRUE, I WON T ACCEPT IT.
...
I ENVY HIM.

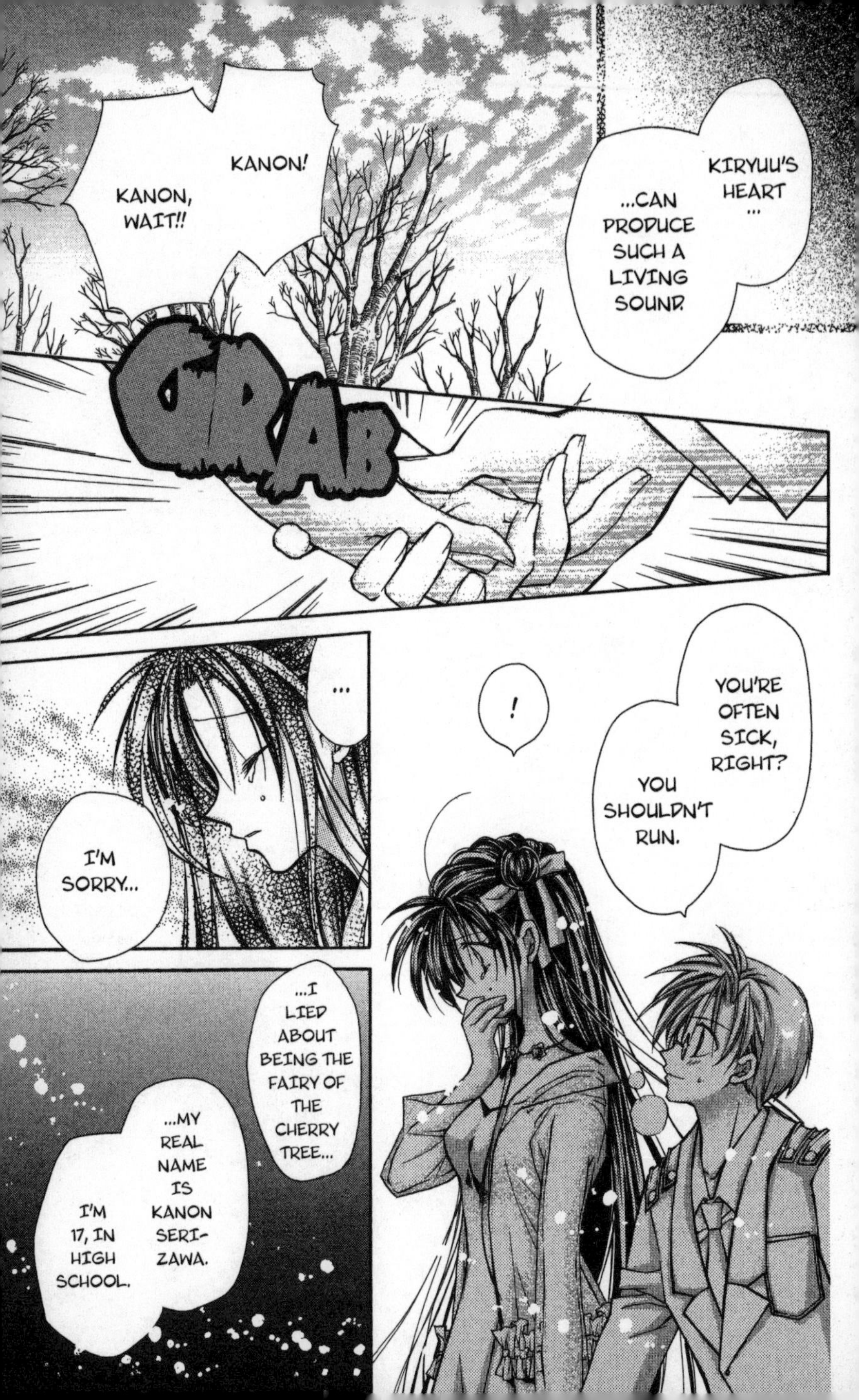
KIRYUU'S HEART ...
...CAN PRODUCE SUCH A LIVING SOUND.
KANON!
KANON, WAIT!!
GRAB
YOU'RE OFTEN SICK, RIGHT?
YOU SHOULDN'T RUN.
!
...
I'M SORRY...
...I LIED ABOUT BEING THE FAIRY OF THE CHERRY TREE...
...MY REAL NAME IS KANON SERI-ZAWA.
I'M 17, IN HIGH SCHOOL.

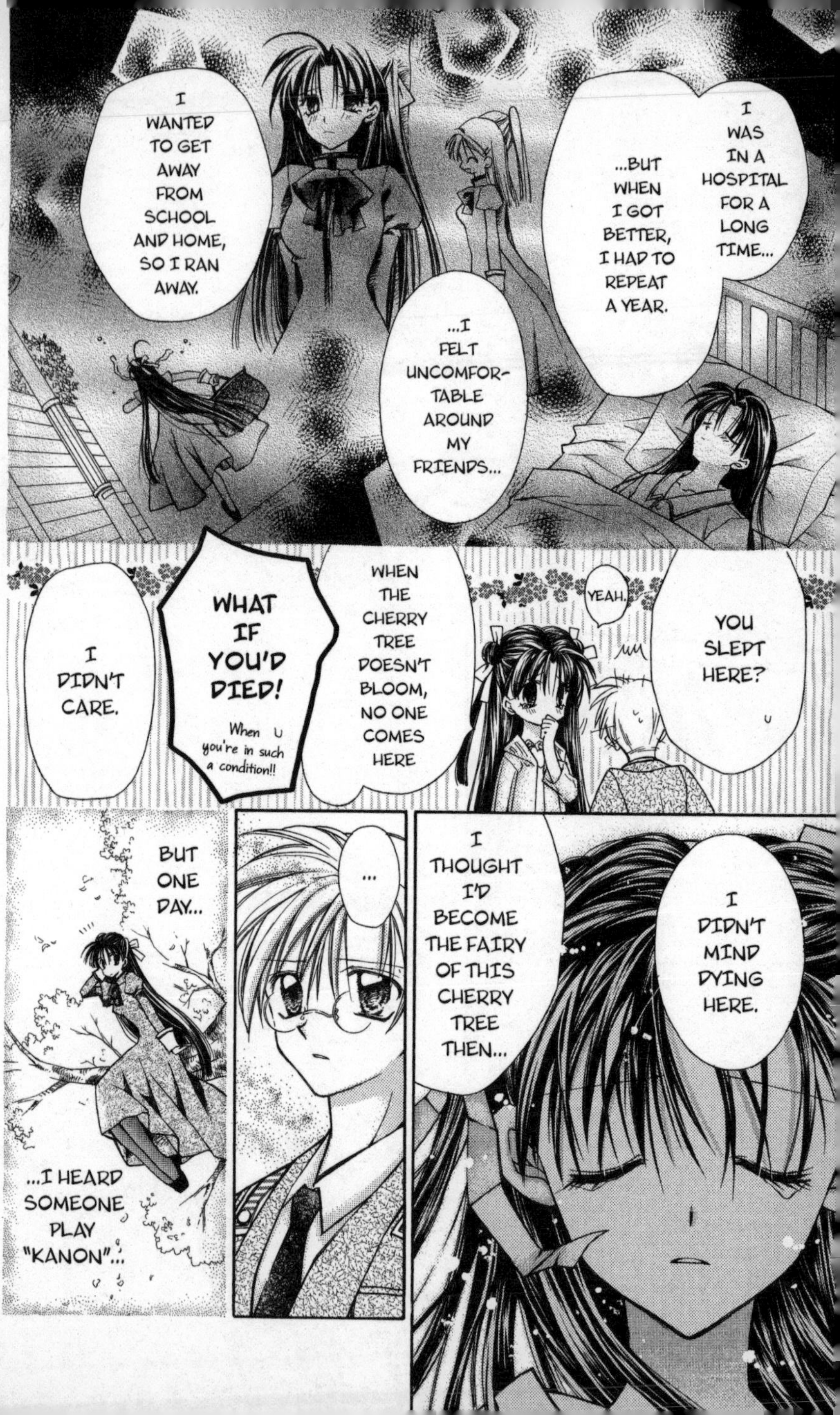
I WAS IN A HOSPITAL FOR A LONG TIME...
...BUT WHEN I GOT BETTER, I HAD TO REPEAT A YEAR.
...I FELT UNCOMFORTABLE AROUND MY FRIENDS...
I WANTED TO GET AWAY FROM SCHOOL AND HOME, SO I RAN AWAY.
YOU SLEPT HERE?
YEAH.
WHEN THE CHERRY TREE DOESN'T BLOOM, NO ONE COMES HERE
WHAT IF YOU'D DIED!
When you're in such a condition!!
I DIDN'T CARE.
I DIDN'T MIND DYING HERE.
I THOUGHT I'D BECOME THE FAIRY OF THIS CHERRY TREE THEN...
...
BUT ONE DAY...
...I HEARD SOMEONE PLAY "KANON"...

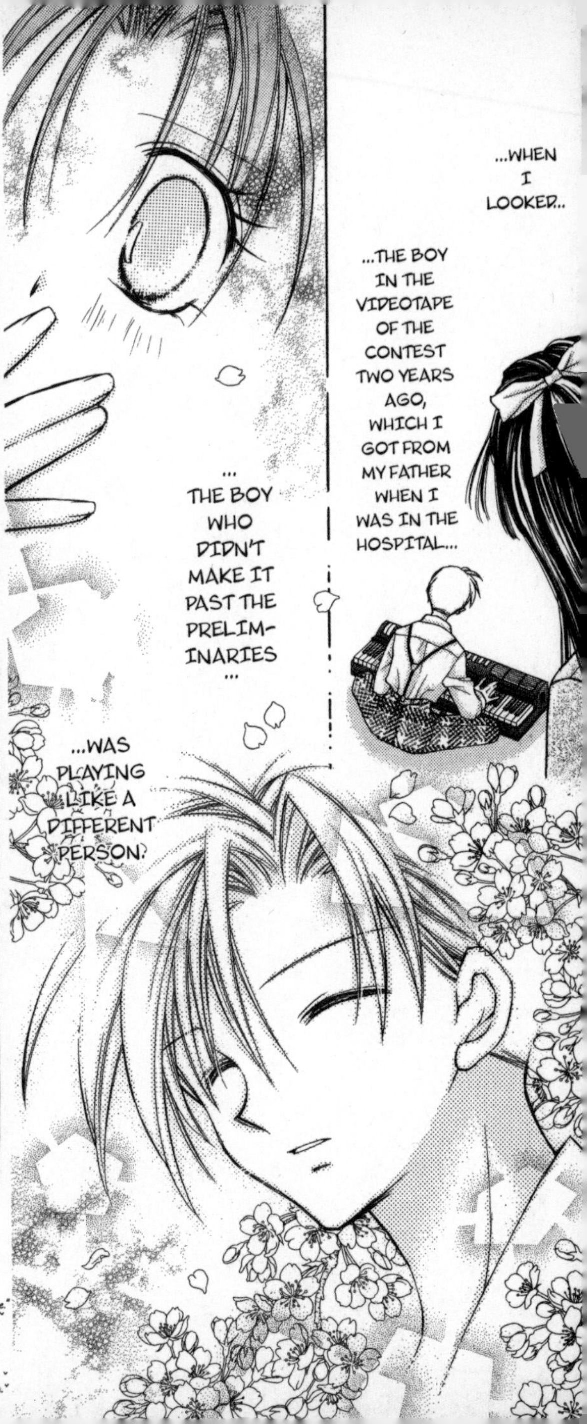
...WHEN I LOOKED...
...THE BOY IN THE VIDEOTAPE OF THE CONTEST TWO YEARS AGO, WHICH I GOT FROM MY FATHER WHEN I WAS IN THE HOSPITAL...
... THE BOY WHO DIDN'T MAKE IT PAST THE PRELIMINARIES ...
...WAS PLAYING LIKE A DIFFERENT PERSON.

ARIIINA TANEMURA'S

PENCHI? SHAKIN!

Episode 54

The Weirdest Person at Work!

I had the work staff choose three weird people at work.
(Weird, or interesting)

Results.

#1 Niki Seisou (By far)
#2 Arina Tanemura ?!
#3 Ai Minase
#3 Kanan Kiseki (a tie!)

#5 Airi Teito (one or two votes)

The other people got no votes.

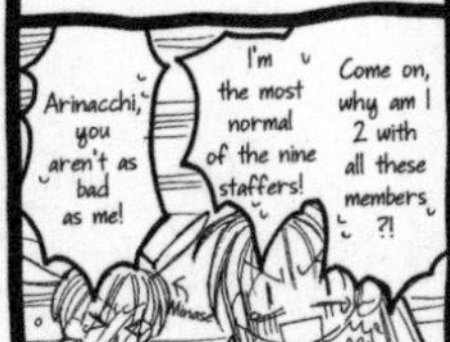
Come on, why am I 2 with all these members ?!
I'm the most normal of the nine staffers!
Arinacchi, you aren't as bad as me!

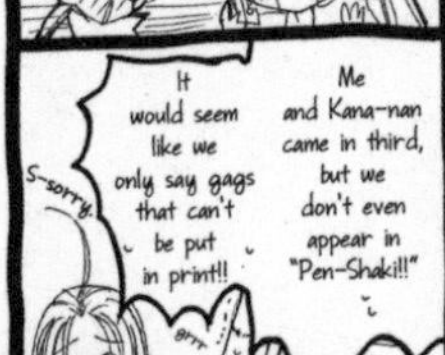
Me and Kana-nan came in third, but we don't even appear in "Pen-Shaki!!"
It would seem like we only say gags that can't be put in print!!
S-sorry.

Special Thanks

- Niki Seisou (sama) bow down before her
- Kanan Kiseki Looking forward to Tokyo Disney.
- Miwa Sawakami ...right?
- Airi Teito Airi is always in my heart.
- Kyakya Asano Do your best in "Hana to Yume."
- Ruka Kaduki Like a beast ♥
- Ai Minase Go for it, # 3.
- Konako Go for Eichi ♥ Mitsuki!
- Akoko Asakura Please assist from now on.

and Ribon!

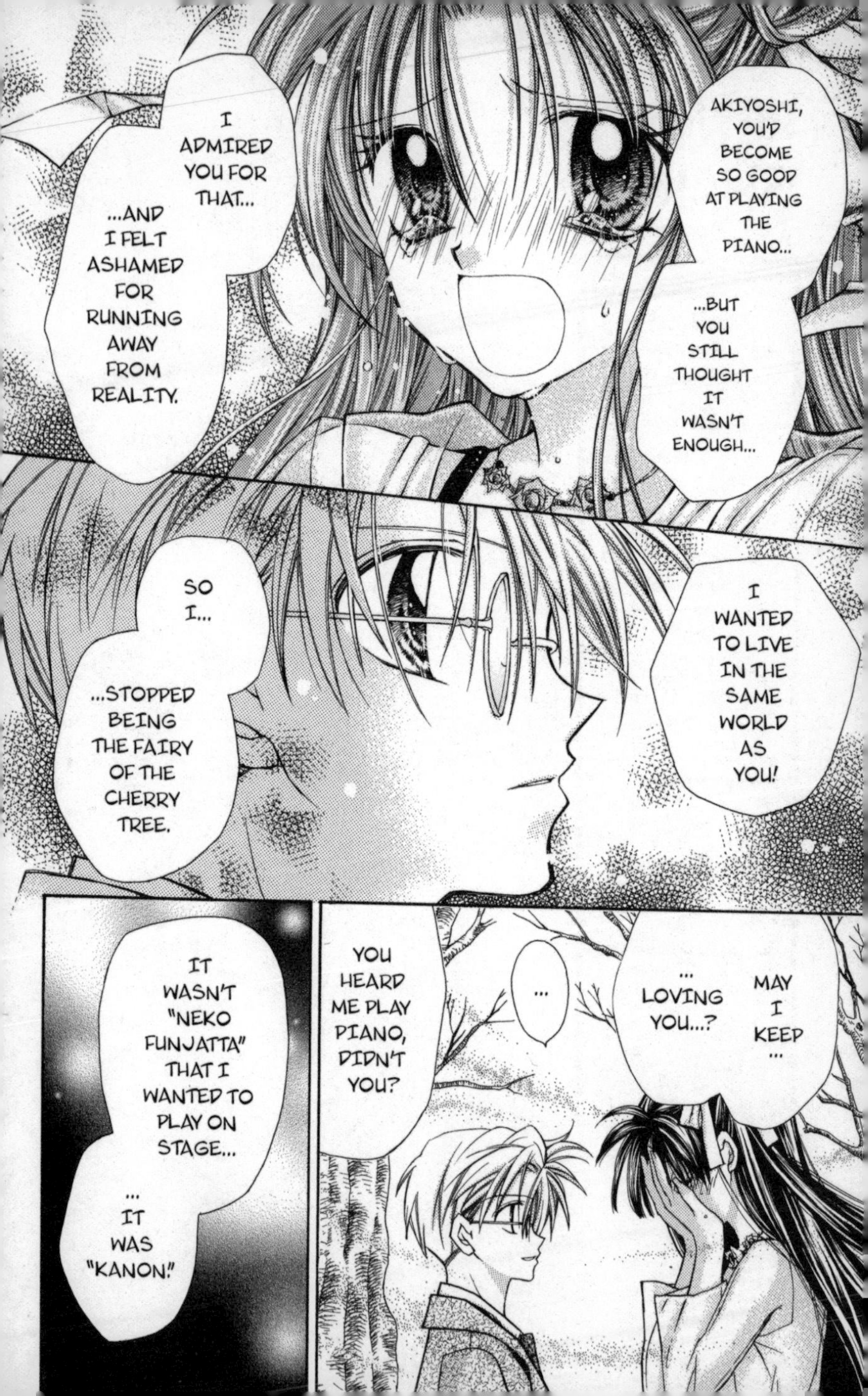
AKIYOSHI, YOU'D BECOME SO GOOD AT PLAYING THE PIANO...
...BUT YOU STILL THOUGHT IT WASN'T ENOUGH...
I ADMIRED YOU FOR THAT...
...AND I FELT ASHAMED FOR RUNNING AWAY FROM REALITY.
I WANTED TO LIVE IN THE SAME WORLD AS YOU!
SO I...
...STOPPED BEING THE FAIRY OF THE CHERRY TREE.
MAY I KEEP ...
... LOVING YOU...?
...
YOU HEARD ME PLAY PIANO, DIDN'T YOU?
IT WASN'T "NEKO FUNJATTA" THAT I WANTED TO PLAY ON STAGE...
... IT WAS "KANON."

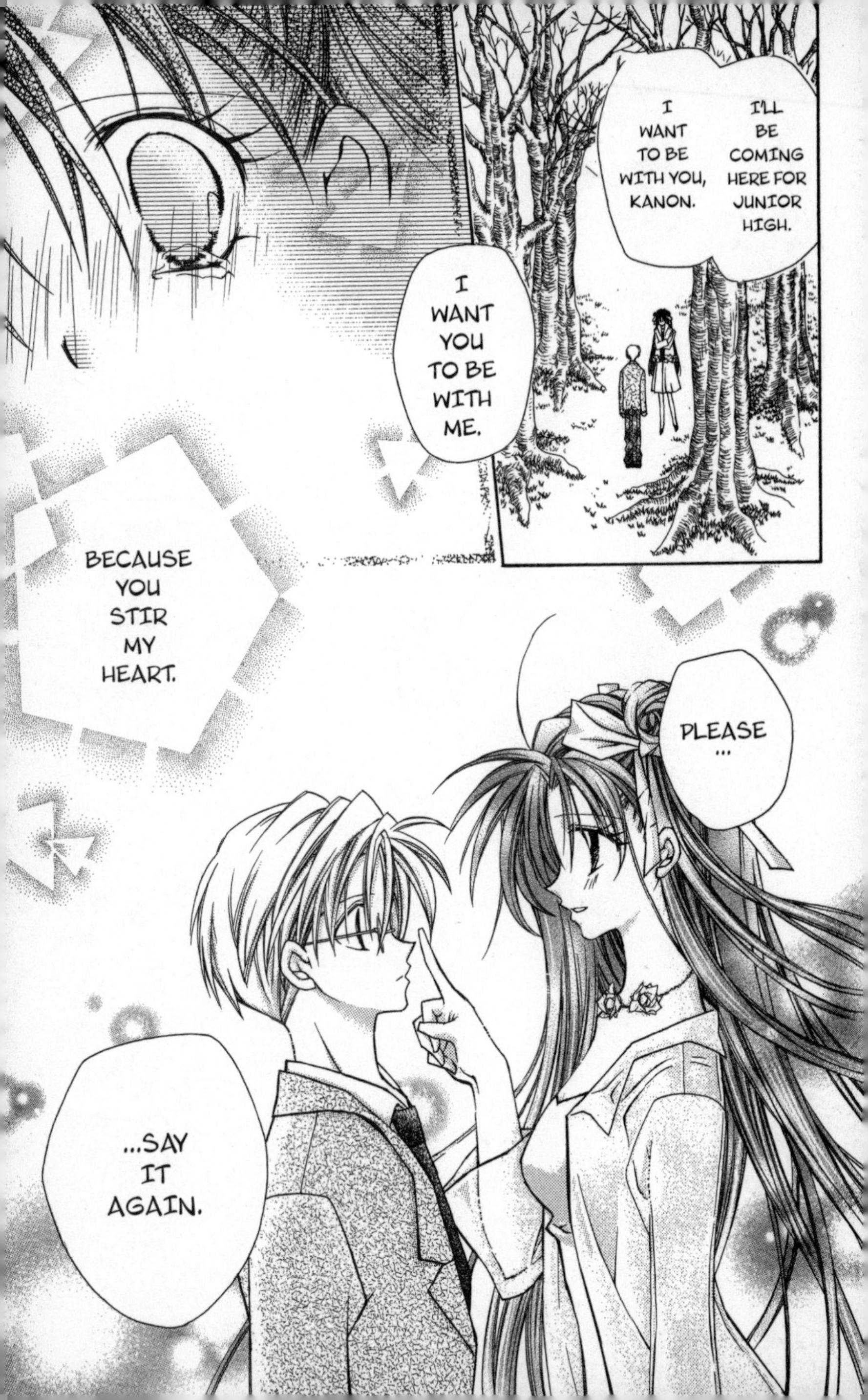
I'LL BE COMING HERE FOR JUNIOR HIGH.
I WANT TO BE WITH YOU, KANON.
I WANT YOU TO BE WITH ME.
BECAUSE YOU STIR MY HEART.
PLEASE...
...SAY IT AGAIN.

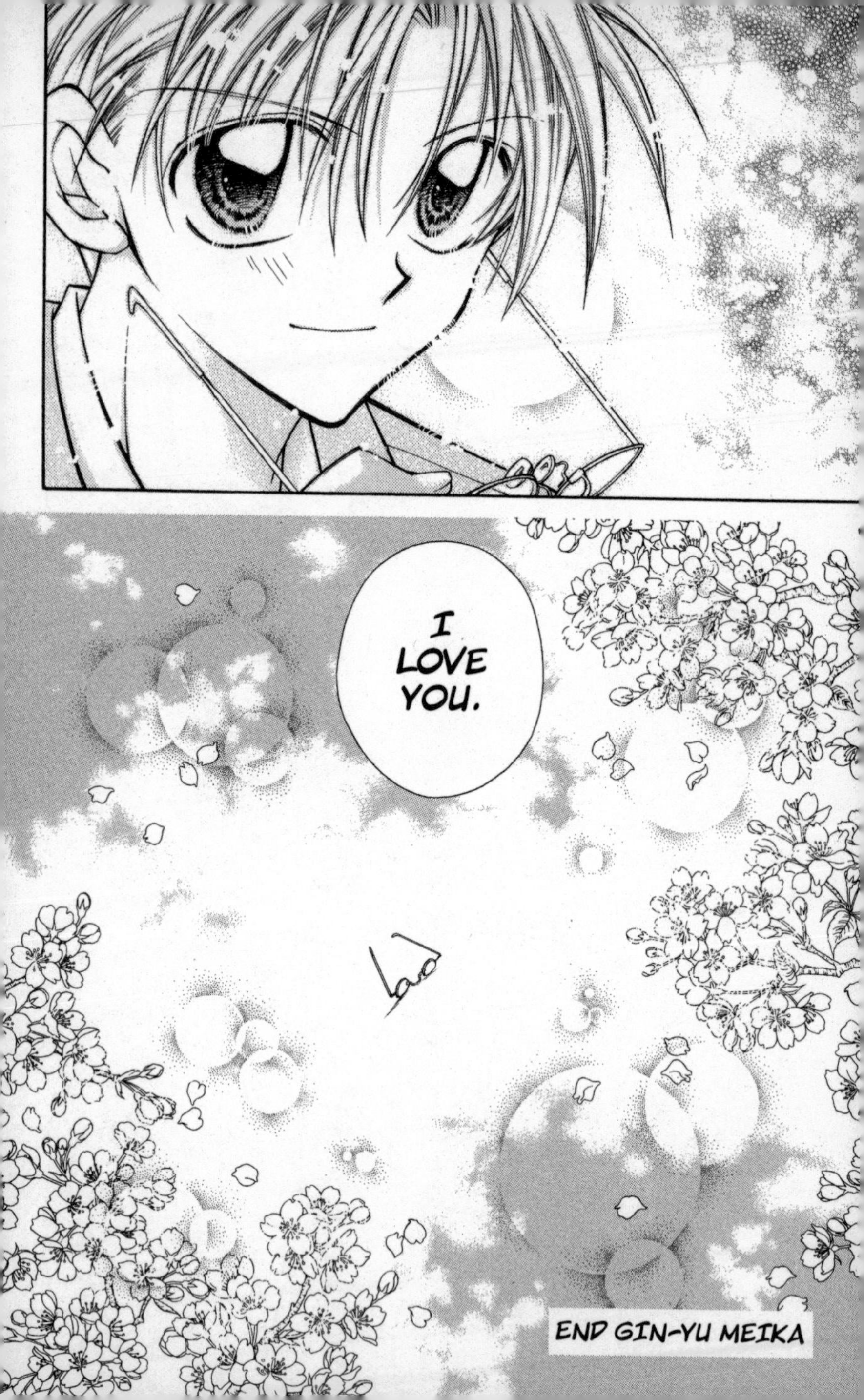
I LOVE YOU.
END GIN-YU MEIKA

Author Bio

Arina Tanemura was born in Aichi, Japan. She got her start in 1996, publishing *Nibanme no Koi no Katachi* (*The Style of the Second Love*) in *Ribon Original* magazine. Her early work includes a collection of short stories called *Kanshaku Dama no Yuutsu* (*Short-tempered Melancholic*). Two of her titles, *Kamikaze Kaito Jeanne* and *Full Moon*, were made into popular TV series. Tanemura enjoyes Karaoke and is a huge *Lord of the Rings* fan.

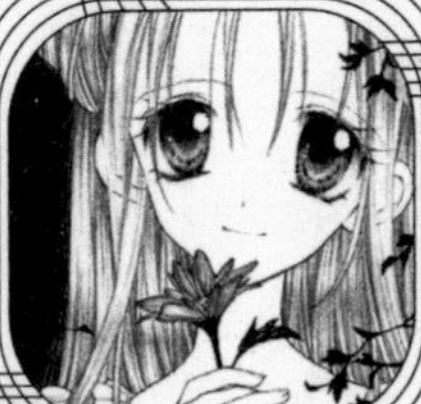

Author's Note

I truly love the four Shinigami (Takuto, Meroko, Izumi, and Jonathan). The more I draw them, the dearer they become and the more I love them. With *Full Moon*, I set myself to really portray the characters, so I am very happy when I'm told, "I love so and so."

Full Moon o Sagashite
Vol. 2
The Shojo Beat Manga Edition

STORY & ART BY
ARINA TANEMURA

English Translation & Adaptation/Tomo Kimura
Touch-Up & Lettering/Elena Diaz
Graphics & Cover Design/Izumi Evers
Editor/Pancha Diaz

Editor in Chief, Books/Alvin Lu
Editor in Chief, Magazines/Marc Weidenbaum
VP of Publishing Licensing/Rika Inouye
VP of Sales/Gonzalo Ferreyra
Sr. VP of Marketing/Liza Coppola
Publisher/Hyoe Narita

Published by VIZ Media, LLC
P.O. Box 77064
San Francisco, CA 94107

Shojo Beat Manga Edition
10 9 8 7 6 5 4 3
First printing, July 2005
Third printing, March 2007

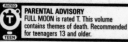